CONTENTS

INTRODUCTION

SECTION 1: CHILDREN AND PEDAGOGY

SECTION 2: TEACHER DEVELOPMENT.

Register of Research in Primary Geography

A Directory of Teaching and Learning Observations in the Primary Classroom and beyond

Researching Primary Geography

edited by

Simon Catling and Fran Martin

Special Publication No 1

ISBN 0-9538154-3-9

First published 2004 by the Register of Research in Primary Geography

Illustrations are provided courtesy of the authors unless otherwise acknowledged.

Published by the Register of Research in Primary Geography
Humber Road, Blackheath, London SE3 7LS
Data Protection Reg. No. Z6741887   Reg, Charity No. 1084895

Edited by Simon Catling and Fran Martin
Set in Plantin OUP and Times New Roman using MS Word
Printed for the Register of Research in Primary Geography by
the Procurement and Business Service Department, University of Greenwich
Cover designed and book bound by The Chameleon Press Limited, West Molesey KT8 2RY

SECTION 3: DEVELOPMENT OF THE SUBJECT.

CONCLUSION

Acknowledgements

We would very much like to acknowledge the work of and thank our many colleagues for their support in enabling this publication to come to fruition. What began in many cases as rough papers, even simply sets of notes, for discussion at a series of Primary Geography Conferences, have been turned into informative and stimulating papers providing a sense of the research that has been and is being undertaken by a large number of primary geography educators from schools and higher education. Without the very hard work of the contributors to this volume, it simply would not have been possible to produce it and reflect the interests and activities of these geography educators. These papers, though, represent more than the work of individual authors; they have benefited greatly from discussions of and comments on them from a much wider group of colleagues, who we wish also to acknowledge and without whom it would have been more difficult to have continued the struggle to research and write. The primary geography network that now exists is very important to us all.

In particular and especially, we want to thank Rachel Bowles for her unstinting encouragement and support in the production of this book. Her expertise in getting us from proposal to draft copy to final versions has been of immense help. Her role as the Co-ordinator of the *Register of Research in Primary Geography* – she is so much more than a Co-ordinator – has been vital in engendering this work and in helping it to completion.

Finally, we would like to thank our families and to dedicate this book to Dawn, Lesley, Emma and Mark. They have put up with much over the years, as we have beavered away at research, development and other activities as part of our contribution to primary geography. Thank you for being so patient and supportive.

Simon Catling and Fran Martin

June 2004.

Contributors

Peter Bloomfield is a Senior Lecturer in the Department of Education at the University of Hertfordshire where he is responsible for Primary Geographical Education, Education for Sustainability and Citizenship and for introducing the Global Teacher Project. Peter is a member of the Geographical Association's Primary and Middle Schools Section Committee and of its Steering Group on *Valuing Places*. He sits on the Development Education Association Initial Teacher Education Group (DEA ITE) and the steering group for Agenda 21 in St Albans District Council. His current research interests are sustainable development and citizenship through gardening in the UK and South Africa. He publishes regularly in *Primary Geographer* and has articles in *New Era in Education and Education 3 – 13*. Among his other publications is, in press, Teaching Education for Sustainability in Primary Schools, to be published by *Peace Child International*, funded by DEFRA.

Rachel Bowles is the Co-ordinator of the *Register of Research in Primary Geography*, which she set up in the mid-1990s to draw together the developing network of teachers, teacher educators and others interested in the development of primary geography. She is an Honorary Research Associate at the School of Education, University of Greenwich. Originally a geography and geology teacher, she has taught geography at all levels in the education system. She is a member of the Geographical Association's Primary and Middle Schools Section Committee and of the ICT Working Group, and was primary editor for the GA's *Guidance* series. A freelance writer and consultant for primary geography and ICT, she has written widely and her publications include a number of locality packs, material on mapwork and guidance on teaching geography for primary teachers and education students. She contributes regularly to Scholastic magazines for key stage 1 and 2 teachers and to *Primary Geographer*.

Simon Catling is Assistant Dean and Professor of Primary Education in the Westminster Institute of Education at Oxford Brookes University. He is a Past President of the Geographical Association and before moving into higher education in the mid-1980s taught for twelve years in an inner London primary school, where latterly he was a deputy head. He has written widely on primary geography and has particular interests in the state of geographical education, children's and students' ideas about geography, geography texts, the understanding and use of maps, and the nature and purpose of primary geography, concerned particularly with children's *natural* and *enhanced* geographical experience. Linked to this he has an interest in the nature of curriculum and curriculum study. His recent research has concerned the state of primary geography, trainee teachers' geographical perspectives and key stages 2/3 transfer in geography. He works in primary geography with undergraduate and postgraduate trainee teachers, on CPD courses for teachers and through local, national and international conferences. He is also a Trustee of the *Register of Research in Primary Geography*, and has organised the Charney Manor Primary Geography Conferences for the past ten years.

Ana Francisca de Azevedo teaches in the Departamento de Geografia e Planeamento in the Instituto de Ciências Socia at the Universidade do Minho, Portugal. She has lectured in education, where she had a particular interest in early years and primary education through children's geographies. However, in 2003 she moved departments to her current post, in which she focuses on the teaching and research in cultural geography. Her research interests lie in the representations of Portugese landscapes, linking geography, aesthetics and symbolic representations. Working with postgraduate students she has been able to maintain the link with primary education and research children's perceptions of landscape, one outcome of which is the chapter in this book.

Anna Disney is a senior lecturer in primary humanities at the Nottingham Trent University. Although primarily a historian, her involvement in a school linking project between Goa and the UK has led to her growing interest in geographical education. She is currently researching the relationship between school linking and global citizenship.

Jane Graham is senior education lecturer in primary geography education at Roehampton University. She lectures on the undergraduate and postgraduate primary teaching programmes and the generic Teaching and Learning courses as well as supervising students in school. She has experience of developing geography in the early years and has provided in-service training for a variety of groups, including playgroup leaders, the British Association of Early Childhood Education seminars and LEA conferences. In collaboration with Greg Walker she produced *Discover Coll, The Real Struay* (2003), the research background for which is the basis for a chapter in this book.

John Halocha is Reader in Education and Head of Geography at Bishop Grosseteste College, Lincoln. His current research interests lie in how trainee teachers are prepared to teach geography in schools. He has also researched ways in which schools have developed links with Europe and the wider world, including the application of ICT to such ventures. He has published widely in the field of primary geography education. This has included two books, numerous chapters in books and a wide range of conference papers presented in a variety of European venues. He has been actively involved with the Geographical Association for eight years and is currently a GA Officer. He is Secretary to the British Sub-Committee of the International Geographical Union Commission for Geographical Education.

Lorraine Harrison is the Deputy Head of the School of Education at the University of Brighton and Course Leader for the PGCE Primary Course.She began teaching in primary schools and now teaches geography curriculum studies and geography subject studies to both primary undergraduate and primary postgraduate students.

Fran Martin is a senior lecturer in primary education at University College Worcester. She is interested in the links between geographical and environmental education and global citizenship, as well as geographical learning in the early years. Her research interests are in beginning teacher development and intercultural learning. She is a member of the Geographical Association Teacher Education Working Group and was leader of the GA Early Years working party responsible for the GA's Position Statement on geographical learning in the Foundation Stage, published in 2003. She is also a trustee for the World Studies Trust.

Margaret Mackintosh lectured in geology in what was then Eastern Nigeria (and being evacuated at the start of the Biafran War), before moving to teach in Humberside for 20 years. More recently she has been senior lecturer in Geography in Primary Education at the University of Plymouth (Rolle Campus). Though she retired in 2001, she now teaches part-time, runs annual students' study visits to The Gambia, leads in-service courses, is Honorary Editor of *Primary Geographer* for the Geographical Association and is involved with its Steering groups and working parties.. Her current research interest is teachers' and trainee teachers' understanding of the nature of geography.

John Moore is a principal lecturer at the Nottingham Trent University. He teaches all four year groups on the BA (Hons) Primary QTS undergraduate course. Year 1 includes a specific geography module taught to the whole cohort. In Years 2 & 3 a Humanities module is taught to the whole year group. In Year 4 a specialist group of 21 geography students study the subject at their own level, and within that group, 11 students are developing their pedagogical knowledge with a view to becoming geography subject leaders. His research interest is in local studies particularly within Nottinghamshire.

Melanie Norman is a Principal Lecturer in the School of Education at the University of Brighton, where she is Route Leader for the PGCE Secondary Geography course. She teaches the geography subject study element on the four-year undergraduate primary course, and both geography curriculum studies and geography subject study elements of the KS2/KS3 undergraduate course and the one-year postgraduate secondary course.

David Owen is a senior lecturer at Sheffield Hallam University and teaches on a variety of undergraduate and postgraduate geography education programmes for trainee primary teachers. He is committed to geographical learning which builds on children's own experiences and values, and has a particular interest in working with children and teachers to develop effective teaching and learning strategies using new technologies in geography. In addition to a number of publications, he is co-author of *Teaching Geography 3-11: The Essential Guide* (2001), published by Continuum.

Paula Owens is currently completing her PhD, entitled 'Fields of Meaning', at Christchurch University College, Canterbury. She currently works as Deputy Head at Eastchurch School, where she has also spent a term as Acting Headteacher. Her responsibilities include Curriculum and Assessment, monitoring NQT's, Music, Eco-school co-ordination and Education for Sustainable Development. She is also mentor to a teacher who is completing research into 'Brain Gym' under the Best Practice Research Scholarship scheme. She is a member of the Geographical Association Early Years Working Party and was a collaborator on the GA Position Statement on geographical learning in the Foundation Stage. More recently, she has represented the GA by working with the Curriculum Partnership on a new Early Years Handbook.

Beverly Plester lectures at the University of Coventry and is a member of the Psychology Subject Group. Her research interests centre on school children's mental representations of location and their ability to use aerial photographs to guide problem solving in the represented space. She also works on the relationship between table-top and real space versions of tasks using aerial photographs and scaled maps drawn from them. She has worked with a number of postgraduate students on related projects, exploring a variety of aspects of children's understanding of aerial photographs, maps and models as representations of real spaces. She has published widely on her research with more than twenty single and co-authored papers in print in the past four years.

Steve Rawlinson is Senior Admissions Tutor for all primary education programmes in the School of Education, Northumbria University. He also has responsibility for issues concerning access, recruitment and marketing across all education programmes. Furthermore, he has responsibility for encouraging under-represented groups to enter teaching. He is module tutor for the foundation subjects on primary education courses, and lectures on geography to primary education trainees. His research interests include the factors affecting entry onto ITT courses, especially as they apply to geography and under-represented groups, environmental education and geographical fieldwork and the use of ICT in geographical education. He has co-authored a number of publications in these areas in recent years.

Alison Ryan is a senior lecturer at Sheffield Hallam University and teaches on a variety of undergraduate and postgraduate ITT courses. Her work focuses on developing expertise and enthusiasm in primary teaching, particularly in geography. She is personally committed to the role of education in encouraging people to recognise the importance of sustainable development and is interested in developing values education, particularly EfSD, both in geography and across the curriculum. She is co-author of *Teaching Geography 3-11 The Essential Guide* (2001), published by Continuum.

Stephen Scoffham is principal lecturer in geographical education at Christchurch University College, Canterbury, where he teaches undergraduate and postgraduate primary student teachers. He is a well established contributor to CPD courses and to conferences on primary geography and geographical education. He has written widely in primary geography and environmental education and is a regular contributor to *Primary Geographer*. His publications include geography texts and other materials for primary and secondary school children, guidance on the teaching of primary geography, and papers linked to his research interests in children's geographical learning, the geography curriculum and resource development in geography. He is editor of the Geographical Association's revised *Handbook of Primary Geography* (2004), a member of the GA Primary and Middle School Section Committee and the GA Honorary Publications Officer.

Chris Spencer is Professor of Environmental Psychology at the University of Sheffield; and has been on the editorial board of the *Journal of Environmental Psychology* from the very first issue. Most of his work has been on children's perceptions of their world, using techniques such as affective mapping and aerial photograph interpretation. He has published widely on children's environmental learning and understanding, including the seminal text, *The Child in his Physical Environment* with Mark Blades and Kim Morsley (1989). With colleagues, he is currently editing a new text on children's geographical and environmental experience.

Colin Storey is an early years teacher at Sherington First School, Buckinghamshire. A scientist by background, he is fascinated by children's engagement in learning and has developed a particular interest in their environmental and geographical learning through his teaching about place and the environment. The chapter in this book has emerged from his work in a TTA funded Teacher Research Project into the use of ICT to support teaching and learning in developing a sense of place in geography. He has recently been awarded Advanced Skills Teacher status.

Greg Walker is a senior education lecturer and primary geography coordinator working on the undergraduate and postgraduate primary teaching programmes at Roehampton University as well as on generic teaching and learning courses. Greg supervises students extensively in school placements and leads in-service training both at Roehampton and in the London borough of Sutton. He has a particular interest in working with small teams of teachers and other educators in producing teaching resources appropriate for National Curriculum geography, including D*iscover Godstone* (1995), *Discover Croydon* (1997), *Discover the River Thames* (1999) and *Discover Coll, The Real Struay* (2003).

Di Wilmot teaches and researches in geographical education in the Education Department at Rhodes University, Grahamstown, South Africa. While her work focuses more strongly on secondary education, she has particular interest in children's developing spatial understanding in relation to geography, which has involved her in research with younger children, which forms the basis for her chapter in this book.

Preface

There has been a long history of geographers gathering at a peaceful retreat in Oxfordshire, at the Charney Manor Conference Centre, in Charney Bassett in the Vale of the White Horse. Here ideas have been aired, discussed and developed from the 1960s to the 1990s by geography educators concerned with the evolving and developing faces of geography and geographical education. During this period, organised by Rex Walford and involving many of his peers, they looked at the state of geographical knowledge and presented the geography education world with principles and models, problems and solutions, approaches and strategies for geography teaching which are still the foundation for serious work at secondary school level and above in geography education. The ideas were able not only to accommodate the curriculum changes in the examination system but also often led such change, and in so doing built a vigorous subject at 14-18 and into higher education.

In 1990 it became clear that with the coming of the National Curriculum there would also be changes at primary level. Initially the national curriculum in primary geography was content rich but did embody a core idea that one had to build upon children's knowledge and experience. This idea developed into an appreciation that there is a continuous progression of geographical learning and understanding from infancy through to becoming a young teenager. Unfortunately, not every primary and secondary educator appreciated this, not least because there was very little evidence available and in print - and what did exist was often in obscure journals and became misrepresented in dissemination.

In the early 1990s Walford saw an opportunity and encouraged past primary teacher, turned teacher educator, now Professor Simon Catling, to use the Charney Manor tradition to provide a focus on primary geography. Thus, as the National Curriculum came up for revision, invitations went out ten years ago, in 1994, to a number of teachers, teacher trainers, LEA geography advisors and geography education researchers involved with developing the geographical understanding of primary children and effective primary geography teaching. The first Charney Manor Primary Geography Conference was held in early 1995. Since then primary geography conferences, organised by Simon Catling, have been held regularly and have attracted both a core and wider group of primary geography educators, as well as fostering and encouraging many others who are helping to research into and develop the quality of teaching in primary geography.

At that first meeting papers were presented on ongoing research and about curriculum development. Amongst other things, discussion began as to how to develop a network of geographers in primary education who could support each other in schools and higher education, and student teachers, in developing ways in which primary children learned and could more effectively be taught. It was clear that there was a need not just for such a conference but also for a larger forum to draw together all those with an interest in the development of primary geography. Thus was borne the *Register of Research in Primary Geography* through someone (guess who), perhaps rashly, saying, "I have a fax and a telephone and can collect correspondents' addresses." Ten years on, most communication is by email; there are nearly a thousand addresses to connect with, and there is now a significant portfolio of papers that have been given at the Charney Manor Primary Geography Conferences.

The *Register*, through immense goodwill and support on the part of TTA, DFES, GA and RGS-IBG, as well as by colleagues at Sheffield Hallam and Worcester University College, has organised four seminar conferences whose proceedings were the core of the Register's *Occasional Papers 1* and *2*. Through individual endeavour, using a variety of routes – not least being the journals *International Research in Geography and Environmental Education* (International Geographical Union [IGU]) and *Primary Geographer* (Geographical Association [GA]) – the limited research into and the debates about primary geography has begun to be more widely disseminated. However, it has become clear over the years that there still is not enough dissemination.

Since this is the year of the IGU Conference in Glasgow – returning to the UK for the first time since 1964 (in London) - it seemed to be timely to publish a range of the work that has been presented at the Charney Manor Primary Geography conferences in recent years. One earlier publication, emerging from studies presented at the Charney Manor conferences and in other venues was *Primary Sources* (Scoffham, 1998), which brought together a number of brief summaries of research projects. It helped to make the point that more was being undertaken than was known. This collection of research papers is a worthy successor to that earlier volume, providing as it does a wide ranging set of detailed reports on some of the recent and current research activity in primary geography. The *Register*, having been born and fostered through the conferences, was asked to publisher the book. This *Special Publication*, edited with care and erudition by Simon Catling and Fran Martin, brings to you the essence of the many deliberations at Charney Manor. In the tradition of Walford and his colleagues, the intention is to set you thinking, with the purpose of taking forward what is represented by this research: to continue to learn more about the learning, teaching and curriculum relevant to enabling primary children to achieve their full potential as natural geographers in and beyond primary schooling.

Rachel Bowles

The Co-ordinator,
The Register of Research in Primary Geography

References

Scoffham, S. (ed.) (1998), *Primary Sources: Research findings in primary geography*, Sheffield: Geographical Association

INTRODUCTION

Chapter 1

The State of Research in Primary Geography

Simon Catling & Fran Martin

Introduction

Much of what is written about children's learning in and the teaching of primary geography is grounded in experience rather than a firm foundation in research studies. This is not to say that 'experience' is not well founded in teachers' awareness and understanding of organising and teaching geography and of children's learning of geography in primary classrooms and outside, but it is to note that the experience on which the advice, directions and guidance that are put forward is informal rather than systematic and disciplined in the study, analysis and evaluation of what is going on. To put it more critically, while much that is taught and learned seems to work and be useful, the acknowledgement that this is so is based on 'gut feeling' rather than rigorous research. Not that this is surprising; there is little opportunity for funding that can enable the focus, extent and depth of research into the teaching of and children's learning in curriculum areas such as language, mathematics and science.

Yet, research into geography in primary education has been underway. Across the world, there have been many who have been interested in, and determined to dig deeper into, the practices of geography teaching and into children's geographical learning. The recent developing academic study in geography of *children's geographies* has helped both to bring forward the nature of children's geographical experience and the contexts and issues in their experience and to provide a developing base that can be applied to geographical experience in school. It is also encouraging interest outside the teaching and teacher education community to investigate children's school and classroom experience to develop a broader and deeper understanding of their lives. This increased awareness, therefore, owes something to the new sociology of childhood (Holloway & Valentine, 2000), as well as to geographical (Aitken, 2001; Phillips, 2001) and anthropological interests (Fog Olwig & Gulløv, 2003).

The focus here, however, is more strictly on research in primary geography education rather than on the broader picture. First, an overview is provided of the sources of information on such research, indicating that more recently this is becoming an area of increased publication. Second, briefly, the context and reasons for developing research in primary geography are considered, in the context of evidence-informed research. Thirdly, the range and quality issues in primary geography research are discussed. In conclusion, a perspective on the current state of research is put forward. There is no attempt to provide a overview or a detailed examination of the range of the research into primary geography that has been undertaken or of what has been learnt from it; there is not the space to do this work justice, whatever its strengths and limitations. Rather, the purpose is to indicate a sense of what has been undertaken and is being explored and to note some of the needs arising from this work, as a basis for future directions and developments.

Some sources for research in primary geography

While research in geographical education has advanced broadly, research into children's learning in and the teaching of geography in primary education is still in a relatively early stage of development. Though geography has been a curriculum subject in English elementary and primary schools since 1870 and earlier (Walford, 2001), rather little research is evident from the first hundred years of publications into *geography in education* (Lukehirst & Graves, 1972). Towards the end of this period, Naish (1972) reviewed a variety of research studies, which included a number of studies exploring aspects of children's geographical thinking, including studies of concept understanding, awareness of vocabulary, their use of maps, ideas about nationality and country, and their sense of international understanding. This indicated a considerable advance on studies noted in earlier reviews (Scarfe, 1949; Long, 1964). A similar situation emerged in a related research review of studies undertaken in the USA (Saveland & Pannell, 1978), with concept learning and map understanding explored in a small number of studies, built around a strongly Piagetian model of children's developing knowledge and understanding. However, this review also noted initial work on children's environmental and spatial learning in geographical contexts, for example the early work of Blaut & Stea (1971).

The development of research degrees in primary geography, curriculum studies, pedagogy, children's learning and related areas during and since the 1970s in the UK and around the world has provided increased opportunities for research into geographical education in and outside schools. The number and variety of studies, not only in research but more strongly in guidance and advice about the nature of geography, its curriculum, its organisation and its teaching and assessment, has increased hugely, as attested in more recent bibliographies (Forsyth, 1995; Foskett & Marsden, 1998, 2002). These sources provide evidence that there has been some growth in the number of research studies into elementary and primary geography in English language publications. Among the summaries and analyses of some of this more recent research the work of Wiegand (1992, 1993), who drew together a range of research to provide a grounding for teaching in relation to the new geography national curriculum in England (DES/WO, 1991), and Matthews (1992), who provided a thorough overview of the state of our understanding of children's place and environmental learning, drawn largely from sources in environmental psychology and cognition and behavioural and phenomenological geography, not school learning in geography.

These studies have been more recently extended by specifically focused reviews of research into particular areas of interest to geographical education. While they encompass understanding and learning across the school age range they also identify aspects of relevance to primary geography. These research analyses cover environmental education (Palmer, 1998; Hart & Nolan, 1999; Rickinson, 2001), children's environmental participation (Hart, 1997), children's environmental experience (Thomas & Thompson, 2004), outdoor learning (Rickinson et al, 2004) and children's understanding of food and farming (Dillon, et al, 2003). There have also been reviews that have linked younger children's environmental and geographical experience and learning to geography in primary education, for instance in relation to children's perceptions of the world about them (Scoffham, 1999) and to children's geographies and the primary curriculum (Catling, 2003).

Alongside these studies there have been few attempts to draw together research and research overviews, linked particularly to primary research activity. The essential context for this approach has been in *children's geographies*. The collections of Holloway & Valentine (2000), Christensen & O'Brien (2003) and Chawla (2002), for example, have been complemented with an educational focus by two useful texts edited by Robertson & Gerber (2000, 2001). These collections have provided some insight into younger children's developing geographical understanding, though the emphasis has been more clearly on older children and youth. To support these publications and to make available more recent work in primary geography, both a collection of brief papers by Scoffham (1998) and two collections of 'up-dates' on ongoing studies edited by Bowles (2000, 2002) have been published. While work has focused often on primary education rather than the early years, this is not entirely the case (Cooper, 2004). Since the mid-1990s two journals, in particular, have provided for the publication of research into geographical education and have ensured that several research studies in other parts of the world relevant to primary geography and children's learning are available. These are the journals of *International Research in Environmental and Geographical Education* [IRGEE] and *Environmental Education Research* [EER]. There are, therefore, a number of sources that are helping to encourage access to research in primary geography.

Towards evidence-informed practice

At the start of this chapter the point was made that much that is done in primary geography is based on experience, and a concern was raised that this might be no more than 'gut feeling'. Yet, more positively, one might see such experientially-based decisions interpreted as built on much personal trial and error in teaching, on personal observations of children learning and on teaching experience and through using the experience gained to improve 'tried and tested' approaches that appear to be of benefit. Such a way of working, especially if related to the work of others, might be seen to be based in professional *wisdom* about teaching primary geography. There is no doubt about the importance and value of such wisdom, but too often in recent years, concern has been raised about under-expectations by teachers of primary-age children in their geographical education (Ofsted, 2002, 2003, 2004). The concern that might be expressed here is that too often the classroom wisdom is inappropriately pitched.

The argument has been growing in recent years for practice in education to be much more effectively evidence-based (Thomas & Pring, 2004). While the focus of the debate lies most strongly in educational policy, the application of evidence to classroom practice is certainly strong, particularly in relation to the core subjects in the primary curriculum. Yet evidence-based practice is a contentious area. In part this arises from the issues around the nature of evidence. For some, 'scientific' evidence is the only valid basis for action; that is, what is undertaken should be grounded fully in experimental testing, which until shown otherwise, provides results that certain activities produce inevitable outcomes, on the basis of proof. However, by no means all scientists adhere to such a narrow interpretation of scientific research. For others, evidence arises through the analysis of records and data to lead to a best-fit thesis, as in historical research or, quite often, in geographical studies. Yet others, in the fields of 'the arts' see 'evidence' in a different light, more open, perhaps more akin to being grounded in 'wisdom'. It is clear from those who write on such matters that while educational research and research with children and in classrooms must be rigorous it can also be varied in its approach and style, dependent upon the focus and context of such studies (McKernan, 1996; Cohen, Manion & Morrison, 2000; Mason, 2002; Fraser et al., 2004; Lewis et al., 2004). Research is a qualitative, not just a quantitative, process.

What is argued is that too often activities in education, from policy judgements to practice decisions, have not been grounded in evidence but based, perhaps, more on preference, whim or prejudice. The need is to ensure that curriculum, teaching and learning decisions are clearly based in research (Sebba, 2004), though there is debate over the nature of the types of research that count or are privileged (Hammersley, 2004). Part of the argument is over the regard for qualitative as against quantitative research, but there is a consensus that research of whichever style should be rigorous and reliable. Thomas (2004) argues that three criteria are important in judging the worth of evidence. It should be *relevant*, in that the information used supports or challenges the arguments or propositions put forward. It should be *sufficient*, in that there is corroboration and reliability with other instances that are relevant; that is, there is a *weight* of reliable evidence. It should have *veracity*, in that the evidence gathered is not prejudiced by distortion or biased through interest. This does not mean that evidence, to be valid, has to be gathered in a particular way; it is more open than that and can take account of tacit understanding as much as of experimental findings. Evidence can, then, encompass personal experience, observation, artefacts, testimony and experiment, but these need to be rigorously gathered, analysed and evaluated.

In one sense classroom practice will always be grounded in evidence, the evidence of experience, personal wisdom and tacit knowledge. Yet it is important that this evidence is examined systematically such that it might be applied rather than remain idiosyncratic. There is, then, an argument for a rigorous approach to understanding the evidence in practice where the interest lies in applying that evidence to inform other people's practice. The development of new ways of teaching and supporting learning in primary geography may come from a considered hunch or through 'inspiration', but they need to be 'tested' in the wider arena of teachers' practical application to understand what enables something to work, if not all the time, at least for many teachers and for many children. The purpose of looking more carefully at what is happening in a classroom, of identifying how a particular approach may most usefully be trialled, of considering the appropriate sequence for a set of tasks to help learning progress, or of evaluating what a variety of related studies might indicate about possible good practice or future lines for development, is to be more explicit, transparent and rigorous in identifying what might be useful for others to apply.

The issue for research in primary geography is that it has been limited and needs to be developed and invigorated. In order to consider what the varieties of best practice might be in planning geography teaching, in identifying the range of practices to help children to understand and learn about geographical experiences, ideas and ways of examining the world, in developing resources that might be helpful in more than one way, and in appreciating how we understand the ways in which children learn, achieve, develop and modify their understandings, the need is to argue for fuller and longer term studies, building from the small scale research that has been undertaken. What has been, and continues to be, done provides the foundation for delving much more fully and with greater care and rigour into the world of geographical teaching and learning.

The range and quality of primary geography research

Concern has been voiced about the quality and depth of much of the educational research undertaken in the UK (Hillage et al, 1998; Tooley & Derby, 1998). This has been echoed in environmental and geographical research more recently (Rickinson, 2001, Rickinson & Reid, 2003) and has led the Geographical Association to develop a new series of publications relating research to practice, *Theory into Practice* (eg Walkington, 1999) and the British Educational Research Association [BERA] to develop a series of *Professional User Reviews* (eg Rawling, 2003; Rickinson et al, 2003). While the range of research into primary geography noted in recent bibliographies on geographical education (Foskett & Marsden, 1998, 2002) indicates that there is a variety of research being undertaken, a reading of the research itself identifies it as usually small scale and spread thinly. While much of the research might meet standards of rigour and be relevant, in Thomas's terms there is a difficulty with much of what is undertaken being *sufficient* and having reliability in that there is corroboration across a number of studies, preferably in differing contexts, even cultures. One issue for quality in primary geography research lies in its internal limited extent.

Areas and topics for research in Primary Geography

1. Geography
Children's and trainee teachers' understanding of the term 'geography'
Children's understanding of 'geographical' vocabulary

2. The physical environmental
Children's emergent environmental understanding
Children's understanding of weather
Children's knowledge of landforms
Children's perceptions of geological time
Children's knowledge of soil, rocks and weathering
Children's conceptions of nature
Children's understanding of rivers

3. The social environment
Children's ideas about work
Children's understanding of farming and food
Children's understanding of trade and industry
Children's experience and understanding of journeys

4. Environmental issues
Children's, trainee teachers' and teachers' understanding environmental issues
Children's, trainee teachers' and teachers' awareness of climate change, the greenhouse effect and the ozone layer
Children's ideas about air pollution
Children's ideas about municipal waste and what is done with it
Children's sense of environmental care
Children's participation in environmental action
Children's sense of and preferences for the present and the future

5. Place
Children's sense of place
Children's knowledge of places
Children's knowledge of environmental features
Children's understanding of settlements

6. Spatial awareness
Children's understanding nested hierarchies
Children's wayfinding in familiar environments
Children's route and layout learning skills and capabilities
Children's construction of spatial layout in familiar environments

7. A global sense and international understanding
Children's ideas about hot and cold places
Children's awareness of, attitudes to and empathy for other peoples and nations
Children's development of international understanding
Children's and student teachers' locational knowledge of places in the world
Children's travel experience and its impact
Children's knowledge of people and places and the impact of stereotypes, partiality, bias and prejudice

8. Fieldwork
The impact of curriculum planning and pupil involvement in fieldwork and outdoor education
Fieldwork as stimulus for learning about the environment
The effectiveness of residential fieldwork on children's learning
Affective attitudes to the environment through fieldwork
Co-operative learning in fieldwork activities
The impact of outdoor education on self-perception
Pupils' engagement in school grounds project participation

9. Graphicacy: mapwork
Children's developing cognitive maps in familiar environments
Children's understanding of map symbols, co-ordinates and scale
Children's ability to locate features on atlas maps
Children's capability in constructing maps
Children's use of maps in the environment
Children's capacity to read and work with aerial photographs

10. Graphicacy: pictures
Children's fieldwork sketching skills
Ways in which children read photographs
Children's understanding from photographs

11. Geography curriculum, pedagogy and assessment
Teaching about local and distant places
Progression within primary geography
Key stage 2/3 progression

12. Resources
The impact of media, such as television, on children's understanding of the world about them
The role of children's family in their knowledge and (mis)understanding of the world, places and environments

Figure 1: Areas of research relevant to primary geography

There is a wide range of research that has been undertaken in relation to primary geography. Such research has encompassed the curriculum, its teaching, learners and resources. However, as Rickinson (2001) notes for environmental education, there are gaps, particularly in the processes of learning geography in classrooms. Figure 1 indicates those areas of primary geography where relevant and related research has been undertaken. The information draws on the bibliographies and analyses of Dillon et al (2003), Hart & Nolan (1999), Forsyth (1995), Foskett & Marsden (1998, 2002), Matthews (1992), Rickinson (2001), Rickinson et al (2004), Wiegand (1992, 1993), Scoffham (1998) and on papers in IRGEE and EER amongst other journals, as well as on some earlier collections of studies (Graves, 1972; Bale, Graves and Walford, 1973).

Within the twelve areas of study identified a wide variety of sub-topics have been researched. While the range of topics appears impressive, it is the case that many of these have been researched in one or very few small-scale studies. The major areas of research, in which studies number in the hundreds are children's environmental experience, particularly in the familiar environment but also in experimental environments (Matthews, 1992), and in mapwork, use and understanding, again linked both to environmental experience in cognitive mapping studies and to skill acquisition, with quite an emphasis in studies in the USA in atlas work and locational knowledge (Forsyth, 1995; Matthews, 1992). Some areas of study have been popular at given times and then interest appears to have been lost in them, for instance studies into understanding of national identity and international understanding were developed in the 1960s but little has been undertaken since, while studies of primary children's awareness and understanding of the world of work were developed in the 1980s but have since fallen by the way. Most recently, environmental understanding and awareness of environmental issues and concerns have been to the fore, developing strongly in the 1990s. The emphasis in much of the research has been into children's knowledge and understanding, but little still is known of the *processes* of geographical learning, whether informally in the environment or through family and the media or formally in the school setting. It is valuable to have a clear sense of what it is that children are aware of, know, understand, feel about and can or want to do, but it is problematic when it remains unclear how this information can be effectively used to enhance the quality of teaching and the capacity to learn effectively. The processes of teaching primary geography are equally under-researched.

As Figure 1 indicates, the curriculum, pedagogic, assessment and resource areas of research are very limited as areas of study. Yet for teachers these are, perhaps, the most important aspects in which that understanding is needed. This seems all the more necessary since research into locational knowledge among children (and, indeed, adults) and into environmental knowledge (as against environmental attitudes) indicates that not only are there considerable gaps in knowledge and understanding but that children have developed misunderstanding, misconceptions and even utterly misconceived ideas by the time they leave primary school. While it appears that children have the potential to learn effectively and to develop high levels of competence, the strong foundations for which can be laid in primary geography, it seems that there are considerable limitations to achieving this at present. There may be *sufficient* knowledge of what children can do or of the difficulties they have in a few areas of relevance to geographical learning, but much of what has been undertaken in primary geography research lacks corroboration.

What becomes clear in examining the aspects of geography curriculum, teaching and learning listed in Figure 1 – albeit of varied depth and quality – is that there are significantly important aspects of geographical education which lack any research base. These key aspects are noted in

Figure 2. It is not that they have not been noted before (Catling, 2000), but that there have been very real limits to undertaking effective research into such topics, the impact of which has been so far to inhibit, to minimise and even to prevent any study in some of them. From Figure 2 it is possible to see the extent of the research that is needed.

Gaps in the research studies in primary geography

1. Geography curriculum and planning
Teachers' attitudes to geography in the primary school curriculum
Primary teachers' knowledge and understanding of the geography they teach
How teacher's geographical understanding affects their geography teaching
Appropriate strategies to develop teachers' geographical understanding
Effective practices in planning the geography curriculum
Effective practices in lesson planning in geography
Creativity in geography curriculum planning and teaching
How teachers select resources and use them in their geography teaching

2. Teaching geography
Teachers' perceptions and expectations of children in geography
The impact of whole class, group and individual learning strategies
The use and impact of enquiry-led teaching in geography
The role of effective questioning in geography teaching
The use of ICT to enhance geographical learning
The use of differentiation in geography teaching
How teachers identify children's misconceptions and use strategies to overcome these
Teachers use of explanation in geography teaching
Teachers' application of higher order thinking skills in geography teaching
Approaches to assessment in geography teaching and learning

3. Aspects of geographical learning
How children's personal geographies affect their learning of local geography
Ways in which children's perceptions and attitudes can be accessed and harnessed in their geographical learning
Children's understanding of specific concepts in geography, such as land use, tourism, transport, rural, and so forth
Children's strategies in the use of different types of resources
The ways in which children respond to geographical displays and other aspects of the school environment
Children's sense of self-esteem in their geographical learning
The affect that different teaching strategies have on children's geographical learning

---

Figure 2: Aspects of primary geography lacking research evidence

There are several significant gaps in our current understanding of primary geography, its planning, teaching and pupils' learning. While this might appear to set an agenda for future studies, it poses the equally significant question about how such research might be undertaken. It is clearly *relevant* and vital to do; but it is important that *sufficient* research is undertaken of a scale and depth that gives it standing in the professional community; and such research needs to be undertaken to ensure *veracity*. To do this requires appropriate resources, something which is problematic in an environment where the non-core subjects of the primary curriculum are not seen as central in research priorities, though the government appears to espouse a rhetoric that argues for a full and broad curriculum (DfES, 2003) and appears to support some relevant research development (Sebba, 2004) and analysis, supported by government (Dillon at al, 2003)

21

or other organisations (Rickinson, 2001; Rickinson et al, 2004). While funding has been accessible for research into children's environmental understanding and activities, it has been much less available for school and classroom-based research related directly to teaching and learning in geography lessons.

Conclusion

The state of primary geography was characterised at the start of this chapter as in a relatively early stage of development. The basis for this assertion is that while there has been a considerable variety of studies undertaken of relevance to primary geography curriculum, teaching and learning (see Figure 1), there has been a lack of *sufficiency* in the studies undertaken and there are important gaps in areas that need to be effectively researched (see Figure 2). Too much of the research in primary geography has 'glanced at' particular topics through small-scale research studies. Only a little – and that largely funded outside geography education, for instance in environmental psychology – has been of a depth and scale that gives it weight as informed evidence. There is still much that needs to be done if primary geography is to become better informed through an evidence base that is extensive, well grounded, rigorous and reliable, in other words, that has *relevance, sufficiency* and *veracity*.

During the latter part of the twentieth century much good work was done in small scale studies of children's familiar environmental experience, of their capacity to make sense of their environmental experience in terms of its spatial organisation, of the variability and partiality of that personal experience and what affected this, of their ability to create maps of their understanding of places, and of their sense of familiar places. Alongside this there have been extensive research into children's capability in understanding the skills of map reading, how they can use and make maps at a range of scales from the immediate and larger familiar environment to national, continental and global contexts (Matthews, 1992). No other area relevant to children's geographical understanding has been researched to this extent; indeed much has been examined only cursorily, not intentionally so but because priorities and funds have been focused elsewhere. In relation to teaching primary geography and to children's experience in and of their geographical learning, there are major gaps in the literature, which have been filled to a large extent by the wisdom of informed experience, through the tacit professional knowledge of teachers. The variety of texts that have provided this informed base for teachers to use, for instance through articles in *Primary Geographer*, is well illustrated in the entries for primary geography in recent bibliographies (Forsyth, 1995; Foskett & Marsden, 1998, 2000). The need now is to search for ways in which this advice and guidance can be studied in practice, such that it is better understood and able to be applied more effectively from teacher to teacher and context to context. Equally, in areas where there is limited advice and little classroom action, such as in differentiation and assessment, this can provide a much-needed fillip to future developments in primary geography.

This book sets out to add in a small way to the totality of research into children's geographical understanding, to support work in primary geography education and to throw some light on teachers' and trainee teachers' geographical learning. The range of chapters that follow indicate the nature and extent of some of the work currently underway, largely from British sources. It is hoped that its contribution may stimulate further studies and encourage those who want to take research in primary geography forward with a stronger base and to higher ground. Certainly, it reflects the determination, efforts and contributions of a wide variety of geography educators who wish to see primary geography better grounded in an informed evidence-base.

References

Aitken, S. (2001), *Geographies of Young People*, London: Routledge

Bale, J., Graves, N. & Walford, R. (eds.) (1973), *Perspectives on Geographical Education*, London: Oliver & Boyd

Blaut, J. & Stea, D. (1971), Studies in Geographic Learning, *Annals of the Association of American Geographers*, 61, 387-393

Bowles, R. (ed.) (2000), *Raising Achievement in Geography*, London: Register of Research in Primary Geography

Bowles, R. (ed.) (2002), *Best Practice in Raising Achievement*, London: Register of Research in Primary Geography

Catling, S. (2000), The Importance of Classroom Research in Primary geography, in Bowles, R. (ed.) (2000), *Raising Achievement in Geography*, London: Register of Research in Primary Geography, 29-38

Catling, S. (2003), Curriculum Contested: Primary Geography and Social Justice, *Geography*, 88, 164-210

Chawla, L. (ed.) (2002), *Growing Up in an Urbanising World*, London: Earthscan/UNESCO

Christensen, P. & O'Brien, M. (eds.) (2003), *Children in the City: Home, Neighbourhood and Community*, London: RoutledgeFalmer

Cohen, L., Manion, L. & Morrison, K. (2000), *Research Methods in Education*, London: Routledge

Cooper, H. (ed.) (2004), *Exploring Time and Place through Play*, London: David Fulton

DES/WO, *Geography in the National Curriculum (England)*, London: HMSO

DfES (2003), *Excellence and Enjoyment: A strategy for primary schools*, London: DfES

Dillon, J., Rickinson, M., Sanders, D., Teamey, K. & Benefield, P. (2003), *Improving the Understanding of Food, Farming and Land Management Amongst School-Age Children: A Literature Review*, [DfES Research Report No. 422], London: DfES

Fog Olwig, K. & Gulløv, E. (eds.) (2003), *Children's Places: cross-cultural perspectives*, London: Routledge

Forsyth, A. (1995), *Learning Geography: An Annotated Bibliography of Research Paths*, Indiana: National Council for Geographic Education

Foskett, N. & Marsden, B. (1998), *A Bibliography of Geographical Education 1970-1997*, Sheffield: Geographical Association

Foskett, N. & Marsden, B. (2002), *A Bibliography of Geographical Education: Supplement 1998-1999*, Sheffield: Geographical Association

Fraser, S., Lewis, V., Ding, S., Kellett, M. & Robinson, C. (eds.) (2004), *Doing Research with Children and Young People*, London: Sage

Graves, N. (ed.) (1972), *New Movements in the Study and Teaching of Geography*, London: Temple Smith

Hammersley, M. (2004), Some questions about evidence-based practice in education, in Thomas, G. & Pring R. (eds.), *Evidence-based Practice in Education*, Maidenhead: Open University Press, 133-149

Hart, P. & Nolan, K. (1999), A Critical Analysis of Research in Environmental Education, *Studies in Science Education*, 34, 1-69

Hart, R. (1997), *Children's Participation*, London: Earthscan

Hillage, J., Pearson, R., Anderson, A. & Tamkin, P. (1998), *Excellence in Research in Schools*, London: DfEE

Holloway, S. & Valentine, G. (eds.) (2000), *Children's Geographies: playing, living, learning*, London: Routledge

Lewis, V., Kellett, M., Robinson, C., Fraser, S. & Ding, S. (eds.) (2004), *The Reality of Research with Children and Young People*, London: Sage

Long, M. (1964), The Teaching of Geography: a review of recent British research and investigations, *Geography*, 49, 192-205

Lukehirst, C. & Graves, N. (1972), *Geography in Education: A Bibliography of British sources 1870-1970*, Sheffield: Geographical Association

Mason, J. (2002), *Researching Your Own Practice: The Discipline of Noticing*, London: RoutledgeFalmer

Matthews, M. H. (1992), *Making Sense of Place: Children's understanding of large scale environments*, Hemel Hempstead: Harvester Wheatsheaf

McKernan, J. (1996), *Curriculum Action Research*, London: Kogan Page

Naish, M. (1972), *Some Aspects of the Study and Teaching of Geography in Britain: A Review of Recent British Research* [Teaching Geography Occasional Paper No 18], Sheffield: Geographical Association

Ofsted (2002), *Primary Subject reports 2000/01: Geography*, London: Ofsted also http://www.ofsted.gov.uk/publications/index.cfm?fuseaction=pubs.summary&id=2870 accessed June 2004

Ofsted (2003), *Geography in Primary Schools: Ofsted Subject Report series 2001/02*, also http://www.ofsted.gov.uk/publications/index.cfm?fuseaction=pubs.summary&id=3163 accessed 5 May 2003 and June 2004

Ofsted (2004), *Ofsted subject reports 2002/03: Geography in primary schools*, London: Ofsted also http://www.ofsted.gov.uk/publications/index.cfm?fuseaction=pubs.summary&id=3523 accessed June 2004

Palmer, J. (1998), *Environmental Education for the 21st Century*, London: Routledge

Phillips, R. (ed.) (2001), *Geographies of Childhood*, Area, 33, 117-189

Rawling, E. (2003), *Connecting Policy and Practice: Research in Geographical Education*, Southwell: BERA

Rickinson, M. (2001), Learners and Learning in Environmental Education: a critical review of the evidence, *Environmental Education Research*, 7, 207-320

Rickinson, M., Aspinall, C., Clark, A., Dawson, L., Poulton, P., Rogers, J. & Sargent, J. (2003), *Connecting Research and Practice: Education for Sustainable Development*, Southwell: BERA

Rickinson, M., Dillon, J., Teamey, K., Morris, M., Choi, M., Sanders, D. & Benefield, P. (2004), *A Review of Research on Outdoor Learning*, Preston Montford: Field Studies Council

Rickinson, M. & Reid, A. (2003), What's the Use of Research in Environmental Education?, paper presented to the American Educational research Association [AERA], April, available through http://www.nfer.ac.uk/research/envsd.asp accessed 5 May 2004

Robertson, M. & Gerber, R. (eds.) (2000), *The Child's World: Triggers for Learning*, Melbourne: ALCER Press

Robertson, M. & Gerber, R. (eds.) (2001), *Children's Ways of Knowing: Learning through experience*, Melbourne: ALCER Press

Saveland, R. & Pannell, C. (1978), *Some Aspects of the Study and Teaching of Geography in the United States: A Review of Current Research 1965-1975* [Teaching Geography Occasional Paper No 30], Sheffield: Geographical Association

Scarfe, N. (1949), The teaching of geography in schools: a review of British research, *Geography*, 34, 57-65

Scoffham, S. (ed.) (1998), *Primary Sources: Research findings in primary geography*, Sheffield: Geographical Education

Scoffham, S. (1999), Young Children's Perceptions of the World, in David, T (ed.), *Teaching Young Children*, London: Paul Chapman Publishing, 125-138

Sebba, J. (2004), Developing evidence-informed policy and practice in education, in Thomas, G. & Pring R. (eds), *Evidence-based Practice* in *Education*, Maidenhead: Open University Press, 34-43

Thomas, G. (2004), Introduction: evidence and practice, in Thomas, G & Pring R (eds.), *Evidence-based Practice* in *Education*, Maidenhead: Open University Press, 1-18

Thomas, G. & Pring R. (eds.) (2004), *Evidence-based Practice* in *Education*, Maidenhead: Open University Press

Thomas, G. & Thompson, G. (2004), *A Child's Place: Why environment matters to children*, London: Demos/Green Alliance

Tooley, J. & Derby, D. (1998), *Educational Research: A Critique*, London: Ofsted

Walford, R. (2001), *Geography in British Schools 1850-2000*, London: Woburn Press

Walkington, H. (1999), *Theory into Practice: Global Citizenship Education*, Sheffield: Geographical Association

Wiegand, P. (1992), *Places in the Primary School*, London: Falmer Press

Wiegand, P. (1993), *Children and Primary Geography*, London: Cassell

SECTION 1

CHILDREN AND PEDAGOGY

Children's geographical understanding

Chapter 2

Children's Understanding of Locality

Rachel Bowles

Introduction: Why question perception?

Discussions with children of different ages and from different contexts show that their ideas about their home area vary from locality to locality. Why should this be? The variations cannot be accounted for entirely through environmental differences. The work of developmental and environmental psychologists, education specialists and planners who have studied the development of spatial and environmental knowledge has been examined to find possible solutions to such variations unaccounted for by geographical studies.

Curiosity about children's locality perceptions began when working with children in different school contexts, such as in the English rural village of Eyam in the Peak District National Park and the cosmopolitan inner metropolitan village of Clerkenwell in Central London (Bowles, 1994b, 1997a). To aid the development of resources for National Curriculum work in the locality, children were asked four simple enquiry questions to see how far they appreciated the features of an area familiar to them through every day activities. The answers, proffered to a stranger, showed a considerable variation in perceptions of the extent and character of the home locality. This provoked the question as to whether this was the consequence of the nature of the environment and the concentration of facilities within the area. Both considerations affected temporal and linear scales of activity (Bowles 1995, 1997b). When inner and outer city suburban children were similarly questioned, social, cultural and community factors began to appear.

Children's geographies

Holloway and Valentine (2000) succinctly describe the two strands of work on children's geographies developed since the early 1970's. On the one hand are studies concerned with the development of spatial cognition and mapping ability, and on the other are those examining the social geographies of children in an adult world, which draw attention to the ways in which children negotiate the *childhoods* constructed in different places, times and scales. The principal concern of the investigators of *children's geographies* is with the street and 'public' space, and with children's access to, use of and attachment to these spaces. These studies have highlighted the uneven geography of such spaces against the background of children's play preferences. (Holloway & Valentine, 2000:11-12). Those researchers considering spatial intelligences are more concerned with the geographical constructs of the individual child, particularly the primary child and how these affect their view of the world about them. Both sets of specialists have come to appreciate that the child's competence and needs in the environment have been underestimated (Aitkin 2001, Holloway and Valentine 2000, Matthews 1992, Spencer et al 1989, 1995).

Martin (1999) succinctly reviewed the contrasting views on locality between children and adults. She pointed out that through Goodey (1971), Matthews (1992) Spencer and Blades (1993), and Hart (1979), there had developed a body of understanding about the nature of children's environmental cognition. Spencer and Blades (1993) showed that children's cognition of environments was connected with active problem solving linked with moving about their locality and developing their own private geographies. Matthews (1992) pointed out that in the course of making sense of their environment children developed an emotional place attachment. In two important studies Hart (1979) and Moore (1986) analysed the way children valued and used their immediate environment. These are studies of intensely private geographies and provide a glimpse into the detail and quality of complex environments that are part of growing up. They encapsulate an element of childhood, of the freedom to create one's own private world, a circumstance that has changed considerably since the mid-nineteenth century.

Hendrick (1997, 60) traced the steady and continued increase 'of the compulsory relationship involving the State, the family, health and public welfare services' since the 1800's. He rightly perceives the developments to be part of realising and paralleling an objective of creating uniformity and coherence 'necessary to unite the urban and the rural, capable of embracing different social-class experiences, and focusing on the supposedly natural state of childhood'. Yet children's geographies are particularly influenced by these different experiences, the urban-rural and social-class, which in turn are compounded by the pervading influence of motor transport, whether personal or commercial.

Childhood spaces have continued to change for two fundamental reasons. One is the continued sociological concern to contain and order the child, in their best interests, by voluntary and official authorities. The other is the concern of middle and working class parents who perceive danger beyond the confines of home and garden. Hillman et al. (1991) have documented the disappearance of children from the street and the increased restrictions placed upon their movement by parents through the changing nature of transport geography. Sibley (1995, 136) has noted that:

> ...the locality is more likely to be experienced from the car, necessarily in the company of adults, rather than alone or in the company of other children. The car then functions as a protective capsule from which the child observes the world but does not experience it directly through encounters with others.

Further, Hillman (1998, 29) has observed that:

> Even apparently laudable initiatives, such as the *Safe Routes to School* projects, reflect the conventional view that children's lives are largely school-oriented...This overlooks the fact that children make many more journeys in their free time to destinations other than school.

These changes have not only affected the private geographies of children but also their public geography which may, or may not, be understood or even perceived by their teacher.

It would seem that academic geographers, public administrators, planners and teachers have had fixed, even unrecognised, perceptions about the way a child thinks, lives and observes within its allotted environment; allotted, because it has no choice about where it is born and brought up. Adults choose the birth or family location, for many reasons which may or may not be focused upon the wellbeing of the child. Consider, at one end of the spectrum, the move of the family home to be near a school of 'excellence' and, at the other, the migration to a country of wealth and presumed cultural safety.

Matthews (1992) has drawn attention to the multi-facetted process of children coming to terms with their environment. He charts the progress of a child's direct experience of outdoor environments both over time and within space. Play spaces, both official and unofficial are considered to be a significant part of environmental experience especially in the context of residential settings and the built environment. Reference is made to the societal context defined and shaped by varying cultural systems. Matthews concluded that:

> ....the opportunities that children have to make sense of place are often beyond their control. Not only is their outdoor behaviour constrained by cultural expectations but also many of the artefacts of place are products of these same cultural mores. (Matthews, 1992, 52)

International research has investigated the nature of these opportunities. Chawla (2002) shows how children can be heard and action taken in a variety of urban environments. Though the aim of the research was to influence urban decision makers, it built on research begun by Lynch (1977) and the research methods, particularly by interview and photographic observation, were used in cities in eight countries. Chawla notes:

> Lynch was surprised by how similar the criteria were that children used to assess their areas, despite great differences in culture, geography and city form...Twenty five years later and in even more disparate environments, most of these constants, in terms of what children like and dislike about their communities, remain substantially unchanged. (Chawla, 2002, 227)

Over the same period children indicated a number of increased concerns – particularly about traffic, environmental changes, crime and the effects of migration. Further the increased access to television could be shown to have influenced the freedom to go into the local community but not the importance of doing so. All of these factors need to be taken into consideration when looking at locality knowledge.

Research approach

Investigations need constant refinement in the light of an available population, favourable environment, suitable tools and the requirement to achieve rigorously analysed outcomes recognisable by an audience with disparate views and concerns.

The material

Initially the contrast in locality perceptions was noticed with year 5 children in three schools in the course of developing resources for the National Curriculum (Bowles 1995, 1997b, 1998). This raised concern about the topic of the study reported in this paper, and a pilot study was initiated. For this four straightforward questions were devised for Year 5 children, and trials were undertaken in London schools in contrasting urban surroundings. The questions relied upon the children remembering responses from a whole class discussion about the locality and asked them to plot the places used and described by the children. Next, using the same four questions but with all available year groups involved, a number of primary schools in London,

Bristol, Blackburn and Derbyshire were studied. Finally, a national survey used the refined methods described below. The locations (Figure 1) ranged from inner city schools, through suburban schools, peripheral urban schools, small town schools, commuter village schools and the New Town of Milton Keynes. They included Middle and First schools, independent and denominational schools and provided a variety of catchment area and social background.

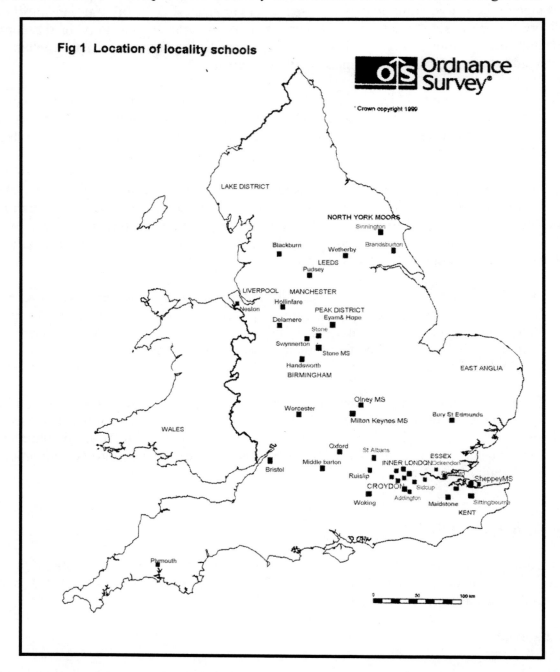

Figure 1: Location of Locality Schools

The sample of primary and middle schools had one common feature. They contained, within the staff, a member known to be in favour of geographical research. Most were aware of the conditions suitable for obtaining unbiased accounts from the children. All gave time and effort and encouraged their colleagues to make time to make sense of the observations in the context of their locality. The sample was determined by location in urban/rural terms and ordered by settlement hierarchy. Within the sample, 32 schools provided cross phase groups of children from Key Stage 1/2, Key Stage 2a /2b or Key Stage 2/3.

By the end of 2000 nearly 1,000 children, in groups of 5, had been interviewed about their perception of their locality, particularly of key landmarks and associated land use. There was no conscious grading by ability, though lower ability at any age may have been shown by the lack of a comparative increase in detail in perception usual for the age group. There was no exclusion; some of the most vivid perceptions, though limited in extent, came from Down's syndrome children. Children identified as suffering Attention Deficit Hyperactivity Disorder (ADHD) also contributed where the teacher and the children had clear coping techniques. All children contributed, whether identified or not as having learning difficulties.

For the study, groups were limited to 5 pupils. Even numbered groups (4 or 6) fell naturally in pairs or into two groups whose dynamics became counterproductive. No school found it difficult to organise groups of 5, but some teachers did not appreciate that groups of 6 provided an unhelpfully different scenario. Odd number sized groups allow for the emergence of a leader. This leader need not be the same person for each activity, e.g. one person may have strengths in making decisions about the significance of specific features, while another can understand the significance of distance and yet another understand priorities in choosing one destination above other destinations. The rest of the group were happy to have this spokesperson make a statement to which they could add their own observations. Even numbered groups, on the other hand, inevitably fall into pairs, with each pair becoming vociferous without enhancing the structure of the enquiry. The lack of a leader to make a statement reduced the variety and depth of evidence freely given. Instead there was competition without rules. Doise et al (1975, cited in Wiegand, 1996, 119) 'established that children perform at a higher level if they are interviewed in groups, appearing to decentre more readily by taking into account the responses of their peers'.

The schools were visited in no particular order, the prime concern being to fit the visit into the most appropriate slot in the school programme. This was usually perceived to be best in the late summer term when the timetable was in a relaxed mode following the completion of the SATS activities of the first part of the term. This was also the time when children move about more freely, with or without supervision.

This random visit approach took no account of the possibility of different authority structures until two primary schools revealed themselves as First Schools and a third school as a Middle School. These three schools became the *raison d'être* for considering three clusters of First/Middle school combinations in North Kent, Buckinghamshire and Staffordshire, and thus extended the study into the perceptions of lower KS3 children. Independent sector involvement arose through contacts with interested teachers and combined curiosity to see how far 'independence' through wealth affected perception and ability to perceive a locality. These children contributed unexpected social elements but blended with the general evidence overall. Awareness of the contribution of denominational schools also arose by chance, but the factor of the school catchment having a range of locality upon which to draw, providing the opportunity to explore similarity and difference, gave added value for the schools' geographical work and reinforced the study's enquiries concerned with children's ability to observe.

The Process

Each school was visited within one day. Up to 90 children could be interviewed in groups of 5 for 15 minutes per group. This period was found to be an appropriate length during which the children could focus well on the task. The youngest children in a school were often interviewed first in the day when they were felt to be at their most alert. When it was necessary to begin the day interviewing the oldest children their alertness often led to 20-25 minute interviews, providing a much more detailed account of their learning about the locality. This approach provided the interviewer with a framework, which guided subsequent scaffolding questions. Interviewing the oldest children in a school at the start of the day only happened when they were involved in other plans later in the day.

Learning about the locality from the children was not a requirement of the study. It was always possible to have made a preliminary survey of the locality to become familiar with the features and place names. A further survey was undertaken at lunchtime when mentioned features in the locality, which were referred to regularly in the interview, were visited. Other, less frequently mentioned features and places were sought out after school, and discussed with the teachers, once the interviews had been completed.

To organise the interview programme from the youngest to the oldest in the school proved the most beneficial approach. It corroborated, through listening to the children, the notion that precision in locating observations increases with age. At the same time, it enabled a superficial measure of any particular group's egocentric perceptions. This was useful for phrasing the scaffolding questions to produce the most efficient descriptions and reduce anecdotal description. Finally, by the time the older children were interviewed, it was possible to concentrate upon filling in the detail of the framework learnt from the younger children.

The interview

Local aerial photographs and the local 1:25,000 map were always available to support the interviews and as an element in the scaffolding of the structured interview. The interviews were based upon *four main questions*:
- Where is the school on the photograph/map
- Where do you live?
- Which places do you visit often?
- What are the main places of interest in your home locality?

Further questions might be added and provided insight into finer geographical detail in children's knowledge (see Chapter 18, where the quantified responses have been used to support a different argument). The older children were asked to specify what they most valued about their area. The places were recorded on the map using different symbols for each year group. The children's responses were recorded using a VOR and by note taking by the researcher.

Findings

Initial evidence

What kinds of understanding do children already have about their home area? What are the factors which may or may not be taken as universal influences upon locality teaching?
Experience, when developing the three study kits on Plymouth, Eyam, and Bury St Edmunds (Bowles, 1994a, 1994b, 1994c) showed that the size of locality and its geographical content was unique to each school. Emerging from these observations arose consideration of the perceptions of children in schools in different geographical contexts. Further enquiry revealed that the 'core'

locality as understood by the children meant those places visited regularly. It appears to be consistent with every age and seems usually determined by walking distance to school, the nearest post office and general stores. The size of the core area is coincident with the concept of the whole locality if it also contains all the needs of the community for special as well as everyday needs. The *idea of locality* begins to expand at an early age if shopping and other amenities require car transport. The narrowest concept of locality occurs in inner city areas where cars are a luxury. The most extended concept of locality is to be found in the outer suburb or rural village seeded with commuter families using the car for work and reaching amenities. Evidence from later interviews with primary children reinforced these findings.

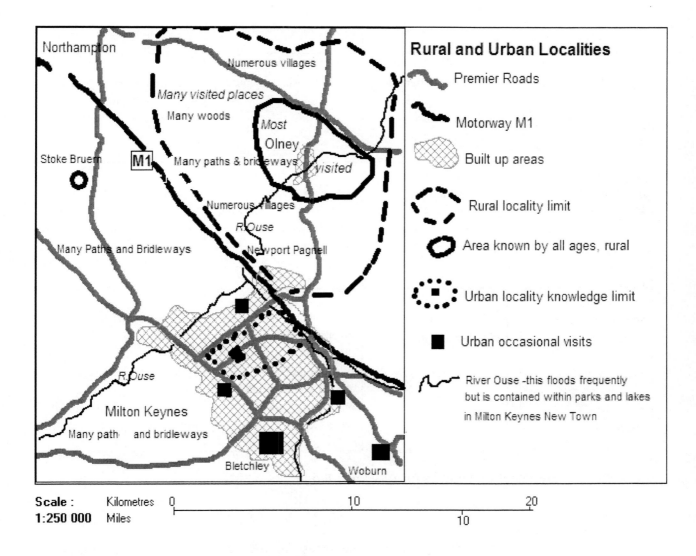

Figure 2: Map of Olney/Sherington & Milton Keynes catchment areas

Main evidence

The initial analysis of the interviews revealed specific themes that cut across the variety of locality contexts. These themes are children's maturation, family constraints, community constraints, community expansion, mobility and children's environmental and spatial awareness.

Maturation

Throughout, there is evidence of progression in the development of children's thought processes with maturation. In answer to the questions, 'Where do you play?' and 'What is there?', the sequence from the first response, through description to more precise location was distinctive for each age group. This sequence is outlined in Figure 3.

4-5 years	5-6 years	7-8 years	9-10 years
1. School or home play area	1. No mention of school or home play area	1. No children's playgrounds admitted	1. No places for any activity were named
2. Nearest swings and roundabouts, which may or may not be in park	2. 'The Park' figured hugely for its space and different areas for different activities	2. 'Park' usually named	2. Specific directions given without prompting
3. Located on a photograph	3. Walking mentioned as an activity, but names of locations not given	3. Leisure centres, especially for swimming, frequently referred to; needed prompting for names	3. Queries about grown-up leisure locations; for example, golf, football, fully answered
	4. located on photograph	4. no specific locations given but finger walking directions on the map frequent and usually correct where aerial photographs covered same area	4. range of activities available in leisure centres and the area generally well known, except by those children who were constrained by cultural concerns or lack of family initiative

Figure 3: Development of a child's locality knowledge

Family constraints

It has become clear that in every school, regardless of the school's type, local context and standing, there are children who come from unsupportive families. Tentatively, these children could be detected through their answers and back chat with their peers, as could, superficially, some of the reasons. Among those reasons appeared to be family divorce, single parent family circumstances (neither a *sine qua non)*, unemployment leading to inertia, and the fears of resettled families (usually migrant travellers or immigrants). Other causes could be found in social mores such as suburban fear through media description of assaults upon young children, a lack of time/willingness to accompany children on locality activities such as walking, cycling and taking part in group activities such as Cubs and Brownies, and, sadly, the working families who use their affluence to take children out of the locality for their leisure activities and who do not make use of the immediate locality. This area requires further investigation using a more sophisticated approach to gathering data and to analysis.

Community constraints
The children, regardless of locality, consistently demonstrated that there are areas of the locality which are *invisible* to them. One has to consider if these are straightforwardly gaps in their knowledge (they have not noticed them at all) or if they are gaps of perception (they 'see' the features but do not have a framework to link the 'information' to). For instance, in most schools the 'work' or employment facet of a locality tended to be invisible and remained invisible despite promptings and despite children appreciating that parents needed to work. It was not associated with their idea of locality

In only two schools did children provide unprompted detailed commentary upon such features and aspects in the local environment. In particular children referred to change in the local area. Children referred to their own observations of local change over time, but they also referred to other relatives' observations and commentary upon those changed features in past times. Both schools had not specifically taught about the particular aspects of local change noted by the children, but both schools were in very stable communities that had many child-friendly activities in which all the family could participate. The children were well used to using their locality. Moreover, the staff of the school came almost wholly from the locality and they were well aware of the cause and effect of change in both the physical and human elements of the locality. Given the stability of these two contexts, there is an important question here. Does this indicate that many communities today have too restless a population to develop a sense of place or to remain long enough in that place to recognise change? This is a theme which needs to be investigated further drawing on a broader and more detailed data base.

Community expansion
The distribution map of the school catchment has an important part to play in providing clues for the paucity or otherwise of locality knowledge. To be 'in-comers' to a community has disadvantages whether the move is from town or country. New estates have their own 'life' – the developers create it so. Most often new housing is for first time buyers with young families and the layout is so arranged that they are often self contained, inward looking and with links only to the nearest shopping parade. In three localities the new estates had been superimposed over the old pathway network, blotting it out and hindering walking in the local area. In another locality the planners had intended to contain the whole community and had succeeded so well that connections were minimal with the surrounding countryside but frequent to the Metropolis, an hour away.

Mobility
The presence or absence of personal transport and the ability to be mobile within a comparatively small area is influential in developing locality understanding. Anecdotal and oral evidence from older generations would suggest that the experience and hence perception, in detail, of one's local area is decreasing. On the one hand, this loss of experience, awareness and knowledge is in part created by the increase in the built environment, the nature of and traffic within inhibit movement about it; on the other, it has been exacerbated by increased regional transport efficiency, which encourages longer distance leisure visits. Figure 4 shows the contrasts between a small rural community (Olney) and the neighbouring New Town (Milton Keynes), and the reduction of use of open spaces by the top junior children in the urban environment. The urban children's experience appears to be both less varied and less frequent,

and this linked, from interview information, to the urban children's more constrained environmental experience.

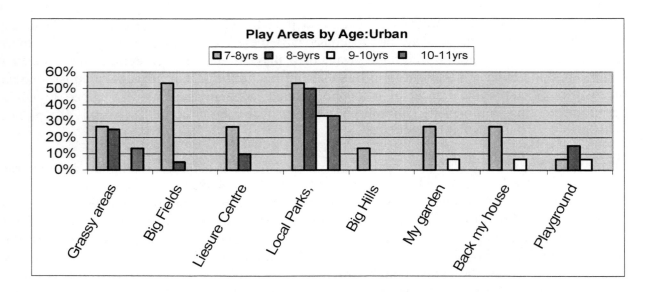

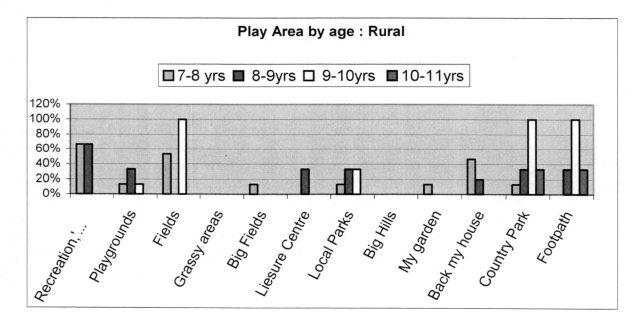

Figure 4: Play Areas by Age

Development of environmental and spatial awareness

Regardless of the type of locality, the children's responses showed a remarkable degree of consistency when describing their area to a stranger. Illustrated particularly by places of play when all features are considered, their observations can be classified as:

1. Absolute certainty of the character of the *core* of the area known by the child. This shows itself as a willingness to describe features without prompting, to debate another's view of those features, and to begin to enquire into the reason for the features, human or physical. This is the area visited most frequently.

2. Acknowledgement of a *fringe* area within which they have secure knowledge of certain features but which they identify discretely, e.g. the toyshop in town, the boat by the river.
3. The key stage 2 child tends to give a fuller picture of the extent of this larger area, define its limits and can be prompted to raise questions about its character. For the older child in key stage 2 this often is their recognised locality.
4. The key stage 3 child tends to go on to express concerns and desires about the future of the locality given the changes that they have observed here or elsewhere. In these cases it was the children who had had rich geographical teaching in their primary years who were most fluent.

Discussion

This research has revealed several factors – including age, parental support and control, maturation, gender, physical and human environmental constraints – which affect the form and extent of a child's perception of the environment. Such perception can be graded from the minimal, restricted form to be found with the inner urban city child and the greater, freer, understanding of the rural child. This leads to a number of questions, among them: Is children's locality perception essentially the result of their environmental experience, fundamentally an informal, personal experience? Can children's perception of their locality be influenced by planned teaching about the locality? What is the impact of the inhibiting changes to enabling children's free movement in their 'home range' during the latter 20th century?

It became clear that the understanding of the character of a locality changes with the age of the user of the locality (Figure 3). This in turn is affected by the concentration of facilities within the locality (Figure 2) and the variations in this concentration have significance. The clearest example is the rural children's intimate knowledge of the path network linking places, rarely mentioned by the urban child even if present. On the other hand the urban child would seem to be fully conversant with built leisure facilities which the rural child has to be prompted to consider. Children are capable of providing vivid locality descriptions and accounts, though not necessarily of the expected features. In one rural school, it was the participation in the local river festival that drew most enthusiasm and associated geographical information. In a New Town, it was the provision of the new leisure and media centre and the prospect of a sports centre of national status which elicited most information, again supported by detailed geographical awareness. Yet, with all groups, the understanding of the locality is more vivid and detailed among children than with the adults who use the area (explored in Chapter 18) – and is thus often ignored.

However, children's locality awareness cannot be taken for granted, nor can it be considered that they are fully informed about an area. What also became obvious during this study – and could only show up through use of the 1:25,000 map as the base for showing the distribution of locality knowledge – was the presence of *invisible* areas. Invisible areas cover a large range of geographical features and landmarks. They are features that a visitor usually notices but which locals take for granted. These features vary in different geographical contexts. Some are invisible because of social factors, for instance those children who never get to explore the local beach or woods because their parents either will not or are too frightened to venture into 'unknown' territory. At the other extreme are those parents who believe they are doing the best for their children by taking them to places outside their locality instead of together exploring places nearby. Some children only get to know their area through visits made by the school.

Other family, cultural and community constraints often make exploring difficult without school initiatives.

Community constraints cannot be ignored. For those schools in rapidly changing areas it is essential to consider where the children live. The distribution map of the school catchment has an important part to play in providing clues to extent, depth or paucity of locality knowledge. It can indicate those areas where some families may be unsupportive. It reveals the location of new developments which have the potential to be overly self-sufficient – for which the developers are largely responsible and, in some cases, where new inhabitants can be likely to be first time buyers with young families. The catchment map shows where it is possible to walk and cycle in safety, or not, and if the regional transport network is useful.

Constrained opportunities in a locality can be compounded by the local school that the children attend. Unfortunately, too often the primary class teacher travels into the locality, is not familiar with the school's locality but only with other locality geographies, and who does not understand the geographies pursued by their children. This is particularly evident in schools whose staff travel to the inner city from the suburbs. This lack of appreciation of the child's good, or poor, knowledge of their home area is often a problem for geography subject leaders, in that too little sense of the children's locality knowledge is taken into account in planning the school's geography curriculum.

Geographers, environmental psychologists and inspired Foundation Stage teachers, have a common principle. Each works on the basis that from the moment of a baby first seeing its surroundings and then exploring its surroundings, sensory information from the environment is stored as a mental map, the foundation of cognition upon which much of the development of the child's other intelligences depend. It is as the child grows and begins to move freely about its neighbourhood, or not, that influences beyond the senses begin to have significant effect upon a child's understanding of the geography of the world about them (Catling 1988). It is here the role of the geography teacher and the environmental educationist is to enable the developing child to look with meaning at this world about them. Teachers have always been aware of this growth or development in children's local spatial and environmental understanding, and good teachers have built their enquiry work around this knowledge.

The efficient Key Stage 1 teacher, regardless of their geographical strengths, will obtain evidence of this understanding through the medium of drawing pictorial maps of the route to school, or to another frequented place such as the library, from home. In many cases the drawing shows both what the child knows and how accurate, or otherwise, their cognitive map can be of their most frequented route.

The National Curriculum progression through the key stages clearly expects a growing ability in the child to observe in increased detail, sorting and classifying evidence, recognising changes, drawing conclusions and making evaluations. This requires a wealth of detail garnered locally by personal observation and experience not learnt by rote. Only this way is a body of knowledge built, against which it becomes possible to recognise similarities and differences in other localities and places. The progression of enquiry has always been an expectation, but only in the latest manifestations of the National Curriculum has it been explicitly stated in terms of children's activity.

Conclusion

This research has focused on children's locality understanding. But should such research be looking solely at children's locality knowledge and what is taught for the National Curriculum? Should it not equally be considering whether the locality lies at the core of children's developing understanding of the wider world about them? Indeed, it needs to examine whether children's understanding can reasonably be constructed in what might seem to be an artificial manner according to the perceptions of curriculum planners and makers? In this context, where does their teachers' geographical understanding and, more particularly, understanding of the school locality affect their learning?

There are other questions to consider. Does size of the locality in which a child lives matter? To what extent does it affect their – and extended – local environmental knowledge and understanding? Does the urban/suburban/rural context matter? Is it important to examine this? In writing about the impact of evacuation to the country of urban children, Ward (1990, 49) noted that during World War Two:

> The immediate effect of evacuation was the revelation of the fact that one nation contained not one or two but half a dozen different ways of living, graduated according to income and opportunity.

Then, children commented upon the changes to their freedom both in the house as well as outside. Does it matter to the primary teacher that there are still such variations in freedom of movement and in different ways of living which should be accounted for in a variable curriculum? Today, what is the impact of such variations on children's locality experience and learning?

Given the intimations that for many children living in urban and suburban localities, knowing and understanding their locality is constrained and inhibited in various ways, it might equally be asked how far planners gone – begun before mid- 20th century – in marshalling people's movements according to their own ideals of tidiness, convenience and safety, and what the impact of such control has been. Does this mean we are seeing a denial not only of children's right to freedom of movement but also of their ability to develop views of their community needs and, indeed, to support their enquiry into matters concerning their local environment.

The most significant finding of this study is that children appear to be more observant than adults. But, to enhance their use of their observations, it is necessary to develop the evidence of children's observation and of the way in which they make sense of these observations before they begin 'to see through a glass darkly' and more deeply into their own locality and into the wider world.

Chawla (2002) outlines research guidelines, a number of which might readily be adapted to be used in a teaching situation. In effect, these take the four questions applied in this study and the use of basic map information further. She suggests using vision maps 'where the children evaluate their area and define their priorities for improving it', child-taken photographs, child-led walks (which would have been eminently possible in this research had time been available), role-play, and, of course, the background data which should have been collected in any case for local studies – census data, photographic records, local histories, government reports and surveys (Chawla, 2002, 243). Such can be the stuff of geography curriculum locality studies, working with and taking forward children's geographical understanding.

References

Aitken S. (1994), *Putting Children in their place*, Washington DC: Association of American Geographers

Aitken S. (2001), *Geographies of Young People: The Morally Contested Spaces of Identity*, London: Routledge

Bowles, R. (1994a), *Geography Study Kits – Plymouth: a waterfront city*, Leamington Spa: Scholastic Publications

Bowles, R. (1994b), *Geography Study Kits - Eyam: An English village*, Leamington Spa: Scholastic Publications

Bowles, R. (1994c), *Geography Study Kits – A Market Town: Bury St Edmunds*, Leamington Spa: Scholastic Publications

Bowles, R. (1995), How well do you know your locality? *Primary Geographer*, 23, 16-18

Bowles, R. & Harrison S. (1997a), *Clerkenwell – An Urban Locality*, Dunstable: Folens Ltd

Bowles, R (1997b), Teaching about the local community: using first hand experience, in Tilbury, D & Williams, M (eds.), *Teaching and Learning Geography*, London: Routledge, 218-230

Bowles, R. (1998), Defining Localities, in Scoffham, S. (ed.), *Primary Sources: Research Findings in Primary Geography* Sheffield: Geographical Association, 24-25

Catling, S. (1988) 'Children and Geography' in Mills D. (ed.), *Geographical Work In Primary And Middle Schools*, Sheffield: Geographical Association, 9-18

Catling, S. (2001) *Children's Developing Spatial Awareness*, Notes for presentation to GeoVisions Project Working Group Geographical Association http://www.geography.org.uk/project/geovisions/places.html   accessed 27 Oct 03

Chawla, L. (ed.)(2002), *Growing Up in an Urbanising World*, London: UNESCO/Earthscan

Goodey, B. (1971), *Perception of the Environment*, University of Birmingham: Centre for Urban and Regional Studies

Hart, R. (1979), *Children's Experience of Place*, New York: Irvington

Hendrick, H. (1997), Constructions and Reconstructions of British Childhood: An Interpretative survey, 1800 to the Present, in James A. and Prout A. (eds.), *Constructing and Reconstructing Childhood*, London: Falmer Press

Hillman, M., Adams, J. & Whitelegg, J. (1991), *One False Move: A Study of Children's Independent Mobility*, London: Policy Studies Institute

Hillman, M. (1998), Neighbourhood Safety, in Scoffham, S. (ed.), *Primary Sources: Research Findings in Primary Geography*, Sheffield: Geographical Association, 28-29

Holloway S & Valentine G. (2000) Children's geographies and the new social studies of childhood, in Holloway, S. & Valentine, G. (eds.), *Children's Geographies : Playing, Living, Learning*, London: Routledge, 1-26

Lynch, K. (1977). *Growing up in Cities*, Cambridge: MIT Press

Matthews, M. H. (1992), *Making Sense of Place*: *Children's Understanding of Large Scale Environments*, Hemel Hempstead: Harvester Wheatsheaf

Moore, R. (1986), *Childhood's Domain: Place and Play in Child Development*, London: Croom Helm

Sibley, D. (1995) Families and Domestic Routines: Constructing the Boundaries of Childhood, in Pile, S. and Thrift, N. (eds.), *Mapping the Subject: Geographies of Cultural Transformation*, London: Routledge

Spencer, C. and Blades, M. (1993), Children's understanding of places: the world at hand, *Geography* 78, 4, 367- 373

Ward C. (1990), *The Child in the City*, London: Bedford Square Press

Wiegand, P. (1996), Interviews, in Williams M. (ed.), *Understanding Geographical and Environmental Education: the Role of Research*, London: Cassell

Chapter 3

Teaching Place: Developing early understanding of 'nested hierarchies'

Colin Storey

Introduction

This chapter relies on the juxtaposition of two disparate texts to explore the teaching of place and the idea of *nested hierarchies*, to look for reflections and resonance between these interconnected ideas and, in hoping to conflate their respective contributions, to illuminate future approaches of research in this area. The two key texts are those of Harwood (1998) and Deacon (1997), the former focused on approaches to the teaching of nested hierarchies, the latter on symbolic representations in language and learning.

Harwood (1998) reviews different methodologies for the teaching of the concept of *nested hierarchies* in primary school geography. A clear example of a nested hierarchy, whereby sets of events, places or features are embedded within each other like Russian dolls, is a postal address:

> *house number is in street, is in town, is in county, is in country, is in UK.*

Harwood goes on to develop a 'meta-methodology' in which the teaching and assessment approaches reviewed are arranged along a continuum of sophistication (Harwood, 1998), as illustrated in Figure 1.

Most difficult	• Arranging and/or drawing symbolic representations • Verbal tests without cues • Pupil's drawing their own maps • Pupil's shading and marking maps already drawn • Verbal tests with cues; eg. multiple choice lessons
Least difficult	• Discussing models or pictures of familiar locations

Figure 1: A sequence of assessment techniques arranged in order of difficulty (Harwood, 1997, 13)

In reviewing these methods I provide a critique for their usefulness with children, that is their 'fitness for purpose'. In this context, Cohen and Manion suggest (1985, 42),

> by methods, we mean that range of approaches used in educational research to gather data which are to be used as a basis for inference and interpretation, for explanation and prediction...

Furthermore, since Harwood himself has approached this in his descriptions of them, I shall go on to examine his continuum alongside a robust model derived from evolutionary linguistics (Deacon, 1997).   I do this because the *most difficult* of Harwood's strategies he claims to be *arranging and/or drawing symbolic representations*. Attaining *symbolic representations* during cognitive development is one of Deacon's central arguments for human language capability. For the purpose of this article I do, however, uncritically accept Deacon's model which can be contrasted with that of Pinker (1994) and others (see Deacon, 1997 for discussion) and derives from the work of Peirce (1897, 1903).

Setting the context

In the study of geography in primary schools *place* is a central theme (Scoffham, 1980; Blyth, 1984; Bale, 1987; Foley & Janikoun, 1992; Matthews 1992; Wiegand, 1992, 1993; Palmer, 1994; Martin, 1995; Tilbury & Williams, 1997; Harwood, 1998). This work has a background in Piaget's work (1929) whereby the child is actively trying to make sense of its environment in order to *adapt*, in biological parlance (Meadows, 1993). Just as all living things must adapt and use a range of strategies and locational placement (Catling, 1998), a mental 'map', derived from experience, is just one of these adaptive strategies, as developmentally it unfolds with growing experience.

The least difficult category Harwood (1998) identifies as *discussing models or pictures of familiar locations*. These two concrete props to instruction, models and pictures, could themselves be further divided. Donaldson (1987), reviewing basic tenets of Piaget's work, finds the three dimensionality of modelling quite different from the verbal reasoning approach, which might be called upon to explain a picture. Giving children the experience, for themselves, of modelling a situation (such as hiding from a policeman) allows them to do very well at placing themselves in space and to *decentre* or to take (literally) another's perspective.

These uses of *concrete*, or external (ie. non-mental or internalised), teaching aids would seem to correspond to Deacon's (1997) lowest level of representations: the *iconic*. He describes two more; the *indexical* and the *symbolic*, which he describes as follows:

> No particular objects are intrinsically icons, indices or symbols. They are interpreted to be so, depending on what is produced in response. In simple terms, the differences between iconic, indexical, and symbolic relationships derive from regarding things either with respect to their form, their correlation with other things, or their involvement in systems of conventional relationships. (Deacon, 1997, 71)

There is a need to be wary of our use of *icon*, since Deacon goes on to differentiate his meaning from vernacular usage:

> ...What we usually mean is that they were designed to be interpreted that way... for example a striking resemblance does not make one thing an icon of another... similarity does not cause iconicity... it is a kind of inferential process based on recognising a similarity. (Deacon, 1997, 71)

So, while it is conventional to accept models and pictures as *iconic*, in Deacon's first step to a fully internalised *symbolic* representation models and pictures are not unless the *relationship*, in this case between picture and place, is truly inferred by the child. This seems to point to the 'least difficult' end of Harwood's scale as not being least difficult enough. The inference is that there may, indeed, be approaches to the teaching and assessment of place understanding that are yet less difficult, and, perhaps, more suited to younger or less experienced children. If so what are they? Two are suggested. One is *first-hand* fieldwork, involving gross motor learning (Donaldson, 1987), to which can be added a second, the *immediate* production and manipulation of images (including sketching: Bartlett, 1999; Martin, 1999; and digital photography, Storey, 2002), alongside this physical exploration of space, direction and distance. In the new curriculum for the youngest children in schooling, set out in the Early Learning Goals - Knowledge and Understanding of the World (DfES/QCA, 2000), this is implied in

> adult support in helping children communicate and record orally *and in other ways*. (QCA,1999, emphasis added)

The intermediate level of Deacon's (1997) route to symbolic representation, *indexical relationships* derives from the first iconic layer. This would seem to be aligned with the median of Harwood's (1998) levels of difficulties, ie.
- pupils drawing their own maps
- pupils shading and marking on maps already drawn

Here there is the possibility of some semantic confusion, because map *symbols* used ordinarily appear more like *icons* as generally used in the vernacular. But here the argument is for treating them, in Deacon's (1997) terminology, as *indices* of geographical experience. According to Deacon's scheme, indices are constructed from iconic representations, but the relationship is not a 1:1 relationship but an *interpretative* relationship. This means that the child's mental processes take the icons as data and rework them into the next level of analysis.

> Indexical reference, however requires iconic reference. In order to interpret something as indexical, at least three iconic relationships must be also recognised. (Deacon, 1997, 79)

So the properties of the icons built into experience can be drawn upon as the data for further re-working. In this respect the experiences of children in
- drawing their own maps, and
- shading and marking on maps already drawn,

would seem to fulfil similar criteria . If the children are truly capable of using maps in this respect, they are drawing upon earlier icon-building experiences (such as gross motor play and investigation, representations of experience through talk, drawing and modelling) and are able to bring these to bear upon the map-work (during construction, coding, 'reading' and interpretation), as Harwood's two median categories imply. In drawing upon these earliest icons, the resulting map-work does not easily correspond point-for-point to the earlier experiences but is a reworking and synthesis of them. In this respect, as measured against Deacon's (1997) scheme, Harwood would seem to have placed them in the correct sequence of temporal (pupil age) order and pedagogic demand.

Finally, Deacon's (1997) third and ultimate category of representations is the *symbolic*. In Deacon's (1997) terms, symbols derive their powers of representation from the *indexical* level but only transiently. Symbols (ie in linguistic development 'words') derive their initial representative power from the learning of individual symbols attached to *indexical* clusters of *icons*. As such they are rooted (and routed) from direct, concrete experience. *But* this relationship is transient while the symbolic system is being built. The relationship serves to 'scaffold' (Vygotsky, 1962) the formation of sufficient symbolic capability until a threshold is reached. Thereafter true or complete symbolic representation is achieved because now the symbols are defined purely in terms of each other, as indeed words are defined lexicographically without (in the use of a mature user of the 'system') recourse to direct experience.

New symbols can be added to the lexicon by mapping them (linguistically) into relationships with existing symbols. Returning to Harwood's (1998) two ultimate categories:
- arranging and/or drawing symbolic representations, and
- verbal tests without cues,

it can be suggested that they be reversed. What Harwood (1998) means by symbolic representation, that is using shapes to stand for countries (a 'spatial test'), is, as discussed above, equivalent to the indexical level of pictograms on maps. He assigns the level of difficulty by comparing results with a verbal test.

> Performances in the spatial test were much inferior to the verbal test. Nearly 75% of the children, who had been able to state correctly that Glasgow is in Scotland did not demonstrate this in the spatial test. (Harwood, 1998, 13)

I would suggest that to be able to state that ' Glasgow is in Scotland' but not to demonstrate this with concrete shapes contradicts the logic of his earlier scheme. The shapes do not approach the same level of symbolic representation as words because in this sense they do not *define each other* as Deacon suggests they should but, instead, are defined by criteria external to their use (probably labels since they were geometric and not map-like). They are not symbols but crude icons used symbolically without the scaffolding (given their appearance as rectangles and circles) or arbitrarily (as with letters and sounds in speech/writing) to cross the threshold to full symbolic representation.

Why then was the 'verbal' test eliciting a higher score? 'Glasgow is in Scotland' could just as easily operate at an iconic level, as a rote learned tag or label without, again, the relationship between Glasgow and Scotland being defined at either of the superior indexical and symbolic levels of representation. Without the eternal philosopher's question, 'It depends what you mean by......', applied to this phrase, we cannot know that its users are indeed understanding the nested relationship, that is, what it means to those who do. One other method in the proposed ranking, the verbal tests with cues, such as multiple choice questions, would seem to be far too low in the scheme to fit with this interpretation unless the 'cues' themselves (uncategorised by Harwood, 1998) are the criteria to be taken into account when establishing the rank order. This category is, it would seem, a subset of the verbal tests and more work could be directed to defining cues and categories of questions according to what they refer in this or any other scheme and so to decide whether and how they should be respectively ranked.

The purpose so far has been to attempt to provide a unitary if not unified framework to set practical studies against and, in doing so, to have illuminated Harwood's (1998) scheme in a way that otherwise would not be possible. This has provided a fresh look at his scheme and suggested sufficient areas for it to be reviewed. Thus the emergent continuum of 'meta-methodology' by which pedagogic devices (teaching methods) are ranked in order of difficulty still holds true, and teachers (Harwood, 1998, 13) can still;

> ...start with the assessment method which they think is most likely to challenge the pupils and then gradually simplify or complicate the process until the child's level of competency is identified.

But my analysis suggests this ranking is not linear. In two places thresholds need to be crossed and moving from one to the next may not be the same sort of step as between two others.

A practical study

In the National Literacy Strategy [NLS] framework for teaching (DfEE, 1998 p61), the inclusion of teaching about a 'pupil's name and address' is listed along with 'high frequency words to be taught as sight recognition words through YR to Y2', that is from Foundation Year 2 [age 4-5 years] (QCA, 2000) to the end of Key Stage 1 [age 5-7] (DfEE/QCA, 1998). Implicit in this NLS requirement is teaching an understanding (through an address) of the concept of nested hierarchies. Harwood (1998) noted that this is 'an important objective of primary geography...', in terms of teaching

> ... young children that places exist in a nested relationship, in which smaller places are located inside larger places... (Harwood, 1998, 12)

Harwood's conclusions point to a developmental and maturational period throughout primary schooling that allows these relationships to be appreciated by children as they approach the age of eleven. While the NLS states that young children should develop a knowledge of the words involved, it would seem that there is little worth in this learning if no development of the idea of nested hierarchies also is involved. In that Harwood infers that the end of Key Stage 1 would be too young to expect this understanding, what can young primary age children understand? This question is the focus of this study.

Harwood (1998, Harwood & McShane, 1996) identifies the approaches used in his studies as
- verbal tests without cues
- pictures and models of familiar situations
- mapping activities
- use of symbolic representations

While all of these approaches have their particular uses, they can also be criticised in relation to age-related appropriateness and usefulness. With younger children the context of a study is important, in that the tasks used should relate to areas of their experience, in order to provide the opportunity to investigate what they might know or understand. Interpreting some of Harwood's strategies for younger children was important.

The study group comprised eleven children, all in Year 1 [5 to 6 years of age], in a mixed-age class with a Reception cohort. These children formed the basis for a larger investigation (Storey, 2002), of which this study was part, and which describes more fully the general nature of this research, the methodology (enquiries embedded in the ongoing curriculum) and the children's familiarity with being observed and the questioning that was engaged in.

The nested hierarchy of an *address* was implicit in the repetitively structured language of a familiar children's picture book, *Funnybones* by Janet & Allan Ahlberg (1980). This book (and others from the series) had been used with the class for work in Literacy. All the children were familiar with the 'cascading' sequence of language, even by rote, from class, small group, paired and (where possible) individual readings. This text provided the research opportunity, using the familiar, to explore the children's appreciation of the relationship of the parts of the 'address' form used in the *Funnybones* picture story book.

The approach undertaken was to develop a number of classroom activities that focused on the key elements of understanding the nested hierarchy relationship: the sequencing of the elements of the 'address'. In the activities the links between the normal, linear relationship of written text in a book (or as listed in the address on an envelope) and the conceptually different 'nesting' of geographical entities this describes, was explored in a series of concrete manipulations. They were based on the text (familiar to the children) initially, then on the use of pictures and drawings. These manipulations were designed to allow children to arrive at the latter, more sophisticated and geographically useful formulation from the simpler and more instrumental former one. The activities evolved in a formative way from the assessment of the success of each activity as the children progressed. They were undertaken as individual activities.

Figure 2: Sequencing pictures and text

Activity 1: The children were given copies of the initial 'paragraphs' from *Funnybones* (words and picture) in random order and asked to reassemble the opening sequence (Figure 2). They were then asked to retell the story. The purpose was to see whether the children recognised and could replicate the pattern of the story.

Activity 2: In this follow-up activity the children were given enlarged copies of the pictures in the story to create a sequence or collage showing the order and relationship of the 'places' in the tale. This was to be done by cutting out and re-arranging the various 'places' in the story. The purpose was to provide an opportunity to reinforce the linguistic 'prop' of the underlying geographical concepts. During this activity a semi-structured discussion was used to elicit from the children their reasons for placing the pictures in the order they did so. The intention was to try to distinguish between the children's reliance upon the literary structure of the text, story and illustrations, including their reading of captions if any-the reason for choosing to approach this topic via the possible scaffolding of the nested hierarchies by the story's opening, and any possible geographical concepts that might be emerging.

Activity 3: This activity involved creating a self-drawn collage of the separated elements of the hierarchy to allow the elements of 'place' to be rearranged. The purpose was to see whether the children could demonstrate an understanding of the intrinsic hierarchy of 'places' in the story. The activity was designed to round-off this series of tasks by allowing the children physically to place representations (drawings in white pencil on black paper) of the features in relation to each other (by eg. sticking the skeletons inside the cellar and the cellar inside the house). This allowed some direct semi-structured questioning around the issue of the nested relationships of the parts to each other and the whole.

In Harwood's continuum these approaches seem initially to fall into the 'least difficult' end of the range, being, as it were, concrete manipulations of a 'model' of the address of the skeletons.

Linguistically, pictures and text, enter into *indexical* and *symbolic* representations of experienced reality (Deacon, 1997) and may need to be reconsidered in this respect.

There were a number of outcomes from the three activities.

Activity 1: This sequencing of the story text was achieved by all the children, whether they were formally able to read the text or not, and all were able to re-tell this part of the story. For example, one child explained:

> *"There's a dark hill where the street is and there's a dark house in the dark dark staircase and down the dark dark staircase there was a dark dark cellar. Because there's a hill with a street on it and there's a house in the street and in the house there's a dark dark staircase there was a dark dark cellar. And I know skeletons live there because they like the dark."*

Here, the first two pictures were initially placed in the in wrong order and then corrected,

> *"because I just did I thought about it for a minute and remembered how the story went. The hill is the biggest, then the street, then the house, then the staircase and then the cellar."*

This example is one of the more full responses and captures the linear sequence set out in the child's own reformulation of the Ahlbergs' patterned structuring of the opening to the story. The rest of the group essentially arrived at a similar, structured relationship with a re-telling of this part of the story.

Activity 2: The children were given the photocopies and allowed to do as they wished in ordering them. All the children remembered the previous work and all either stuck the pictures in a linear sequence directly or asked if they could do so, without prompting. If the sequence was not correct then the child were asked to look again and say if they were happy that this was the sequence. Finally, the children were asked to say why they had chosen that arrangement and how they had done it.

After the sequence was established, the questions used to probe the geographical and locational issues were:
- why does this one come first?
- which one is the biggest place?
- where does this one fit in?

They were applied to whichever sequence the child had created.

The majority of the children did not intuitively make the connection between the literary scaffolding that accommodated the representation of a nested hierarchy and the explicit description of the nesting. Further comments are noted in Figure 3.

Activity 3: Initially, the children used their drawings to recreate the illustrations. However, they were then encouraged to cut them out and stick them together so as to make an overlapping collage in which the 'nested' element of the sequence could be physically demonstrated. Eight of the eleven children were able to move from a purely linear conception of the skeleton's address to a form of 'nested' representation (Figure 4). A more detailed outline is given in Figure 3.

Child	Activity 2: Sequencing the photocopies of features	Activity 3: Creating a collage of drawn features
AL	Sequence completed using illustrations	Linear arrangement maintained overall but skeletons moved forward earlier in sequence to align with cellar and house [*]
AK	Sequence completed using illustrations and text	Linear sequence maintained to establish relationship and could describe this [+]
LS	Sequence completed using illustrations and text	Linear arrangement limited to the street and the skeletons clearly moved to positions under houses where the cellar would be [*]
JB	Sequence completed using illustrations	Stairs, cellar and skeletons moved inside and overlapping one of the drawings of the houses [*]
SB	Sequence completed using illustrations	Maintained linear sequence and did not add any overlapping qualities [#]
AB	Sequence completed using illustrations	Arranged pictures in a vertical rather than horizontal sequence to demonstrate the nested arrangement of the elements and could explain this [*, +]
SG	Sequence completed using illustrations and text	Stairs, cellar and skeletons moved into overlapping relationship and could explain this [*, +]
TC	Sequence completed using illustrations and text	Drawings arranged as the sequence not revealing the nested arrangement but could describe nesting verbally [+]
FS	Sequence completed using illustrations	Broadly repeated the linear sequence but not so accurately and did not add any verbal indication of understanding a nested arrangement [#]
RC	Sequence completed using illustrations and text	Persisted in the linear arrangement but was able to explain the nested relationship [+]
ES	Sequence completed using illustrations	Showed the skeletons out of sequence and fitting into a house but could not explain any further [#]

Activity 2 Comments
All the children were able to complete the sequence. There were no restrictions due to the manual skills required to cut, stick and assemble the sequence.
The use of illustrations and/or text to order the pictures follows an expected correlation with individual reading skills and proclivities at this time. All children, additionally, relied upon saying (often chanting) the opening passage and all could independently 'read' the text to an adult from prior familiarity. There was no overt expression of the nested arrangement of the sub-localities within the opening of the story and all appeared to be relying upon the linear sequence.

Activity 3 Comments
The activity allowed the previously linear outcome of the sequencing to be relied upon and then elaborated either practically or verbally to indicate the understanding of any nested relationships.
The previous collage using photocopies introduced the idea of possibly rearranging the pictures to express further ideas of the text. It was more flexible in that it allowed a majority of the children to progress toward the appreciation of the nested arrangement either by pictorial [*] or verbal [+] means. Three [#] could not be said to have progressed this far.

Figure 3: Comparative outcomes from activities 2 & 3

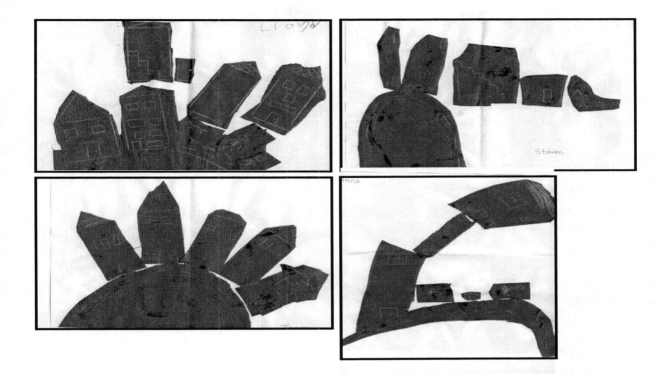

Figure 4: Drawn collages of the opening sequence of *Funnybones*

Discussion

Clearly, when we consider Harwood's (1998) developmental sequence – however it might be modified for younger pupils – the recitation of an address by a child aged between 4-7 years is, of itself, unlikely to mean that they have any internalised *geographical conception* of the nested arrangement of places within places, which adults would accept without question. Yet, it appears that the teaching activities described here have, to some extent, enabled a majority of the Year 1 children to begin to *approach* this conceptually difficult aspect of learning. Reciting their address would seem to be instrumentally supportive initially in helping young children, Literacy Strategy notwithstanding, but it is not sufficient to be left unexplored if the nested hierarchy *idea* behind an address is to begin to be understood. However, the more elaborate sequence of activities outlined above, in terms of pedagogic efficiency, may not fit easily into the Year 1 curriculum, a matter which needs to be addressed for true geographical learning to develop effectively.

One way forward, using Deacon's (1997) scheme and the concomitant argument that has been developed, is to extend Harwood's (1998) continuum of teaching and assessment methods and to reconstruct it as shown in Figure 5. A further point emerges from this thinking about methods themselves as being ranked in a hierarchical 'meta-methodology'. At any point along the continuum the child/learner can be asked to comment upon or consider the methodology being used. Harwood (1999) does not consider the degree to which meta-cognition may develop along this series. While this aspect may be what Leat (1997) describes as over-used, nonetheless, for children, learning for most children is helped by clear and focussed help, particularly if they are helped to reflect upon their own thinking (Weedon, 1997). The value of this lies in :

...helping children to be conscious of what they know and can do and then teaching them how to draw purposefully on that knowledge and to deploy it when working on problems." (Knight, 1993, 35)

Deacon (1997) argues that even at an early age, in their language capabilities young children have crossed the threshold for symbolic linguistic representation. This occurs before children enter formal schooling and are engaged in geography or any other curriculum subject. Children, coming into the curriculum, already have the symbolic tools to engage in thinking about thinking from the very beginning of the range of activities to which they will be exposed. To engage them with the processes of their learning in this way, at whichever level of teaching and assessment, has the potential to make available their already considerable capabilities in symbolic representation. In such a pedagogic scheme, symbolic representation is the ultimate goal for subject-based knowledge and skills, enabling integration across the learners' experience by virtue of untying them from the limits of concrete, iconic experience. As such, symbolic representation becomes available for reordering learning in novel ways that allow personal and socially recognised progress.

Harwood's original continuum (Harwood, 1998)	Redrawn scheme	Deacon's levels of representation (Deacon, 1997)
Most difficult	*Most difficult*	*Most sophisticated or mature*
• Arranging and/or drawing symbolic representations • Verbal tests without cues • Pupils' drawing their own maps • Pupils' shading and marking maps already drawn • Verbal tests with cues, eg. multiple choice questions • Discussing models or pictures of familiar locations	• Verbal tests without cues/verbal tests with cues, eg. multiple choice questions • Arranging and/or drawing pictorial representations • Pupil's drawing their own maps • Pupil's shading and marking maps already drawn • Discussing pictures of familiar locations • Gross motor play, investigation and modelling	• Symbolic -area of overlap where 'thresholds' are crossed • Indexical -area of overlap where 'thresholds' are crossed • Iconic
Least difficult	*Least difficult*	*Simplest or least mature*

Figure 5: Harwood's hierarchy of pedagogic methodologies redrawn.

Conclusion

For the purposes of teaching geographical understanding, however, there has been value in investigating the intertwining relationship between language, literature and the learning of the geographical conceptions of nested hierarchies. Children are more sophisticated learners of language at ages rather earlier than schooling attempts to inculcate broader concepts about the world. They have the foundation for tackling more sophisticated and challenging ideas than is usually recognised, based on scaffolding learning in the way that the activities used in the study above show can be undertaken, a potential in relation to learning through language well discussed elsewhere (Daniels, 2001). Linguistically, children may be capable of operating at a quite sophisticated *symbolic* level (Deacon, 1997) though day-to-day teaching seems to rely – inhibitingly – over much on more explicitly concrete experiences. Indeed, since young children, as language users, are already juggling symbols, grammar and meanings in attempting to understand their world, perhaps those showing understanding through the third of the activities used in this study are indicating a greater level of symbolic sophistication than is recognised. But perhaps more interestingly still, arising from this study, might there be greater opportunity for common ground to be attained and greater understanding to be attained by young children in reading *symbolic* texts of all kinds, whether they be books, maps, musical scores or algebraic formulae?

References

Ahlberg, J. & A. (1980), *Funnybones*, London: Collins

Bale, J. (1987), *Geography in the Primary School*, London: Routledge and Kegan Paul

Bartlett, K. (1999), Field sketching; an appropriate skill for upper primary children? *International Research in Geographical and Environmental Education*, 8(2), 199-207

Blyth, J. (1984) *Place and Time with Children Five to Nine*, London: Croom Helm

Carr, W. & Kemmis, S. (1986), *Becoming Critical*, London: Falmer Press

Catling, S. (1998), Children as mapmakers, in Scoffham, S. (ed.), *Primary Sources*: *Research findings in primary geography* Sheffield: Geographical Association

Cohen, L. & Manion, L. (1985), *Research Methods in Education*, London: RoutledgeFalmer

Daniels, H. (2001), *Vygotsky and Pedagogy*, London: RoutledgeFalmer

Deacon, C (1997), *The Symbolic Species*, London: Penguin

DfEE (1998), *The National Literacy Strategy*, London: DfEE

DfEE/QCA (2000), *Curriculum Guidance for the Foundation Stage*, London: DfEE/QCA

Donaldson, M. (1987), *Children's Minds*, London: Fontana Press

Foley, M. & Janikoun, J. (1992), *The Really Practical Guide to Primary Geography*, Cheltenham: Nelson Thornes,

Harwood, D. (1998), Children's understanding of nested hierarchies, in Scoffham, S. (ed.), *Primary Sources*: *Research findings in primary geography* Sheffield: Geographical Association,

Knight, P. (1993), *Primary Geography, Primary History*, London: David Fulton

Leat, D. (1997), Cognitive acceleration, in Tilbury, D. & Williams, M. (eds.). *Teaching and Learning Geography*, London: Routledge

Martin, F. (1995), *Teaching Early Years Geography*, Cambridge: Chris Kington Publishing

Martin, F. (1999), Developing geographical skills of field sketching with Y3/4 pupils, paper presented to the *Primary Geography Research Conference*, Sheffield Hallam University, 13 November

Matthews, M. H (1992), *Making Sense of Plac: Children's understanding of large scale environments*, Hemel Hempstead: Harvester Wheatsheaf

Meadows, R. (1993), *The child as thinker*, London: Routledge

Palmer, J. (1994), *Geography in the Early Years*, London: Routledge

Piaget, J. (1929), *The Child's Conception of the World*, London: Kegan Paul

Peirce, C. (1897, 1903), Logic as semiotic; the theory of signs, in J Buchler (ed.), *The Philosophical writings of Peirce*, New York: Dover Books

QCA (1999), *Early Years: Early Learning Goals* London QCA

Scoffham, S. (1980), *Using the School's Surroundings*, London: Ward Lock Educational

Storey, C.(2002), Using ICT to support the teaching of 'Place' in geography, in Bowles, R. (ed.),

Best Practice in Raising Achievement, London: Register of Research in Primary Geography

Tilbury, D. & Williams, M. (eds.) (1997), *Teaching and Learning Geography*, London: Routledge

Vygotsky, L. (1962), *Thought and language*, Cambridge: MIT Press

Weedon, P. (1997), Learning through maps, in Tilbury, D. & Williams, M. (eds.), *Teaching and Learning Geography*, London: Routledge

Wiegand, P, (1992), *Places in the Primary School*, London: Falmer Press

Wiegand, P. (1993), *Children and Primary Geography*, London: Cassell

Acknowledgements

I wish to thank the following: Liz Browne who read an earlier version of some of this material and for her teaching in the methodology of action research; Simon Catling who has been a mentor for several projects over some years and who took part in the practical aspect of this work; the Teacher Training Agency who provided a Small Scale Research Grant that facilitated this and other work; the children in this study and their parents at Sherington CE School who have been a constant inspiration and delight to work with through these and other teaching idea

Chapter 4

Children's Understanding of Rivers: Is there need for more constructivist research in primary geography?

Margaret Mackintosh

Introduction

Talking about a river Daisy, aged four, said that 'the wind' made it flow, but on a walk she observed a small stream. She pointed in the direction of flow, which happened to be downwind. Asked if the stream could flow the other way, she said 'no, because it would come back down again'.

Ten year old Kathleen was standing on Keadby Bridge over the River Trent. She exclaimed, 'Eh, there's water on both sides!' Was it the concept of 'river' or 'bridge' or both that Kathleen had not grasped?

In the classroom teachers use many geographical terms which are in common everyday use, such as river, bridge or town. They assume a shared meaning, but Kathleen's and Daisy's comments indicate that children can construct different meanings.

The research reported here was initiated by May (1996). using a constructivist approach in geography to explore children's visualization, understanding or 'alternative conceptions' of 'river'.

Literature review

Constructivist ideas have been traced back to the early 1770s when Vico (Hunter & Benson 1997) said that knowledge is not a representation of objective reality; it is a personalized sense-making construction of the experiential world . . . dependent on the situation and purpose, the person's unique experience, and the process involved in actively constructing meanings. It is, therefore, an active, cultural process, contextually bound and personally and historically informed. More recently these ideas have been developed, notably through the work of Piaget, who talked of 'cognitive adaptation', the learner assimilating and accommodating experiences into 'action schemes'. These ideas also underpinned the Plowden Report (CACE, 1967) and have been developed by several authors since, especially in the field of science education (for example Driver et al (1994), Nussbaum (1985), and the S.P.A.C.E. project (Russell *et al* 1993)

As well as being used extensively to elicit children's concepts in science, constructivist approaches have also been used as a model for teachers' development in science (Bell & Gilbert 1996) and mathematics (Jaworski 1984). But they have been little used in geography. However, in recent years Harwood & Jackson (1995) and Platten (1995a, 1995b) have adopted this approach, the latter usefully summarizing the work in science. Dove (1999) has also briefly discussed constructivism in a geographical context.

Children's sense-making of rivers arises from their direct and indirect experiences of rivers, their indirect experiences through television and books and their conversations about them at home and in school.

What do we know about children's ideas about rivers?

Piaget (1929, 1930) reported that children's early ideas show a tendency to artificialism, that everything is artificially made, the river bed, even the water. Later they believe that the river is dug out by men but the water is natural, eventually moving to an acceptance that the river is entirely natural. In trying to explain the current in rivers children invoked animism (ascribing a living soul to natural phenomena), for example water (internal animist force) obeys man (an external artificialist force). They then believe that the current is due to stone, wind or spontaneous movement, eventually accepting that the weight of the water and the slope makes the water move along.

Lunnon (1969) found that children could interpret photographs of rivers but had difficulty in explaining their understanding in words. As he asked children for a definition of 'river' this is not, perhaps, surprising considering the experience and skills of generalization and visualization that a definition requires.

Platten (1995a,b) and Harwood and Jackson (1995) analysed children's responses to a selection of oral, picture recognition and drawing tasks about the physical and human landscape into four categories of understanding, but did not attempt to recognise 'stages' in children's conceptual understanding of 'river' in the way that Sharp (1999) did with children's ideas about the Earth. Wilson and Goodwin (1981) and Harwood and Jackson (1995) agreed that children's perceptions of rivers are guided by local experience. The latter concluded that 'children's experience and understanding of physical landscape features are likely to be very restricted, even by years 5 and 6 of primary school'. They expressed the fear that 'both teaching and assessment of physical landscape concepts will be superficial and inadequate'. What does this mean, particularly for the urban child? What ideas about rivers do children hold?

Perhaps it is useful not only to try to identify progression in children's understanding of rivers, but also the hierarchy of concepts required to understand them. Gunning, Gunning and Wilson (1981) referred to a ' concept ladder', illustrating the idea with the concept of 'castle'. Wiegand (1993) suggested: rivers are water; this water is of considerable size; the water moves; it moves along some course in its surroundings. Bale (1987) and Wiegand (1993) stress the importance of establishing and using as a starting point that water flows downhill. The national curriculum Key Stage Two (for 7-11 year olds) programme of study (DfEE/QCA 1999) identifies the processes of erosion and deposition as important, but what level are these on a 'river' concept ladder? What other concepts must be understood before these can be integrated into a child's conceptual framework? This will be returned to later.

Research method

Standard elicitation methodologies, based on the work in science mentioned above and described by White and Gunstone (1992), were used in this research.

Children in a Year 5 class (9-10 years) in a town at the mouth of a major estuary were engaged in six activities. The first five involved the children in a variety of tasks, as follows:

(i)   **List rivers**. To list known rivers and state location, so as to encourage the children to start thinking about rivers, to remember those they 'knew' or had heard of and, perhaps, to recall visually rivers they had seen.

(ii)   **River definitions**. To defining 'river' and 'estuary', in order to see if children could generalize about rivers, and discover which aspects they selected as significant.

(iii)   **Word association**. To encourage the children to think about the features and processes associated with rivers.

(iv)   **Drawing a river**. To draw 'a picture of a river from its beginning to its end', in pencil on an A4 sheet of plain paper. This was photocopied for use in Activity (v).

(v)   **Concept mapping**. To use words highlighted from the word-association activity (Activity (ii)) or cards with the words 'Rain', 'Stream', 'Estuary', 'River', 'Sea', together with blank cards for their own words and arrow cards on which to explain their linkages. The children moved the cards around and labelled the arrows until they were happy with their concept map. The cards were stuck down as a final recording and the map explained to the researcher. Some children preferred not to use the cards but to write directly onto paper. Some chose to work individually, others in pairs or small groups, arriving at a consensus map.

The final research activity was an interview with each child:

(vi)   **Interview**. To undertake a semi-structured interview. The children were interviewed individually about their drawing. It was known that each child had been on a field-visit to the local river estuary. The interview was semi-structured, children's responses being recorded on a photocopy of their drawing, so that the original was not defaced.

- Tell me about your picture / drawing.

Then, depending on what was revealed:

- Is the water moving?
- Can you tell me which direction? (If given, direction of movement was marked on the photocopy by an arrow.)
- Can you tell me what this movement is called? (If given, word label was written on the flow arrow.)
- What do you think causes this flow? Word 'flow' introduced if not used by the child.
- (Interviewer points upstream) Where do you think the river / water is coming from?
- (Indicating downstream) Where do you think the river / water is going to?
- (Pointing to the river banks) What do you think is on each side of the river, on the river banks?
- Could the river be flowing through a town or city / the countryside?
- What do you think is at the bottom of the river?
- What do you think is in the river?
- If the river's flowing to the sea, do you think it could run out of water . . . . like when you empty a bath? Why / why not?

Integral to the interviews were the following:

- Depending on the response to a question, the interviewer followed up, in a non-judgemental way, with 'That's interesting. Why do you say that?, and avoided correcting or 'teaching' the child. The children were encouraged to use as much river-associated vocabulary as possible, linking this with aspects of their drawing.
- The children sorted some photographs into 'river' / 'not river' and were asked to explain their sorting.
- Finally they were asked 'Is there anything else you'd like to tell me about rivers or about your drawing?'

The activities were completed before the class study of rivers, although all the children had been on a walk to the estuary and engaged in some fieldwork activities and didactic teaching. They had also been taught about the water cycle in the previous school year.

Findings

The findings are reported in the same sequence order as the elicitation tasks described above.

(i) **River lists**. The 31 children made 63 references to rivers in Devon and Dorset, with the local rivers Exe and Dart being named by 28 and 19 children respectively. There were 29 references to rivers elsewhere in the UK, the Thames being named by 16 children and one child naming rivers in Scotland. There were 14 references to just five rivers worldwide, with the Rhine being located in Scotland. Ten children could only name two rivers, whereas one child named seven.

(ii) **River definitions**. All definitions of 'river' (31) referred to water. Ideas frequently mentioned included movement (10), shape (9), contains things (9), and that a river runs through a course (9).
Definitions included:

- wet water running down
- a long blue thing that's wet
- a thing with water in a long ditch
- something that flows and has fish and water
- a lot of water in a line
- something that runs through a hole
- a long tube shape full of water which is not man-made
- water that runs around a bank
- a long stream of water which has a strong current which pulls everything along
- if you didn't have a river you probably wouldn't have any water
- between valley (May 1996)
- a ditch or hole that filled up with water, something in the river absorbs water

This selection gives insight into the alternative frameworks into which children try to accommodate their new learning, perhaps about erosion and deposition.

Definitions of 'estuary', by children who live very close to the mouth of a major undeveloped, non-industrial estuary, included reference to where the river meets or joins the sea, the river's mouth or the sea's mouth. Mud, sand, pollution and sewage, birds and marine life were mentioned several times but only one child mentioned tides.

(iii) **Word association.** Whereas all children (31) had mentioned water in their definition of river, only 22 gave it in word association. The other most commonly mentioned words were fish (14) cold (12) wet (12) boat (10) stone (9) stream (6) swim (6). Fifty-nine words were given by less than six children.

(iv) **Drawing a river.** Most children drew just a section of river, a picture postcard view from the river bank. The children's drawings were predominantly of rivers flowing through rural settings with grass, hills, wildlife and recreational uses such as picnics and fishing. Stones, boats, fish and crabs were shown in the water. Clouds and rain were often included.

The illustrations of those children who had attempted to draw the whole river from 'its beginning to its end' showed progression in the form of the river. This could be described as 'dumb-bell' to 'bow' to 'klaxon', 'funnel' and finally 'river' (see Figure 1)

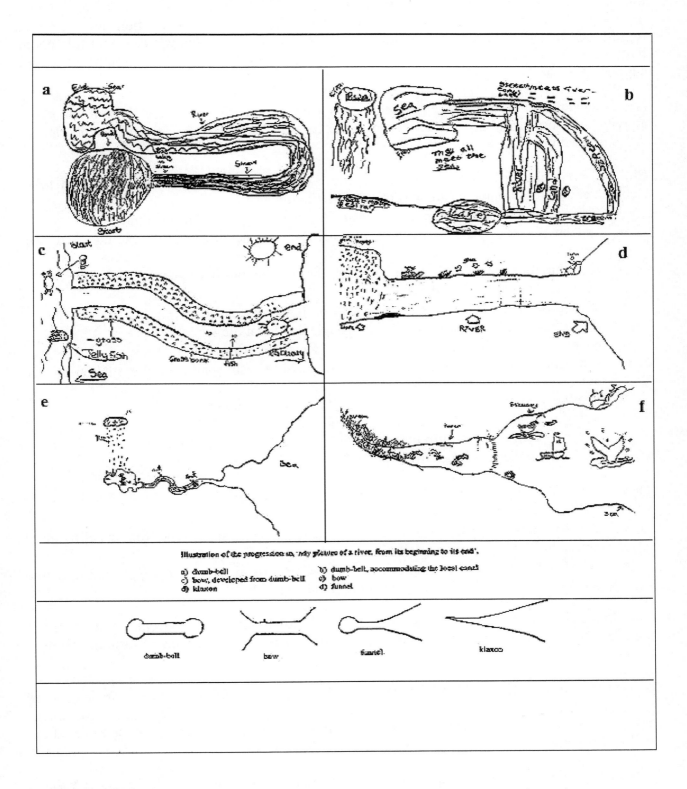

Figure 1: Progression in children's pictures of a river from its beginning to its end

(v) **Concept mapping**. The concept maps frequently showed knowledge of the rain → stream → river → estuary → sea sequence and some knowledge of the relationships between flow, drainage, erosion, transportation and deposition, although not using all the terms. There was mismatch between the drawings and the concept maps - showing the importance of using a range of research strategies for triangulation - with the quoted sequence or relationship not being represented in the children's visualization of a river. It must be acknowledged that this could have been a function of graphicacy or representational skills, but this interpretation was not supported by the interviews.

(vi) **Interview**. The interview, focused on each child's drawing, was the most illuminating activity. In most cases information given in the concept maps was *not* repeated, supported or demonstrated to be understood at interview.

Children were shown to have strong alternative frameworks, particularly with regard to flow, channel, source, environment (urban/rural) and destination:

- a river flows into the sea (not vv) because the sea is bigger and needs more water
- at then end of a river there'd be a wall across, river gets deeper because there's a wall blocking it
- rivers might flow through towns in Italy or France, but not in England
- the wind or stones make the river flow
- 'I've never seen the end of a river' (child who lives adjacent to one)
- rivers are bigger than streams because people dug them bigger
- a stream is small because they only dug out what they wanted
- a stream is smaller than a river because some of the rain soaks into the mud on the hill but a river is faster so it hasn't got time to soak in
- river gets bigger and bigger because salt gets in it from the sea
- water in the river comes from the sea (tidal estuary?)
- water in the river comes from rain that falls on the river, not on the land
- the water in the sea comes from rain water and toilet water

They also exhibited some confusion over erosion and deposition:

- 'mud comes from the river grass bank',
- 'the river gets bigger by wearing away the sides, mud and sand come from the cliffs, mud comes in from streams and rivers'
- 'when water goes out to another place (like Cornwall) it gets muddy and shallower; the sea brings the mud in and the river brings mud from a lake'

Questioned closely, not all children showed a grasp of the fundamental concept that water flows downhill, which surely must be the bottom rung on a concept ladder leading to understanding rivers.

Using the photographs provided of water in the landscape, the criteria used to sort into 'river' included big; long; meanders; in a natural (rural) setting. 'Non-river' criteria included too small; has signs of human intervention (rubbish, walls). In their sorting some children contradicted the artificialist perspective they had previously expressed.

In the interviews children showed that they had tended to learn the water cycle (taught in Year 4) by rote, with varying accuracy of recall, but without understanding. Only one pupil could relate the water cycle to his drawing with understanding. The children are not recalling direct experiences or visualizing the river and, apparently, not being encouraged to use these strategies in their sense-making of river features and processes. They seem to be trying to recall classroom teaching.

Discussion and Conclusions

Teachers who want their pupils to know about rivers have their own personal construct of rivers, they know about *it* and want their pupils to know *it* too. *It* is well defined, *it* exists, *it* can be conveyed to students so that they will know *it* too. If the pupils' *it* differs from their *it* in any substantial way then the teaching is regarded as less than successful. But can we agree on what *it* is anyway? What model; of 'river' do we start with? (Jaworski 1994)

This describes a top-down, guess-what-teacher-knows, model possibly required by the national curriculum and assessment system. But a concept ladder (Gunning, Gunning and Wilson 1981) would give us a, to me preferable, bottom-up approach. 'Top-down' dictates to the teacher a progression in teaching, as when working to a prescribed examination syllabus, but 'bottom-up' is more allied to progression in learning which, with knowledge of children's ideas and alternative frameworks, can guide teaching. It lets the children have some control over their learning.

How can pupils assimilate the concepts of erosion and deposition, mentioned in the national curriculum, into a framework not ready to receive them, if there is a conceptual gap, if rungs are missing from the concept ladder? Constructivist research helps to identify the rungs and the gaps.

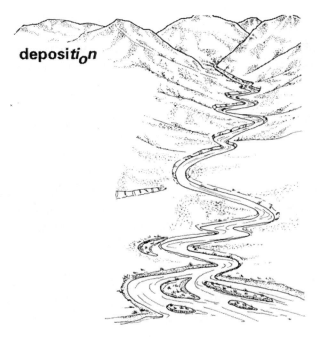

Figure 2:   Two-dimensional representation of a river
Can children see this as a river flowing towards them?
Does the perspective suggest to them that it's flowing away from them?

Experience suggests that a result of a top-down approach leads primary teachers to rely on their recollections of secondary school geography and the use of largely inappropriate 'so-what' activities with primary children. This includes relying on pictures and diagrams which children might not have sufficient graphicacy skills to interpret, such as in Figure 2. For example, are we sure they can see and interpret a two-dimensional representation a three-dimensional structure? The top-down approach also fails to consider the ideas children bring with them to their study of rivers. As this paper has shown, these can often be decidedly 'alternative' conceptual frameworks. We used to use the horrid expression 'start where the children are at', but we seem to have lost sight of this good advice in geography. And we failed to adopt Gunning, Gunning and Wilson idea of concept ladders. But we must not overlook or forget the importance of experience or, in geographical terms, of fieldwork.

Constructivist research is time consuming but it provides valuable indications of 'where the children are at' and of 'starting points' for teaching and the gap between these and suggested national curriculum content. In the research reported here Piaget's findings and those of subsequent researchers were confirmed.

The findings suggest implications for the classroom. Instead of concentrating on the terminology for features and processes, it seems that it is of paramount importance to give children experience of rivers, visiting sites from source to mouth in urban and rural environments. This is particularly true for urban children for whom rivers are often in concrete channels or even underground. These experiences should enable them to make three-dimensional models of rivers and encourage them to visualize rivers, to make mental reconstructions. Without this children have no cognitive or environmental image on which to locate, or with which to associate, the terminology and processes they encounter, whether taught in the classroom or met with through fieldwork.

Teachers have mentioned having difficulty providing appropriate activities during fieldwork. Do children need to play Pooh sticks or do other 'so-what' activities if they cannot fit their significance into their conceptual framework? Should their thinking be focused beyond the immediate context?

The children's drawings suggest that, even when they have visited a river and stood on its banks, they register just the framed view of the section of river directly in front of them. They must be encouraged to notice flow, to consider why this is, where the water is coming from and where it is flowing to. They must consider what happens to rainfall over extended 'natural' and built landscapes and compare this with the analogy of rain falling on the school and its grounds - recognise downhill flow, roof ridges as 'watersheds', guttering as streams, drains as rivers. They should be encouraged to think of, to visualize, a river and its catchment area as a system through which water flows.

Recent research in science has explored how children's alternative ideas develop towards the currently accepted scientific ones within conceptual themes. I would argue that there is a place for this model of research in primary geography, indeed that it is long over-due.

References

Bale, J. (1987), *Geography in the Primary School,* London: Routledge & Kegan Paul
Bell, B. & Gilbert, J. (1996), *Teacher Development: a model from science education*, London: Falmer Press
DfEE/QCA (1999), The *National Curriculum: Geography,* London, QCA

Central Advisory Council for Education (England) (1967), *Children and their Primary Schools*, London: HMSO

Dove, J. (1999), *Theory into Practice: Immaculate Misconceptions*, Sheffield: Geographical Association

Driver, R., Guesne, G. & Tiberghien, A. (eds.) (1985), *Children's Ideas in Science*, Milton Keynes, Open University Press

Gunning, S., Gunning, D. & Wilson, J., (1981), *Topic Teaching in the Primary School*, London: Routledge & Kegan Paul

Harwood, D. & Jackson, P. (1995), Why did they build this hill so steep?: problems in assessing primary children's understanding of physical landscape features in the context of the UK National Curriculum, *International Research in Geographical and Environmental Education*, 2(2), 64-79

Hunter, W.J. & Benson, G.D. (1997), Arrows in time: the misapplication of chaos theory to education, *Journal of Curriculum Studies*, 29(1), 87-100

Jaworski, B. (1994), *Investigating Mathematics Teaching: a constructivist enquiry*, London: Falmer Press

Lunnon, A. J. (1969), A Further Case for the Visual, *Geographical Education*, 3, 331-339

May, T. (1996), Children's Ideas about Rivers, *Primary Geographer*, 25, 12-13

Nussbaum, J. (1985), The Earth as a Cosmic Body in Driver et al (1985) *Children's Ideas in Science*, Milton Keynes, Open University Press et al

Piaget, J. (1929), *The Child's Conception of the World*, London: Routledge & Kegan Paul

Piaget, J. (1930), *The Child's Conception of Physical Causality*, London, Routledge & Kegan Paul

Platten, L.B. (1995a), Talking geography an investigation into young children's understanding of geographical terms Part 1, *International Journal of Early Years Education* 3 (1), 74-92

Platten, L.B. (1995b), Talking geography an investigation into young children's understanding of geographical terms Part 2, *International Journal of Early Years Education* 3 (3), 69-84

Russell, T., Bell, D., Longden, K. & McGuigan, L. (1993), *Science Processes and Concept Exploration Project Research reports: Rocks, Soils and Weather*, Liverpool, Liverpool University Press

Sharp, J. (1999), Young children's ideas about the Earth in Space, *International Journal of Early Years Education*, 7(2) 159-172

White, R. & Gunstone, R. (1992), *Probing Understanding*, London: Falmer Press

Wiegand, P. (1993), *Children and Primary Geography*, London: Cassell

Wilson, P. & Goodwin, M. (1981), How do twelve and ten-year-old students perceive rivers? Geographical Education, 4, 5-16

Chapter 5

Researching the Development of Children's Environmental Values in the Early School Years

Paula Owens

Introduction

In 1998 I left a full time teaching post to take up a research studentship for three years, driven by questions that would not go away about the ways in which young children developed their understanding of the world around them. I had had responsibilities as geography, environmental education and Eco-schools coordinator and it was through close encounters with these areas of learning that my questions grew. I was concerned that many young children starting school appeared to have limited first- hand experience of the world around them and this appeared to be reflected in their vocabulary and knowledge of the outdoor environment. These early years of schooling are crucial in laying firm foundations for future values and attitudes and so I wanted to know how we as practitioners could best help children develop.

My overarching aim was to investigate how children's environmental values developed during the early school years within school contexts. The key questions of the research were:
- What aspects of the environment did children value and why?
- How and why did these values develop and/or change?
- Was there any evidence that long-lasting values were being developed?
- How were environmental values translated into action?
- How relevant (for all the above questions) was school context in terms of provision, access, ethos and curriculum?

Literature review

In the impressionable years of early schooling, educators have opportunities to enable children to construct meanings and form values from outdoor experiences that may last into adulthood. However, the fabric of social and family life has greatly changed over the last three decades. There are less opportunities for first hand outdoor experiences during childhood than thirty years ago, the reasons being a complex mix of parental fear of 'stranger danger', restricted access to the natural environment because of dangerous boundaries, e.g. main roads, or increased building and enclosure, and increased car travel (Hillman, 1998).

The last ten years have seen an explosion of media culture reach overwhelming proportions in modern society. Now, most families have television, personal computer, mobile phone and video or DVD players. Nearly two decades ago when Spencer et al (1989) explained that children used a combination of mediated and first hand experiences to learn about the world it was perhaps unimaginable that such rich sources of mediated experience would be available in modern society and begs the question *what outcomes are there when this balance is tipped in favour of the mediated world at the expense of first hand experience?*

While it is true that learning about our immediate environment can be done through a variety of sources, really *knowing* a place arguably involves a range of cognitive, physical and emotional responses. Tuan (1977, 184) summed the fullness of this process in the following passage:

While abstract knowledge about a place can be acquired quite quickly, feeling about a place takes longer as it is made up of a succession of experiences repeated day after day, year after year. It encapsulates blends of sights, sounds, rhythms (natural and artificial), and is even apparent in the way that our bodies have learned to respond to the physicality of place e.g. through developing certain muscles.

Indeed, the role of place attachment in the development of self – identity has been well documented in environmental psychology literature (see Bonnes & Sechiaroli, 1995, for a comprehensive reading list) while significant research has suggested that positive experiences in the outdoor natural settings, in early childhood have been instrumental in developing pro-environmental attitudes and behaviours, (Palmer et al, 1998; Tanner, 1998; Chawla, 1998). In this contested body of research, termed Significant Life Experiences, adults identified as having either pro-environmental attitudes or behaviours gave autobiographical accounts of early childhood experiences that they claimed had a significant effect on their later thinking.

However, the term, 'pro-environmental behaviour' is one that is, by its value-driven nature, difficult to define. For example, while Palmer has applied the term to encompass those in careers concerned with the environment, such as teachers and with those who have a regard and concern for the environment, Tanner (1998) argued that only environmental *activists* exhibited such behaviour and that Palmer et al's definition was too loose. Other criticisms of these research findings have included Gough's (1999) comments that the research neglected to recognise that the contexts of children growing up today are vastly different to those a generation or more ago, while Chawla (1998) has suggested that in order to lend credence to this theory, investigations should be made into children's memorable experiences as all research has hitherto concentrated on the recollections of adults. The healthy debate in this area has emphasised its prominence in environmental education research.

Key research into children's perceptions of place and environmental preferences, for example Hart (1979), Moore (1986) and Matthews (1992), has been particularly valuable but there has been, and still is, a great deal of controversy about the perceived 'gap' between environmental attitudes and action, (see Scott, 2002). It was with these thoughts that the research was designed to discover what kinds of environmental experiences young children were having, how these had been laid down into memory and how this affected the development of their values, skills, knowledge and capacity for action. The school setting was chosen for this research because of its common frame of reference for all children and potential for influence on their development.

Research methodology
In the past, researchers in environmental education have been orientated towards a belief in the doctrines of logical empiricism and positivist thinking (Gerber, 1996). Tilbury and Walford (1996) described this orientation as being partly to blame for the reason that the goals of environmental education had not been fully realised, although Williams (1996) suggested that the positivist tradition in geographical education was relatively underdeveloped. Generally, there has been a growing rejection of positivistic approaches in environmental education because of a perceived lack of applicability to the real questions and sought answers of today's researchers. For example, Robottom (1999) has stated that the behaviourist perspective of the positivist

tradition meant that within a deterministic framework, researchers sought to impose their values whether social, environmental or educational, upon practitioners and pupils in a way that disempowered them. Today there is a growing emphasis on an educational approach in which the empowerment of pupils is desirable and learning is constructed rather than given (Hart, 1997; Catling, 2003; Owens, 2003), and so the climate of thinking has tended to influence researchers away from a positivistic approach.

While positivism is associated with the predominant scientific approach characterised by elements of predetermination, behaviourism and quantifiable methods of data collection and analysis, the newer paradigms have reflected a move towards qualitative studies. However there are some, for example Norwich (1998), who have argued that both the 'old' and 'new' paradigmatic approaches could be constructively interwoven. Such views concur with Slater's (1994) view that rather than take note of the differences between the various paradigmatic approaches, which she offered as comprising essentially scientific, interpretative and action research, we should be considering common elements and how each adds to the other.

Tilbury and Walford (1996) made a similar point, and argued that for example, while research in environmental education has been hampered by the dominance of a positivistic approach, there is no advantage to be gained by the total rejection of quantifiable methodology. Tilbury and Walford (1996) advised that research methodology in environmental education should reflect the diverse and wide ranging area of the subject, and that we should therefore, be prepared to use a 'range of disciplinary perspectives and conceptually diverse frameworks of investigation' (Tilbury and Walford, 1996, 53).

Since the aim of this research was to access individual children's thoughts, memories and voices of outdoor experiences and to analyse them individually as well as compare them across age ranges and school settings, it was considered beneficial to use a combination of qualitative and quantitative approaches. The former would enable individual voices to be heard whilst the latter would afford generalisations or permit themes to emerge.

Research methods

Tools
Matthews (1992), authoritatively summarised a number of methodological approaches undertaken with children, and warned that when working with young children it is a problem to find suitable methodologies that will reflect the true extent of their environmental capabilities. However, Matthews (1992) suggested that a study of the content of children's maps, or of their drawings gives an indication as to what children consider important in their world through what he termed ' affective imagery' (Matthews, 1992, 102).

Barraza (1999) also favoured a graphical approach, using a drawing technique to elicit the environmental perceptions of Mexican children aged seven to nine years, and concluded that children's drawings were a useful tool for this purpose. Barraza's rationale was that most children enjoyed drawing, it was a relatively tension free activity and it provided a way to compare groups of children with different languages and abilities. Prompted by this particular piece of research and by the knowledge that a graphical approach would be especially useful with young children, a key research tool was developed and successfully trialled, (Owens, 2000), to test its efficacy in accessing children's memories of important outdoor environmental experiences. This 'concept drawing' tool was adopted as the main research tool and was used in conjunction with questionnaires, informal interviews and observations of practice and documentation.

School	Type	Location	Participants	Research Methods
East	First YR – Y4	Village	135	▪ Concept drawings and taped interviews with all Foundation and KS1 pupils, (carried out at the start and end of an academic year.) ▪ Informal interviews with staff and observations of practice ▪ Case study
Town	First	Urban centre	88	▪ Concept drawings and taped interviews with all Foundation and KS1 pupils (carried out at the start and end of an academic year.)
Edge	First	Urban periphery	87	▪ Informal interviews with staff and observations of practice
City	Primary Nursery – Y6	Inner city	20	▪ Concept drawings and taped interviews with a sample of Nursery and Reception children carried out once ▪ Informal interviews with staff and observations of practice ▪ Snapshot study

Figure 1: Research Overview

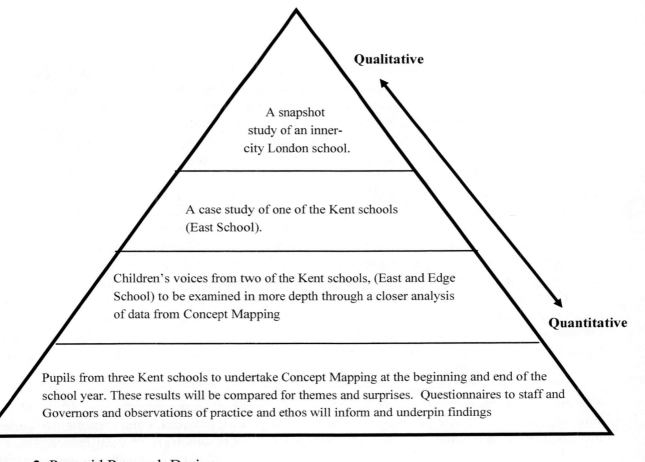

Figure 2: Pyramid Research Design

Research practice

The research was undertaken as follows:

- For the Concept Drawings, the children were arranged randomly within classes into small groups of four to six pupils and were asked if they could draw and talk (from memory), about things that were special and of value in the school grounds. This was an important stage of the research as it normally involved a negotiation of meaning with the children to ensure that they understood what was involved. All the sessions were taped.

- Questionnaires were given to staff and governors similar in design to those given by Palmer and Suggate in determining the environmental orientation of adults in their SLE studies, (Suggate, 1998). While these questionnaires contained some closed questions they also invited open comments. School staff were also observed teaching and notes from informal interviews were kept in a research journal.

- For the case study, many days were spent in school as a 'participant observer'. This involved observing lessons, teaching lessons, attending school council and staff meetings and speaking to parents, teaching assistants and older children. Policy and planning documents were examined for content and use.

Four schools gave their informed consent to participate in the research and an outline of the participants and research methods used is given in Figures1 and 2.

Findings

Concept Drawings

Analyses of the concept drawings were undertaken on two levels. First, a quantitative analysis was undertaken to compare the data between and within schools generally. Second, a more in depth qualitative analysis was undertaken to probe individual and group trends and relate them to specific learning contexts. The second stage was more complex, involving the integration and evaluation of the evidence from children's comments, schools' practices and documentation within *and against* the more generalised quantitative framework

Quantitative Analysis of Concept Drawings

A quantitative analysis was done which summed the total drawn and named features by each child for each phase of the research. This was then used as the basis to work out a *pupil feature ratio* (PFR) using different criteria. For example, the sum of *all* features for *all* year one children in *all* schools was divided by the total number of these children to give an average number of features drawn by this age group. These features, or remembered images from the children were also classified as either 'natural', 'constructed or man-made' or 'activity' dependant on the child's given meaning. These categories permitted further comparison between schools and year groups as to what kinds of memories were significant and how they related to discernible teaching and practice. Figure 3 summarises the total number of features remembered by the children at the beginning (Phase 1) and end (Phase 2) of the year.

The number of features remembered and valued by children increased with age. While this result was expected as children's communicative ability and environmental experience generally increases between the ages of four and seven years other results were of significance. There was considerable variation between schools, East School having a much higher number of remembered features from all year groups than did the other two schools. For example in Phase

1, East School Year One pupils gave almost twice as many features than Year One pupils at Edge School did (Figure 3). The abundant significant memories of environmental experiences at East School appeared to be linked to a mix of active outdoor teaching and the school ethos which promoted children's participation in their environment.

Data from Concept drawings			Total features drawn		Expressed as a Pupil Feature Ratio		
SCHOOL	**Year Group**	**Number of Pupils**	**Phase 1**	**Phase 2**	**Phase 1**	**Phase 2**	**Difference between Phase 1 and Phase 2**
Edge School	*Reception*	14	44	57	3.1	4.1	0.9
	Year One	39	137	138	3.5	3.5	0.0
	Year Two	35	180	204	5.1	5.8	0.7
	All	88	361	399	4.1	4.5	0.4
Town School	*Reception*	17	61	68	3.6	4.0	0.4
	Year One	36	145	147	4.0	4.1	0.1
	Year Two	34	160	190	4.7	5.6	0.9
	All	87	366	405	4.2	4.7	0.4
East School	*Reception*	41	167	178	4.1	4.3	0.3
	Year One	45	269	262	6.0	5.8	-0.2
	Year Two	49	292	289	6.0	5.9	-0.1
	All	135	728	729	5.4	5.4	0.0
All Schools	***Reception***	**72**	**272**	**303**	**3.8**	**4.2**	**0.4**
	Year One	**120**	**551**	**547**	**4.6**	**4.6**	**0**
	Year Two	**118**	**632**	**683**	**5.4**	**5.8**	**0.4**
	All	**310**	**1455**	**1533**	**4.7**	**4.9**	**0.3**

Figure 3: Differences between and within schools in the number of features drawn and described as being valued

The predominant category of response from pupils at all schools was that of natural elements of the environment (see Figure 4). Within this category, references to animals (other than humans) and to humans only were separated in order to compare these memories more accurately against practice. For example, at Edge School the Year Two children initially gave very few animal references but following a sustained active investigation of their pond the children's responses increased in number and contained a great deal of specific animal names.

Qualitative analysis of concept drawings
Following transcription of the children's comments, key responses were collected in tabular form for ease of viewing and comparison. For example, Figure 5 gives one such table for one group's responses. This phase of the research proved particularly useful in highlighting children's voices within the research, something which Catling, (2003) has suggested we should pay more attention to, and allowed children to explain not just *what* they valued but *why*.

The key findings can be briefly summarised as follows:
- First hand experience and contexts were linked to enhanced vocabulary acquisition.
- The reasons for valuing features could be simply and consistently categorised. For example, children generally valued features because they could offer one or more of the

following: play, access, movement, warmth, comfort, safety, friendship and learning, (extrinsic value). Or, features were valued just because they existed, (intrinsic value).

- The types of features mentioned by the children were often linked with playtime opportunities as this was a predominant and constant outdoor experience.

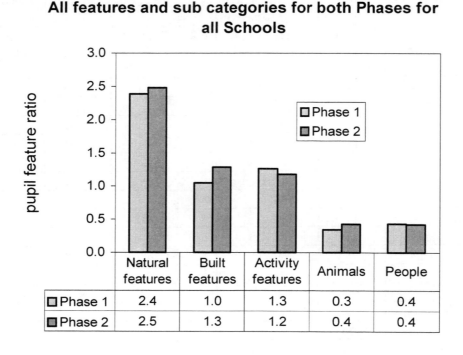

	Natural features	Built features	Activity features	Animals	People
☐ Phase 1	2.4	1.0	1.3	0.3	0.4
☐ Phase 2	2.5	1.3	1.2	0.4	0.4

Figure 4: Average number and types of environmental feature given by all children

- Children valued rules that they had been given and where they saw them being consistently applied, they derived positive connotations from them. For example, while the youngest children in East school said that you *mustn't* put litter on the floor, older children at the same school said that bins were valued because you *could* put litter in them.
- Where outdoor curricular learning had taken place it was apparent in the additional learnt vocabulary of the children, for example groups of Year Two children at Edge School had mentioned mostly playtime activities at the start of the year but in July, after a successful topic investigating the school pond, their drawings reflected the learning and specialised vocabulary they had acquired. Their reasons for valuing these features were mostly intrinsic, e.g. frogs because they were living things.
- Collaborations between children and adults were valued by children, for example the joint community building of a gazebo at Edge School was mentioned by a high proportion of pupils from all age groups at the school.
- Some outdoor learning experiences were long lasting, for example a group of Year Two children at East School fondly recalled gathering autumn leaves and looking for animals with their Reception teacher.
- Children remembered and valued activities that they had fully participated in, for example at East School a large proportion of children valued the planting of a willow shelter and knew that it helped other animals to live.

- There was a strong peer effect at work in groups across all age groups and schools. In nearly all groups there was evidence of the same feature or features being drawn within groups. This enabled the sharing and joint construction of existing and new knowledge *and* misconceptions.

The peer effect within groups was very interesting. Invariably, there would be at least one occasion, and sometimes several, where in each group a feature drawn and described by one child would be picked up by others who copied it. Sometimes a child would give the same reason for valuing it as their neighbour. In a few extreme cases, children next to each other would have almost identical elements to their drawings. There are three suggested explanations for this, although they may not be mutually exclusive:

- One is that a child does not understand the task and so copies another's ideas so as to please the researcher by producing something rather than admitting that they have no idea what is required of them.
- Second, a child understands the task but may not be able to think of anything that they consider special and so relies on another's ideas.
- Third, while they are searching their memory and thinking what to draw; they hear or see a feature that reminds them that they too, like that particular thing. In some examples, children drew similar things but gave different and plausible reasons for valuing them.

The last scenario was the most commonly observed where children appeared to be acting as catalysts for each other; prompting memory recall and sharing language as they fed on and extended ideas. Where such group activity occurred, a vibrant and animated exchange was created that produced a wealth of responses. *The common denominator for such an exchange was always a shared memorable experience outdoors.*

Sometimes children would drift into reverie once the structure of their responses had been established. For example, when recalling a shared pond activity, one child had remembered similar features to others in the group but was alone in drawing gravel and stones around the pond. He said:

I like the pond because the birds come. There is gravel and stones by the pond and I want to walk on it. I wish I could go back there.

As well as appreciating the wildlife around the pond, the boy's comments implied that he wanted access to this area but that this was not possible. Another child then said:

...the pond is quiet but we can't always go there.

The inference that children had little access to the pond was drawn from a mixture of knowledge about prior events, school rules and geographical layout as well as the children's comments. Comments taken out of geographical and historical context are difficult to analyse and so every effort was taken to understand the way in which children's comments were embedded in their day to day lives and settings. The class had visited the pond in the previous school year for a small project in which they looked at the development of tadpoles. Outside of directed curriculum time however, the pond was out of bounds as is normal practice in schools due to health and safety regulations.

| Phase 2 (July 2000)   East School   Reception   Group 3 | | | | | |
| How drawings were classified | | | Analyses from child comments whilst doing drawings | | |
Natural	Activity	Built	Child comment	Reasons for value	Comments
Clouds, sun, me, flowers, tree		playground	A tree so they make the school look nice. Flowers, I like them. Clouds 'cause they make the sun come out. Me playing on the playground.	Intrinsic play	Still lots of 'natural' features but with abundant reasons given much more confidently since previous interview.

There are intrinsic reasons, lots of play reasons, e.g. you can hide, you can run, you can race, make daisy chains.

There are misconceptions about the sky, e.g. the clouds make the sun come out, the cloud makes the sun. One of these comments came after a comment from another child and shows how easily misconceptions can be passed on. Children are very ready to absorb ideas and explanations given by their peers.

The sun is a common thread, whether, as mentioned before, because of peer influence, genuine individual importance or a mixture of both. It is valued for the same reasons as given by other groups. The sun is valued as an important feature in children's lives because of its basic life giving properties, something that we as adults often take for granted. |
Clouds, apples, grass, flowers, field, sun,	Race track	Sun cream	Clouds … it makes the sun. Flowers, you get to make daisy chains. Field you get to play on it. Grass, you can hide. Racetrack, you get to do races. Trees with apples, you can grow them and you get to eat them.	Play, access, hide, grow, race	
Me, sun, cloud		playground	The playground 'cause we get to play on it.	play	
Blue sky, sun, me, trees, flowers			The sun .. it gives you a sun tan. Me racing .. I'm going past the trees and the flowers. Flowers, you can make daisy chains. Trees, they keep growing.	Racing, intrinsic	
Trees, clouds, apples, flowers, sun, children	Making a daisy chain		Sun, it makes it sunny and all lovely – if it rains .. it won't look all blue. Tree 'cause I love the pretty flowers and apples it grows, and it grows birds. Cloud 'cause it makes the sun.	Warmth. Access, intrinsic, aesthetic	

Figure 5: Responses from children during the construction of their Concept Drawings

Case study

The case study of East School, (reported in full in Owens, 2003), revealed the ways in which pupils were given a say in their school through their School Council. Since their initial Eco-School, award in 1998, the school had worked to continue to fulfil seven criteria established by Eco-Schools (ENCAM, 2003). These are:

- Establishment of a committee prominently made up of school pupils who make real, purposeful decisions;
- The development and use of an Eco–code which shows the key principles held by the school;
- An annual environmental review of the school;
- An action plan made each year from the review;
- A commitment to informing and involving the local community;
- Adapting and using the school curriculum to deliver Eco – school objectives;
- Continuous monitoring and evaluation of the Eco – school process.

From discussion with teachers and pupils, observation of curricular and extra curricular activities and an examination of planning and policy documents a picture emerged of school ethos, policy and practice. When this was combined with the knowledge gleaned from the quantitative and qualitative aspects of the research, a clearer understanding of the educational processes at work emerged. The key findings were:

- The apprenticeship mode of learning was valued by practitioners and children alike. The ethos and aims of the school were transparent and reiterated throughout school life in many different guises.
- Relationships between staff, pupils and parents were good.
- The school grounds were stimulating and developed through ongoing participative structures.
- Children were given responsibilities for environmental practices, for example Energy Monitors patrolled the school and kept account of meter readings, Recycling Monitors collected used paper daily from each class in school, Playtime Buddies helped children play at playtimes and each class had School Councillors who reported to and from classes.
- Pupil's self esteem was generally high and they spoke with pride about their school.
- The school had a high profile within the local community and had regular community helpers, for example some senior citizens worked within the school grounds with pupils to grow vegetables that were used in the school kitchen, sold to staff and parents and entered for local gardening competitions.
- The school worked regularly with local bodies, such as Groundwork UK, on environmental projects.
- School ethos was important in defining children's relationships with the environment and each other, for example the value bestowed upon the School Council at East School gave a greater significance to its actions.

Overall, the children at East School appeared to have a higher degree of involvement in the running of their school through the democratic and participative structures in place. The children appeared to be more confident and have more critical skills, i.e. they were more willing to question environmental practices in their school and suggest alternatives. Arguably, these critical thinking skills were better developed because of the responsibility they have been given to make creative choices concerning their own environment. The active involvement in their school environment may also explain why these children had a greater vocabulary relating to outdoor features, as shown by the greater number of responses in their Concept Drawings. The recall of some Year Two children suggested that positive environmental experiences in the outdoors with supportive practitioners during the Reception Year remained with children over time. These memories appeared to be reinforced by school ethos and resulted in concerned motivation from the pupils to maintain the status quo. This was evidence of early awareness of the concept of stewardship, i.e. valuing, evaluating and striving to conserve the environment.

It was also evident that children experiencing the Foundation Stage Curriculum were given more opportunities for curricular-linked outdoor experiences than were children who followed the National Curriculum. This was a common theme throughout all the schools.

Snapshot of an inner city school

Briefly, this stage of the research revealed that while the children had beautifully cared for and stimulating outdoor provision they had little opportunity for direct decision making within it. This appeared to detract from both their environmental perception and vocabulary acquisition, with Foundation Stage children indicating a greater affective bond and knowledge of their environment than older children did.(reported fully in Owens, 2004) In this way, the outdoor curriculum provided for the Foundation Stage proved more supportive than the National Curriculum although neither was supported by environmental interaction such as that evidenced by Eco-school participation at East School.

While it had been expected that the English language used by children for whom it was an additional language would be sparse, the potential for accurate and detailed environmental vocabulary acquisition was revealed through the children's concept drawings. In these drawings and discussions, children with the least environmental access, (playtime access only) had been unable to name or recall but one environmental feature, the climbing frame. However, some of their memories contained a rich mix of mediated sourced images, particularly from television cartoons and the language base used was rich, detailed and precise. For example, some children gave complex cartoon character names, (even spelling them out), recalled storylines and used appropriate adjectives. Arguably, if this propensity for language acquisition had been harnessed to stimulating play situations in the outdoors then they could have just as easily acquired a vocabulary base that reflected environmental features. Instead in their recalls they were utilising mediated rather than real experiences of the outdoor environment. Indeed, when observed outdoors, these children spent the majority of their time enacting fictional situations within what could be termed conceptually, a 'fantasy space', within the given physical parameters of their real environment.

Conclusions

Children appear to value environmental features and experiences for a mixture of extrinsic and intrinsic reasons which are driven by simple basic needs and an appreciation of other life forms, the latter being enhanced and extended through practical teaching activities in the outdoors. Where teachers modelled values, the learning was all the more effective, a point made by Siraj-Blatchford (1996). It is not merely enough to provide stimulating school grounds if the children are not shown how to investigate and participate in them. The most enthusiastic children were those who had been motivated and involved in their surroundings.

Children construct their ideas jointly and peer interaction is a very important part of the hidden curriculum, helping to shape values and attitudes. In this way, positive and negative ideas can quickly grow or wane in popularity so practitioners need to be aware of the values and ideas that pupils hold at any time and challenge or reinforce positive concepts and attitudes. This necessarily involves an investment of time allotted to discussion and investigation and stresses again the need for jointly constructed knowledge rather than didactic teaching methods

Peer groups can be powerful learning spheres and should not be underestimated in their propensity to fuel children's natural thirst for learning so it is important that we recognise and listen to children's voices.

Nearly all of the features that children said they valued came from the sphere of their first hand experience and were fed by the school ethos in which they operated. There was also evidence to suggest that memories of significant experiences were sustained over time. This once again stresses the overwhelming importance of first hand environmental experience in developing language and other connotations of place. Above all, it demonstrates the importance of setting such experiences within a context of a school ethos that reinforces and encourages value acquisition through a sense of shared community and purposeful participation.

Implications for teaching, learning and future research

As practitioners, we need to ensure that we make the best possible use of outdoor areas, both in school and the locality. As well as providing exciting, stimulating and sensory surroundings for our children we also need to ensure that they are given the responsibility to make real decisions about their environment and that their views are valued. A truly democratic format, when applied with transparency and real participation, permits children the luxury of challenging other views in a safe environment. A safe environment in this case describes a space where children feel that they can equally contribute to learning and decision making processes without fear of ridicule and know that their ideas are important. It is in these kinds of contexts that children can be encouraged to risk new and radical ideas, collaborate with others and become critical and creative thinkers and doers.

Several questions stand out from many at the end of this period of the research, (does research ever have an end?) What kind of citizens will these children make as adults? How concerned will they be about their environment? What early outdoor experiences will they remember as being of particular significance? While we may believe that, as educators, it is important to educate children to value the environment from an early age it is, as previously stated, difficult to define and measure pro-environmental behaviour. This is problematised because the outcomes of our efforts are only truly gauged in the long term. In the meanwhile, perhaps we can hope that our best efforts lay in teaching and developing knowledge, attitudes, values and skills that give children the potential to act responsibly in a range of diverse and varied cultural contexts. I will end this chapter by suggesting we use first hand environmental experience to concentrate on four such attributes: enquiry, evaluation, empathy and empowerment.

References

Barraza, L. (1999), Children's Drawings About the Environment, *Environmental Education Research,* 5 (1), 49-66

Bonnes, M. & Sechiaroli, G. (1995), *Environmental Psychology: A Psycho-social introduction* London: Sage Publications

Catling, S. (2003), Curriculum contested: primary geography and social justice. *Geography,* 88 (3), 164-210

Chawla, L. (1998), Research Methods to Investigate Significant Life Experiences: Review and recommendations. *Environmental Education Research.* 4 (4), 383-397

ENCAM (2003),http://www.eco-schools.org accessed 20 November, 2003

Gerber, R. (1996), Directions for Research in Geographical Education: the Maturity of

Qualitative Research, in Gerber, R. & Lidstone, J. (eds.) (1996), *Developments and Directions in Geographical Education*, Clevedon: Channel View Publications, 131-150

Gough, A. (1999), Kids don't like wearing the same jeans as their Mums and dads so whose 'life' should be in significant life research?, *Environmental Education Research*, 5 (4), 35-48

Hart, R. (1979), *Children's Experience of Place*, New York: Irvington

Hart, R. (1997), *Children's Participation, The theory and practice of involving young citizens in community development and environmental care*, London: Earthscan/UNICEF

Hillman, M. (1998), Neighbourhood Safety, in Scoffham, S. (ed) *Primary Sources: Research Findings in Primary Geography*, Sheffield: Geographical Association, 28-29

Matthews, M. H. (1992), *Making Sense of Place: Children's understanding of large scale environments*, Hemel Hempstead: Harvester Wheatsheaf

Moore, R. C. (1986), *Childhood's Domain: play and place in child development*, London: Croom Helm

Norwich, B. (1998), Research methods in educational psychology: traditional and new paradigms, *Educational and Child Psychology*, 15 (3), 8-14

Owens, P. (2000), Where has all the wonder gone?, in Bowles, R. (ed.) *Raising Achievement in Geography*, London: Register of Research in Primary Geography, 79-84

Owens, P. (2003), A Case Study of an Eco-School: practice and evaluation, in Hill (ed.), *New Directions in Environmental Education*, Hong Kong Centre for Urban Planning and Environmental Management, 76-92

Owens, P. (2004) Voices from an inner city school, in Bowles,R.(ed.) *Place and Space* London Register of Research in Primary Geography 65-76

Palmer, J. A., Suggate, J., Bajd, B. & Tsaliki, E. (1998), Significant Influences on the Development of Adult's Environmental Awareness in the UK, Slovenia and Greece *Environmental Education Research*, 4(4), 429-464

Robottom, I. (1999) Beyond Behaviourism: Making EE Research Educational http://www.edu.uleth.ca./ciccte/nacceer.pgs/pubpro.pgs/alternate/pubfiles/11.Robottom.rev.htm accessed 16 June 1999

Scott, W. (ed.) (2002), Special Issue: Exploring the Gap, *Environmental Education Research* 8 (3)

Siraj-Blatchford, I. (1996), Why understanding cultural differences is not enough, in Pugh, G. (ed.), *Contemporary issues in the Early Years, Working Collaboratively for Children*, London, Paul Chapman

Slater, F. (1994) Do our definitions exist? *Reporting Research in Geography Education* Monograph No 1, 5- 8. Department of Economics, Geography and Business Education Institute of Education, University of London

Spencer, C., Blades, M. & Morsley, K. (1989), *The Child in the Physical Environment*, Chichester: Wiley

Suggate, J. (1998), Interview with Jennifer Suggate, Durham University, June

Tanner, T. (1998), Choosing the right subjects in significant life experience research, *Environmental Education Research*. 4 (4), 399-418

Tuan, Y.F. (1977), *Space and Place: The Perspective of Experience*, London: Edward Arnold

Tilbury, D. & Walford, R. (1996), Grounded Theory: Defying the Dominant Paradigm, in Williams, M. (ed.), *Environmental Education Research: Understanding Geographical and Environmental Education: The Role of Research*, London: Cassell, 51-64

Chapter 6

Place Attachment, Place Identity and the Development of the Child's Self-identity: Searching the literature to develop an hypothesis

Christopher Spencer

Introduction

In this chapter, I would like to use a specific argument about place and identity (encapsulated in the title) to offer a generalizable example of how to use published literature to develop and formulate one's research hypothesis. When starting off, one may either feel that one's new idea will have no predecessors, and thus ignore 'standing on the shoulders' of other thinkers; or alternatively, one may be awed by the amount of research which exists, and wrongly presume that there will not be room for one's own contribution. For practically any area that you might think of, if you search the literature, you will probably find already existing research which is relevant; but it is also likely that you will not find exactly the thoughts that you are pursuing, or the application that interests you. So there is, indeed, a need for your research to take its place alongside the existing work, and to fill in one further part of the wall of knowledge.

How to start? Do not assume that you can search the library or use a web search engine with just your terms of reference in mind. Think what synonyms and associated terms might lead you to fellow researchers' work; free associate around the initial idea. Equally, do not presume that relevant articles will all be found within just the one discipline or area: by the time you finish the chapter, think back to this point, and see where the trail has lead. My whole point is to tempt geographers to look beyond Geography!

How to go about scanning articles? When reading a research report, you will find that it often has, in addition to a title, several key words listed to help in your search, followed by an abstract which will enable you to check beyond the title and key words for relevance. [In my own area, I may find 'environment' or 'architecture' jumping out from titles, only to find that the terms are being used in completely other ways than those I need.] Having found those interesting and relevant articles, then get a general idea of the line of argument, rather than at first getting bogged down in the study's details [these can come later if necessary]. Many journals help you to do this by putting these details in smaller print! Take notes as you go [but again, of main ideas only at this stage]. And always make a note of authors, title and where you found the article. [I have wasted more time than I care to admit chasing back on incomplete references, when if I had taken care when first finding an article….] Fairly soon, even if you find the whole process bewildering to start with, a pattern will emerge; and you will find articles cross referencing each other, or mentioning some obvious 'ancestor' reference that sounds like you should seek out. Indeed, other people's reference lists at the end of articles can be an excellent source of further leads. But do not get obsessive: develop a feel for knowing when enough is enough for your purposes. [You are not about to write an encyclopaedia!]

Keep a notebook or file for the project and, if that is your way of working, perhaps a graphic diagram of interconnections that are emerging. And make a running log of your own thoughts about what the literature says about your own particular area of interest. Sometimes the omissions are as interesting as what is down on the page [remember the Sherlock Holmes story about the Dog that didn't Bark!]. These may reveal the assumptions that the author or whole area may have, but which you might not share. [Often, if you are a professional teacher, your classroom experience will have you saying: Yes, but....]. Use these professional insights to develop testable hypotheses: ideas, which go beyond anecdote. Anecdotes may be good starting points for new ideas, but often they are about the exceptional, not about the usual: so ask, under what conditions...?

What do I mean by 'testable hypotheses' and what would count as a test? What kind of study would lead to my being able to suggest firm and generalizable statements? What kind of data, quantitative and qualitative, should I look to? Here again, the literature will help, but should not have you so constricted that all you do is an exact replication of someone else's study.

Now to my example.
- Ask yourself: Why are we **all** geographers?
- And what value has the subject within education?

Most of the defences, the *raisons d'être* for geography and its teaching that we customarily mount against the philistine horde are, quite understandably, couched in terms of the importance of the subject matter we deal with, from local-place studies through to an understanding of geo-politics and conflicts between nations over resources. We talk, again quite rightly, about the transferable skills that the study of geography develops: from observation and recording through analysis of findings to presentation of an argument; and the evidence-led scholarly approach to issues and questions.

Without wishing to take any of this away, I want to argue in this paper that, in 'doing geography' with the child, one is participating in a process which is even more fundamental and therefore more important still: namely, one is in a humble way facilitating the child's very personal development of self identity which will shape much of their lives, their values, sense of belonging and self-worth.

A little bit about identities: social- and self-identity

If we were first meeting, you and I, it would be natural that we would introduce ourselves ... but how would we do it? Probably, having given our name, we would select from a whole possible array of self-descriptors, part of the social identity. Which we selected would probably reflect the context of the meeting: if aware of our common educational interests, we would most likely give our institutional affiliation. But had we been first meeting with other parents at the school gate, it would be more likely be: "Hello: I'm Tom's dad" [fill in the blanks as appropriate]. Encountering each other as 'Brits' Abroad in some touristy place, almost certainly home town, region, etc., would be early-mentioned. [Although perhaps without the vigour with which Americans-abroad seem to pursue that particular self-presentation!] And indeed, were you to be asked to write a little bit about yourself for some reason or other [again fill in the blanks here: for a job application, for the lonely-hearts advert in *Private Eye* or whatever], you would be selecting some parts of that social identity, probably carefully crafted for the purpose in hand. But in that self-presentation or description, I think its also quite likely that you would start including more personal descriptors: not only would you like the world to know that you are from Bakewell, have a nice job and good prospects, but also that you have a GSOH…and all the other very positive acronyms which you flatter yourself that describe you.

Who you are and how you think of yourself are linked but not at all the same: publicly ascribed social identity and personal identity have an interesting relationship with each other, and with experienced well being. If our aim as people concerned with children's development and well-being, it is probably worth spending just a little time talking about how social and personal identities develop, and how they relate to well-being, health and fulfilment. Here, we do not have to speculate: there are good research literatures for each

How do social identities develop? The social psychologist Henri Tajfel (eg 1981) saw social categorisation as the pivotal mechanism in the ways people relate to each other: we see people in terms of their perceived social group membership, and react to them accordingly. In a way, it is how stereotypes work: we see the 'typical member of a group' rather than an individual when we first hear of someone, or first encounter them. Tajfel demonstrated that it takes minimal information about someone [and the group they belong to] for us to start attributing characteristics to them. In many cases, social groups do have a long history [think Loyalists and Nationalists in Northern Ireland]; but one can easily demonstrate the very beginnings of an in-group/out-group identity by allocating groups of strangers to one or other 'team' by something as obviously random as a coin-toss, and then getting them to describe a 'typical person' from own 'team' and comparing them with a 'typical person' from the other 'team'. Frighteningly, instead of saying that we are all just alike, or that they cannot judge, people are willing to see 'own' as in some way 'better' than 'other'. And if allowed, they will differentially allocate rewards between 'own' and 'other' group members (Tajfel, 1981)

So in a way we see who we *are* as being defined by those we *are not* [and often as a result feel superiority to]. And just as with social identity and how it develops, so there is an extensive literature on personal identity and its development: not only from developmental psychologists and educationalists, but also, more profoundly, from philosophers

Daniel Dennett, the philosopher suggested that a human being first creates – unconsciously [the way a spider creates a web] – one or more ideal fictive-selves and then elects the best supported of these into office as her Head of Mind. A significant difference in the human case, however, is that there is likely to be considerably more *outside influence*. Parents, friends, and even enemies may all contribute to the image of "what it means to be me", as well as – and maybe over and above – the internal news media (Dennett, 1981). He continues that we are almost constantly engaged in presenting ourselves to others, and to ourselves, and hence *representing* ourselves – in language and gesture, external and internal. *"Our* fundamental tactic of self-protection, self-control, and self-definition is …telling stories – and more particularly concocting and controlling the story we tell others – and ourselves – about who we are"(109).

So what if we ask, what is a self? Since Descartes in the 17th Century we have had a vision of the self as a sort of immaterial ghost that owns and controls a body the way you own and control your car (Figure 1). Personal identity as a product of others' opinions, as described by Daniel Dennett, is an idea with a long ancestry: as for example G H Mead's concept of the 'looking glass self' in sociology (Mead, 1934). The idea that self (and later identity) is formed mainly on the bases of information attained from other people got its full power in the symbolic interactionist theory (Mead, 1934). However, the self is not a passive acceptor of feedback. Instead, the self actively processes and selects information from the social world the concept of identity process refers to a phenomenon extending from the deep unconscious roots of a person's psyche via shared intra-group stereotypes to the 'outside' of social and personal identities imposed and/or perceived by the public.

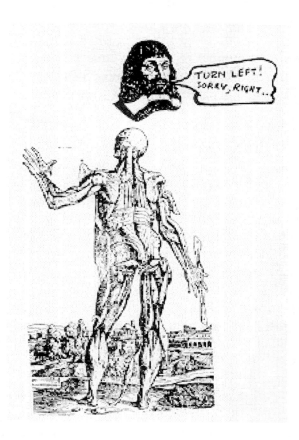

Figure 1: The Cartesian representation of self

Developmental psychology has however not always followed this 'social' line: for instance, George Butterworth (see Butterworth & Harris, 1994) constructs a plausible explanation for the origins of the self in infancy. Breaking from a long history of ideas that formulates both the definition of the self and the origins of the self in social and cultural terms, Butterworth argues that the self exists prior to, and perhaps independent from, social experience. According to Butterworth, the self is directly perceived without cognitive mediation as part of sensory information related to body movement: "the self originates in the fact that we are *embodied*." (Butterworth & Harris, 1994,102)

So how do place attachment, place identity and the development of the child's self-identity link?

The geographically-inclined reader will by now have become impatient. *Nothing* of what we have seen of the literature on self and identity has, as yet, mentioned place explicitly: *but this is the point, this is where geography fits in!*

So far in this chapter, we have seen the individual developing their identity as a member of a group, gaining social identity from the contrasts between own and other groups; as an individual, being shaped by others' responses to them as an individual; and from a biological self-awareness from infancy. So it is indeed striking that nothing much is said in the standard accounts of self, in either social or developmental psychology, about *place* as part of the shaping of self and identity; though in many cases social group identity may include places as identifiers of social group distinctiveness ['We are the boys from the Bronx'].

But continuing in our survey of existing literatures on self, we find that there *is* a new and cohering literature from *environmental psychology* on place attachment.

Place Attachment

We find in this literature that environmental psychology does see *place attachment* as integral to self-definitions, including individual and communal aspects of identity; it therefore follows that disruptions threaten individuals' self-definitions. Place attachment would seem to function by providing the individual with a sense of stability amid change. Place attachments involve the individual's behaviour, cognition *and* affect, and they may operate at several levels of scale.

The early definitive text for environmental psychology has been Altman & Low's book, *Place Attachments* (1992). This is a collection of essays on a whole miscellany of topics, including children's attachment to places; and the importance of childhood places as remembered in adulthood – valuable chapters by Louise Chawla and by Clare Cooper Marcus, each of which summarises many studies.

Chawla (1992) describes four traditions within the literature she reviews: *psychoanalytic theory*, which has a surprising amount to say about the role of places and things within their social context; *environmental autobiographies*, sieved through memory for their significance; *behavioural mapping*, which records where children and adolescents congregate; and *favourite place analysis*, derived from interviews, essays and drawings. She offers a useful developmental sequence of the types of places which feature with increasing age.

Cooper Marcus' (1992) chapter then amplifies the adult memories category, reminding us that for many individuals, their most powerful memories revolve round places. As she notes, these might be the house where they grew up, the secret places of childhood and adolescence, "the setting where they first fell in love, the neighbourhood where they established their first home, the dwelling where they raised their children, the summer house they built in the woods, the garden they first nurtured" (87). She has collected hundreds of 'environmental autobiographies', essays by adults about their most fondly recalled significant places of childhood: it is clear that these earliest places remain powerful images into adulthood. Three categories of remembered places predominated in her sample's essays:
- purpose-built adult spaces, such as culverts, shacks or porches, taken over (one could almost say subverted) by children for their own use;
- hiding places, moulded out of the natural landscape, such as nests, dens or lairs;
- places specifically constructed for play, such as forts and tree houses.

Adaptation and creation of places would seem to be a significant dimension for many adults recalling childhood places, an observation consistent with the various published studies of children's actual patterns of use of their neighbourhoods: eg the classic studies by Hart (1979), Wood (1985), Moore (1986), Torrel (1990), etc., in which behaviour mapping meets almost a street anthropology of childhood. Happily, there is now a second wave of such studies to keep us in touch with what children actually do and what they value: notable amongst which is the many nations study of urban children's activities and participation co-ordinated by Chawla (2002); and the new British studies of the rural experience by Tucker (2003). [See also: Matthews, 1992; Hart, 1997 on children's participation, and the volume edited by Spencer & Blades, 2002, summarising recent work on children's environments in three continents.]

How can one prove that, above and beyond favourite and vivid memories of childhood, attachment to places is actually important to the development of self and security? One way one can often demonstrate the effect of a factor is by looking to 'breakdown' situations, and seeing what is their effect. Thus, the Altman & Low book (1992) includes several such chapters where own place has been disrupted or even violated. In it, Brown & Perkins (1992) review the literature on various ways in which disruptions of PA can take place. A summary of these follows.

Burglary: there are reports of often severe reactions to the intrusion itself, revealing "how many victims had been caught off guard, mistakenly assuming that home is a safe extension of self that is both stable and under the resident's control" (285).

Voluntary re-locations (eg going to college) seems a less severe but still potentially significant factor: a combination of 'losing' home and having to rapidly acquire new place-knowledge leads for more students than will admit to it to levels of homesickness. How disruptive the re-location will be would seem to relate to prior loosening attachments and obligations to home; and the extent of anticipating and connecting with new life.

Involuntary disruptions: eg refugees from disasters: not surprisingly may well have major consequences for psychological well-being; and studies of those who cope best with such disruptions often stress their efforts to establish new identities; or alternatively to re-establish identities reminiscent of the old identities among the exiled groups.

But as we know, people do manage to survive these disruptions; and one way they do it is by bringing a little bit of 'home' with them. As an example of the *importance of objects in transitions between places*, the Taiwanese psychologist Herng-Dar Bih (1992) interviewed Chinese postgraduate students who had been in New York for one semester in 1992. He showed how important certain physical objects, both old and new, were to the person's adjustment in their new setting. He suggests that the importance of objects can be categorised as follows:

- objects have more than functions: symbolic meanings may accrue from eg: "Who gave this to me?";
- objects may manifest values or ideals: religious items; professional symbols (eg a business suit);
- objects as an extension of memory: eg photographs of key people and places; old diaries;
- objects for deepening experience: eg a cherished tea-set, which gave warmth and peace;
- new objects, representing desired changes in role and attachments;
- objects as a place of release from the alien environment: maintaining cultural continuity.

[There is a whole further literature on the psychology of place as 'home': this will not be reviewed here, but to see how it could link with our current concerns, see for example the work of Manzo (2003, 57):

'My research interests have focused on people's emotional relationships to place. I have explored concepts of place attachment and place identity in an effort to learn about the kinds of places that are meaningful for people, the role these places play in their lives and the impact they have on people's identity and well-being. I have sought to understand the foundational, existential qualities of being "at home" in the world and to learn about what places support this way of being. Traditional understandings of home have focused on the residence and positive affect. My research seeks to broaden that understanding to include a wide range of places and to incorporate the role of negative and ambivalent feelings and experiences in places to appreciate the full magnitude of people-place relationships'.]

From this kind of evidence, of disruptions and of repairs and copings, one can see how the case for arguing the importance of place attachment in personal well being and self-identity can be made. We now need more work, both with adults and with children, which examines the nature of the relationships with place [eg are there desiderata for the elements of place for us to become attached to, or is it a case of the familiar becoming positively evaluated whatever its nature?]. We also need to sort out the definitional muddle that has existed in this area.

Some thoughts towards a definition

For some time, the main difficulty the researcher has encountered when dealing with the study of place attachment has been the diversity of approaches available at the theoretical level as well as the empirical. There was no agreement regarding its name, description or the methodological approach best suited to deal with it. There are many similar terms such as community attachment, sense of community, place attachment, place identity (Proshansky, Ittelson & Rivlin, 1976), place dependence (Stokols & Shumaker, 1981), sense of place (Hummon, 1992), etc., such that it is often difficult to tell whether we are talking about the same concept with a different name or different concepts. On occasions we see that one of the terms is used as a generic concept which embraces others [for example, for Lalli (1992), place attachment is a component of place identity]. On other occasions some authors use them without distinction as if they were synonyms. This terminological and conceptual confusion has seriously blocked advances within this field as many authors have pointed out (eg Lalli, 1992).

Currently, there seems to exist a certain consensus in the use of the term `place attachment'. In general, place attachment is defined as an affective bond or link between people and specific places (Twigger-Ross & Uzzell, 1996). For example, for Stokols & Shumaker (1981, 233) it is `a positive affective bond or association between individuals and their residential environment'. Hummon (1992, 256) considers it `emotional involvement with places', and Altman & Low (1992, 165) describe it as 'an individual's cognitive or emotional connection to a particular setting or milieu'.

These descriptions may be appropriate to describe this special feeling toward certain places, but they have the drawback of being too ambiguous and do not allow us to differentiate attachment from other closely-related concepts such as, for example, residential satisfaction, which has been described as 'the positive or negative feeling that the occupants have for where they live' (Weidemann & Anderson, 1985). For this reason, we consider it necessary to further delimit it. Towards this aim, we fall back on what we understand to be the main characteristic of the concept of attachment: the desire to maintain closeness to the object of attachment (see Smith, Cowie & Blades, 2002). This characteristic, although it is implicit in many definitions and operationalizations of the concept, has rarely been explicitly emphasized. If we incorporate this specific property into the previous definition of place attachment, it could take the following form: a positive affective bond between an individual and a specific place, the main characteristic of which is the tendency of the individual to maintain closeness to such a place.

We can only find one description of place attachment in these terms, although under a different name. Sarbin (1983) speaks of the Spanish term *querencia* which reflects the frequently observed tendency of people to prefer to stay near to specific places. It is the propensity of human beings and other animals to seek out the place where they were born or find a place in which they feel comfortable and secure. However, with the exception of this author, rarely has place attachment been described in these terms. On the contrary, many other aspects have been incorporated in its description, for example, the role that attachment plays in the development of identity, its influence on the sense of community, etc. In our opinion, these other aspects are not inherent to attachment or definitive, but the tendency to stay close to the object of attachment is.

But it is clear that the plausible, intuitively persuasive, case for the importance of place in the development of a complete, rounded self-identity has begun to be made. And it is also clearly arguable that the subject of geography, and its early-years teaching, can have a major role to play in partnership with parents and peers and personal exploration of the neighbourhood. If, as Catling (2003) has argued most persuasively, geography teaching starts from children's own geographies, rather than being a slave to theoretically driven curricular, then I would argue we have a really strong argument for the importance of geography teaching in the enhancement of personal well-being (see also Spencer, 2003; Roberts, 2003; Valentine, 2003). One could also make a parallel case for its importance for the sense of community and citizenship, and one moves the focus from individual well-being to that of the wider social world of the child: but that is a whole further literature!

References

Altman, I. & Low, S.M. (1992), *Place Attachment*. London: Plenum

Bih, H.-D. (1992), People, Places and Possessions, *Journal of Environmental Psychology*, 12, 135-147

Brown, B. & Perkins, D. (1992), Disruptions in Place Attachment, in Altman, I. & Low, S.M. (eds.), *Place Attachment*. London: Plenum

Butterworth, G. & Harris, P. (1994), *Principles of Developmental Psychology*, New Jersey: Erlbaum.

Catling, S. (2003), Curriculum Contested: Primary Geography and Social Justice, *Geography*, 88, 164-210

Chawla, L. (1992), Childhood Place Attachments, in Altman, I. & Low, S.M. (eds.), *Place Attachment*, London: Plenum

Chawla, L. (ed.) (2002), *Growing up in an Urbanising World*, London: Earthscan; Paris: UNESCO

Cooper Marcus, C. (1992), Environmental Memories, in Altman, I. & Low, S.M. (eds.) *Place Attachment*, London: Plenum

Dennett, D. (1981), *The Mind's I: Fantasies and Reflections on Self and Soul*, with D. R. Hofstadter, New York: Basic Books

Hart, R. (1979), *Children's Experience of Place*, New York: Irvington.

Hart, R. (1997), *Children's Participation*, London: Earthscan; Paris: UNESCO

Hummon, D.M. (1992), Community Attachment, in Altman, I. & Low, S.M. (eds.), *Place Attachment*, London: Plenum

Lalli, M. (1992), Urban-related Identity, *Journal of Environmental Psychology*, 12, 285-304

Manzo, L. (2003), Beyond home and haven: Toward a reconceptualization of place attachment, *Journal of Environmental Psychology*, 23(1), 47-61.

Matthews, M. H (1992), *Making Sense of Place: Children's understanding of large scale environments*,Hemel Hempstead: Harvester Wheatsheaf

Mead, G. H. (1934), *Mind, self, and society from the standpoint of a social behaviourist* Chicago: University of Chicago Press.

Moore, R.C. (1986), *Childhood's Domain: play and place in child development*, London: Croom Helm.

Proshansky, H.M., Ittelson, W.H. & Rivlin, L.G. (1976), *Psychology*, New York: Holt, Rinehart and Winston.

Roberts, M. (2003), *Learning through Enquiry*, Sheffield: Geographical Association.

Sarbin, T. R. (1983), Place identity as a component of self, *Journal of Environmental Psychology*, 3, 337-342

Smith, P. K., Cowie, H. & Blades, M. (2002), *Understanding Children's Development*, Oxford: Blackwell.

Spencer, C.P. (2003), Why has the Geography Curriculum been so little attuned to the child's geographical enquiry?, *Geography*, 88, 232-233

Spencer, C.P. & Blades, M. (eds.) (2002), Children and the Environment, *Journal of Environmental Psychology*, 22, 7-220

Stokols, D. & Shumaker, S.A. (1981), People in places; A transactional view of settings, in J.H. Harvey (ed.), *Cognition, Social Behaviour and the Environment*, Hillsdale, NJ: Erlbaum.

Tajfel, H. (1981), *Human Groups and Social Categories*, Cambridge: Cambridge University Press

Torell, G. (1990), *Children's Conceptions of Large-Scale Environments*, Sweden: Department of Psychology, University of Goteborg.

Tucker, F. (2003), Sameness or Difference? Exploring Girls' use of recreational spaces, *Children's Geographies*, 1, 111-124

Twigger-Ross, C. & Uzzell, D. (1996), Place and Identity Process, *Journal of Environmental Psychology*, 16, 205-220

Valentine, G. (2003), Boundary Crossings: transitions from childhood to adulthood, *Children's Geographies*, 1, 37-52

Weidemann, S. & Anderson, J. (1985), The affective criterion in homes: Satisfaction, in I. Altman & C. Werner (eds.), *Human Behaviour and Environment 8: Home Environments, Advances in Theory and Research*, New York: Plenum Press

Wood, D. (1985), Doing Nothing, *Outlook*, 57, 3-20

Chapter 7

Children's Geographical Understanding: The perception of landscape and sites of representation

Ana Francisca de Azevedo

Introduction

This chapter describes a geographical investigation focused on an interdisciplinary approach that has the child's world at its centre. Evolving a conceptual revaluation of landscape at the same time helps to put in perspective those symbolic representations that are intrinsic to the idea of landscape. The study was undertaken with 9-10 year old children in an industrialised rural area of the north-west of Portugal: the Ave Valley. The analysis was based itself on the children's interpretations of geographical sites. It is part of a wider study that will be extended to other sub-cultural groups of children. A key outcome has been the realisation that different objects and ideas can be combined with spatial co-ordinates to produce a better understanding of an individual's or a group's attitude towards a given geographical place, particularly when considered through the prism of its symbolic representations.

The point of departure for this study was the assumption that the special relationship people establish with the places where they choose to live is increasingly culturally determined (Duncan, 1993; Blyth & Krause, 1995; Crang, 1998). A particular instance of this is the environment's increasing artificial nature, which is something that may be understood in terms of modem society's patterns and, particularly, of automation (Appleton, 1996). This subtle process of the de-territorialisation of the individual is something that, understandably enough, eludes children, for they are still unaware that territory, along with the perception of landscape and the acquisition of a sense of space, lies at the very heart of the process that leads to the development of identity. The prime objective of the study was to consider the way landscape was perceived by a very specific group of children. Considering the way in which children perceived, analysed and interpreted images representing various geographical places that they might be more or less familiar with, provided a better understand of the ways in which children from that age group and social background acquire their 'sense of place', introducing us to their cultural landscapes (Palmer, 1994; Scoffham, 1998).

The research approach

For the research, a sample of eighty fourth-grade primary school children, from four schools of the region was selected. Two sheets of paper, each showing a reproduction of a picture postcard were then presented to them (images A and B in Figure 1). These photographs showed two geographical sites with marked and contrasting characteristics, in essence, two stereotypes with strong and different potentials to stimulate the imagination. The children were invited to examine each picture carefully for a few minutes. Having done this, they were asked to provide a title for each image and to write a composition about what they had seen in the photographs.

These tasks were undertaken individually. While doing them the children were not allowed to ask any questions. Finally, a semi-structured interview took place with each child about what they saw in the photographs and about their own perceptions of landscape.

Image A

Image B

Figure 1: A rural and an urban scene

The acquisition of sense of place and the perception of landscape

The guiding principle throughout this investigation was to consider whether groups with different cultural backgrounds necessarily have different ways of perceiving the world (Crang, 1998). What this implied is awareness of the various ways in which people interact socially with each other in their respective environment and of the different meanings they attribute culturally to geographical locations.

While being fully aware that the data can only provide a very fragmentary view of the children's representations, it is nevertheless the case that our results from this particular sample group showed that the children found it difficult to state their perceptions of the landscapes. Despite being familiar with the types of landscape that they were shown, the children experienced a certain amount of difficulty in expressing themselves clearly and with an appropriate choice of words. Whenever they were asked to elaborate on their idea of landscape the children resorted most frequently to language that expressed feelings of happiness and beauty, rather than stating information about what they could see as modified landscapes. It was as if they referred to an Arcadian world, where nature itself appeared to be uncontaminated by any human practices. However, it cannot be assumed that the children's perceptions of landscape completely ignored human interference in the landscape, since there had been not only occasional references to urban spaces viewed in terms of landscape, but also a number of individual statements that referred, for instance to "*when one thinks about landscape, it is of children at play that one is reminded of*" or, that one should bear in mind those "*books that suggest to us many landscapes, that inspire us*".

The children's written statements led us to the conclusion that the farmer had a pivotal role in their interpretations of the rural world. There were, in fact, a good number of references to 'labourers tilling the land', and in many cases the titles the children gave the pictures echoed this perception.

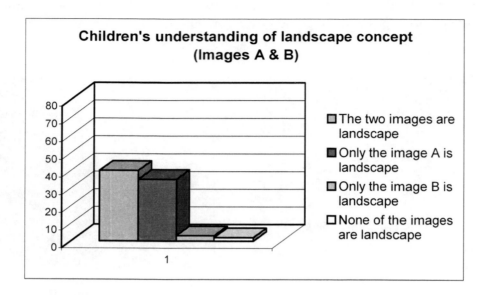

Figure 2: Children's understanding of the concept of landscape, arising from Images A and B

While assessing what the children had to say about the two pictures that had been shown to them, a number of points emerged (Figure 2). While almost half of the children considered both photographs showed landscapes, there were also thirty-five children who only qualified the rural image A as such. Three children thought similarly about the picture B, and there were two children who thought neither of the images conformed to their notion of landscape. The principal reason given by children who saw both images as landscapes was that "*the two photographs are views of places*". For the second group, who focused only on photograph A, on the other hand, what constituted the decisive factor was the presence of *nature* in the photograph. According to one of the children's statement,

> "*the fact that it was calm and full of plants means that it was landscape. In a town, on the contrary, there are no fields and there is too much confusion and pollution*".

The three children who thought that only image B qualified as landscape justified this by saying that "*the town was very pretty*", and also that in it

> "*one could see blocks of flats, cars, cabs and people, whereas in the other picture there were no people to be seen*".

The two children who considered that neither photograph showed a landscape said that

> "*there were no mountains and rivers to be seen, whereas in a landscape one should have plenty of trees, flowers and animals and to be able to rest and to listen to the sounds of nature*".

The emergent meanings of cultural landscapes

In order to gain a better insight into their cultural landscapes, and considering that this sample of children belong to a specific cultural subgroup, namely that of the factory workers, the children were asked to elaborate on various other types of landscape through semi-structured interviews. In common with many families in the Ave Valley region, the children's grandparents had been farmers and their parents were still deeply in touch with the land. It seemed only natural that these children were likely to retain a close relationship with rural life and, particularly, with its symbolic meanings. From their statements, the children revealed a close understanding of the vital role that the "land" has to play in terms of survival, and they appeared able, at the same time, to interact in a creative and almost organic way with the multiple settings that form the background to their daily lives.

Each child's perception of landscape was, indeed, informed by a complex process of social construction and by very specific cultural values, namely those of his/her spatial and temporal co-ordinates. Throughout this investigation, the intention was to emphasise the idea of *geography* as an interpretative art. This made it possible to discern how specific groups of children refer to the landscape and provided the opportunity to analyse the mental processes of deconstruction of places to complement with their material and aesthetic interpretations. While interviewing the children, their imagination was appealed to by proposing that they travel to various destinations and also that they imagine themselves making a photographic coverage of each of them. The perception of landscape that they were able to derive from that exercise was a very important complement to the first of the written compositions, because it indicated some key points about the constitution of a groups' identity, related to the very sense of belonging and to spatial references, as well as alluding to the excluded and marginalised.

The children's favourite landscapes were those where nature and the rural world appear to be inextricable entwined with each other, but it was their parish landscape, first and foremost, that they chose above all others. This type of cultural landscape seems to act as a kind of blueprint for their identities, which are already rooted in a deep sense of place.

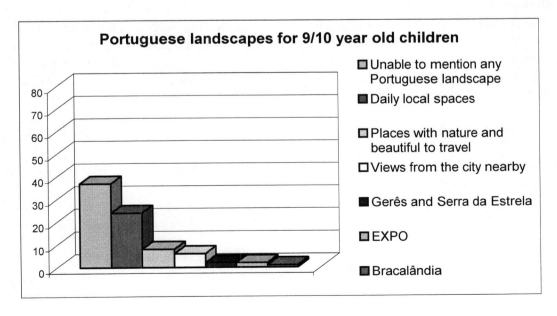

Figure 3: Portuguese landscapes identified by 9-10 year olds

The children were asked about landscapes they could remember and liked in Portugal, their home country (Figure 3). However, the children clearly lacked information. Thirty-seven children who could not recall a single favourite Portuguese landscape. In contrast, twenty-four children identified their favourite places from their daily lives. Two other children talked about Gerês and Serra da Estrela, while for eight other children the landscape of their choice would have to be not only "*a natural one, but also a nice one to go for a stroll*" though they did not refer to a particular place. There were six children who referred to particular views and places in Guimarães. Finally, two children considered EXPO (in Lisbon) to be their favourite Portuguese landscape, and another child pointed to Bracalândia.

The children were asked about their perceptions of landscape across the world. Fifty-three children, more than half the sample group, could not identify a landscape of their choice. Eleven children mentioned places from their daily lives (including the view of their school, house, or "from here"). Thirteen children referred to natural landscapes, and another three mentioned Londres, Brasil and Amazónia.

The children in this study had access to many sources of information about their country and the world generally, sources that contain a wide range of visual representations of distant and exotic places, images that are full of meaning and which the children are capable of interpreting. Yet, the children experienced a certain amount of difficulty in making sense of, and even remembering these images of places and landscapes. Could it be that such images' specific symbolism is too remote for them to assimilate? Or, could this difficulty have its roots in the complexity of the idea of landscape, which makes it difficult for children to recall a large number of places often visualised (Gombrich, 1996)? Or, is that because they see so much, the landscapes they see make little impact on them?

For these children, the perception of landscape is strongly bound up with such notions as those of beauty and nature, as noted above. In fact, what proved to be the most recurring aspect of each exercise was, indeed, the aesthetic/ethical criteria of children's interpretations and the emotional value of the sites linked to the idea of nature and "what is natural". The results point also to a contemplative, idyllic and enjoyable attitude towards the places chosen to be considered as landscapes. The collective memory also has an important role to play here. Their sites of representation are truly located on a few precise co-ordinates. It also emerged that for many of these children an urban area may be qualify as a landscape. But, of what type? And what parts of that urban area may be implied here? Furthermore, from the interviews, the children showed a great deal of concern for the environment. But, for what kind of environment?

Figure 4 indicates the views children expressed in relation to a number of types of urban environment. For the large majority of these children (seventy-four), views of shantytowns and slum areas do not qualify as landscapes, because, among other reasons, they are not seen as real towns and also because

> "*they are very ugly views of places where there is too much poverty and drug-addicts and no gardens or nature nor culture*".

The rest of the sample of children, however, considered them to be landscapes, but ugly and sad ones. This perception related closely to their viewing such places through photographs.

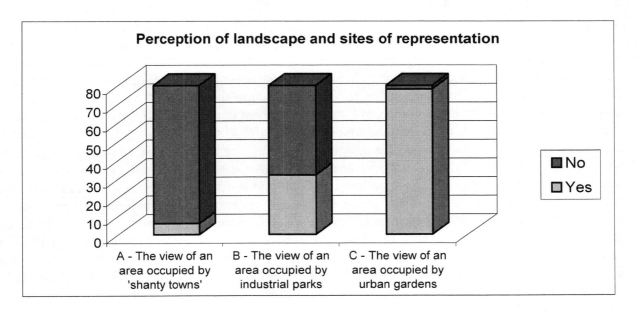

Figure 4: Perception of landscape and sites of representation

There was also a marked division of opinion among the children about views of industrial areas on the urban perimeter. Over half of them (forty-eight) thought that those images could not be landscapes, due to the pollution and the lack of nature, but also to the fact that they considered them ugly. The rest of the children, on the other hand, considered those areas to be landscapes, since there were factories and paths to be seen, not to mention the fact that they often compared to their neighbourhoods.

There were only two children for whom city gardens did not qualify as landscapes, and this, for the simple reason that there was too much traffic noise and burglars in them. For the other children, they were expression of the landscape idea itself because "*they were nature*". What this implies is a perception of landscape in picturesque and aesthetic terms, and where nature itself is represented as a kind of scenic backdrop. All this is reminiscent of Palladian landscapes, which were fundamental in the formation of the western world's idea of landscape (Cosgrove, 1988; Daniels, 1994).

Elements towards a biography of landscape

Just as in the past, the perception of landscape appears to be imbued with contemporary meanings and values. The children's imagination, along with their judgements about what is or is not a landscape, in a way, are predetermined by the dominant western culture. If a landscape is to be understood in terms of its territory, it is important to take into account that it is shaped by the energies and practices of the population according to the beliefs and the meanings the inhabitants invest in it, and through the values that are at the core of the society. What this implies, for one thing, is that industrial areas or shantytown views are to be regarded as landscapes, just as much, in fact, as the two images that had first been shown to the children, or, indeed, as much as urban gardens or the children's parishes. If landscape is to be considered as a symbolic system (Cosgrove, 1988; Cosgrove & Daniels, 1988; Duncan, 1993), it might be a better basis for understanding the apparent inconsistencies in the children's interpretations of landscape.

What the children did, while undertaking the exercises, was to transform visual images into verbal ones; they worked out ideas and elaborated narratives about those images. They attributed their own meanings and interpretations to them, according their sites of representation of those visual images. In effect, these could not but elicit different reactions from the children than those that might be expected from adults. Nonetheless, the children were able to share certain emotional responses arising from the images. In a way, an individual is only able to perceive truly whatever has a certain meaning for him/her, and this is true for children just as much as for adults. All the rest stay's out of the perceptive field; that is always the result of a peculiar *way of seeing*. This is due to the fact that each individual's perception presupposes a very specific intellectual and intuitive approach and attribution of meaning to the world. While doing the exercises, the children were able to identify the stereotypes, those conventional symbols that inform the perceptions of rural and urban areas. However, only by moving on from this iconographic level to that of iconology, is it possible to access deeper levels of symbolic meaning and, by the same token, reach a better understanding of the children's interpretation about places and their sites of representation.

The perception of landscape as a kind of palimpsest, in which the different cultural artefacts and techniques superimpose themselves continuously on the territory, is apparently giving way to a post-modern concept that envisages landscape as a way of seeing, as if it were a text being digitally processed on a screen from which we can create, extend, transform and, finally, obliterate meanings (Cosgrove, 1988; Daniels, 1993). The children involved in this study, either by proposing their own ideas of landscape, or by actually interacting with it in a creative and practical way, engaged themselves actively in what one may call a biography of landscape. In that sense, the school with all its range of experiences and curricular areas seems to be one of the most important places where the different sites of representation could be worked on to extend the children's cultural landscapes and their geographical understanding.

References

Appleton, J. (1996), *The Experience of Landscape,* Chichester: Wiley

Blyth, A. & Krause, J. (1995), *Primary geography: a developmental approach,* London: Hodder & Stoughton

Cosgrove, D. (1988), *Social Formation and Symbolic Landscape,* London: Wisconsin Press

Cosgrove, D. & Daniels, S. (eds.) (1988) *The iconography of landscape*, Cambridge: Cambridge University Press

Crang, M. (1998), *Cultural Geography,* London: Routledge

Daniels, S. (1994), *Fields of Vision: Landscape Imagery and National Identity in England and the United States* Cambridge: Polity

Duncan, J. (1993), *Place/Culture/Representation,* London: Routledge

Gombrich, E. (1996), *Art & Illusion: A study in the psychology of pictorial representations*, London: Phaidon Press Ltd

Palmer, J. (1994), *Geography in the early years,* London: Routledge

Scoffham, S. (ed.) (1998), *Primary Sources: Research findings in primary geography*, Sheffield: Geographical Association

Chapter 8

Urban Children's Perceptions of Rural Villages in England

Greg Walker

Introduction

This chapter reports a piece of small-scale research that sought to add to the existing body of knowledge about how children come to know and understand distant places, places of which they have not usually had direct experiences. Distant places are 'known' by children, the result of indirect, second hand experiences such as written and visual media and the stories of family and friends. But what are children's ideas about these places and what are their attitudes towards them and the people who live there?

In response to the National Curriculum geography requirements for Key Stage 2 to teach children about 'a contrasting locality in the UK' (DES, 1991, 36) a team consisting of three teachers, a local authority advisory teacher and a university tutor produced a Geographical Association award-winning photographic resource pack *Discover Godstone* (Walker & Wetton, 1995). It supplied a range of information, teaching ideas and resources about a Surrey village designed to represent a 'contrasting locality' for schools in urban areas. One section provided ideas for fieldwork in the village for schools located close enough to Godstone to consider affording children first hand experiences. By 1996 its use in schools was reported by Roehampton trainee teachers including that some schools were also supporting learning with field visits.

Literature review

A research framework relating to children's knowledge and understanding of places was established by Piaget and Weil (1951). They theorised that children's understanding of places involved a complex relationship between development in both the cognitive and affective domains. The former involved categorising different kinds of knowledge and skills whilst the latter was concerned with learning values and attitudes. A key concept was 'reciprocity' or 'the ability to look at the world from someone else's point of view' (Wiegand, 1992, 36) and Matthews believed that 'children have a strong affective sense of place' and that they develop feelings and emotions which 'induce powerful positive and negative images' (Matthews,1992, 236).

Wiegand (1992) reported extensively on a wide range of research evidence about children's understanding of places including spatial relationships between places, children's developing sense of their own national identity and their attitudes to distant people and places. At the heart of much of the research reported (Jahoda, 1962; Carnie, 1972; Wiegand, 1992) were ideas about, and between nations. Harrington (1998) investigated children's images of Africa and the effect of a teaching programme upon those images. Pre-testing revealed a great number of shared, stereotypical images. After a nine-week period of study about rich and poor areas of Nairobi re-testing revealed the continuing strength of ideas like hot weather, deserts and poverty but the children now drew images of cities including wealthy houses, high-rise buildings and busy roads. Amongst Harrington's conclusions were that it is important for children 'to be taught about distant lands in a positive way at school, right through the primary years'(1998, 47).

Little research was found that focused on young children's ideas about unfamiliar places within their own country. An exception was a study by Baldwin and Opie (1998) whose investigation with a Year 3/4 class in rural Devon revealed something of their ideas about cities. The majority of children had visited a city at least once but even when drawing on direct experiences Baldwin and Opie concluded that they had only gained superficial understanding of city life. They had little appreciation of 'the wide cross-section of people living in cities' and when considering city life children were not positive because of 'the perceived crowding, noise and fumes' (1998, 40).

A number of studies into the benefits of fieldwork have been reported (Mackenzie and White, 1982; Gwilliam,1987; Nundy, 1999). All suggested positive findings, for example, on long-term memory and enhanced cognitive outcomes. Nundy claimed that, when completing the same tasks, children who had first hand experiences outperformed children who had been involved in similar, passive work inside the classroom.

The literature review led the research to be underpinned by these assumptions:
- children in English schools have existing, and probably muddled, fleeting and improbable ideas about unfamiliar places;
- there exists potential for teachers to challenge these perceptions towards more clear, stable and probable ideas;
- fieldwork has the potential to extend children's understanding of the real world.

The following research questions were proposed for children in the Year 3/4 age range:
- What ideas do children who live in urban areas have about villages in England?
- To what extent does the classroom use of a case study photographic resource pack, *Discover Godstone*, change their ideas towards a clearer view of what a village is like?
- How effective is geographical fieldwork as a means of extending children's understanding of villages and village life in England?
- Does a case study offer children opportunities to develop more positive values and attitudes towards the lives of people in villages?

Research method

A case study strategy, defined by Robson (1993, 5) as

> a strategy for doing research which involves an empirical investigation of a particular contemporary phenomenon within its real life context using multiple sources of evidence,

was applied with a range of data collection tools. White and Gunstone (1992, 14) have argued that it is best not to rely on a single approach, advocating "the informed use of many different probes", as this was likely to give a more insight into children's ideas.

Data collection tools

Data was collected over three consecutive days using these tools in this order.

Drawings
Choosing a drawing first was planned as it offered children a familiar activity. Atkinson and Bannister argue that drawings 'offer the opportunity for an alternative form of expression to children who may well hold ideas, but who find it difficult to express them in words'(1998:3). The children were asked to draw what they thought they would see in a village in England and to annotate it to help clarify what they had drawn. Support for spelling was available from adults in the class.

Word association
Word lists were completed next as both teachers considered it a relatively simple written activity that was within the children's capability. Word lists were structured around what Ghaye and Robinson called 'concept clues' (1989, 121). The five clues were 'the people', 'the buildings', 'the work people do', 'the 'landscape' and an open ended 'other things' category. The need for lists of single words was stressed.

Concept mapping
Concept maps were designed (Ghaye & Robinson, 1989) to explore the added dimension of how children link ideas and individual facts. The same concept clues used in the word lists were provided around which the children could make their maps. The children were asked to write words first and then to make linear and written links.

Interviews
Individual, structured interviews were completed at a time when the children had become familiar with the researcher in their classroom. Pre-set questions probed knowledge and attitudes with responses recorded in writing:
- Can you tell me the names of any villages in England that you know?
- Have you ever been to a village in England?
- Do you know anyone who lives in a village in England?
- What do you think a village is?
- What would you think you would see / hear / smell if you visited a village in England?
- What sorts of people live in villages in England and what kind of work do they do?
- What do you think people who live in English villages like to do in their spare time?
- Can you tell me ways a village is different from a city in England and are there any things that are the same?
- What do you think life is like for people who live in a village in England?
- Would you like to live in an English village? Why would you like to / not like to?

Photograph sorting
Photograph sorting was the final probe used so that the images would not influence other activities. Eleven photographs taken in Surrey villages and with varied content were used. They included a village green and timbered houses but also modern flats and roads with heavy traffic. Sorting was into three categories:
- those images children thought they would see 'in a village' in England;
- those 'not in a village';
- if uncertain, a 'don't know' category.

To encourage close observation the children were advised that category choice would require explanation. Photographs placed in each category were noted by letter and explanations recorded in writing.

Data collection

Data was collected at two schools in heavily urbanised parts of south London, referred to as school A and school B. Children in school A acted as the control group taught entirely in the classroom. Children in school B were taught in the classroom and they also visited Godstone. Children's work was identified by their register number.

Initial, or phase one, data was gathered over three days before the start of the teaching period. Re-testing, or phase two, occurred afterwards using the same methods in the same order. There were 22 children of mixed ability in school A and 23 in school B who completed both phases in full.

Between phases one and two the class teachers taught the children about a village in England using *Discover Godstone*. Teaching time was similar in both schools and the teachers were encouraged to assist the children to answer the enquiry questions 'Where is Godstone?', 'What is Godstone like?', 'Why is Godstone like it is?' and 'In what ways is Godstone similar to, and different from our place?'. There was no external support during the teaching programme and the teachers were encouraged to choose their own path through the enquiry.

Findings

Question 1. What ideas do children who live in urban areas have about villages in England?

Phase one results revealed a few children who were able to provide a range of clear observations about villages. In all but one case they were children who had knowingly been to a village in England. Child 21 from school A exemplified this group. He drew, in colour, a village with houses, police station, road, shop and a tree. His word list included 'cotages'(sic), 'old people', and 'small streams'. His concept map (see Figure 1) showed attempts to link ideas. He explained during the interview that he knew of the village of Evercreech in Somerset where he had visited his grandmother. He defined a village as "a little town with small houses in it", specified work in a Somerfield supermarket and thought that life for villagers was 'sometimes quiet and sometimes, not usually, noisy'. When photograph sorting he confidently rationalised his choice into categories 1 or 2, for example, because 'those are the sorts of houses you get in villages'.

A much larger group of children had some clear ideas but also gave some muddled responses. Child 2, school B exemplified this group. He drew a village consisted of just a house and tree. He listed words with village associations such as 'barn' and 'hills' but others, included 'hospitals' and 'jumper making', less so. His concept map (see Figure 2) confirmed muddled ideas with limited links between categories. He could not name a village, defining one as 'a bigger form than a cottage, more than a building'. He named work as a 'teacher' but also 'collecting firewood to heat their homes because they don't have radiators'. Differences between cities and villages were the greater number of buildings, cars, and people in cities. However, he thought villagers would have 'a hard life, they have to go out to get fruits and food and the school doesn't have much technology'. Photograph sorting was done confidently and accurately and amongst his explanations was 'because it looks like a house in a village because of the flowers and the old fashioned style'.

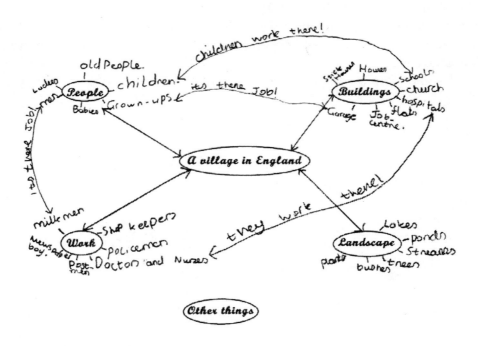

Figure 1: Child 21's village concept map

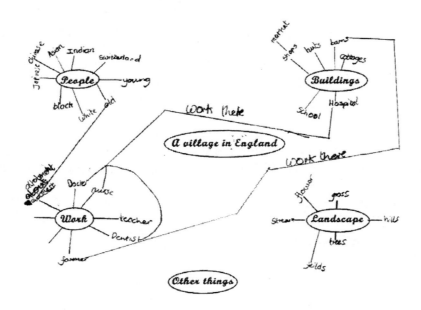

Figure 2: Child 2's village concept map

The biggest group proposed largely muddled, often improbable ideas and a narrow range of responses. Child 10, school A exemplified this group. He completed a drawing with considerable content including a cottage and a pond but also high-rise flats, tents and a wigwam. His word list repeated 'wigwam', 'tents'. 'block of flats' and also 'huts'. 'Work' would be in 'hopital'(sic), 'offices' and 'schools'. His concept map (see Figure 3) exemplified word list ideas with few attempts to make links. He could not name a village and defined one as 'like with tents in, a little amount of houses'. Amongst work in a village would be in a hospital (a large hospital is located very close to school A) and he did not want to live in one 'because a village has sand and some people don't wear shoes and half the buildings are wooden and you'd get splinters'.

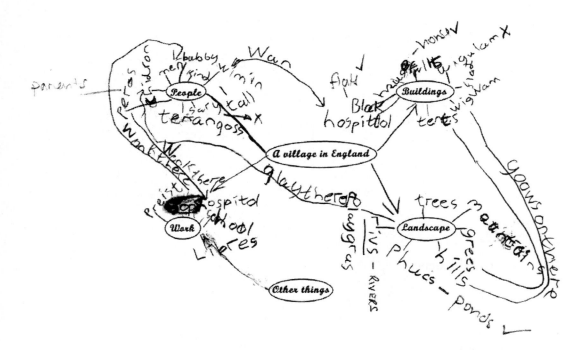

Figure 3: Child 10's village concept map

Word coding exercise.
A coding exercise was applied to the children's word lists. Coding was based on sixteen words that three primary teachers thought Year 3/4 children might use about English villages:

> **People:**   Farmers/Men/Women/Shopkeepers/Old
> **Buildings**:   Pub/Cottage/Shops/Church
> **Work:**   Farmer/Shop work/Pub work
> **Landscape:** Field/Trees/River/Pond.

The frequency with which these words appeared in the children's lists produced quantifiable data (Figure 4).

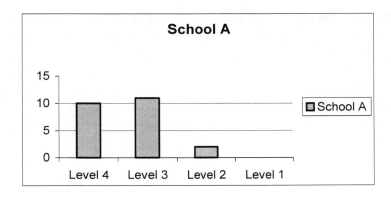

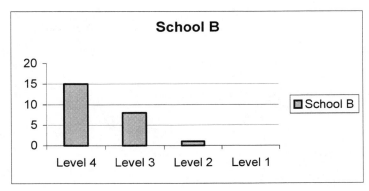

Figure 4: Frequency of words in children's lists.
Levels were awarded according to the number of coded words listed:
Level 4 = 0-4 words
Level 3 = 5-8 words
Level 2 = 9-12 words
Level 1 = 13-16 words

In both schools at least half of the children failed to record even a quarter of the coded words. The majority scored half or less suggesting many children initially had unclear ideas about villages.

Question 2 To what extent does the classroom use of a photographic resource pack, *Discover Godstone*, change their ideas towards a more geographically accurate understanding?

Phase two data analysis revealed considerable change to results.

Child 21, school A, again drew confidently but content changed to a playing field with pond labelled 'playground' 'slide' and 'swing', remarkably like photographs 9 and 10 in *'Discover Godstone'*. His word list was longer with words from the photopack like 'florist' and 'bakers'. The concept map (Figure 5) was briefer but content also reflected the teaching programme, for example, 'butcher', and 'bungalow'. Connections between ideas were no more effective. Godstone was named alongside Evercreech at interview and answers often reflected the teaching programme like the 'smell of fruit from the farm'. He was now positive about living in a village 'because there's not many roads so I could go to my friends and where I live I can't because the roads are too busy'. Photograph sorting used a mix of existing knowledge, 'when I went to my grandmother's there were lots of farms' and classwork, 'there's usually churches in villages, there's one in Godstone'.

Child 2, school B, showed change in both the range and clarity of ideas. He drew a detailed graveyard with features seen in Godstone parish church including its lychgate. His word list reflected both classwork and field trip such as the 'club house', 'cemetry'(sic), and 'doctor'. His concept map (Figure 6) showed greater clarity although links showed no improvement. He named Godstone, listed work 'cutting grass' that he had observed and thought that life for villagers would be a 'fun life because they've got fields and lots of open spaces'. Confident photograph sorting included responses like 'in Godstone some houses looked old-fashioned and these are old fashioned'.

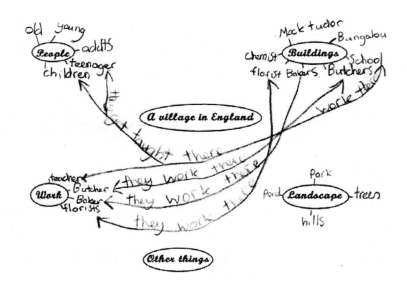

Figure 5: Child 21's Godstone village concept map

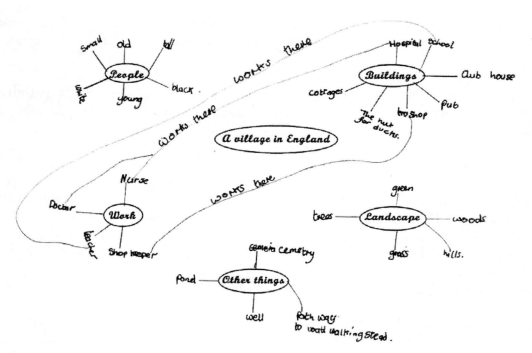

Figure 6: Child 2's Godstone village concept map

Child 10 typified the children who made the greatest progress in clarity of understanding. His colourful drawing showed a church with gravestones, a farm with sheep, a pond and a house. His word list included 'bungalows', 'terraced house' and 'cottages'. Work included on 'farms' and in 'shops' and 'pubs'. His concept map (Figure 7) still showed weaknesses in spelling but content reflected the teaching programme. He named Godstone, defined a village as 'it's got stores, houses and rich people' and he thought there would be work in shops. Life in a village was 'nice because they can enjoy going out to play and to the shops and they can relax' but he still didn't want to live in one 'because its much smaller and they don't have flats and a post office'. Photograph sorting was completed confidently but orally he showed no particular insight that might have reflected the teaching programme. Responses were utilitarian, for example, there would be schools 'for the children to go and learn stuff'.

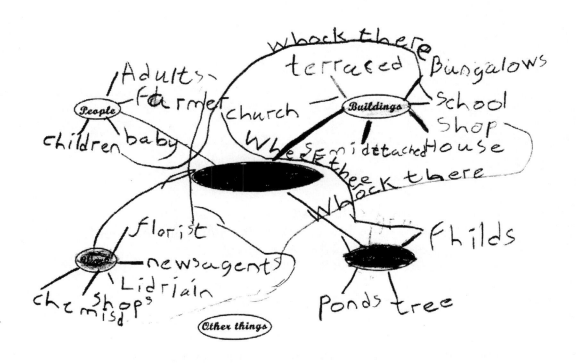

Figure 7: Child 10's Godstone village concept map

Word coding exercise.
The coding exercise was completed with phase 2 data (see Figure 8). Both schools showed improved results with school A showing greater change than school B. No child reached level 1 but this may reflect the composition of the coding words. School B results showed little movement into level 2 but, for example, one child at level 4 wrote a long list of appropriate words but just three were coded.

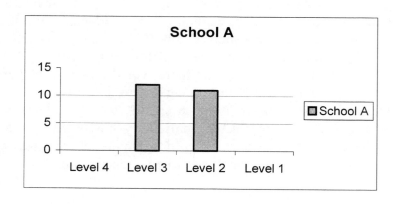

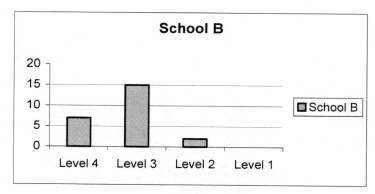

Figure 8: Frequency of words in children's Godstone village lists
Levels were awarded according to the number of coded words listed:
Level 4 = 0-4 words
Level 3 = 5-8 words
Level 2 = 9-12 words
Level 1 = 13-16 words

Question 3 How effective is geographical fieldwork as a means of developing children's understanding of villages and village life in England?

Results from all data collection strategies showed the impact of fieldwork. Specific reference to Godstone was common in responses from school B, especially photograph sorting where over 80% explained their choices because of what had, or had not, been seen on the trip. For example:

Child 1: *'because when we were in Godstone there were lots of lorries like that one'.*
Child 16: *'because when we got off the coach the first thing we saw was a pond'.*

School B drawings showed more varied content including images not in the photo pack. For example, graves of a 'pirate' and that of a child younger than them had been seen in the graveyard and they proved powerful images appearing in several drawings. Word list and concept map content confirmed wider knowledge with words like 'estate agent' and 'surgery' appearing, neither found in *Discover Godstone*. Connections between ideas in concept maps were more varied. Explanations for both photograph sorting and to questions were generally longer, with insights that could only have been the result of the visit.

Question 4. Does classroom teaching enable children to develop more positive values and attitudes towards the lives of people in villages?

At interview the final two questions explored values and attitudes. In both schools in phase one there was a mixture of negative and positive attitudes to village life (see Figures 9 and 10). Positive ideas included 'quietness', 'happiness' and the proximity of services such as shops, for example:

Child 1, school B – '*nice, hardly any noise, few cars each day and you can play in the fields*'

Negative ideas were particularly about the hardness of village life, for example:

Child 10, school B – '*like African people they beg for food and water*'

Both schools showed considerable change in attitudes in phase two with just a single child in each continuing to express negative views. Changed attitudes included:

Child 10, school B – '*good because they have spare time*'

Despite the changed attitudes in school A, there was no similar change, in response to the final question, in the children **themselves** wanting to live in a village.

Phase 1.

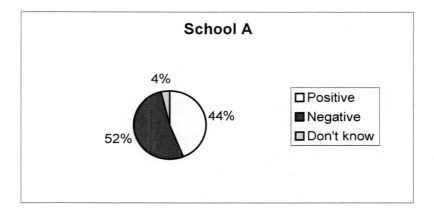

Phase 2.

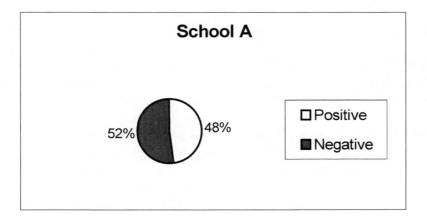

Figure 9: Attitudes to villages at School A

Phase 1.

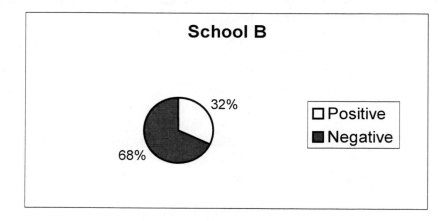

Phase 2

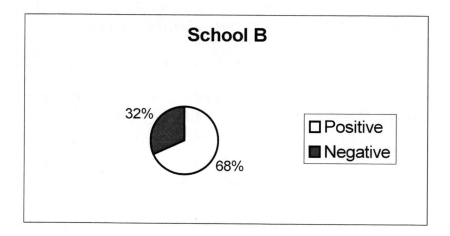

Figure 10: Attitudes to villages at School B

In school B there was an almost direct reversal of results in response to the final question. First hand experiences seemed to have influenced positive attitudes.

Discussion

Ideas about villages in England varied from child to child, but not greatly from school to school. Children who had knowingly experienced village life, usually when visiting family members, showed greatest clarity of understanding but they are likely to be few in number in this age group. Most children drew on indirect experiences and had muddled and in some cases very improbable ideas about English villages and the people who live in them.

The majority of children in both schools showed considerable improvement in clarity of ideas about villages and village life after the teaching programme. The children in school A were heavily influenced by the content of the photographs of Godstone. The children from school B made greater progress in their range of ideas with fieldwork influences clear. Observations, related to the visit, gave individual and often unique dimensions that were absent from school A responses.

Class-based work was reinforced in the field including confirmation that images seen in the classroom existed in reality. Children's drawing, writing and talk revealed extended understanding of the real world that could only have been the result of the fieldwork. Sensory awareness, especially aural, was enhanced. Evidence from all the data collection strategies revealed a clearer and wider understanding of villages and village life.

On completion of the teaching - programme every child confidently expressing an opinion about village life, Attitudes were more positive towards life for village residents, even if children felt negative about living in a village themselves. Children who visited the village were much more positive about living in one themselves than the children whose work was classroom -based. Peace, quiet and safety were common arguments in favour of living in a village.

General findings including the benefits offered by distant place studies

Teachers should first establish how children conceptualise this part of their world and any subsequent 'concept modification' needs to take into account existing ideas. Case studies of real places and people should be used to teach children about distant and unfamiliar places. This may present images and ideas in conflict with some children's initial ideas and they should be encouraged to reconsider them. Within a teaching approach seeking to give a balanced view of a place teachers should ensure that positive aspects are apparent. Activities that explore children's values and attitudes, providing opportunities for them to express opinions should be sought. Photographs should be at the core of place studies in class-based tasks. Fieldwork enhances children's understanding of the real world and schools, in key stage 2, might seek a contrasting UK locality that affords such opportunities. *Discover Godstone*, a village case study photo resource pack, was effective in developing children's knowledge and understanding. A village case study offers links in a spiral study of urban children's own place, contrasting places in their own country and places in very distant localities.

Conclusions

While this small-scale research project answered, in part, the research questions, it also posed many others:

- Some children initially painted a picture of English villages as 'low technology', 'developing world' or 'dull'. What are the sources of those ideas?
- What ideas do key stage 1 children have of unfamiliar places and what is the impact of a study of a 'contrasting' place?
- Should schools introduce distant places studies in the early years curriculum and what are effective teaching strategies and resources for this age group?
- What are the most effective teaching strategies and resources to help children to know and understand distant places when the place to be studied is too far distant for first hand experiences?

Each of these is a potential area for further research.

References

Atkinson, H. & Bannister, S. (1998), Concept maps and annotated drawings: a comparative study of two assessment tools, *Primary Science Review* 51, Jan/Feb, 3-5

Baldwin, H. & Opie, M. (1998), A child's eye view of the city, in Scoffham, S. (ed.) *Primary Souces: Research findings in geography*, Sheffield: Geographical Association, 40-42

Carnie, J. (1972), 'Children's attitudes to other nationalities' in Graves, N.J. (ed) *New Movements in the Study and Teaching of Geography*, London: Temple Smith, 121-135

DES (1991) *Geography in the National Curriculum (England)*, London: HMSO

Ghaye, A. & Robinson, E (1989), Concept maps and children's thinking: a constructivist approach, in Slater, F. (ed) *Language and learning in the teaching of geography*, London: Routledge, 115-139

Gwilliam, P. (1987), "Beyond the Wild Wood", *Teaching Geography*, June 1987

Harrington, V. (1998), Teaching about distant places, in Scoffham, S. (ed) *Primary sources: Research findings in primary geography,* Sheffield: Geographical Association, 46-48

Jahoda, G. (1962), 'Development of Scottish children's ideas and attitudes about other countries', *Journal of Social Psychology*, 58, 91-108

Mackenzie, A. & Whiter, P. (1982), Fieldwork in geography and long-term memory structures. *American Education Research Journal*,19 (4), 623-32.

Matthews, M. H. (1992), *Making Sense of Place: children's understanding of large-scale environments,* Hemel Hempstead: Harvester Wheatsheaf

Nundy, S.(1999), The Fieldwork Effect: The Role and Impact of Fieldwork in the Upper Primary School, *International Research in Geographical and Environmental Education.* 8 (2) 190-199

Piaget, J. & Weil, A.-M. (1951), 'The development in children of the idea of the homeland and of relations with other countries', *Institute of Social Sciences Bulletin*, 3, 561-78.

Robson, C. (1993), *Real World Research.* Oxford: Blackwell

Walker, G. & Wetton, S. (1995), *Discover Godstone, a study of a village in England,* Farnborough: NRSC

White, R. & Gunstone, R. (1992), *Probing Understanding,* London: Falmer Press

Wiegand, P. (1992), *Places in the Primary School,* London: The Falmer Press.

CHILDREN AND PEDAGOGY

Processes of learning in geography

Chapter 9

Computer Supported Collaborative Mapmaking and Children's Talk: Developing a research focus

David Owen

Introduction

This chapter reports the process of developing a research project investigating how children represent their local geography using Information and Communications Technology (ICT). The central aim of the initial stage of the research project was to gather exploratory empirical data across several possible research themes, in order to select a final more discrete research focus for the main research study. Initial interest in the area of children's environmental mapping and their use of computer based mapping tools stemmed from professional practice and small scale evaluation of primary school and student mapping projects. My previous teaching role in a primary environmental education centre involved setting up map making activities. These activities involved children using and making maps for outdoor orienteering and reporting the results of geography and science fieldwork. The children also made use of an early computer based mapping resource, the BBC Domesday disk.

This interest in children's environmental mapping using new technology continued in work with primary geography development in initial teacher education. A small scale evaluation of primary children's environmental mapping using a simple computer mapping program was carried out (see Owen, 1997), and primary geography students evaluated the effectiveness of using simple geographical information system (GIS) software to report the results of geographical fieldwork enquiries (see Owen, 2000). Recent curriculum guidance (BECTa, 2002; Ordnance Survey, 2002; ESRI, 2003) suggests the use of electronic mapping software and GIS gives learners the advantages of interactivity, flexibility, accuracy and ease of use when engaging in mapping tasks previously done by hand. However, little research has been completed on the teaching and learning strategies needed to capitalise on the potential advantages of such new technologies. The combination of an interest in curriculum development in the area of electronic mapping, and the identification of a gap the relevant research literature, led to plans to develop a PhD proposal in this area.

Literature review

The initial stages of the development of a research question focused on empirical data collection in a classroom situation. However, it quickly became apparent that an initial review of the literature was needed to further inform the development of the study .The study focused on two main areas: children's mapping ability and the role of talk in paired mapping activity at the computer. The following sections outline relevant research in these areas.

The development of children's mapping ability

Children's ability to create maps has been linked their development of spatial cognition (Matthews, 1992). Spatial cognition is the ability of children to make sense of the environment around them. No single explanation of the development of spatial cognition is accepted by all researchers, and three competing positions of *nativism, empiricism* and *constructivism* can be identified. Nativists believe spatial ability to be an innate part of human experience, and that it develops in similar ways to language acquisition. Children are, it has been claimed, natural mappers (Blaut et al, 2003). Empiricists believed such cognition is derived directly from experiences of the environment (Tolman, 1948), although this stance is not now seen as reliable. Constructivists believe spatial cognition is created by the action of the child attempting to make sense of the world through the construction of structures (or schemas) to model their understanding of the real world. Interpretations of the work of Jean Piaget (Piaget and Inhelder, 1956; Piaget et al, 1960) have had a profound effect on the interpretation of primary children's mapping and on the curriculum available to primary children over the last thirty years. His four stages of cognitive development are well known, but Piaget also proposed a developmental sequence of how children construct spatial relationships. Children first comprehend *topological* spatial relationships involving proximity and separation of objects, how features are ordered, and the degree of openness or closure. They then develop the ability to describe *projective* space, in which they perceive the interrelationships of objects from different views and are able to project themselves into another viewpoint. At the same time as developing this *projective* view of space they also begin to perceive space as *Euclidean*, with characteristics such as size and proportion portrayed relatively accurately, and landmarks positioned relative to each other as if viewed from above. These stages have been used to define curriculum progression in the primary school (Catling, 1996) as well as classify children's maps. Empirical research on children's mapping ability (Catling, 1979; Matthews, 1992; Sowden et al, 1996) has since been selected (see Scoffham, 1998) to prompt teachers to build on young children's natural mapping skills in formal schooling and to disregard a rigid progression through Piaget's stages. However, some authors (Liben et al, 2002) continue to report the potential difficulties junior school children have with complex map displays, symbolisation strategies, and aerial photograph interpretation.

The role of speech in pair or group learning

Much of the work on children's developing mapping skills suggests that learning is an individual activity which occurs via interplay between reason and experience. However, theorists influenced by social constructivists such as Vygotsky (1962) and Bruner (1966) see learning as initially a social activity. Vygotsky argued that thinking was first shared between people as interpersonal communication, then later internalised as individual thought. Crucial to this internalisation is the role of speech. Learners must communicate with a teacher or more able peers to move into their zone of proximal development (ZPD) when attempting to master a concept or skill they cannot comprehend individually. Bruner coined the term scaffolding to describe the role of the teacher, adult or more able peer when supporting learning in and through the ZPD.

Mercer (1995) focused on the role of the teacher in structuring talk in a classroom situation based on social constructivist principles. He identified three broad types of pupil talk, which are summarised below:
- cumulative talk which reflects an orientation to share and understand each other but without any critical grounding of shared knowledge;

- disputational talk where individuals treat dialogue as a competition which they seek to win;
- exploratory talk which is oriented to sharing knowledge like cumulative talk but with the addition of critical challenges and explicit reasoning.

Wegerif (2001) identified exploratory talk as most likely to support peer or group learning, but also claimed that such talk does not readily occur without overt teaching. There is a limited amount of published research on using such collaborative approaches in children's map work development, but results from this research suggest a cautious optimism in continuing with such approaches. Leinhardt et al (1998), and Bausmith and Leinhardt (1998), found that paired map construction was more effective than individual or group map-making. Wiegand (2002), working with secondary school students, analysed the discourse generated by a collaborative mapping task and found a relationship between the quality of map and the type of talk used whilst making it. Higher quality maps were related to reasoning and questioning talk for older children, who also discussed more cartographic concepts whilst making the maps. However, this relationship was not as strong for younger children.

This review of literature framed the initial proposal for the research. It provided a justification for investigating primary children's collaborative mapping, as very little work was found on primary children's use of new mapping technologies.

Research method

Initial classroom based research used a range of methods to both test the effectiveness of these methods and to generate and refine research questions and methods for the main study (as suggested by Punch, 2000). Development of the final proposal involved two separate empirical data collection sessions in school. These were an exploratory study, followed by a more formal pilot study which built on lessons learned from the first work in school. The impact of the exploratory study is discussed in more detail in the following sections.

Research strategies for both the exploratory study and pilot study built upon the approaches of Catling (1979) and Matthews (1992) who asked children to draw maps then classified them and interviewed the children about what they had created. Data were obtained through video and audio recording the electronic map creation enabling the processes involved, including the children's talk, to be captured. This approach was based on the work of Leinhardt et al, 1998; Wegerif, 2001; and Wiegand, 2002. A semi-structured interview technique was used to gather data in the exploratory study showing the children's reflections on the process of mapping and the maps they created.

Procedure for the exploratory study

School based work was conducted with the children (ten pupils aged 9-10) over a period of one week, in both the children's classroom and a smaller workroom. The initial sessions focused on establishing a rapport with the children and explaining the task. In the next activity the children were asked to draw a map of a forty-minute walking tour starting and finishing at the school. The purpose of this walk was to introduce new pupils to the locality of the school. The tour had to include up to six places of interest for the new pupils. This task was completely individually by the pupils on paper.

The third stage of data collection involved introducing the whole group to the electronic mapping application. The software used was *Local Studies*, published by Soft Teach Educational. The five pairs of children were then given the mapping task that required them to jointly create a walking tour for the pair of new pupils. Two of the five pairs of children were given a vertical aerial photograph of the school as a prompt in the map making process. The mapping episodes were recorded on video tape and the finished maps were saved electronically and printed in colour for analysis. After the two mapping tasks were completed, I returned to the school several days later with copies of the paper and computer drawn maps for the children, and carried out semi-structured interviews with the pairs of children.

Mapping analysis

A range of classification structures have been developed to describe the quality of children's maps (see Hart and Moore, 1973; Matthews, 1992). Harwood and Usher (1999) summarised these approaches and proposed their own system which graded maps using the following six criteria, giving a score of 0 to 5 to each aspect of the map:

- spatial arrangements;
- scale and proportion;
- perspective;
- level of abstract/symbolisation;
- amount of content (1): everyday features, houses, roads et cetera;
- amount of content (2): understanding of the wider area.

Both paper and pencil maps were graded using a modified version of Harwood and Usher's system.

Analysis of paired talk

Video tape data for four pairs of children were transcribed and analysed by focusing on what the children were doing, what they were saying about spatial relationships in the mapped area, what they were saying about how to represent space on the map, and evidence in the interchange about how they supported or hindered each other during the map making process. The study adapted Pilkington's DISCOUNT scheme (Pilkington, 1999) which was devised to record the structure and content of an argument as speakers talk with each other. Content of the argument was recorded under two categories; talk about spatial representation and talk about symbolisation of space.

Interview data

Conducting semi-structured interviews with children is a well-established technique in geographical as well as general educational research (Cohen et al, 2000). The interview transcripts were analysed to reveal relevant themes and show how the children talked about the space represented on their maps, explained their choice of representation of that space and gave their views on paired working, the software and the pedagogy used.

Findings

The exploratory study generated much quantitative and qualitative data, which in turn formed a strong basis for both evaluating the research tools and further developing the research questions for the main study. Only the analysis of the children's computer drawn maps and the analysis of their talk are presented here.

The children's maps drawn on the computer

The general and specific standards of computer based map drawing appeared to be of lower quality than the pencil drawn maps when judged by the same criteria. The prominence of pictorial symbols in the software led to children who drew mainly abstract symbols for houses using paper and pencils, to choose pictorial symbols in their paired map work, thus lowering their scores in the abstract symbolisation category.

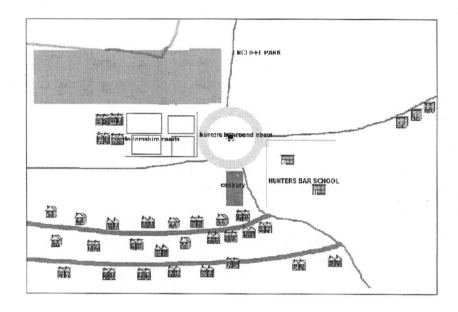

Figure 1: Rueben and Josh's *Local Studies* map

The pairs with the highest scores included Reuben and Josh (see Figure 1). Reuben and Josh had access to an aerial photograph, which explains their higher scores for spatial arrangement. Reuben and Josh's map has the most evidence of abstract symbolisation. Reuben made extensive use of the drawing palette in *Local Studies*, so shops, tennis courts and the roundabout are shown as abstract symbols in plan view. Houses are shown as pictorial symbols and are located in areas of terraced housing. The trail however is not evident on the map, due to lack of time and many revisions of the map. Although in general the standard of paper based mapping was higher; the work produced by individuals did vary. Reuben's work on the paired mapping task was far superior to his work on pencil and paper. His paper map could be interpreted to reveal that he possessed only a topological understanding of spatial representation, yet he was responsible for Euclidean or metric mapping in his paired work.

Talk during paired mapping

In general, the higher quality maps were characterised by higher levels of talk categorised as informing statements, but this is not significant due to the very small sample and the exploratory way in which data collection was carried out. What may be significant, however, is the overall lack of talk classified as reasoning or challenging, which suggests that most of the talk could be classified in Mercer's (1995) terms as cumulative or disputational. The lack of exploratory talk, in which reasons for action are presented and challenges given and accepted, may suggest that advantages of peer working and joint problem solving were not being exploited to the full in much of the mapping collaboration.

Analysis

The analysis of the children's performance in drawing pencil and paper maps will be presented first, followed by a discussion of the factors involved in the paired electronic mapping. The fact that the children's individual paper based maps were in general of a higher standard than the paired computer based maps is significant in terms of the choice of the mapping tools for the final project. It also served as reminder that use of ICT does not necessarily guarantee improved standards.

The individual paper drawn maps were very useful in identifying the extent of prior mapping competence of the children. The small number of children in this pilot study showed a range of mapping styles from topological/fantasy drawing to a range of Euclidean or metric maps. Children had already developed conventions of representing roads, pavements, buildings and spaces, and using keys and locational grids. Any use of electronic media should be able to build on and potentially improve children's mapping. For this to happen, electronic drawing tools need to at least equal the strengths and limitations of pencil and paper sketch mapping. This point will be taken up in the discussion.

Two factors are worthy of discussion when considering the paired mapping episodes. These are the use of appropriate technology and the role of talk in peer scaffolding the map making process. Each factor will be discussed in turn. The design of the *Local Studies* software strongly influenced the maps produced by the pairs of children. The prominence and ease of use of the drag and drop pictorial symbols and the basic nature of the drawing tools in the Palette directly affected the quality of maps produced. Not all pairs used the application in the same way, but even Reuben who had most experience with drawing packages, was unable to quickly manipulate the drawing tools to produce effective map drawing. This was the first time that the children had used the software, so it is possible that amount of content and perhaps the quality of mapping would improve during future attempts. However the data from the interviews reveal that a more sophisticated drawing tool is needed, which allows the user to rotate objects, drag and reshape lines, points and polygons, and undo and redo drawing and writing actions easily and quickly. Without the use of an effective, interactive and intuitive mapping tool, any benefits gained from paired collaborative work may well be masked.

When reflecting on their own mapping, all children stated that paired mapping was their preferred approach to the mapping tasks. This partially reflects the findings of Bausmith and Leinhardt (1998) and Leinhardt et al (1998) yet the evidence from analysis of the paired maps showed that Helen's individual map was of higher quality than her joint map created with Annie, whereas the quality of Reuben's work was much improved when working on the computer with Josh. A key finding related to this discrepancy between attitude towards paired working and performance in paired working was the lack of Mercer's exploratory talk in analysis of the discourse.

These findings led to the creating of the first formal set of research questions proposed for the main study, shown in Figure 2.

Initial research questions for main research project:

1. What role does peer scaffolding play in the construction of collaborative maps?
2. Is the quality of children's talk whilst mapping related to quality of the maps they make?
3. What interventions could teachers make to scaffold the map making process?

Figure 2: Initial research questions for the main project

Discussion

The results from the exploratory study generated appropriate initial research questions and prompted a review of the research tools. This section explains the how the research tools were changed as a result of the exploratory study, and how a new pilot study was designed to answer new research questions. The results of the exploratory study were written up as a formal research report and presented at appropriate conferences and seminars. Much useful formal and informal feedback was obtained from peers in the primary geography and cartography communities. Presenting work in progress is always potentially a daunting process, but it gives the researcher the opportunity to verbalise their thinking and discuss problems in a supportive environment. After writing up and presenting this exploratory work, the focus of proposal development shifted to library based study. Two formal literature reviews were written to develop a more detailed understanding of both collaborative learning and the analysis of classroom discourse. The results of these reviews then fed into discussions with my supervisor, and plans for a more formal pilot study working with eighteen Y3 and Y5 children were then drawn up.

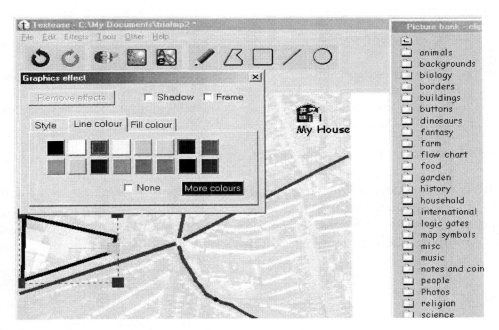

Figure 3: The *Textease* drawing application.

The task given to children (planning a route for a pair of new pupils to places of interest in the local area) was retained but some changes were made. Children in the exploratory study who created a map without the aid of an aerial photograph spent much time discussing the location of features rather than symbolisation issues. In the subsequent pilot study children drew their computer based map over a 'transparent' aerial photograph image which formed the background to the mapping screen.

The mapping tool used in the first study was not seen as an effective tool by the children involved. The use of a popular drawing tool in a KS2 software suite (see *Textease* software illustrated in Figure 3) was adopted as it provided the facilities that the children had requested. *Textease* allows for the creation of a clipart bank of symbols which gives the children more flexibility in the way they symbolise places on their trail. The clipart bank was augmented by creating a range of symbols that represented the key landmarks around the school. For example, children had the opportunity to symbolise the sweet shop opposite the school using a variety of symbols such as small digital image of the shop, a pictorial symbol (a cartoon drawing of a shop), a more abstract symbol (a sweet), and a text symbol (the letter S). The choice of a range of symbols provoked much discussion between the pairs of children and was used in the formal pilot study to reveal the children's symbolisation strategies.

The video recordings of the exploratory study were transcribed by hand and the transcriptions analysed separately from the moving images of the mapping episodes in the first data collection episode. This was changed in the second formal pilot to use video transcription and qualitative analysis software (see Woods, 2001). This software allows the user to build up a library of video and audio data which can be sorted to show the processes involved in the different types of symbol creation and pupil talk. The pilot study gave rise to a second, more focused set of research questions which are shown in Figure 4.

Final questions for main research project.

How do children symbolise selected point, area and line features when mapping on paper and the computer?
1. What explanations do they give as to how they have represented the features of the locality using each technology?
2. Do they intuitively use cartographic design principles to symbolise environmental features?
3. Do they draw upon a shared social notion of how symbols should be drawn?
4. Is there evidence of a developmental progression in symbolisation strategies between years 3 and 5?

Figure 4: Final questions for the main research project

This set of research questions focuses specifically on the children's symbolisation strategies when engaged in environmental mapping. The explicit focus on the children's collaboration has been dropped in response to feedback from colleagues who advised a single research focus, as well as the depth and quality of children's discussion of symbolisation during the pilot project.

Conclusion

The flow chart below (see Figure 5) illustrates the progress to date of research proposal development. The empirical work in school has been essential in moving from a broad interest in curriculum development to a series of more focused research questions which will be answered in the main research project. The exploratory study focused on in this paper has revealed much in terms of the children's mapping strategies using paper and computer based technologies.

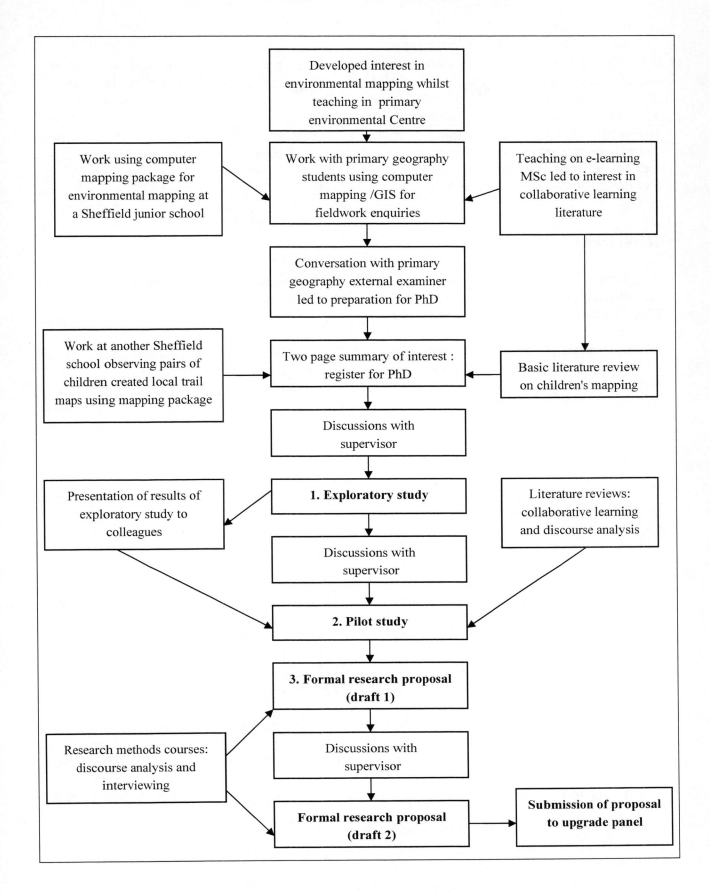

Figure 5: Flow chart to show development of the research proposal

The children's competence in paper and pencil mapping provided useful data on their prior experience of mapping and their conceptions of how a mapping task should be undertaken. The children's maps produced in paired electronic mapping provided guidance on the selection of appropriate electronic tools for plotting the spatial arrangements of the space around the school. Children's views on their maps and mapmaking processes gave insight into their attitudes towards collaborative work, electronic map making and their use of computers in their school and home lives. Indeed, one of the challenges for future work may be keeping up with the technological sophistication of the children involved.

References

Bausmith, J.L., and Leinhardt, G. (1998), Middle-School Students' Map Construction: Understanding Complex Spatial Displays, *Journal of Geography*, 97, 93-107

BECTa (2002,) *Introduction to GIS*,: http://vtc.ngfl.gov.uk/docserver.php?docid=4011. accessed 10 Feb 03

Blaut, J., Stea, D., Spencer, C., and Blades, M. (2003), Mapping as a Cultural and Cognitive Universal. *Annals of the Association of American Geographers*, 93 (1), 165-185

Bruner, J.S. (1966), *Towards a Theory of Instruction*, New York: Belnapp Press.

Catling, S. (1979), Maps and cognitive maps: the young child's perception, *Geography*, 64(4), 288-296

Catling, S. (1996), Technical Interest in Curriculum Development: A Programme of Map Skills, in Williams, M. (Ed), *Understanding Geographical and Environmental Education,* London: Cassell, 93-111

Cohen, L., Manion, L. and Morrison, K. (2000), *Research Methods in Education* (5th Edition), London: RoutledgeFalmer

ESRI (2003), *A road map for schools and libraries,*:http://www.esri.com/industries/k-12/roadmap.html.   accessed 10 Feb 03

Hart, R.A. and Moore, G.T. (1973), The development of spatial cognition: a review. In R.M. Downs and D.Stea (Eds.). *Image and Environment,* Chicago: Aldine, 246-288

Harwood, D & Usher, M. (1999), Assessing progression in primary children's map drawing skills, *International Research in Geographical & Environmental Education.* 8 (3), 222-238

Leinhardt, G., Stainton, C., & Bausmith, J.M. (1998), Constructing Maps Collaboratively, *Journal of Geography*, 97, 19-30

Liben, L.S., Kastens, K. A., & Stevenson, L. M. (2002). Real-world knowledge through real-world maps: A developmental guide for navigating the educational terrain. *Developmental Review*, 22, 267-322

Matthews, M. H. (1992), *Making Sense of Place: Children's understanding of large scale environments* Hemel Hempstead: Harvester Wheatsheaf.

Mercer, N. (1995), *The guided construction of knowledge: talk amongst teachers and learners*, Clevedon: Multilingual Matters

Ordnance Survey (2002), *The GIS Files* : http://www.ordsvy.gov.uk/gis-files/. accessed 10 Feb 03

Owen, D. (1997), That's me on the screen. *Primary Geographer* 30, 26-27

Owen, D. (2000), Using Geographic Information Systems (GIS) to develop enquiry based learning. *International Conference on GIS in Education*, California State University , San Barnardino.: http://www.shu.ac.uk/schools/ed/teaching/dho/ .accessed April 2004

Piaget, J., & Inhelder, B. (1956), *The Child's Conception of Space*. Translated by F.J. Langdon and J.L. Lunzer . London: Routledge and Kegan Paul

Piaget, J., Inhelder, B., Szeminska, A. (1960), *The Child's Conception of Geometry*. Translated by E.A. Lunzer, London: Routledge and Kegan Paul

Pilkington, R.M. (1999), *Analyzing Educational Discourse: The DISCOUNT Scheme*. Version 3, January 1999. CBL Technical Report No. 99/2 Leeds: University of Leeds Computer Based Learning Unit

Punch, K. F. (2000), *Developing Effective Research Proposals*, London: Sage

Scoffham, S. (1998), *Primary Sources: Research findings in primary geography*, Sheffield: Geographical Association

Sowden, S., Stea, D., Blades, M., Spencer, C. and Blaut, J.M. (1996) Mapping abilities of 4 year old children in York, England. *Journal of Geography*, May/June, 107-111

Tolman. E.C. (1948), Cognitive maps in rats and men, *Psychological Review*, 55, 189-208.

Vygotsky, L.S. (1962), *Thought and Language*, Cambridge, MA: MIT Press

Wegerif, R. (2001), Applying a Dialogical Model of Reason in the Classroom, in Joiner, R., Faulkner, D., and Littleton, K. (Eds.) *Rethinking Collaborative Learning*, Free Association Press, 119-139

Wiegand, P. (2002), Analysis of Discourse in Collaborative Cartographic Problem Solving, *International Research in Geographical and Environmental Education*, 11, 2, 139-159

Woods, D.K. (2001) *Transana Tutorial*. Downloaded from http://www.transana.org/. accessed November 2003

Acknowledgements
Many thanks to Descalie Baldwin, Shirley Harrison and the children who took part in the pilot. Pseudonyms have been used throughout the report. I am indebted to geography education colleagues and Patrick Wiegand, my supervisor, for feedback on the development of this project.

Chapter 10

Geography, Learning and the Brain: An example of literature-based research

Stephen Scoffham

'Our present-day knowledge of the child's mind is comparable to a fifteenth century map of the world – a mixture of truth and error...vast areas remain to be explored.'

Arnold L Gesell (cited in Fisher, 1990, 1)

Introduction

From the nineteenth century onwards scientists have been aware that specific parts of the brain control particular physical and mental activities. Although the early phrenologists (as those who proposed this view were called) were unable to locate the control centres with any accuracy, more recent studies have confirmed the value of this approach. Case studies of accident victims and patients with selective brain damage have shown how our sense of taste, smell and other cerebral functions can be traced to precise locations. Furthermore, new techniques like Positron Emission Topography (which measures the fuel intake of different areas of the brain using a radioactive marker in the blood) can show the areas which 'light up' when we do particular tasks. This has revolutionised our knowledge of how we think the brain works.

Brain-based research has potential implications for primary geography. As yet these are unexplored, and the purpose of this chapter is to set out some of the possibilities that might emerge from a review of the area. This is a literature-based survey that draws on a range of work in brain studies to set the scene and indicate the range and state of development in relevant brain research. It is selective and limited in scope, as an introduction to this developing area. The first part of this chapter focuses on providing a background understanding about the brain and its multifaceted role in our thinking, not on particular and detailed aspects of brain-based research in recent years, such as on the hippocampus and spatial cognition and skill (O'Keefe & Nadel, 1978; Millar, 1994). This provides a basis for illustrating some of the connections to teaching primary geography, which forms the latter part of this chapter. As such, this chapter is interpretative of research and speculative in making an argument relating this vitally important area of research to geography in primary education.

Some evidence from brain-based studies

How the brain works

The brain is divided into two linked hemispheres. Some activities, such as language processing, tend to be located in the left hemisphere, while the right often deals with music and spatial awareness. Whether this specialisation is biologically determined or whether it is influenced by social and cultural forces is not entirely clear. Whatever we are doing, however, both sides of the brain are nearly always involved in some way, and information flows back and forth in a continual dialogue. In addition, it also appears that there are different layers or areas of the brain relating to different periods in our evolutionary past. McLean (cited in Jensen, 1995) has proposed a threefold structure to explain this:

- The *reptilian brain* is the oldest part of the brain and is responsible for survival, motor functions, mating rituals, social hierarchies and role behaviour.
- The *mid-brain* or limbic system controls our emotions. It regulates our eating and sleeping cycles, sexuality and immune system and is the site of long-term memory.
- The *upper brain* or neo-cortex is the 'thinking' part of the brain. It is divided into four key areas dealing with problems and planning, sensory information, vision and hearing and language. The neo-cortex is much larger than the other areas and occupies about five sixths of the space in the cerebrum.

McLean believes that each part of the brain has a different agenda and behaves in its own way. It is the interplay between the three parts that accounts for some of the contradictions and complexities of human behaviour. Ultimately, though, the need for survival dominates, and when our lives are threatened the reptilian brain takes charge and we react instinctively.

Recent thinking has modified and extended McLean's theory. It seems that the limbic system plays a bigger part in processing information than was previously supposed and that we attribute value to data at the same time as we interpret it. The hierarchical structure has also been challenged and replaced by a more sophisticated notion of modules (Slywester1995). Nevertheless, McLean's ideas continue to be useful; not least because they provide a comprehensible model of what is in fact an enormously complicated and subtle structure.

Although the brain is only about a litre in volume, it contains 100,000 million active cells. The cells which create brain activity are called neurons and consist of a nucleus with a single shoot at one end (axon) and lots of root-like fibres at the other (dendrites), a little bit like a sprouting onion. The point of contact between cells is called a synapse. When a cell fires it sends an electro-chemical pulse up the shoot and excites the roots of another cell. Whether the cell actually fires or not depends on the balance of messages it receives. Some pulses are trying to urge it into action while others are trying to silence or inhibit it.

Learning and cognition appear to consist in establishing patterns between brain cells. Modern scientists believe that the cortex is organised into several hundred million neural networks or modules. These extend vertically through the cortex in small columns, which are then linked up into more complex structures. Once cells have fired together a few times a chemical change occurs which makes them more likely to trigger each other in future. This is called 'Hebbian learning' after the Canadian psychologist Donald Hebb.

Brain-compatible teaching

If this account of the brain is correct, it follows that experience has a vital part to play in promoting our development. The things that we see or do are sculpted into the pattern of connections between the neurons inside our heads. Rich experiences can promote brain growth while sensory deprivation can inhibit it. Furthermore, because the brain is actually physically changed by the circumstances in which it operates, we can mould it to our needs. Robertson, a psychologist, explains:

.... it is the gift of natural selection, and the secret of our enormous success as a species, that we can programme and reprogramme the very apparatus that controls our behaviour. (Robertson, 1999, 138)

However, what is important as far as learning is concerned is not simply the quantity of crude stimulation. Feedback is also vital. By confirming the child's first tentative attempts to make sense of their experience, parents and teachers can reinforce the first weak connections in a new neural network. An unresponsive adult leaves the child uncertain and the newly formed links are not confirmed and may even be undermined. The notion of collaborative learning (Geekie et al., 1999), in which teachers and pupils co-operate to construct new knowledge, thus appears to be supported by research evidence. The value of fieldwork and first hand investigations also becomes apparent.

The role of experience in developing our knowledge and understanding is an issue that has been discussed by philosophers for centuries. The doctrine that human beings are born with innate ideas was strongly contested from the seventeenth century onwards by Locke and other empiricist thinkers. One of the notions for which Locke is famous is the idea that the human mind is like a 'tabula rasa' or blank sheet. He put it this way:

> Let us then suppose the mind to be, as we say, white paper, void of all characters, without any ideas; how comes it be furnished?.... To this I answer, in one word, from *experience*. In that all our knowledge is founded and from that it ultimately derives itself. (Locke, 1689 [1971], 89)

Discussing this same question three centuries later from the standpoint of a cognitive scientist, Hart (1983, 82) declares 'as a general rule, the more brainpower an animal has, the more it learns after birth'. As we know from comparative studies, one of the defining characteristics of human beings is that we are creatures with very large brains.

The role of emotions

Our growing knowledge about the structure of the brain has led to another highly significant conclusion. Learning does not simply occur in the neo-cortex, it also requires an input from our emotional or limbic system. Some of the evidence for this comes from neurological studies. For example, LeDoux (cited in Goleman, 1996) has demonstrated clinically how rats can learn emotional reactions without any cortical involvement. Furthermore, as Sylwester (1995) points out, there are many more neural fibres leading outwards from the limbic emotional centre of the brain into the cortex than there are going in the reverse direction. This suggests that, although the limbic system is relatively small, it has a powerful influence on the rational part of our brain. When we behave illogically it is often because we are making decisions on an emotional basis. Why else, for instance, do so many people purchase lottery tickets when they know they have a negligible chance of winning?

Even the recognition of simple sensory stimuli involves an emotional dimension. When we perceive an object for the first time it seems that the incoming stimulus, rather than going to a single destination, is split into several different streams. These are then processed in parallel in different parts of the cortex and limbic system assembled in an association area. Thus, when we recognise a knife we perceive not only its shape, colour, size and the material from which it is made; we also associate it with a range of concepts such as stabbing, eating and slicing. In this way our perception is the result of a combination of images. It follows that we construct different versions of reality from the same external stimulus depending on a range of factors such as our previous experience and natural disposition.

Theories such as these have led researchers to conclude that the limbic system plays a very important role in the operation of the mind. Indeed, as Jensen (1995, 27) observes, our mid-brain area may well be the 'glue' that holds the different parts of the brain together. Certainly, when the link with our emotional system is severed, the effect is devastating. Carter (1999) for example, describes the unfortunate case of a patient who lost part of his limbic system in an operation to remove a growth. Although his capacities were otherwise unaffected, the patient was no longer able to live a normal life. Carter reports:

> He found it hard to make the simplest decision or to pursue any single plan to a fruitful conclusion......Once at work he might fritter away a whole day either trying to decide what to do first or attending diligently to some unimportant detail while urgent tasks went unheeded. (Carter, 1999, 81)

It seems that emotions are crucial because they focus our attention, which in turn drives our learning and memory systems. The strong implication is that teachers need to get their pupils to engage emotionally as well as cognitively in learning activities. Damasio (cited in Jensen, 1995) goes further than this. He argues that the brain, mind, body and emotions form a linked system. Certain aspects of emotion and feeling are indispensable for rationality. Emotions he says, are not separate, but rather enmeshed in the neural networks of reason.

One aspect of emotional learning which is particularly important for teachers concerns attitudes and prejudices. Robertson (1999, 174) talks about how some emotional events are particularly potent since they can create links in the brain which are more or less indelible. Traumatic events are, as he puts it, woven into our minds with stitches of 'steel thread'. Just as phobias can be contagious, so hate can be passed from person to person, infecting whole groups.

Carter (1999) is rather more hopeful pointing out that the cortex can control the emotions emanating from the limbic system. However, the connections take time to grow. It is the relative weakness of cortical signals which causes children to have far more emotional outbursts than adults. 'The young brain,' she declares, 'is essentially unbalanced – the immature cortex no match for the powerful amydala' (Carter, 1999, 90).

It seems then that Descartes, and other rationalist philosophers whose thinking ultimately provides the philosophical underpinning for the National Curriculum (Naish 1996), may well have been mistaken when they argued that the mind could be separated from the body. The two are, it would seem, inextricably linked. Furthermore, there is good reason to suppose the brain is poorly designed for academic models of learning that focus chiefly on the intellect. What appears to be needed is a more holistic approach that involves the mind, heart and body. Hart sums up the matter when he declares that the way that:

> ...curriculum builders and teachers try to devise logical methods of instruction, assuming logical planning, ordering and presentation of the content matter or skills, is the plainly correct and only respectable approach to take.... It can be stated flatly, however, that the human brain is not organised for linear, one-path thought. (Hart, 1983, 52)

Hart (1983, 56) concludes with some scathing criticism of the 'undeserved respect' educators have given to Greek-type sequential logic which he believes in practice 'guarantees severe learning failure' for most young students. Robinson (2001) too expresses similar concerns and argues that the school system conflates academic ability with intelligence. Education, he contends, needs to take account of the creative abilities of all people. Apart from anything else, this will be vital to our success as a nation in the knowledge-based economies of the future.

There are other reasons to be optimistic. Those who believe intelligence is located in the cerebral cortex have often argued that it is genetically determined and cannot be changed by life experiences. If, however, we admit there is a significant emotional component, then there may be other opportunities for enhancing performance. Goleman (1995) highlights a number of abilities which he believes are significant qualities in those who excel. Encouragingly, they can all be taught to children.

Changes with age

Research into neuro-biology is also beginning to shed light on how the brain changes with age. One key finding is that children have many more synapses than adults do. These are gradually pruned back through learning and experience as we grow older. Another discovery, is that during the first twenty years of life nerve pathways acquire a kind of insulation called myelin which helps keeps pulses confined and allows them move much faster. These two processes may go some of the way towards accounting for the plasticity which researchers note in the brains of children and young adults.

Until recently it was believed that the number of neurons in the brain decreased from birth onwards. However, the latest research suggests that there may also be an unsuspected period of neural growth in early adolescence. This could provide a 'critical window' for learning which needs to be used when it is available before the opportunity is lost (Giedd, 1999). The development of the pre-frontal lobes is another factor that accounts for the differences between age groups. Research by the Soviet scientist, Luria (1975) indicated that the pre-frontal lobes only fully mature in the late teenage years. It is this area of the brain which is responsible for our concept of future time and ability to concentrate.

It is instructive to relate these findings to established learning theory. Thus, when Piaget suggested that children only become capable of formal or abstract thought in adolescence he may well have been responding to what we now know are physiological changes in the structure of the mind. As Hart (1983, 115) remarks, 'it is easy here to see a probable relation to Piaget's stages or periods, and again to realise that individual variations have great practical significance'.

Indeed many key theorists such as Vygotsky, Bruner and Gardner appear to have illuminated our understanding in a way that is entirely consistent with our new neurological knowledge. If educational theory can be matched to empirical findings the implications could be very considerable, especially as it is now established that the first ten years of childhood are 'highly significant in the development of the brain's capacity to learn.' (Gipps and MacGilchrist, 1999, 51)

Some implications for geography teaching

Any future geography curriculum will need to take account of recent research about the functioning of the brain by cognitive scientists. If we wish to accelerate learning then we will need to adopt strategies that reflect our increasing knowledge about the workings of the mind.

Some important conclusions appear already to be emerging. For example, it seems that we learn in highly individual ways and extract meaning from our environment in a rather random manner, rather as young children acquire language. What we learn is heavily influenced by previous experience and involves an emotional as well as an intellectual content. Our brains work particularly well in rich, multi-modal environments. We cope rather badly with sequential logic and the manipulation of symbols, and are much better adapted to activities that have a practical outcome. Some of the evidence from research to support this perspective is outlined in Figure 1.

	What we know about the brain	**Implications for geography teaching**
1	We learn in highly individual and often random ways and our understanding develops in fits and starts (Hart, 1985, 52).	Identify broad teaching objectives, rather than step-by-step stages.
2	Children learn at very different rates. For example, all five-year-olds should *not* be expected to perform at the same level (Jensen, 1995, 12).	Use whole class instruction judiciously and try to differentiate activities for different ages and abilities.
3	The optimal learning pattern for ten-year-olds consists of 10 minutes focused work followed by a short diffusion activity (Jensen, 1995, 48).	Do not devise lessons where children have to listen to the teacher for long periods without a break.
4	All new learning is heavily influenced by previous experience via stored biases in the neurons (Hart, 1983, 100).	We need to discover children's existing knowledge and abilities and tailor our teaching to this.
5	Children need to actively *engage* in what they are learning (Robertson, 1999, 44).	Provide children with practical activities and first hand experiences and encourage them to take charge of their learning.
6	The novelty, challenges and feedback of the real world help to promote brain growth (Hart, 1983, 102).	Use a variety of learning strategies, especially fieldwork and real world environments.
7	Questions generate sustained and enriching brain activity (Jensen, 1995, 168).	Use enquiry questions to draw children into a problem and makes them restate it.
8	The most effective learning often leads to practical outcomes (Hart, 1983, 124).	Focus on real-life problems and get pupils to make models and plans as well as written reports.
9	Learning needs to be associated with a purpose which the learner has set (Smith, 1996, 17).	Help children to identify questions and strong personal goals which they think are meaningful.
10	Repeating what we have learnt helps our limbic (emotional) system to *feel* it is true (Jensen, 1995, 131).	Give pupils plenty of opportunities to reinforce their learning by presenting it in different ways, eg by teaching a peer, by role-play, by writing a journal.
11	Try to make children aware of their thinking skills and strategies (Robertson, 1999, 159).	Transferring programs from one situation to another greatly speeds learning.
12	Intellectual learning and emotional involvement are linked together in the fabric of the brain (Carter, 1999, 81).	Provide pupils with material that is appropriate to their interests and which they can relate to personally.
13	A learner under stress is likely to resort to primitive responses and be resistant to innovation or new information (Hart, 1983, 110).	Try to create a supportive classroom environment and use techniques such as team building which develop self-esteem.
14	Male and female brains are structurally different (Jensen, 1995, 87).	We need to acknowledge the differences between the sexes, as well as providing equal opportunities for learning.
15	We learn with our minds, hearts and bodies (Jensen, 1995, 38).	We need to pay good attention to the social, emotional and physical well being of our pupils.

Figure 1: Applying new knowledge about the brain to geography teaching

While it may be tempting to produce a 'brain-compatible' curriculum based on the different stages in our evolutionary history, this approach is fraught with difficulties. Not only is the approach backward looking, it is also runs into the dangers of bio-determinism. How we use and apply our mental powers is heavily influenced by social and cultural factors, as Vygotsky (1962), Geekie (1999) and others have demonstrated. A knowledge of the mechanics of the mind says nothing about how our capacities should be applied. That is why it is so important to recognise that the curriculum is underpinned at a fundamental level by a set of common values and beliefs.

On the other hand, there are clear advantages in understanding the structure of the brain. We now know, for example, that there are neurological differences between the sexes. Females show a faster rate of language development and score better at some language tasks than males. By contrast males generally appear to perform better at spatial tasks (Jensen 1995, Baron-Cohen in Carter 1999). Whether these differences are culturally transmitted or biologically determined is still unresolved. What matters is that teachers are alerted to these differences. Similarly, while there are still great areas of uncertainty about the nature of learning, our increasing understanding of the operation of the mind should help us to devise modes of instruction which favour the acquisition of knowledge.

Geography educators have a long tradition of linking classroom learning with the outside world to make schooling more personal and meaningful. They have also pioneered methods of learning which encourage pupils to ask question, test hypothesises and transfer ideas from one situation to another. Practitioners know these techniques are effective (Geographical Association, 2002). The new discoveries from cognitive science about the workings of the mind are beginning to explain *why* they work. This can be illustrated in the following ways.

Mapwork
Mapwork develops spatial awareness, which is a key survival skill. In the wild, creatures have to be able find their way around their environment in order to locate food and safe places in times of danger. This propensity appears to have been built into human capabilities through evolution. It is developed uniquely through geography which the only subject that distinctively explores the notion of location. Practical mapwork activities in the classroom, school grounds and surrounding areas are established features of good practice in geography teaching.

Fieldwork
Fieldwork engages children with the real world on many different levels. This matches the way the brain appears to work best, since we are designed to process information from a variety of different modes – sight, sound, smell and so forth – simultaneously. Furthermore, fieldwork provides an essentially free setting in which pupils can respond in different ways according to their needs. Fieldwork is fundamental at all levels of geography.

Geographical enquiry
Enquiry questions draw pupils into a problem so that they relate new learning to their previous knowledge and understanding. Without this link, the patterns between brain cells are not properly established. Enquiry questions have long been advocated by geographers and are used extensively in the QCA geography schemes of work (DfES/QCA, 1998/2000).

Direct experience
First hand experience provides immediate feedback which is a key component in learning, as it allows children to check whether the connections they are making are valid. Over a period of time, first hand experience can gradually remould children's thinking. Practical activities are given a high profile in geography and serve to underpin many of the components of the

Geography National Curriculum. As a recent Ofsted subject report observed, some of the best work in geography 'involved pupils in practical activities linked to relevant and real issues.' (Ofsted, 2002, 3)

Role play and drama
Role-play and drama involve children emotionally. This is vital because we all need to engage in what we are learning, and we achieve much better results when fully engaged and motivated. Role plays also help pupils to see other viewpoints, thus extending their understanding. Leat (1998) uses strategies such as these in his innovative work on geography thinking skills.

Real-life problems
Thinking about real-life problems harnesses the brain's natural capacities, especially if they involve practical skills and abilities. The most effective learning is often associated with a tangible outcome or a goal that learners have set for themselves. Geography, being the study of the contemporary world, involves the study of current issues. Introducing problems and conflicts in a meaningful way to young children is one of the challenges which geographers have begun to take extremely seriously over the last few decades. However, as Catling (2003) argues, there is much more to be done.

Teamwork
Teamwork helps to develop intrapersonal and social skills. Geography, along with other subjects, provides contexts in which pupils can work to investigate an issue, communicate findings or solve a problem. The importance of collaborative learning and groupwork is also extolled in the current debate about creativity and thinking skills.

Communicating
Communicating findings helps to consolidate learning and make it meaningful. Indeed, one of the best ways of learning something is to explain it to another person. There are frequent opportunities for children to report their findings in geography lessons. Higgins (2002) is one of a number of researchers who argues that one of the best ways to enhance children's thinking is to encourage them to talk about their findings.

Graphical and visual presentations
Charts, diagrams and other visual presentation techniques serve to extend pupil's skills beyond the rather narrow confines of linguistic and logico-mathematical thought and to explore links and connections that might not otherwise be apparent. They are employed extensively by geographers who use the term to *graphicacy* to cover a wide spectrum of non-verbal communication techniques.

Generic concepts
Over-arching concepts such as change, pattern and process provide pupils with notions that help to structure their experience. Labelling and sorting are fundamental parts of learning. Introducing children to appropriate categories helps to organise their thoughts and raise their level of attainment. Identifying concepts is also important if we are to build progression into the geography curriculum in a meaningful way.

Conclusion

The current interest in creativity and thinking skills is pointing the way ahead. Leat, an enthusiast for cognitive acceleration, is clear that 'learning needs to be made more visible to pupils in classrooms' (Leat, 2000, 150). Interestingly, he argues strongly in favour of big concepts and skills, not only because they emphasise connections between subjects but also to promote better practice in assessment. Further research is needed into ways of raising levels of achievement. The ways in which findings from neuro-science can be applied to primary geography also needs to be explored much more fully. Both these areas appear to offer exciting possibilities for the future and provide good links with the current interests and concerns.

References

Carter, R. (1999), *Mapping the Mind*, London: Seven Dials

Catling, S. (2003), Curriculum Contested: Primary Geography and Social Justice, *Geography*, 88 (3), 164-210

DfES/QCA (1998/2000), *Geography A Scheme of Work for Key Stages 1 and 2*, London: QCA

Gardner, H. (1993), *The Unschooled Mind*, London: Fontana

Geekie, P. et al. (1999), *Understanding Literacy Development*, Stoke on Trent: Trentham

Geographical Association (2002), *Finding Time for Things That Matter: Geography in Primary Schools*, (leaflet), Sheffield: Geographical Association

Giedd, J. et al. (1999), Brain Development During Childhood and Adolescence: A Longitudinal MRI Study, *Nature*, 2 (10), 861-863

Gipps, C. and MacGilchrist, B. (1999), Primary School Learners, in Mortimore, P. (ed.) *Understanding Pedagogy and its Impact on Learning*, London: Paul Chapman

Goleman, D. (1996), *Emotional Intelligence*, London: Bloomsbury

Hart, L. (1983), *Human Brain and Human Learning*, New York: Longman

Higgins, S. (2002), Learning to Learn, *Primary Geographer*, 47

Jensen, E. (1995), *Brain-based Teaching and Learning*, Del Mar CA: Turning Point

Leat, D. (2000), The Importance of 'Big' Concepts and Skills in Learning Geography, in Fisher, C. and Binns, T. (eds.), *Issues in Geography Teaching*, London: RoutledgeFalmer

Locke, J. (1689) [1971], *An Essay Concerning Human Understanding*, London: Fontana

Luria, A. (1973), *The Working Brain*, New York: Basic Books

Millar, S. (1994), *Understanding and Representing Space*, Oxford: Oxford University Press

Naish, M. (1996), The Geography Curriculum: A Matyr to Epistomology?, in Gerber, R. and Lidstone, J. (eds.), *Developments and Directions in Geography Teaching*, Clevedon: Channel View

Ofsted (2002), *Geography in Primary Schools: Ofsted Subject Reports Series 2001/2*, London: Ofsted

O'Keefe, J. & Nadel, L. (1978), *The Hippocampus as a Cognitive map*, Oxford: Clarendon Press

Roberstson, I. (1999), *Mind Sculpture: Your Brain's Untapped Potential,* London: Bantam

Robinson, K. (2001) *Out of Our Minds* Oxford: Capstone

Slywester, R. (1995), *A Celebration of Neurons*, Alexandria VA: Association for Supervision and Curriculum Development

Vygotsky, L. (1988), *Thought and Language*, Cambridge, Mass: MIT Press

Chapter 11

Education for Sustainable Development and Citizenship through Outdoor Education: Gardening as a focus

Peter Bloomfield

Introduction

The geographical rationale for this research is embedded in the development of skills and the themes embracing the environment, citizenship and sustainable development, all integral to the national curriculum and Agenda 21. It focused on three primary schools in St Albans and was a partnership project between Hertfordshire County Council (HCC) Department of Environment (who funded the research) and the Department of Education at the University of Hertfordshire (UH). At a local level were the schools, and St Albans District Council (SADC).

The project had . These were to investigate:
- whether through sustainability and citizenship 'growing activities' at Key Stages 1 and 2, the school can engage and involve the local community;
- whether sustainability and citizenship can be integrated into the current national curriculum without detracting from targets already in place;
- whether through these activities it is possible to maintain continuity in school and the community, post-project;
- the effect gardening has on children's motivation, values and attributes, self-esteem and general behaviour.

An additional aim was to engage final year teacher education students, following a B.Ed. degree at the University of Hertfordshire and taking a course in Education for Sustainable Development [ESD], in the planning and delivery of ESD through the gardening activities in the core curriculum in the three schools.

The project has been ongoing for over 3 years, has outlived its funding and is now in the post project stage identified above. It has been an eventful period and the research has not been straightforward.

Literature Review

Since the conception of this research, the rationale outlined in the introduction has come to appear rather dated. Initially, the rationale provided a clear foundation for the study, but thinking about ESD has moved on substantially in the past four years. The underpinning of ESD and citizenship in school has, or arguably should, move outwards from geography toward whole school thinking and policy, with geography an excellent vehicle for underpinning some of the finer detail. Thinking generally needs to be more holistic and embrace the statement in the national curriculum as to its 'values, aims and purposes':

Education is also a route to equality of opportunity for all, a healthy and just democracy, a productive economy and sustainable development (DfEE/QCA, 1999, 10).

Indeed, the argument for and role of ESD is set out in a full paragraph in the same document (DfES/QCA, 1999, 23). There is a clear mandate for its inclusion in the wider curriculum of the school.

But why gardening? Gardening is a practical, outdoor activity, which can provide creativity in any subject (Bloomfield, 2003a). It can also begin to provide children with alternative understandings of where food comes from at a time when, for them, most food seems to come directly from the supermarket. This 'reality' seems totally unsustainable. Gardening, as an approach, can engage children in the sustainability discussion.

Accepting that there is a need to develop, understand and teach ESD, Fein (2003) argues that ESD is not an extension of environmental education or an integration of development and environmental education, as others have stressed. He sees the debate moving into a second stage where ESD is

> a catalytic process for social change that seeks to foster- through education, training and public awareness – the values, behaviour and lifestyles required for a sustainable future (Fein, 2003, 3)

In attempting to make sense of this for the primary school teacher, it is useful to consider the components of ESD. The seven key concepts, presented by Sterling (2001) and outlined by QCA are:
- interdependence
- citizenship & stewardship
- needs and rights of future generations
- diversity; quality of life
- equity and justice
- sustainable change
- uncertainty and precaution in action.

These key concepts can underpin all the schools teaching, but it is useful to integrate them with 'the three pillars of sustainable development', *society, environment and economy*, as outlined by Harrison (2002) an advocate of an holistic approach to the future. The holistic model is a dominant theme taken by Sterling (2001, 11), where he argues for a transformation of all education. One strand to attain this, he says, is

> Realization of a sustainable education paradigm requires vision, image, design and action – at all levels – from all concerned with achieving healthy societies and ecologically sustainable lifestyles.

He draws attention to the way in which education is preoccupied by assessment and asks: what is being assessed and how it is being assessed? Sterling is, in effect, posing the questions about what we do not assess, and argues that naming and shaming does nothing to develop reflective, critical thinkers, or responsible citizens. Teachers and children who engage in practical (gardening) activities can engage with the curriculum, in many subjects, reduce the stress from assessment and inspections and integrate good practice across the school, as did the schools in the research project. He continues by presenting five key success factors for sustaining change in schools by citing Symons:

- raising staff awareness of sustainability issues
- taking a whole school approach
- involving pupils in the decision-making processes
- increasing involvement with the broader community, and
- taking one step at a time (Sterling, 2001, 68).

These factors figure either in the aims of this research or in the process developed during the project. If the first point is deemed most important, and it may well be, perhaps not enough attention was paid to it throughout this project. Huckle (2003, 34), in an unpublished paper for the Teacher Training Agency, mentions this point when he writes, 'Beyond a 'converted minority' there is limited awareness of ESD amongst teachers'. He continues, 'but what good practice exists is more likely to be found in primary rather than secondary schools' (34). Huckle also expresses concern at the 'significant mismatch between ESD as an aim of the national curriculum and ESD as delivered in teacher education and school classrooms' (33).

Built into the project was an expectation that children would become motivators of local and global citizenship (Clough and Holden, 2002; Young, 2002). They have a vested interest, as Hicks (2001, 2) states:

> As children well know, their future adult life will greatly be affected by what is happening in the world today. It is important, therefore, for teachers and pupils to develop some sense of the current state of the world (where we are now) and also the future (where we want to be).

Given the links with environmental education, it is important to recognise why there is a need for ESD and to build on that foundation. Palmer et al (1996), in the extensive work on *emergent environmentalism,* and specifically on *environmental cognition* in young children, found

> that as children mature between the ages of four and seven, they are able to take a longer term view of issues and consequences and to make meaningful links between cause and effects problems. ... the research sample shows children to be active thinkers in the realm of environmental issues. (Palmer et al., 1996, 328)

ESD has moved through the political and academic agenda with great speed since the inception of this project. Many of the authors and researchers quoted here have contributed to current thinking and will, no doubt, have differing views on recent developments. In late 2003, Ofsted published *Taking the first step forward ... towards an education for sustainable development: Good practice in primary and secondary schools* (Ofsted, 2003). In the same month the DfES published its 'Sustainable Development Action Plan for Education and Skills' (DfES, 2003). These two documents could be taken to be a turning point in ESD and education as a whole if they are 'followed through'. However, this presumes a radical change in thinking and, as Sterling (2001, 77) comments, 'education for change is by definition a long-term process', which also presumes that all the parties involved want the same changes. He suggests change begins at a micro level, where 'the exchange you next have with a child or adult might be transformative immediately', as in his experiences of working with teachers on in-service courses. This perspective underpinned the model used in this research.

Research pathway and methods

From the outset a delicate balance existed between the 'real work' of the schools and the ESD/gardening research. The head teachers of the schools were committed to the project and were very supportive. They saw an opportunity to develop a vision of their school, backed by good pedagogic practice. At the outset they suggested that to monitor motivation and achievement, the Hertfordshire PSHE framework, which was already in existence, be used. This provided them with a known method of data collection.

The researcher played a multi-functional role in that the research and development project was framed as action research in the sense that the data was gathered at various points to develop the next stage, inform thinking about progress and move forward accordingly. The structure of the research was written into the funded agreement:
- UH convene meetings of lead teachers in schools to discuss methods and set targets.
- Schools to put procedures in place to meet targets.
- UH and HCC meet with schools to monitor progress.
- UH, HCC and school lead teachers to meet, share and process data and to assess whether targets have been met, problems and way forward.
- UH and HCC write report.

The methods of monitoring the research were agreed by the schools and set out in the project bid:
- teachers and researchers keeping diaries of events, feedback from children, parents and other participants;
- teachers keeping evidence of children's work (gardening, ESD & Citizenship);
- monitoring local press coverage;
- keeping records of numbers and categories of participants involved;
- keeping records to sessions taught, clubs attended, events, etc.

As 'research facilitator', the researcher's role included convening and facilitating meetings between the partners, setting targets for the schools, acting as go-between with the local council and HCC and contractors, schools and students and at times getting involved in the gardening with the children and teachers. It also involved setting up staff development visits, which were project funded. The meetings were rotated between the schools so that the participants could share ideas and support each other. This was all perceived as data collection.

In the final stages of the project interviews were held with children, teachers, parents, students and others who were involved. This proved to be a rich source of information and data. Children were given the option of completing a storyboard to illustrate how their learning had progressed or to enter into a dialogue with the researcher about the project. The children were quite articulate and relaxed about providing data. This was supported by some of their parents who also volunteered to be interviewed. They saw the process of recording their feelings as an important way of being involved and considered. Where possible, teachers were also interviewed, but less formally. A caretaker, who had taken a major role in the project, was also interviewed.

The researcher taught a lead-in session at one of the schools, attended the 'Growing Schools' conferences, and the teacher development visits to Spitalfields City Farm (Coriander Garden), London and Coombes School, Reading. The research has been summarised as 'work in progress' in several publications (Bloomfield, 2000, 2001, 2002, 2003a, 2003b, 2003c). The World Education Fellowship conference, in 2001, (a WEF event) established links between St Albans schools and township schools in South Africa who had gardening projects and the WEF conference, Mumbai 2004, allowed discussion of the transfer of intergenerational skills from this project.

Two themes emerged from the research, the data from the participants and the rewards and challenges of the research. These are the twin foci of the rest of this chapter.

Research findings

The research findings are presented as two distinct data sets, that from the perspective of the main school partners and that from the interviewed children and adults. Full data is appended to the HCC Report (Bloomfield, 2003c).

Rewards and challenges

Most of these data were abstracted from diaries and anecdotal evidence supplied by the schools, from evidence of children's work, and from links with the local and global community. The following emerged.

School 1
- Children have an overwhelming interest in the project. It had to accommodate twice as many as expected
- Less able children have realised that they too can make a vital contribution – something special. Some very co-operative work has been led by a child who is not especially liked.
- The school was awarded Beacon Status for 'Education for Sustainability' and 'Citizenship' and 'the outdoor classroom'.
- A teacher has been designated to oversee the above, including 'the plot'.

School 2
- Enthusiasm of Foundation Stage staff and children beginning to permeate to other teachers; 50% now enthusiastic.
- A group of parents and the Family Learning teacher showing interest despite not having a garden.
- Y4 particularly enjoyed their 'habitats' work with the UH students.
- Willow arbour extended to 'willow village'.
- Allotment plot prepared by St Albans District Council.
- Plans for school grounds, especially the allotment, drawn up by final year students at local F.E. College.
- Very strong, ongoing, links made with school in South Africa.

School 3
- Opportunity to visit other schools e.g. Coombes School.
- Group meetings, which give a focus and a target to the project.
- Having new equipment (e.g. digital camera).
- Having the allotment rotovated and laid out by SADC.
- A parent and the Caretaker very involved.

- Strawberries from allotment sold to pupils via the breakfast club.
- Teachers used the allotment during 'School Grounds Week'.
- School fully accepted by the 'allotment community', including 'Camphill Trust' who also have an allotment.
- Links established with South African school garden project.
- Teachers expressed interest in continuing allotment after retirement of Head Teacher.

All schools identified that the university students integrated gardens into the school plans for core subjects and shared these with the teachers. Written evidence was given regarding increased motivation and achievement especially with regard to the less able children, for example in School 1. In school 3 one child was so motivated by the allotment that his work in English (writing about the gardening) improved dramatically. A girl in year 5 was overheard saying that she could not miss school, to attend hospital, because *"they're doing an ICT project about designing a shed for the allotment"*! Schools naturally saw the acquisition of new equipment (digital camera, tools, sheds, etc) as a positive outcome. The cameras were used in part to record progress of the project. All felt the meetings and the targets useful in progressing the work.

The schools also identified ways forward. All three saw the need to get more adults involved in maintenance of the plots and more teachers using them. They also wanted to get more children involved, but did not identify how this might be achieved. This raises the issue of whole school, or even class, curriculum involvement in the garden project.

The interviews

The following is a synopsis of the interview data.

Children
- Great fun, exciting way to learn, not really school;
- Acknowledged integration with the curriculum, mainly science;
- Recognised inter-generational links with parents and grandparents;
- Strong links between school and home gardens;
- Good to work together;
- Sense of achievement in growing and eating own produce.

Teachers (one school)
- 'Highly motivating for children.'
- 'We should not have to justify it in the curriculum, but we could.'
- 'It gives the children a sense of responsibility (citizenship).'
- 'It should be timetabled to allow each class gardening time each week.'
- 'It needs to be in the plans; teachers need to know when to include it in the curriculum.'

Parents
- Gardening should be developed with all classes; other children *want* to be involved.
- 'I'm sure that *if asked* lots of parents would help, and grandparents; there are a lot of them and they have lots of time!' 'Feeling you're helping, like a community thing'.
- 'He's very proud and tells us everything, far more than other school stuff. It helps his communication with other children'.
- It gives responsibility to the children for growing food.

- It's practical; helps children develop enthusiasm toward school.
- 'For the future we'd like the children to develop a holistic view of the world; develop life skills, environmental skills; it's the world isn't it?'

Students from University of Hertfordshire
- 'Teaching in the environment showed me just how much it inspired children and motivated them.'
- The ICT, English and Maths activities facilitated an 'awe and wonder of the world and local environment'.
- Benefits include real, concrete experiences to enhance learning and enjoyment. ESD and Citizenship need to be planned into all subject areas.
- The activity helped me plan and make cross-curricular links throughout the six areas of development in the Foundation Stage.

Caretaker
- Children see a different side of adults and get some benefits, the strawberries, for example.
- It develops better relationships in the whole school. There's a definite 'spin off' in school.
- It has developed positive relationships with other allotment holders.
- Children queue up for jobs, eg watering, at dinnertime. It's often 'scallywags' who come for jobs! Children become part of the school, develops a sense of belonging.
- Gardening is an adventure to the children.

In summary, these children found gardening fun, rewarding and part of the curriculum. The teachers saw it as motivating, and stated that it should be planned into curriculum and timetabled. The parents want their children to be involved, want to be involved themselves, and see it as developing important life skills. The students identified gardening as an excellent vehicle for motivation in core subjects and geography, as well as for fostering 'awe and wonder' from Foundation Stage to Year 6. The caretaker identified a strong citizenship and school ethos as outcomes.

Discussion

Rewards and challenges

The head teachers of the schools attended meetings, which were important arenas for sharing ideas and for detailed discussion. Indeed, these were often the only times when such involvement took place. The integration of the garden project into the curriculum, by the students in the summer term, was praised by the teachers as a positive step forward, and upheld the head teacher's wishes for planning ESD into the curriculum. When teachers used one of the gardens (during School Grounds Week), both they and the children thoroughly enjoyed the experience. These are all outcomes that should be celebrated and encouraged.

All was not rosy though. It was unfortunate that the council sub-contractors failed to meet their targets for site preparation, since this de-motivated the staff and parents in one school, such that the project was deviated from the original direction. Equally unfortunate was the lack of take-up when it was suggested that each school had an excellent case to submit to the Best Practice

Research Awards, with the majority of the work already completed and a university link in place. However, these examples may serve more to illustrate 'researcher frustration', than negative outcomes!

Realising that there was a willingness to tackle targets as set and negotiated with the researcher, further targets were set out in an interim report, ready for September 2002. These targets strove to delegate much of the responsibility for the project to the children by way of the school council:

- contacting the local community and press to celebrate their successes;
- contacting other local and South African schools to share and compare their work;
- using the school newsletter to get more parents involved and generally sharing responsibility for the projects.

The thinking was that the children should take greater ownership and responsibility for the project. New targets were negotiated in October 2002 between HCC and the head teachers, which resulted in visual and written action plans for future development.

The interviews

Data from the interviews was very positive, as is indicated above. The children and the parents interviewed were highly motivated and enthusiastic. The limitation is that only the children who had participated (and their parents) were interviewed and, therefore, it is not known what other pupils thought about what they saw happening. That aside, the teachers and student teachers were equally enthusiastic, and they were the ones who would implement visionary and future plans. They agreed that they could justify planning ESD, environment and citizenship, from geography, into and across the curriculum via gardening. Yet, the teachers did question whether they should have to justify this; surely, they said, we should just be able to do it because we believe in it as a good pedagogic activity. The caretaker and parents also identified many other 'whole school' advantages.

In this context the key concepts of ESD, (e.g. citizenship, interdependence, rights and responsibilities) were seen to be of benefit to all and were deemed attainable. The parents identified this when in two schools they stated that parents and grandparents would help if asked and that parents enjoyed the allotment, giving them a feeling that they were helping the children in the community.

As in many educational situations, the project organisation, partnerships and action research formed a complex set of inter-related data. For the most part, these were identified with their origins. However, who can say whether the less able child who became motivated through being allowed a major role in a gardening activity would not have become motivated if given a lead part in a school play or responsibility in other extra-curricular areas? Only when projects such as these become more accepted (dare it be said, inspected?) will sufficient data be generated on which to base more specific conclusions.

Conclusion

The evidence collected has indicated many successful outcomes from the garden project. Whether teachers, and in particular, head teachers are yet ready or able to 'grasp the nettle' (to coin a gardening pun!) and develop curricula in such a way that underpins ESD as good geographical pedagogy and whole school thinking, is debatable. Using the expertise in schools and the motivation of the children to promote ESD and citizenship in the curriculum, through school based community gardens, may be too radical or simply too demanding in a climate of national strategies, core subject testing and league tables. However, the example of Coombes School (2003) is good evidence of what can be achieved in the state system if teacher vision and motivation are positive and lateral thinking is allowed expression. Maybe *Excellence and Enjoyment: A strategy for primary schools* (DfES, 2003a) provides just the vehicle to allow geography to bring projects such as this into core teaching.

In this project, it was often hard to define the researcher's 'role'. On one hand, it included facilitating and collecting data, on the other the 'wanting it to succeed', which was hard to suppress! The project is ongoing. This is work in progress, but much has been achieved and most of the aims of the project have been met. As Chairman Mao famously said, 'Every journey starts with the first step'. Considering the recent 'Sustainable Development Action Plan for Education and Skills' (DfES, 2003b) and 'Taking the first step forward … towards an ESD' (Ofsted, 2003), there is good reason to suggest that these 'steps', and these schools, are already working toward the aims of both papers, and the UN decade of ESD.

References

Bloomfield, P. (2000), Spencer Junior School Allotment Project, in Bowles, R. (ed.), *Raising Achievement in Geography*, London: Register of Research in Primary Geography, 93

Bloomfield, P. (2001), The root of success, *Primary Geographer*, 43, 26-27

Bloomfield, P. You are what you eat: the sources of food as a source of education for citizenship sustainability, *New Era in Education*, 83 (1), 8-22

Bloomfield, P. (2003a), Local, national and global citizenship, *Education 3-13*, 117 (3), 59-67

Bloomfield, P. (2003b), Growing Up, *Primary Geographer*, 52, 38-39

Bloomfield, P. (2003c), *Report to Hertfordshire County Council, Forward Planning Unit, Environment Department*, August, unpublished

Clough, N. & Holden, C. (2002), *Education for Citizenship: Ideas into action*, London: RoutledgeFalmer

Coombes School (2003), http://www.thecoombes.com, accessed September 2003

DfEE/QCA (1999), *The National Curriculum Handbook for Primary Teachers in England*, London: DfES/QCA

DfES (2003a), *Excellence and Enjoyment: A strategy for primary schools*, London: DfES

DfES (2003b), Taking the first step forward … towards an education for sustainable development: Good practice in primary and secondary schools, http://www.dfes.gov.uk/sd/ accessed September 2003

Fein, J. (2003), Toward the UN decade: looking backwards, looking forwards. *Development Education Journal*, 9 (3), 3-6

Harrison, D. (2002), *Be the change! Introducing Sustainable Development*, Buntingford, Herts, Peace Child International/ Defra

Hicks, D. (2001), *Citizenship for the Future, A practical classroom guide*, Godalming: WWF-UK

Huckle, J. (2003), *Education for Sustainable Development, A briefing paper for the Teacher Training Agency* (May 2003 draft unpublished in this version) quoted with author's permission.

Ofsted (2003), *Sustainable Development Action Plan for Education and Skills*, http://www.dfes.gov.uk/sd/action.shtml accessed Sept 2003

Palmer J., Suggate J., & Matthews, J. (1996), Environmental cognition: early ideas and misconceptions at the ages of four and six, *Environmental Education Research*, 2 (3), 301-330

Sterling S. (2001), *Sustainable Education: Re-visioning Learning and Change*, Dartington: Green Books Ltd.

Young, M. with Cummins, E. (2002), *Global Citizenship: Handbook for Primary Teaching*, Cambridge: Chis Kington Publishing

Chapter 12

Children's Developing Images and Representations of the School Link Environment

Anna Disney

Introduction

Over the last few years, the government of the UK has promoted the development of global citizenship within the primary curriculum and has provided funding for schools to link with partner schools in places around the world in order for pupils to develop values of global citizenship. The research discussed in this chapter was developed within the context of one such school-linking project between Richard Bonington School in Nottingham and St. Anthony's High School in Goa, India. The link was initially funded by the Department of Primary Education at the Nottingham Trent University as part of a small-scale research and curriculum development project within the context of its Initial Teacher Training (ITT) Partnership Programme. Within the Department there was a growing concern to develop the global dimension within the humanities modules in order to prepare students for their future careers in primary schools. Many local schools were addressing global citizenship through setting up school linking programmes and it was becoming increasingly important that this aspect was reflected in the ITT curriculum.

The project has developed as a three-way link between the two schools and the university and is very much led by the curriculum development needs of all three institutions. The research focus has strengthened this development and fed back into the work of the schools, as well as raising wider research issues for future consideration. The link has provided a variety of curriculum development and research opportunities including teacher exchanges and a student study visit. The work has been disseminated locally through presentations for teachers, tutors and research students. This chapter focuses on one aspect of this school linking experience.

Literature review

The revised National Curriculum (DfEE/QCA, 1999) placed a greater emphasis on the global dimension in the primary curriculum and on the development of citizenship. The publication of a guidance document (DfEE et. al, 2000) for head teachers, senior managers and LEAs published in the following year, urged schools to 'place the school curriculum within a broader, global context'. It also advocated 'incorporating a global dimension into the wider life of the school with particular attention being paid to school linking and the opportunities that this offers for learning across the curriculum.'

Increasing numbers of primary schools have developed links with schools abroad, many of which are in economically developing countries, and support and guidance from the Central Bureau, the former educational branch of DfID, has been readily available to facilitate these projects.

The nature of global citizenship

Definitions of global citizenship and the value of including it in the primary curriculum have been well documented in recent publications (Oxfam, 1997; Grimwade et. al, 2000; Young & Cummins, 2002) and these promote a welcome emphasis on process and ways of working as well as on knowledge and understanding. However, as Tsolidas (2000) asks 'How do we teach and learn in times when the notion of global citizenship sounds like a cliché?' As Graves (2002) has argued, there is a need to question some of the assumptions and premises on which effective practice is based and query whether addressing such a complex subject in the primary school without the provision of extensive school based training and staff development is an appropriate path to take.

Central to the concept of global citizenship is a commitment to the idea of personal reflection and critical thinking, processes which need to be informed by accurate information about the world and knowledge of how that information is constructed and communicated. In an overburdened curriculum which prioritises the acquisition of basic skills and sidelines the arts and humanities, surface coverage of many important areas of children's learning about the world is a major cause for concern. In order to explore the notion of global citizenship and raise young children's awareness of issues such as sustainability, social justice and poverty, a context needs to be provided.

History and geography, as traditional school subjects, provide rich opportunities to develop these understandings and it is ironic that the downgrading of these subjects in the primary curriculum has occurred at the same time as global citizenship is being increasingly promoted. School linking seems to be developing as a preferred context for such work. The opportunities provided by geography, as a national curriculum subject, to address these key concepts are abundant but there has been a significant reduction in the amount of geography being taught in many schools and the latest indications are that the quality of geography teaching has declined (Ofsted 2002). Ashley (1999) has referred to citizenship as being 'the new humanities' and it undoubtedly shares a common concern with the experiences of people in society. However there may also be a danger that in subsuming much humanities learning within the citizenship curriculum, the rigorous methodologies of history and geography will be lost. The focus in primary history and geography on the enquiry process and the use of evidence has a particular contribution to make to the development of the global citizen and school links which aim to develop global citizenship need to consider the particular contribution that the geography curriculum can make.

Teaching about distant places

The study of a distant locality provides children with opportunities to develop key geographical skills and concepts. Through comparing and contrasting their own locality with another in a distant place, children can develop concepts of similarity and difference and come to an understanding of shared humanity and environmental processes. When the distant locality being studied is located in an economically developing country, issues relating to the effectiveness of teaching resources and approaches are of particular significance. The messages which children absorb through the images, and materials they are exposed to, will have a major impact on their attitudes and perceptions (Wiegand, 1992).

With restricted curriculum time available for distant locality teaching, it becomes even more urgent that the approaches and materials used are of an appropriate nature. Resources such as the Chembakolli locality pack (Action Aid 2002) are widely used in schools and although it has many attractive features and has been usefully updated, it needs to be used in a cautious and selective way if the stereotypical image of an Indian village is not to be seen as representative of the lives and experiences of all Indian people. Used with care and supplemented with a wider range of images and other resources, it is possible to portray the more complex mixture of modern and traditional, rich and poor, urban and rural contexts that make up India today. School linking can offer another approach which enables children to learn about the real lives of real people in a real place and can be developed to enable children to communicate meaningfully with each other about their own lives. Weldon (1994,16) argues that

> …forming overseas links has the potential to develop in children a greater sympathetic and caring attitude to other peoples and ways of life, a sense of responsibility for the environment, both locally and globally, and helps to counteract prejudice.

In such circumstances, the similarities children find when they share experiences about their lives often outnumber the differences but there are difficulties. Challenging children's perceptions that all people in India live in poverty and have no possessions, can be powerful but if it reinforces their view that to be a person of value, it is necessary to possess western consumer items and be as similar to themselves as possible, the lessons of global citizenship are not being learned. As Tsolidas (2002, 222) argues,

> teaching and learning needs to be premised on the understanding that there is an ongoing and productive tension between sameness and difference. Rather than construct a pedagogy which aims at either sameness or difference we should be teaching to the relationship between these by focusing upon what is shared as a means of making difference more familiar to all students.

This emphasises the importance of teachers widening the study of a distant place to include teaching global issues in a way which enables children to consider underlying political and moral issues and which focuses their thinking on the impact which lifestyle choices in the UK have on the experiences of others.

Research method

The drawing of clear distinctions between curriculum development and research in the field of education is always problematic and can be unhelpful. The nature of this research context, which involves the complex interaction and experiences of children, teachers, parents and communities required an approach which would not exclude all participants in the setting of directions or priorities. My role as researcher was far from being a cool observer of the events and central to my role was the relationship I was forming with all concerned. In many ways, I acted as original initiator in bringing the schools together and providing funding, in accompanying staff on exchange visits and providing curriculum support and advice. I worked with teachers and children in their classrooms to support the geographical aspects of their teaching and learning and it was the 'insider' nature of my role which enabled me to gain a deeper and more informed view of the value of what was being undertaken and achieved. In becoming so much an insider and an actor in the unfolding drama, certain objectivity could be forfeited but the advantages of this role far exceed these limitations. Cohen, Manion and Morrison's (2000) conception of action research as 'a small scale intervention in the functioning of the real world and a close examination of the effects of such an intervention' match well with some aspects of the research process undertaken.

The research discussed in the following sections was all focused on 9/10 year old children in Year 5 (UK) and Standard 6 (India). Three aspects of their developing images and representations of the school link environments have been explored. In each case, analysis of the data has focused on the emerging characteristics and dominant features of children's work rather than on the tracking of changes in the work of individuals. It has also been the case that it was not possible, or desirable, to duplicate exactly the way in which the tasks were set up in each school context. The cultural and contextual differences in the English and Indian curricula meant that the tasks which the children undertook, although essentially the same, were adapted to fit as much as possible with the children's known curriculum and ways of working. The case study nature of this research limits the extent to which wider claims can be made but it raises issues for further research and hopefully provides a resource for teachers and other researchers to develop in their own contexts. The work was produced within the first three years of the project and its function needs to be seen as exploratory and establishing a basis on which more in-depth research will be built as the project continues to develop. It should also be noted that there are many other aspects of the project which are not referred to in this chapter.

The main source of data on which the findings are based is the work produced by the children themselves. This includes their drawings, writings and map work. These data have been supported by classroom observations and discussions with teachers about the work produced.

Findings

Children's initial perceptions of each other's localities

During the early stages of the project, two classes of Year 5 children at Richard Bonington and a similar number of children in Standard 6 of St Anthony's were asked to draw pictures of what they imagined the locality of their linked school to be like. Children in both schools were fairly hesitant about the specificity of this task and the instruction had to be broadened and expanded upon to include the terms 'India' 'England', 'town' and 'village.'

The English children's representations matched fairly consistently with the findings of other researchers. (Graham & Lynn, 1989; Gill, 2002) Their images tended to fall into four major categories:

- *The stereotypical, traditional, rural Indian village.* This was the predominant image amongst the children and the key features were the straw and mud 'huts', people carrying baskets on their heads, wells and animals.
- *The exotic.* This was less common but the features of this include domed buildings, snake charmers and minarets; images in keeping with stories from the Arabian Nights and representative of a more 'middle eastern' cultural style.
- *Undifferentiated.* Again this was not a common response but characterised by drawings which could have easily been of England – the supermarket, road, houses.
- *Complex.* These included flat roof houses, blocks of flats with balconies, markets, palm trees and bicycles. This was the second most common category and revealed that children had images that were based on some knowledge and had not only focused on the more traditional stereotype.

What was most interesting was what the images did not include – there were no representations whatsoever of any form of modern technology and several children categorically stated that there were no cars or buses. There were no TV aerials, computers, cars. The only buildings represented were houses or flats and one supermarket and a couple of temples. There were no schools even though children knew they were going to be communicating with children in an Indian school.

The Indian children's representations were equally fascinating and fell into the following categories:
- *Snowy scenes*. This was the largest category and the children drew rural and urban scenes dominated by snow. The people in these scenes were often depicted on skis or snowshoes and well dressed up against the cold.
- *Skateboarding*. Many pictures included children skateboarding and roller-skating.
- *Urban scenes*. Many of the pictures reflected a predominantly urban environment with cars, buses, bus stops, traffic lights and shops. There was a fair range of buildings including the Houses of Parliament, the Prime Minister's house, schools, churches and shops. Most of the buildings were depicted in the traditional Goan Portuguese architectural style.
- *Rural scenes*. These were less frequent but showed hills and rivers, flowers and trees.

Changing perceptions?

Two years later, at a stage when the link was well established, and both the deputy head and head teacher from Richard Bonington had visited St Anthony's and the teachers and children in both schools were familiar and involved in the project, this activity was repeated with two Year 5 classes at Richard Bonington. These children had been exposed to the link through whole school assemblies which drew on their teachers' visits to St. Anthony's and through displays and their involvement in the general life of the school but had not as yet undertaken any focused teaching through geographical or other curriculum work. The children were again asked to draw what they thought of when they imagined India and /or the locality of the school in Goa. The images drawn by the children were far more varied and idiosyncratic than before and it was difficult to slot them so easily into categories. There were still many of the stereotypical, traditional pictures depicting a life of rural poverty but these were by no means the majority. The majority depicted elements of the real locality particularly the school environment. There was widespread reference to modern technology including computers and multinational brands. The pictures reflected knowledge and understanding of key aspects of life in Goa such as tourism and the presence of water and crops. A much wider range of buildings was depicted and there was more detailed representation of people, in both western and traditional clothes and of people engaged in particular activities such as sport. The pictures were more diverse and informed by more knowledge. Images of the partner school were very strong.

Letter writing

In the initial stages of the project, Year 5 and Standard 6 children were matched up as pen pals. This individualised communication has often been regarded as problematic within the context of a school link as children can become disappointed if the exchange is not kept up. However there were strong support systems in place to ensure letters were written and the benefits of this personal level of communication have proved extremely powerful in that it was through the letters that the similarities in children's lives came through most strongly. Their shared focus on family, friends, school and hobbies has probably done more to challenge stereotypes and assumptions about each other's lives than any other aspect of the link. One feature of the letters, which was of particular significance in terms of the research focus, was the significant difference between the two groups of children in the extent to which they made reference to the local, regional and national context to locate themselves in place. The English children frequently gave their address and identified the area they lived in. None gave information about where this was in England or any information about Nottingham as a place or about England as a country. There were a far larger number of Indian children who communicated information about the locality of their home within the context of Goa and India and gave descriptive detail about the place where they lived, both locally and regionally. It was also significant that many Indian children gave information about their religion and the languages they spoke which were aspects entirely missing from the letters of the English children

Exchange of maps

As part of the children's distant locality study in geography which focused on the locality of St Anthony's in Goa, children were asked to draw a representation of their own school environment which would show children in the partner school what their school was like. Children at Richard Bonington had already focused on developing maps of their own local area as a preparatory stage in the collection of local area resources to support the project. Children at St Anthony's school were approaching the task with less experience of 'map' drawing. The children had a clear communicative purpose in drawing their representations as the actual outcomes were to be taken to the partner school for their peers to study. Both schools have large grounds and a variety of buildings and space for outdoor activities and gardens. Richard Bonington's main building is the more complex of the two buildings, being spread out, irregular and one storey. St Anthony's, whilst the main building is of a more compact and regular design, has the added complication of three storeys. Drawing a representation of their school environment in order to give their peers a sense of what it was like was a challenging task and children were creative and imaginative in addressing the problem.

The English children, although the task was set up in such a way as to allow them to develop their own representations, which could be pictorial, tended to draw something which approximated to a standard plan view. This reflected their prior experience of map work and their own developing expectations of what a map should be. As is usually the case, the group reflected the whole range of ability in terms of the key features of mapping, ranging from 3D pictorial representations of a limited number of features to incredibly sophisticated and complex plan views.

The Indian children had opportunity to study these plans and identify the features of Richard Bonington School and compare them with those of their own school. They were then asked to draw a representation of their own school environment to send back to the English children. Their representations were almost entirely drawn pictorially and there were fewer elements of the plan view. The pictures however were just as effective in identifying and communicating a real sense of the configuration of the layout of the school and all its main features. Ingenuity and imagination were evident as many of the children had overcome the problem of identifying the individual rooms in a three-storey building and labelling was used to great effect. These pictures were studied by the Richard Bonington children who were also able to make comparisons between the two schools. When used alongside photographs of the schools, children were able to develop mental models of each other's environments, based on accurate information - information which they had shared in constructing.

Discussion

This research has been a small part of a wider research and curriculum development project focused on the effectiveness of school linking in developing global citizenship. It is premised on the belief that geography, as a subject in which the interaction between people and places and their relationships with each other form the foundation for understanding our globalised world, needs to be at the heart of the school linking process. The skills of enquiry and interpretation of evidence, which are the tools of the geographer, are also instrumental in affecting attitudes. It is essential that activities of the type outlined above, are utilised not just to inform the wider field of academic research, but also to help teachers explore and develop the understandings of their pupils in a meaningful geographical context.

The research has raised many questions and in this it has been successful, as one of the initial aims was to explore the possible issues and experiences through a case study approach. An insider's perspective has been particularly useful in facilitating the identification of further questions and in establishing clearer themes for future investigation. The complexity and multi-faceted nature of the relationship between school linking and the development of global citizenship has been highlighted, as has the role of geography as a focus for developing understanding of the processes involved. The relationship between particular geographical activities such as mapping and representing places and the process of developing and changing attitudes has been brought into focus and the relationship between geography and global citizenship has been consolidated and strengthened. With reference to the particularities of the activities described, several key issues have been raised:

Equality and social justice

Issues of social justice are never far from the surface in projects which link UK schools with those in the poorer countries of the South. We may be uncomfortable with children in the UK having predominantly stereotypical images of life in India and we know this is not the whole picture of life in the country. We want to portray the whole diversity of urban, rural, rich and poor that make up modern India and we need initially to challenge the predominant stereotype. However, this research has raised the possibility for me that we can change children's predominant imagery by showing them more of 'the other side of the coin'. We can show them that children in India have computer suites in their schools, speak fluent English and have televisions in their homes. However this is no more an accurate image than the traditional stereotype and the research indicates that children have rapidly latched on to the idea that there are western appliances in India and these in turn become the predominant image. There is some indication from this research context, that children's estimation of the worth of their peers in the partner school is affected by the extent to which they possess modern consumer items such as computers and Nike trainers and this is an aspect which deserves further investigation. Teachers may also latch on to this, as it is a much more comfortable image with which to work. There is a possibility that we select our images in such a way as to airbrush out the very real poverty, the shantytowns and the beggars in the street. We cannot afford to dismantle some stereotypes and replace them with others. School linking projects can provide images of real people in real places but it is still possible to select the aspects of the surrounding locality with which we feel comfortable to deal. There are no simple solutions to this problem but grappling with the issues has to be a central focus in any school-linking project and is central to the role of geography in developing the global citizens of the future. There are also implications for providers of initial teacher training, to ensure their courses are preparing students to be able to deal confidently with these issues. The work of The Global Teacher Project, established by the World Studies Trust to help university tutors, students and mentors develop a global dimension in the curriculum, is an important initiative in this field.

Representational skills

The research has made me question whether or not we place an over emphasis on a particular approach to map drawing within the primary curriculum. Children need to develop their skills of representation and to find ways of recording and communicating their mental models of localities and routes. However, the effective and communicatively sophisticated representations drawn by Indian children who had less exposure to maps and little experience in drawing them, indicates that teaching the standard ways of map drawing with a focus on plan view, may not be the factor which best develops representational competence. Knowledge of the environment and an understanding of communicative purpose may be more valuable attributes to develop. Graphicacy in its widest sense can be developed within meaningful, communicative contexts through effective geographical work as part of a school-linking project.

Conclusion

The research has been small scale and tentative in its conclusions. Evaluation of its outcomes has been effective in identifying key issues for further research and in raising some problematic issues which deserve further consideration. The effectiveness of school linking in developing children's awareness of global issues would seem to depend largely on the extent to which the link becomes embedded within the school curriculum in a meaningful way but this raises huge questions about whether the purpose of the link is predominantly forged in order to resource the UK school's curriculum. Unless school links are developed as shared endeavours in which both schools have an equal opportunity to articulate and communicate their own needs and feel that they have an equal amount to gain from the project, they can come dangerously near to epitomising a new form of colonialism which endorses the traditional stereotypes of the dependency of people in the South and the exploitative nature of western culture. There is also a danger that the school link is seen as the sole focus for the global citizenship curriculum and that children's understandings are unduly influenced by their knowledge of one particular locality. Teachers may work so hard to challenge stereotypes and provide positive images of this locality that they end up presenting a partial and simplistic view and avoid confronting real issues such as poverty. Unless our teaching and learning really does grapple with global issues and help children understand the complexities of cause and effect on a global scale, school linking projects will do little more than provide yet more surface learning and have little impact on children's development as global citizens. The knowledge base of teachers is crucial to the effectiveness of school linking projects and the inclusion of the global dimension on ITT courses is of the utmost importance. Teachers need to think deeply about the nature of global citizenship, about their own role as global citizens and about what constitutes good practice. There is a strong case for more research both at the case study level and on a wider scale to develop a foundation of expertise on which staff development can be based.

Not all aspects of the project and associated research have been discussed in this chapter and are ongoing. The findings, although only indicative, have endorsed the view that there is a direct and essential relationship between the geography curriculum and the development of global citizenship. If respect for diversity and for people of other cultures is a central attribute of a global citizen, then activities which help to challenge preconceptions, develop communication and stimulate learning have to be present in the educational experience of young children.

Whilst a school link can provide opportunities for expression and development in all subject areas, geography has a key role to play in ensuring that children are provided with activities which require them to engage in structured enquiry which relates to the real experiences of real people and which is based on a rigorous exploration of the evidence.

References

ActionAid (2002), *Chembakolli – Life and change in an Indian Village*, Chard: ActionAid

Ashley, M. (1999), *Improving teaching and learning in the humanities*, London: Falmer Press

Cohen, L., Manion, L. & Morrison, K. (2000), *Research Methods in Education*, London: Routledge

DfEE/QCA (1999), *The National Curriculum Handbook for Primary Teachers in England*, London: DfEE

DfID/DfEE/QCA/DEA/Central Bureau (2000), *Developing a global dimension in the school curriculum*, London: DfEE

Gill, C. (2002), Concepts of Africa, *Primary Geographer*, 48.18-19

Graham, J. & Lynn, S. (1989), 'Mud huts and flints': children's images of the third world, *Education 3-13*, June, 29-32

Graves, J. (2002), Developing a global dimension in the curriculum, *The Curriculum Journal*, 13 (3), 303-11

Grimwade, K., Jackson, E., Reid, A. & Smith, M. (2000), *Geography and the New Agenda* Sheffield: Geographical Association

Ofsted (2002), *Primary Subject reports 2000/01 – Geography*, London: Ofsted

Oxfam (1997), *A Curriculum for Global Citizenship*, Oxford: Oxfam

Tsolidas, G. (2002), How do we teach and learn in times when the notion of 'global citizenship' sounds like a cliché?, *Journal of Research in International Education*, 1 (2), 213

Weldon, M. (1994), *Discovering Distant Places*, Sheffield: The Geographical Association

Wiegand, P. (1992), *Places in the primary school*, London: Falmer

Young, M. with Commins, E. (2002), *Global Citizenship: The handbook for primary teaching*, Cambridge: Chris Kington Publishing

Acknowledgement
Acknowledgements are due to the children and teachers at St Anthony's High School in Goa, India and at the Richard Bonington Nursery and Primary School, Arnold, Nottingham.

CHILDREN AND PEDAGOGY

Mapwork and spatial cognition

Chapter 13

Small People Thinking about Big Spaces: Young children's navigational use of aerial photographs

Beverly Plester

Introduction

Primary geography focuses on the child in the environment, children's curiosity, enquiry and knowledge about their personal environment, and considers children's knowledge, beliefs, attitudes, and values regarding their wider, global environment, with a central aim of encouraging responsible stewardship in that environment: How does children's thinking inform their action in the environment? Developmental cognitive psychology also considers children's knowledge, beliefs, attitudes, and values regarding their environment, but the central aim is understanding of the processes of children's thinking: How is it that children can think the way they do? How does that thinking develop through time, and what might influence it? And, with geography, how does children's thinking inform their action in the environment?

Simple maps are suggested as resources for geographical education from the earliest units and activities of the English National Curriculum at Key Stage 1, addressing children's work from five and six years old, as, for instance, in the guidance for a Geography Scheme of Work Unit 1 (DfEE/QCA, 1998/2000). Locality photographs are also suggested, but it is not until Unit 6, with children of seven and eight years, that aerial photographs are introduced. Psychological research has shown that children from four years old have begun to understand the symbolic nature of simple maps (Blades and Spencer, 1987), but also that children somewhat older continue to have difficulty with non-realistic icons (Downs and Liben, 1988; Liben and Yekel, 1996). Children from three years have begun to understand aerial photographs (Blaut, 1997) as representations of real spaces, although their understanding continues to develop into adolescence (Downs and Liben, 1997; Liben and Downs, 1997).

Young children's understanding of aerial photographs

DeLoache (1989, 2002) has outlined the development of children's understanding of symbolic artifacts, and Liben (1999, 2002) has proposed a developmental trajectory for understanding of spatial representations. An analysis of these positions, with respect to aerial photographs, is presented by Plester, Blades and Spencer (2003). To make use of any spatial representation in the real space, two kinds of correspondence need to be made: feature correspondence, matching the objects in the representation with the objects in the referent space, and spatial correspondence, matching the spatial relations among objects in the representation with the spatial relations in the real space. These require cognitive transformations of scale and perspective before a child can make use of a representation within the referent space.

The research presented here addresses the difficulty young children have with maps in 'eeing through'symbols that are not perceptual equivalents of their referents, a difficulty that is less problematic with aerial photographs. The cognitive needs remain for shift to the aerial perspective, and scale transformation between representation and referent spaces, and reviewed here is research that has investigated children's competence in these cognitive transformations.

Muir and Blaut (1969) tested five- and six-year-old American children with vertical black and white aerial photographs, at a scale of 1:2700, including photographs of the schools attended by these children, and found that children taught about the aerial photographs demonstrated map interpretation ability above untaught peers. Stea and Blaut (1973) asked Puerto Rican five-year-olds from four types of community to interpret 1:5000 scale vertical aerial photographs of these communities, centred on the children's schools. The children in all groups gave more accurate identifications than inaccurate ones. They concluded that the children had no trouble 'reading' the content of the photographs.

Blaut, McCleary and Blaut (1970) tested five- to seven-year-old children in both Puerto Rico and the United States, using black and white vertical aerial photographs of scales 1:2000 and 1:3000 respectively. The children identified features, and then were asked to trace a map on acetate from the photograph, identify the features they had drawn, and to plot a route on their maps. Most children successfully completed the tasks. In this report, Blaut et al also found that there was no enhancing effect of working with a larger scale oblique aerial photograph first. From these studies and other related work, Blaut (1997) drew the conclusion that interpretation of aerial photographs and using them in problem solving were untaught skills, perhaps incidentally learned. Indeed, in one study, only mentioned briefly in Blaut et al (1970), they found that children from a remote peasant village, who had had no experience with such images, were also able to interpret the photographs. The stance Blaut (eg Blaut, 1997) and his colleagues took was to emphasise the competence of the very young child. Spencer, Harrison and Darvizeh (1980) used copies of the photographs used in the US and Puerto Rico by Blaut and Stea (1969) with children as young as three years, and found they responded to them as depictions of real places, and could identify features.

Liben and Downs (1997) acknowledged these putative understandings, but drew more cautious conclusions, emphasising the limitations of young children. They showed three to six-year-old children a black and white vertical aerial photograph, with scale 1:12,000, of Chicago, an unfamiliar city (Liben and Downs, 1989). In other work (Liben and Downs, 1992) children were shown aerial photographs of their own town. In these studies, they found scale errors and confusions over the representational function of the photograph, such as referring to boats on Lake Michigan as fish, believing a line could not be a road because it was too narrow for two cars, a building could not be an office because a real office was as big as the whole map, or a field could not be grass because it was not depicted in green.

Errors of these kinds, however intriguing, are exceptions to young children's overall representational competency, and indicate incomplete understanding, but not complete misunderstanding. Blades et al. (1997) found a few misinterpretations, and a very small proportion of scale errors, with children from three and a half years to five years of age, using an aerial photograph of 1:1300 scale. Further, Blades et al. (1998), in a study involving children in five cultures across the world, found little evidence of young children's inability to make the scale and perspective transformations required.

Blades et al (1997) also investigated children's understanding beyond mere comprehension of feature correspondence, with a proposed navigation task, asking children to draw a proposed route over the photograph from one place to another, either using a familiar or unfamiliar real space. Children familiar with the space were considerably more able to plot a plausible route.

Where the latter work is important for assessing the functional aspects of the children's understanding of representations of familiar and unfamiliar spaces, it falls short of fully assessing the children's pragmatic ability to make use of that understanding because the children were not present in the space at the time of testing. Bluestein and Acredolo (1979) and Liben and Yekel (1996) had children use maps in the referent space, but the maps were simple ones, and the space enclosed.

Research method

The present investigations take the children into a much larger, perceptually rich referent space for actual tasks of navigation, finding hidden objects, and placing objects in the space, using aerial photographs as aids as they moved within the space. The two methods employed, and the findings from each, are reported below, followed by a general discussion, drawing the findings together. Three experiments, using the hidden object paradigm, have been reported by Plester, Richards, Blades and Spencer (2002). Findings from an experiment using the object placement paradigm have been reported by Plester, Blades and Spencer (2003).

Search for Hidden Objects

Three experiments asked a total of 128 four- and five-year-olds to use colour aerial photographs of their schools and grounds, ranging in scale from 1:400 to 1:1100, either oblique or vertical projection, to find hidden objects around their school playgrounds. In each case, children were questioned individually about their understanding of the correspondence between the photograph and the real space, and prompts given to establish feature correspondence and orientation before the search tasks began. The children were asked to find hidden objects in a variety of hiding places indicated on the aerial photographs.

Hiding place targets were of three types:
- distinctive targets, where the target was marked by a nearby, unique environmental feature, visible in both photograph and real space;
- non-distinctive, marked targets, where the target was marked by one of a set of similar or identical environmental features, visible in photograph and real space;
- non-distinctive, unmarked targets, where the target was not marked by any environmental feature, and indicated only on the photograph by an arrow.

The photographs are shown in Figures 1, 2 and 3.

For the distinctive targets, feature correspondence was necessary and sufficient for success. For non-distinctive, marked targets, feature correspondence was necessary, but not sufficient, and correspondence of spatial relations among similar features, or between the target and other features, was necessary to disambiguate among alternatives. For the non-distinctive, unmarked targets, feature correspondence was only possible to identify a general area for search, and close spatial correspondence was necessary for success.

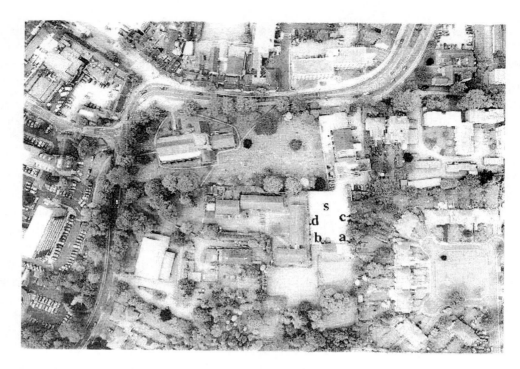

Figure 1: Vertical aerial photograph used in Hidden Object Task, scale 1:1100, used in Plester, Richards, Blades & Spencer (2002). [**S** = starting point for searches. **a** and **b** show distinctive hiding places. **c** and **d** show non-distinctive hiding places.]

Figure 2: Oblique aerial photograph used in Hidden Object Task, scale equivalent to 1:475, based on central features, used in Plester, Richards, Blades & Spencer (2002). [**S** = starting point for searches. **a** and **b** show distinctive hiding places. **c** and **d** show non-distinctive marked hiding places; each child looked for one **c** and one **d**. **e** and **f** show non-distinctive un-marked hiding places.]

Figure 3: Oblique aerial photograph used in Hidden Object Task, scale equivalent to 1:400, based on central features, used in Plester, Richards, Blades & Spencer (2002). [**S** = starting point for searches. **a** and **b** show distinctive hiding places. **c** and **d** show non-distinctive marked hiding places.]

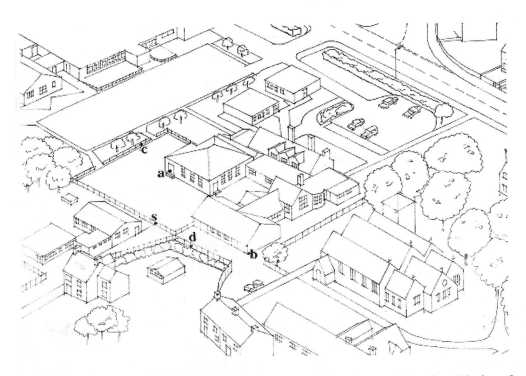

Figure 4: Oblique map drawn from Figure 3, used in Plester, Richards, Blades & Spencer (2002). [**S** = starting point for searches. **a** and **b** show distinctive hiding places. **c** and **d** show non-distinctive marked hiding places.]

A further aspect of one study was to compare children's success using an aerial photograph with their success using a map drawn from it, shown as Figure 4. Half of the children used the photograph first, then the map for a further set of comparable targets, and half used the representations in reverse order.

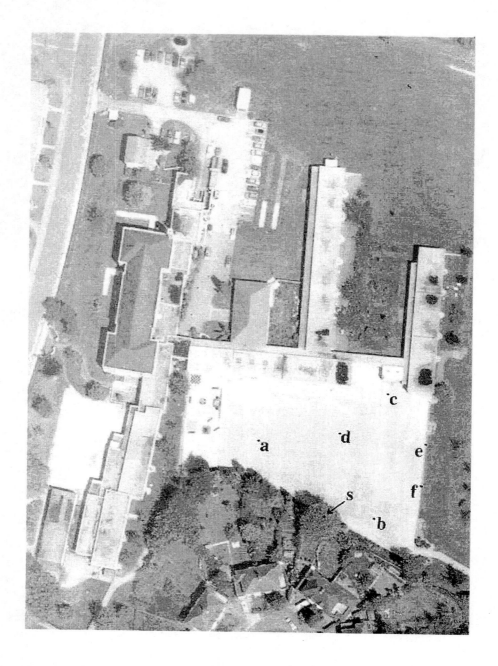

Figure 5: Vertical aerial photograph used in Object Placement Task, scale 1:750, used in Plester, Richards, Blades & Spencer (2002). [S = starting point for searches. **a** and **d** show targets nearer the centre than the borders. **b** and **c** show targets nearer the borders than the centre. **e** shows the 1-dimensional target closer to the endpoint than the centre. **f** shows the 1-dimensional target closer to the centre of the border than the endpoint.]

Object Placement

Because of the low rate of success in finding unmarked targets, because a success/fail scoring system does not describe relative accuracy, and because it was desirable to track levels of success developmentally across a wider age range, further research concentrated on unmarked targets, using an object placement task, with 135 children ranging from five through ten years. A small adult sample was also included for comparison. The photograph used is shown in Figure 5.

Participants were taken individually to a starting point on the playground of their school, shown the aerial photograph, and questioned using a set of prompts to establish feature correspondence and orientation. A soft toy dog was introduced, and participants were asked to "take him for a walk" and put him down on the playground at locations indicated on the photograph by dots. There were no corresponding markings on the playground. There were four targets in the open space of the playground, two closer to the centre and two closer to borders, with two further targets along one border. The placements, measured relative to peripheral landmarks in two directions, made were recorded using grid references. Accuracy was measured in three ways: displacement from the exact target location; amount of distance error relative to the true distance from starting point to target along a direct path; and amount of directional error, measured by degrees of deviation from the direct path to the target.

Findings

Search for Hidden Objects

Little difference was found between oblique and vertical projections, and, looking at the three studies together, five-year-olds were more competent than four-year-olds, as expected, although in some cases the difference was small. Distinctive hiding places were found 62%, 88% and 92% of the time; non-distinctive, marked targets were found 67% and 72% of the time; non-distinctive, unmarked targets were found 40% and 44% of the time. The lower success rate for distinctive targets in the first study may be attributable to mismatch between what adults felt was distinctive and what young children perceived as such. One distinctive target was found 77% of the time, the other 47%. The less frequently found target was at a corner, which had been deemed marker enough, and children found the general vicinity, but often not the hidden object. Children have been shown to use corners as landmarks implicitly in other tasks (eg Plumert and Hund, 2001).

It was clear that the presence of landmarks, with which feature correspondence could be made from the aerial photographs, was helpful to these young children when using the photographs as navigation aids, and that the children depended upon feature correspondence in their problem solving. Landmarks also served to attract drift in unsuccessful searches in unmarked spaces. But because there was some success in even the most difficult searches, it was also clear that the children had some ability to map spatial relations from the representation onto the real space.

It was also found that using an aerial photograph before using a derived map led to greater success using the map to find equivalent targets, whereas using the map first did not affect success with the photograph. This is compatible with the findings of Muir and Blaut (1969), and suggests that the use of the photograph may scaffold the feature correspondence needed to orient the user to a map, by providing features with greater perceptual likeness with which to make the correspondence.

Object Placement

Every adult and child, except a very few of the youngest, used a strategy that reinforced the earlier finding that landmark features were central in thinking about large spaces. They did not treat the playground as a single, homogeneous space; they subdivided it into wedges originating at the starting point and subtended by a portion of the playground boundary that might be represented by a particular landmark such as a set of benches or a distinctive part of the building. The placements around all targets are illustrated in Figure 6. The importance of landmarks in spatial thinking was further reinforced, by the finding that landmark features again attracted drift away from accurate placements. This was particularly true with respect to the two targets nearer the edges than the centre of the playground, and with one of the targets along a border.

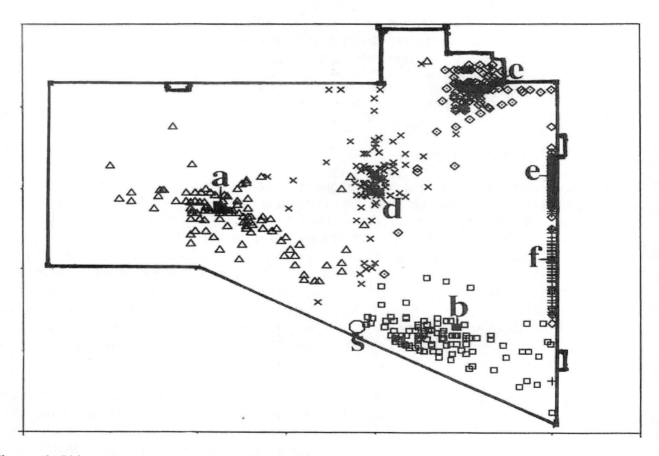

Figure 6: Object placements made at all targets [O indicates the starting point **S**. All targets are indicated by solid black squares. Δ indicates placements around target **a**. ☐ indicates placements around target **b**. ◈ indicates placements around target **c**. **X** indicates placements around target **d**. ◊ indicates placements around target **e**. + indicates placements around target **f**.]

There was continual, gradual improvement through childhood in all measures of accuracy, as expected, with significant differences not generally appearing between adjacent years.
Placements by children from five through seven years were significantly less accurate in actual distance from the target than were older children and adults. Looking at accuracy in distance from the starting point, only adults and ten-year-olds were significantly more accurate than younger children. A similar trend showed for directional accuracy, and adults were not significantly more accurate than eight- through ten-year-olds.

Discussion

Two overriding impressions from this study have been that young school children do have considerable ability to make feature correspondences between aerial photographs and the referent large spaces of their school grounds, and that they develop the ability to make spatial correspondences gradually over the primary school years, reaching competence approximating that of adults by the age of eight to ten years. Whereas previous research with aerial photographs had demonstrated young children's understanding of feature correspondences, without actually testing the children in the depicted space, it had not been possible to assess their ability to make spatial correspondences in large spaces.

Accurate spatial correspondence by young children had been shown to be relatively poor in smaller spaces, such as classrooms or enclosed experimental spaces (eg Liben and Yekel, 1996; Uttal, 1996), or the even smaller spaces of desktop tasks (eg Blades, 2001). One study had attempted a systematic comparison between spatial correspondence in a desktop task and a large outdoor equivalent (Bell, 2002), but this study depended upon spatial memory and did not make use of a spatial representation such as a map or aerial photograph. We have seen here that in large outdoor space tasks using aerial photographs, spatial correspondence lags behind feature correspondence in development, but that it does reach adult levels before the end of the primary years. Ongoing research will make direct comparisons between desktop tasks using aerial photographs and outdoor tasks using the photographs in the actual space.

Another overriding impression from the present work is that children and adults were resolutely situated beings, utilising the landmark features of their environment in problem solving as and when they could. Landmarks were fundamental to thinking about these large spaces. Whereas adults and older children may be capable of representing space mentally in abstract terms, through use of a coordinate system, as Piaget and Inhelder (1956) found, they did not always do so if they were able to utilise landmarks as representations of spatial categories, and calculate location by projective spatial relations to those landmarks. Adults and older children appeared to integrate information from more projective relations than did younger children, compatible with Piaget and Inhelder's model, and this was associated with greater accuracy in placements. Further research will investigate whether training will improve children's use of information from more than one projective dimension.

Uttal (2000) proposed that map use might enhance children's development of adult spatial cognition, mentally representing space in an abstract, plan view, representing multiple spatial relations not yet experienced directly. Finding here that the use of an aerial photograph enhanced young children's ability to use a map in problem solving leads to the further proposal that early experience with aerial photographs might be a doorway to the enhancement Uttal proposed. If children can make spatial correspondences more easily when feature correspondences are more transparent, as they are with aerial photographs, then it would seem fruitful to explore the use of aerial photographs alongside the simple maps suggested for primary geography Key Stage 1 units. Further research might profitably test this proposal against learning outcomes in Key Stage 1.

Conclusion

It has been seen that young school children possess considerable competence in relating aerial photographs to the referent spaces while they are active in the depicted spaces. Their greater competence appears to be in making feature correspondences, and their ability to make spatial correspondences develops rapidly, reaching adult standard before the end of primary education. Both children and adults appear to make practical use of landmarks in location tasks, even when over-attention to landmarks decreases accuracy. Further, there are indications that children's use of an aerial photograph may improve ability to use an equivalent map. Several suggestions have been put forward for further research into the ways that younger children think about large spaces.

References

Bell, S. (2002), Spatial cognition and scale: A child's perspective, *Journal of Environmental Psychology*, 22, 9-27

Blades, M., Blaut, J. M., Darvizeh, Z., Elguea, S., Sowden, S., Soni, D., Spencer, C., Stea, D., Surajpaul, R. and Uttal, D. (1998), A cross-cultural study of young children's mapping abilities, *Transactions of the Institute of British Geographers*, 23, 269-277

Blades, M. (2001), Preschool children's failure to consider configural spatial information in a map task, *Poster presentation at the Society for Research in Child Development Biennial Meeting*, Minneapolis, MN

Blades, M. and Spencer, C. (1987), The use of maps by 4-6 year old children in a large scale maze, *British Journal of Developmental Psychology*, 5, 19-24

Blaut, J. M. (1997), The mapping abilities of young children: Children can, *Annals of the Association of American Geographers*, 87, 152-158

Blaut, J. M., McCleary, G. S., and Blaut, A. S. (1970), Environmental mapping in young children, *Environment and Behavior* 2, 335-349

Bluestein, N. and Acredolo, L. (1979), Developmental changes in map reading skills, *Child Development*, 50, 691-697

DeLoache, J. (1989), The development of representation in young children, *Advances in Child Development and Behaviour*, 22, 1-39

DeLoache, J. S. (2002), Early development of the understanding and use of symbolic artefacts, in Goswami, U. (ed.), *Handbook of Childhood Cognitive Development*. Oxford: Blackwell

DfEE/QCA (1998/2000), *A Scheme of Work for Key Stages 1 and 2: Geography*, London: DfEE/QCA

Downs, R. M. & Liben, L. S. (1988), Through a map darkly: Understanding maps as representations, *Genetic Epistemologist*, 16, 11-18

Downs, R. M. & Liben, L. S. (1997), The final summation: The defence rests, *Annals of the Association of American Geographers*, 87, 178-180

Liben, L. S. (1999), Developing an understanding of external spatial representations, In I. E. Sigel (Ed.) *Development of Mental Representation*. Mahwah NJ: Lawrence Erlbaum Associates

Liben, L. S. and Downs, R. M. (1989), Understanding maps as symbols: The development of map concepts in children, *Advances in Child Development and Behavior*, 22, 145-201

Liben, L. S. & Downs, R. M. (1992), Developing an understanding of graphic representations in children and adults: The case of GEO-graphics, *Cognitive Development*, 7, 331-349

Liben, L. S. and Downs, R. M. (1997), Can-ism and can'tianism: A straw child, *Annals of the Association of American Geographers* 87, 159-167

Liben, L. S. and Yekel, C. A. (1996), Preschoolers' understanding of plan and oblique maps: The role of geometric and representational correspondence, *Child Development*, 67, 2780-2796

Muir, M. & Blaut, J. (1969), The use of aerial photographs in teaching mapping to children in the first grade: An experimental study, *The Minnesota Geographer*, 22, 4-19

Piaget, J. and Inhelder, B. (1956), *The Child's Conception of Space*. London: Routledge

Plester, B., Blades, M. and Spencer, C. (2003), Children's understanding of aerial photographs, *Children's Geographies* 1(2), 281-293

Plester, B., Richards, J., Blades, M. and Spencer, C. (2002), Young children's ability to use aerial photographs as maps, *Journal of Environmental Psychology*, 22, 29-47

Plumert, J. M. and Hund, A. M. (2001), The development of memory for location: What role do spatial prototypes play? *Child Development*, 72, 370-384

Stea, D. and Blaut, J. M. (1973), Some preliminary observations on spatial learning in school children, in Downs, R.M., and Stea, D. (eds), *Image and Environment*. Chicago: Aldine

Spencer, C..P., Harrison, N. and Darvizeh, Z. (1980), The development of iconic mapping ability in young children, *International Journal of Early Childhood*, 12, 57-64

Uttal, D. H. (1996), Angles and distances: children's and adults' reconstruction and scaling of spatial configurations, *Child Development*, 67, 2763-2779

Uttal, D. H. (2000), Seeing the big picture: map use and the development of spatial cognition, *Developmental Science*, 3, 247-286

Chapter 14

The Skills Children Use when Encoding and Decoding Spatial Information about the Environment: A case study

Di Wilmot

Introduction

Graphic literacy is identified as one of the critical outcomes of South Africa's first post-apartheid national curriculum (National Department of Education, 1996). For graphic literacy to become an achievable outcome of the new curriculum, it is vital to investigate the skills and concepts underpinning this key form of communication.

This chapter describes a case study, the goal of which was to investigate graphicacy as a form of communication in a South African primary school. The primary aim of the study was to illuminate and describe the spatial skills, combinations of skills and level of skill competency displayed by the seventeen 10/11 year old children when encoding spatial information about the environment through a series of practical and drawing tasks. It sought similarly, to identify and describe what skills were utilised and how they were utilised and applied when children decoded spatial information contained in pictures. Secondly, this study set out to illuminate, describe and explain the difficulties children experienced when reading and interpreting pictures as well as the factors which may have impeded or enhanced the sense-making process.

Although it is recognised that this research is a case study located within a specific context, the research findings, evaluated according to existing and emerging theoretical perspectives on graphicacy, help to illuminate the current situation regarding the graphic literacy of South African primary school children. The study may contribute to wider international debate about graphicacy and the development of graphic literacy, from a South African perspective.

Literature review

Children, as social beings, need to communicate with each other through four forms of communication. According to Balchin & Coleman (1965, 85), literacy, numeracy, oracy and graphicacy are the *four aces* in the 'pack' of education. They claim that education is incomplete if any one of the four aces is left out of the pack. Balchin (1985, 8) contends that 'in a brain as highly evolved as that of the human being, the potential for all types of ability in communication is inborn but none of them can come to full fruition without education'. In South African primary schools, graphicacy is a neglected skills area (Van Harmelen & Boltt, 1995).

Graphicacy is a complex form of communication in that it utilises some form of symbolic language to convey information about spatial relationships (Balchin, 1985). Graphicacy is underpinned by a complex and interconnected network of spatial perceptual skills and spatial conceptual skills (Boardman, 1976, 1983; Spencer et al, 1989; Van Harmelen & Boltt, 1995). The following spatial perceptual skills and concepts are relevant to this study:

- recognising and understanding *what* objects are in terms of shape, colour, size, pattern, texture, and discerning objects in the foreground/background;
- recognising and understanding *where* objects are (location) and how they are arranged (distribution); distance, depth and direction;
- recognising and understanding *spatial relationships*, making sense of patterns; orientation; perceptual constancy, and the position in relation to self and other objects;
- distinguishing between and drawing objects from different *perspectives*;
- making judgements about what, where and how objects are *spatially*.

Of significance to this study is the recognition that the ability to communicate spatial knowledge is dependent on the extent to which an individual has *both* spatial perceptual skills and spatial conceptual understanding. If spatial perceptual skills are poorly developed, an individual will not be able to develop spatial understanding. Conversely, if spatial conceptual understanding is poorly developed or lacking, then an individual will not be able to utilise and apply spatial perceptual skills efficiently. To communicate spatial information effectively in graphic form requires that an individual not only recognises and utilises spatial perceptual skills but also has the ability to apply these skills. The latter requires spatial conceptual understanding. Thus the importance of the interconnectedness and interdependency of spatial perceptual skills and spatial conceptual understanding needs to be recognised (Boardman, 1976, 1983; Catling, 1995).

While the human brain has the capacity to utilise four forms of communication, the efficiency and level of sophistication with which it is able to do so is seen as dependent on education. Procedures for each have to be taught (Balchin, 1985). It follows that primary education has an important role to play in developing the skills and concepts underpinning graphicacy as a form of communication. This should be done as early as possible whilst a child is still in the skill-learning stage of his/her education.

Graphicacy involves encoding information in some type of graphic representation (for example, maps, photographs, pictures, diagrams, cartoons, sketches, posters and graphs), which is conveyed to the reader through some or other form of symbolic language. The reader then decodes the representation in order to understand the information being communicated. Molyneux and Tolley (1987) and Catling (1995) contend that to develop graphicacy, children need to be given the opportunity to practise both encoding and decoding information.

Given the scope of a research project of this nature, it was decided that rather than dealing with the entire spectrum of graphic representations, pictures, as the most frequent and concrete graphic representation encountered by young learners, would be focused on. Whilst pleas (Wright 1989) have been made for the teaching of pictures [the decoding aspect of graphicacy], far less has been said about the teaching of the encoding aspect of graphicacy, drawing or picture composition. According to Boltt & Van Harmelen (1995), in a South African context, little has been done to establish how children process the information contained in pictures, what skills they need to do so and how these are acquired.

The findings of research carried out in Britain on children's graphic abilities has challenged the orthodoxy of conventional developmental psychology perspectives. There is a growing body of evidence which suggests that Piagetian age and stage theory of cognitive and spatial development may have under-estimated young children's competencies (Spencer *et al*, 1989; Matthews, 1992; Spencer, 1995). For many years the Piagetian contention that children develop sequentially and according to age-related stages has guided or perhaps mis-guided thinking about children's spatial knowledge and skills. Uncritical acceptance of this theory has influenced curriculum design in South Africa and may well be the reason why graphicacy has been a neglected skills area, relegated to the position of 'discard' in the pack of education.

Research methods

The goal of this research is to illuminate and understand the graphic skills children utilise and apply when encoding and decoding spatial information using symbols. This study is best described as a small-scale interpretive case study (Cohen, Manion & Morrison, 2000; Denzin & Lincoln 1994). According to Stake (1995) a case study method is well suited to rich interpretation and thorough understanding, the purpose of which is to understand the case rather than to seek to establish generalisations about the wider population to which the case belongs. This case study used one Grade 5 class consisting of seventeen 10/11 year old boys within an independent South African primary school. The children who constituted this case, while from diverse cultural and linguistic backgrounds, were nevertheless from the more affluent and privileged sector of society. In that it was age, gender and economic class specific, this case does not constitute a representation of all South African primary school children.

Data was gathered in the field from multiple sources including the class teacher and pre-service trainee teachers, and the verbal and written responses and drawings of the children. Data collecting techniques included direct observation, two diagnostic activities, field notes and interviews. Following Yin's (1989) recommendation, multiple sources and techniques were used for triangulation purposes, as a means of overcoming problems of construct validity and reliability associated with interpretive research. The study was undertaken in two stages, outlined below (see also, Wilmot, 2002).

Stage One

The study initially focused on the entire Grade 6 class as a case study. This enabled trends and patterns within the class to be identified and described. For this purpose, two diagnostic activities were conducted with the class. The first was based on a number of practical drawing and mapping tasks set up in the classroom as 'islands'. The tasks were based on those used by Van Harmelen & Boltt (1995) with in-service primary school teachers. Working in pairs and individually, the boys completed eight different tasks as they rotated from one 'island' to another. The first four tasks were:
- A shape sorter activity;
- Puzzle building (with picture);
- Puzzle building (no picture);
- Tangram construction.

These were selected since they are based on varieties of practical activity in which the same or similar spatial skills or combinations of skills need to be recognised, utilised and applied.

The next four tasks were as follows:
- Drawing observable objects (a glass beaker and rectangular box) from: 'normal' side view and reversed, obscured side view;
- Drawing observable objects (a gas burner and cup) from aerial view;
- Drawing a side view of a familiar but un-observable scene (the interior of the school hall);
- Drawing a route map from memory.

These activities sought to illuminate both the children's spatial skills and understanding and their ability to communicate spatial concepts through using symbols. They required the children to encode spatial information through a variety of drawings and by means of a map.

During *Diagnostic Activity One*, the researcher assumed the role of participant observer. The student teachers and class teacher, as non-participant observers, observed how the children set about the tasks and recorded their observations by means of field notes. These, together with the children's drawings, provided the empirical evidence of what the class could do and constituted the raw material for the identification of patterns and trends. The data was analysed according to the individual child's ability to recognise and utilise the spatial skills and concepts listed in the preceding section.

Diagnostic Activity Two, a picture-reading activity, was designed to illuminate how the children utilised and applied the same spatial perceptual skills and concepts as *Activity One*. The children were asked to respond to eight colour photographs in writing. The photographs were selected purposely to include different perspectives (side, oblique and aerial) and scale (small, medium and large). *Activity Two* illuminated how the children decoded spatial information communicated through pictures. The following criteria, suggested by Wright (1989), were adapted for the analysis:

1. Recognise individual features shown in the pictures. This is linked to an ability to recognise and understand: 3-D reality in 2-D form; shape; colour; pattern; texture; size, and perspective.
2. Read the picture by skimming and/or scanning. This is linked to an ability to attend to both the individual parts as well as the whole of what is shown in the picture.
3. Describe what they see in little/moderate/rich detail. This is linked to an ability to recognise and understand the size, shape, colour, *etc.*, of objects, and to express this understanding using appropriate vocabulary.
4. Express their ideas lucidly using simple or sophisticated/technical language. This is linked to the ability to communicate effectively in the written form, using appropriate language and correct syntax.
5. Discriminate between foreground and background (linked to criterion 2 above). The particular concern was to illuminate what children focus on and what they ignore when reading pictures.
6. Identify/explain relationships. This is linked to the ability to identify and understand size, scale, patterns, distance and position. It requires of the children an ability to juxtapose objects using familiar views from unusual perspectives.
7. Interpret what they see (deduce, infer, speculate).

The class teacher's role was that of non-participant observer. Construct validity was increased through triangulation by the non-participant observer. The empirical data obtained from this diagnostic activity was analysed using both quantitative and qualitative methods, in order to identify trends and patterns and to identify individual cases which did not conform to the 'typical' patterns which emerged. The analysis was shown to the teacher for crosschecking purposes and the selection of the purposive sample was discussed. Internal validity was increased through triangulation by multiple investigators.

Stage Two

Guided by the patterns and trends identified in both the diagnostic activities, four children were selected as a specific sample because they represented the spectrum of skill competency within the case study class. The researcher interviewed each child to probe, clarify and explore their responses to the diagnostic activities and to gain more insight into the factors which may have impeded or enhanced the sense that they had made, and to corroborate responses obtained from other sources.

Findings

A number of informative findings emerged from this study (see also Wilmot, 2002). These are outlined in relation to the two diagnostic activities described above.

Diagnostic Activity One

Overall, the children managed the four practical tasks, albeit with varying degrees of efficiency and success. Further, the findings revealed that the ability of an individual child to identify, utilise and apply skills and combinations of skills was consistent throughout the various 'island' tasks.

The range of times and scores recorded suggests that despite the children knowing what to do, the level of efficiency, consistency and success with which they were able to apply what they knew varied considerably. Typically, most of the children were able to apply the skills to a lesser or greater extent, from which it was inferred that they possessed spatial conceptual understanding, but not at a high level of development. Atypically, a small number of children experienced serious difficulty when applying the skills, from which a low level of spatial conceptual understanding was inferred. This group was described as having a low level of skill competency. Also atypically, a small number of children were able to apply the skills efficiently and effectively and in so doing they achieved a high level of success. They were seen as possessing a high degree of skill competency.

The findings suggest that when children work co-operatively and collaboratively, they achieve higher levels of learning than when they work on their own. The findings support the claim that development is age-related, but challenge the notion that cognitive and spatial development is innate and dependent on maturity and that it occurs in an invariant sequence.

Most importantly, the findings support the notion that if formal education is to play a role in developing and extending the young child's ability to communicate effectively through symbols, then the importance of the skills *and* the concepts underpinning graphicacy need to be recognised and understood. Further, the teaching of graphicacy needs to emphasise the development and understanding of the conceptual basis in which the skills are located.

Diagnostic Activity Two

This activity sought to investigate the children's ability to read and interpret spatial concepts as shown in and communicated through a variety of pictures. Making sense of spatial information requires that one 'sees', recognises and understands what is shown, implied or suggested. Reading thus takes place on two levels: on a literal level of 'seeing' what is there, and on another level as 'reading between the lines' or making inferences and contextualising. This in turn requires that one recognises, utilises and applies spatial skills. The claim to be graphically literate can only be made if one not only reads but also understands what has been read. This is only possible if one has a conceptual grasp of what has been read.

The children's written responses to the picture reading activity revealed the following:

- All the children recognised and identified individual features in most of the pictures.
- The class mostly read the pictures by skimming for gist as well as scanning for specific features. Individual children tended to be consistent in the procedures they employed for reading the pictures.
- The class mostly described most of the pictures in little to moderate detail. Individual children tended to be consistent in the amount of detail they provided.
- The class mostly experienced difficulty in expressing their ideas or did so using simple language. Individual children tended to be consistent in terms of language proficiency.
- The class mostly discriminated between foreground and background in most of the pictures. Individual children tended to be inconsistent in their discriminations from picture to picture.

The findings corroborate those of *Diagnostic Activity One*, namely that the children were all able to 'read' the pictures in a literal sense in that they recognised, identified and described what they saw, albeit in varying amounts of detail. However, the efficiency with which they were able to interpret what they had read was linked to and dependent on their level of conceptual understanding. Typically, most of the children read and interpreted the pictures to a greater or lesser extent, which suggested that they possessed some conceptual understanding. Atypically, a small number of children who were able to recognise and understand the spatial attributes and relationships, decoded the spatial information contained in the pictures with the highest level of efficiency and offered the most sophisticated and articulate descriptions and interpretations. By and large, this group comprised the same children who displayed a high level of skill competency in *Diagnostic Activity One*. Again, atypically, the children who experienced difficulty in identifying and describing information about space contained in the pictures were the same children who experienced difficulty when required to encode such information in drawings and a map. By and large, this group comprised the same children as the group which displayed the lowest level of skill competency in *Diagnostic Activity One*.

Discussion

The findings of both diagnostic activities support the claim that graphic literacy is not dependent so much on the ability to identify and recognise spatial perceptual skills as it is on the ability to apply those skills when encoding and decoding spatial information through the use of symbols.

The findings of *Diagnostic Activities One* and *Two* revealed a number of pertinent points. Generally, the children who were of a similar age, recognised and were able to utilise spatial perceptual skills and combinations of these. But their efficiency in performing the tasks was dependent on their ability to apply the skills. The ability to apply a skill, it was argued, is dependent on spatial knowledge. Knowing something means being able to communicate one's knowledge; without this ability, a claim to knowledge is spurious. In looking at graphicacy as a form of communication, we are essentially looking at a tool through the use of which we are able to communicate and share our spatial knowledge with others. The spatial knowledge which graphic literacy enables us to communicate undoubtedly involves certain skills, but these skills cannot be seen as separate from the conceptual basis in which they are embedded. The most significant disjunction came not in the children's ability to identify and use skills, but in their concept-dependent ability to apply them.

This study shows that children who have the spatial skills but lack the conceptual understanding in which the skills are embedded, are inhibited in their ability to communicate spatial information about the environment through symbols. It also became apparent that when a child lacked spatial conceptual understanding, it not only affected his ability to communicate in graphic form but also limited him in his ability to utilise other forms of communication, namely oracy and literacy.

The second stage of the study focused on four children selected as a specific sample because they represented the spectrum of skill competency within the case. The findings highlight the importance of early childhood experiences and the nature of the social interactions children experience through their informal education in the home and in the pre-school. There is evidence that higher levels of learning and skill development are achieved when a child has enjoyed a rich and stimulating childhood; where he has been supported, encouraged and guided by more experienced learners, most important of which are the parents; where there has been freedom to explore the environment through active, first-hand encounters of it; and when a child has consequently acquired the confidence and social skills necessary for interacting with others.

The evidence suggests that the children who displayed the highest levels of skill competency do so as a result of having been taught the skills and concepts informally through social interactions with 'significant others', the most important of which were parents. These findings support the Vygotskian claim that knowledge is socially constructed and that higher levels of cognition are possible when a child is guided and supported by more mature learners. The findings thus support the notion that spatial cognition and skills utilisation can be accelerated through teaching. The implications of this within a multicultural and multilingual South Africa are significant. Many of our children come from materially poor homes; many have illiterate or semi-literate parents. The scaffolding necessary for spatial conceptual and skill development may not take place. Unless these children are taught the skills as embedded in conceptual understanding, there is a danger that these children's chances of succeeding have been reduced. Teachers need to guard against making age-based assumptions about children's levels of spatial conceptual understanding.

It has been revealed that the pre-school and junior primary section of formal school have an important role to play in supporting the development and acquisition of spatial skills and concepts necessary for graphic literacy. However, these skills need to be taught in such a way as to include their conceptual basis. In this way, children can become more effective communicators and thus achieve the goals of graphic literacy. Teachers should recognise and accept that children bring different experiences and prior knowledge; they should start by establishing what children know *and* understand, and how they apply their knowledge and understanding when communicating in general and, more specifically, when communicating through symbols.

The findings support the notion that schools have an important role to play in ensuring that all children are afforded an equal chance to succeed in a technologically advanced world, and that they are taught the skills necessary for effective communication, including those associated with graphicacy.

Conclusion

This study has afforded a glimpse into what goes on inside the minds of children within a South African primary school classroom. It has revealed how children actively construct knowledge both individually and through interactions with others. The findings suggest that higher levels of knowledge are achieved when learning has been socially constructed. What has emerged from the findings of the study can also be seen to support the growing body of international opinion which challenges the orthodoxy of traditional theoretical perspectives on learning and development. This study has revealed that within a South African context, we may well be mis-informed about children's spatial conceptual ability in general.

It is acknowledged that the findings of this study are tentative and limited for the following reasons. The focus on graphicacy was narrow. The case was age, gender and economic class specific. As such it cannot constitute a representation of all South African primary school children. By virtue of the nature of qualitative research an element of subjectivity was unavoidable in the study.

References

Balchin, W. and Coleman, A. (1965), Graphicacy – the fourth 'ace' in the pack, *Times Educational Supplement,* November 5, 1965

Balchin, W.G.V. (1985), Graphicacy comes of age, *Teaching Geography* 11(1), 8-9

Boardman, D. (1976), Graphicacy in the curriculum, *Educational Review,* 28, 118-125

Boardman, D. (1983), *Graphicacy and Geography Teaching.* London: Croom Helm

Boltt, G., & Van Harmelen, U. (1995), Text illustrations: An aid or an obstacle to learning? Experiences with South African teachers, Grahamstown: Rhodes University, Education Department, unpublished

Catling, S. (1995), Mapping the environment with children, in De Villiers, M. (ed.) *Developments in Primary Geography: Theory and Practice.* Sheffield: The Geographical Association

Cohen, L., Manion, L. & Morrison, K. (2000), *Research Methods in Education,* London: Routledge

Denzin, N.K., & Lincoln, Y.S. (1994), Entering the field of qualitative research, in Denzin, N.K., & Lincoln, Y.S. (eds.), *Handbook of Qualitative Research,* Thousand Oaks: Sage, 1-22

Matthews, M. H. (1992), *Making Sense of Place: Children's understandings of large-scale environments,* Hemel Hempstead: Harvester Wheatsheaf.

Molyneux, F. & Tolley, H. (1987), *Teaching Geography,* London: Macmillan.

National Department of Education (1996), *Curriculum Framework for General and Further Education and Training.* Pretoria: Government Printer

Spencer, C., Blades, M., & Morsley, K. (1989), *The Child in the Physical Environment: The development of spatial knowledge and cognition,* Chichester: Wiley & Sons

Spencer, C. (ed). (1995), *Readings in Environmental Psychology: The child's environment*, London: Harcourt Brace

Stake, R.E. (1995), *The Art of Case Study Research,* Thousand Oaks: Sage

Van Harmelen, U. & Boltt, G. (1995), Primary teachers and science and technology: The role of graphicacy in an in-service programme for South African teachers, Unpublished paper, Grahamstown: Rhodes University, Education Department

Wilmot, D. (2002), Investigating Children's Graphic Skills: A South African Case Study, *International Research in Geographical and Environmental Education,* 11 (4), 325-340

Wright, A. (1989), *Pictures for Language Learning,* Cambridge : Cambridge University Press

Yin, R.K. (1989), *Case Study Research: Design and Methods,* Newbury Park: Sage

SECTION 2

TEACHER DEVELOPMENT

Beginning teacher development

Chapter 15

Primary Student Teachers' World Map Knowledge

Simon Catling

Introduction

It has been traditionally regarded that the ability to locate features and places accurately on a map of the world is the province of geography (Lewis & Wigen, 1997; Gregg, Stainton & Leinhardt, 1997; Elkin, 1997). The National Curriculum Geography Programmes of Study in England have included since 1991 the requirement to teach to pupils "the locations of places and environments they study and other significant places and environments" (DfEE/QCA, 1999, 19), and the examples include features to locate on maps of the world, Europe and the British Isles (DES, 1991; DfE, 1995; DfEE/QCA, 1999). As part of their background understanding, trainee primary teachers need to be aware of ways in which they can teach such locational knowledge (Catling, 2002a). Inevitably, however, the question arises as to how well student primary teachers can locate places and environments on maps. There has been limited research in the England and elsewhere into primary student teachers' world map locational knowledge, though several studies have examined college students' and adults' knowledge. The purpose of this study was to consider whether primary student teachers were any less or better informed than previous research indicated.

What do we know of student teachers' world map knowledge?

Adults' world locational knowledge, including that of pre-service teachers, has been the subject of a number of studies. Saarinen (1976) found that university students in different parts of the world tended to exaggerate their home country and region when drawing world maps, a finding also identified by Gould & White in their place preference research (1974). Saarinen also identified that the 'centring' of the world map which students became used to was influential; students in the Americas drew an 'Americas-centred' world map, while Iranian and African students drew a 'European-centred' world map. Gould & White recognised that, while findings about adults' locational knowledge about places are difficult to generalise from, the impact of personal experience and knowledge and of perceptions of places both affect locational competence. They note that adults may *know of* places but not necessarily *know where* they are with any accuracy, if at all, even though they may have been there! In other words, going to places does not mean that adults set them into their 'world map framework', though it does appear that adults have a general mental map of the world.

Helgren (1983) challenged this view, using a world map on which non-geography university students had to mark places named by him. Though scored 'generously', in that close approximations of correct locations were accepted, over half the students could not locate more than half the features accurately and over a quarter could not locate a quarter of the features correctly. Indeed, only the location of the North Atlantic Ocean, Miami and the USSR (Russian Federation) were known by 90% or more of the students. This raised national concern in the USA. A follow up survey, which excluded geography students, by Cross (1987) produced similar though not such dramatic results, with over a third of students unable to locate accurately less than half the countries listed. He argued that gender was an important factor, with males locating countries more accurately than females, as was students' familiarity with media news reports. Cross stated that travel experience was not significant, though students who had travelled to a greater extent in and beyond the U.S.A. located more countries accurately, inferring that greater experience of travelling was advantageous.

In 1988, Gallup conducted an international survey of adults' geographical knowledge. As with many such studies (see: Gould & White, 1974; Saarinen, 1976), the survey used both maps and question & answer techniques. Among their findings about USA citizens were the following:
- adults could only identify half the named places on a world map and on their national map;
- adults could identify only about a third of places in other continents;
- one in seven could not identify their home nation on a world map.

A similar set of findings emerged for citizens of the UK, though several other European nationals fared better. For a number of commentators the results indicated that world map locational knowledge was not strong (eg see: Wilby, 1988; Anon, 1988). It should be noted that the places to be located on the world were mainly countries and were predominantly in the Western world. A similar study, undertaken for National Geographic in 2002 with 18-24 year olds, drew broadly the same conclusions (National Geographic/RoperASW, 2002), though it noted some improvements in world and national map knowledge among those young Americans who had taken a geography programme. British young people, getting just over 50% of world map locations right, fared little better than young Americans did and rather poorly in comparison to Swedes, Germans and Italians. They performed no better on European and Asian maps. Essentially, finding places on world maps remained a problem. The press made similarly critical comments as in the late 1980s (eg Radford, 2002).

Research into teachers' and student teachers' locational knowledge has been conducted in the USA. Chiodo (1993) asked students to draw a free-hand world map. He found that female elementary school student teachers drew the least competent maps compared both to their male counterparts and to secondary colleagues and that their mental maps of the world seemed the least developed in his survey. He comments that his study reinforces Drumheller's (1968) findings that the quality and content of teachers' maps was little different from those produced by 11-12 year olds. However, this contradicts Schneider's (1976) findings, using multiple choice questions, that elementary teachers performed better than 11-12 year olds, though they indicated many of the same map skill and locational problems. Giannangelo & Frazee (1977) also found that elementary teachers had locational knowledge weakness. Cross (1987) identified in his world map location study that teacher education students in the USA were significantly less knowledgeable about place location than students on other courses. More recently, Gregg, Stainton & Leinhardt (1997) identified that student teachers were much weaker at locating states than experienced teachers and primary grade children.

Wiegand and Stiell (1997), in asking post-graduate teacher education students to draw a free-hand map of the British Isles, identified a significant gender difference, with males drawing more accurate maps. They also found that the degree subject of students and their home location were significant, but they found no difference between primary and secondary students. Geography graduates were the most accurate group, though there was variation between these students.

These researchers and other geography educators have argued that student teachers need to develop skills in helping children to learn the locations of places and features on world maps (eg

Lockledge, 1991; Stimpson, 1991; Kapp, 1991; Wiegand, 1992; Weeden, 1996; Gregg, Stainton & Leinhardt, 1997; Catling, 2002a). Some have made the point that student teachers need to develop their own competence and knowledge in order to be able to undertake such teaching effectively (Schneider, 1976; Giannangelo & Frazee, 1977; Chiodo, 1993).

There has been no study of primary student teachers' world map knowledge in relation to the places and environments included in the primary geography national curriculum list (DfEE/QCA, 1999). The purpose of this study was to test, straightforwardly, student teachers' ability to locate accurately places and environments on the world map. In mind was the question: are student primary teachers are poorly informed as the studies cited above indicate?

Research method

The research was undertaken with a group of undergraduate student teachers in the first year of their primary teacher training course in a university in England. They were all following a generalist primary teacher education course and none had a subject specialism. During their programme, all the students undertake a short (12 hour) geography course to introduce them to the national curriculum primary geography requirements. The data were gathered during their first geography sessions.

It was decided to use a similar approach to that used in several of the earlier studies (Helgren, 1983; Cross, 1987; Gregg, Stainton & Leinhardt, 1997). This involved asking respondents to mark on maps the location of named places, to test the accuracy of the student teachers in their location of places and features. As with the Gallup (1988) and National Geographic/RoperASW (2002) studies and with map drawing research (Chiodo, 1993: Wiegand & Stiell, 1997), this method of gathering data relies on the students' memory of places learnt. Testing in this way is a recognised form of research (Cohen, Manion & Morrison, 2000), which provides access to the respondent's remembered knowledge or understanding in a particular topic. The approach to be used was a criterion-referenced test, in which the accuracy of the location of features would be assessed and scored against set criteria. While not focused on individuals as such, the range of respondents' scores would provide a basis for tentative conclusions in relation to the group's overall capability in locating map features from memory as well as providing information on the range of capabilities in the study group.

The research involved two tasks, given one week apart. The student teachers were not informed prior to either test that they would take them; they were unaware that a second test would follow the first. The tests were given at the start of two teaching sessions as part of their initial geographical activities and conducted individually in silence. The first task involved a test of specified locations. The second required students to name their own locations. The students were tested in three groups. Sixty-six students completed the first task and sixty-two students completed the second task. The purposes and formats of the two tasks are outlined below. Both tests were anonymous; individual comparisons could not be made. No background information on the students was gathered.

Task 1: Specified recall

In the first task students were tested on their ability to locate and name specified features. The purpose of this task was to ascertain some sense of their general world locational knowledge. The features selected were considered to be among those likely to be known to the students. All but one (Madagascar) of the features have appeared in the lists of places and environments in the primary geography curriculum (DES, 1991; DfE, 1995; DfEE/QCA, 1999). The specified places and environments are listed in Figure 1.

The features selected for the test represented a range of world features, with a spread of continental locations. They are likely to have been included on world maps and in many cases to have been heard of in the news and to have been encountered in school geography lessons. The types of features included:

- the two basic features of the planet: a continental area and an ocean area;
- four major features on the Earth: a mountain region, an extensive river, a large desert and a large island;
- two countries: the student's home nation and a populous country large in area;
- two major world cities.

Australasia	(continent)	Himalayas	(mountain range)
Arctic Ocean	(ocean)	Sahara	(desert)
New York	(city)	UK	(home country)
Moscow	(city)	China	(country)
Amazon	(river)	Madagascar	(island)

Figure 1: The ten features used in the *Specified Recall* location task

The students were given a blank equal area world map, which contained only an outline of the world's landmasses. They were asked to mark the ten features on the world map, as accurately as possible, by indicating each feature by shading, a line, ringing or another appropriate means and writing its name alongside. The students were read the ten locations, which were also displayed one-by-one on an overhead projector, so that by the end of the test all ten were visible. Students then had a short while to check and complete their map. The test was completed in ten minutes.

The maps were analysed in two ways. Each feature was scored for accuracy of the location on the world map, ranging from 'wild inaccuracy' to 'accurate'. Each map was given an overall feature location score, to indicate the individual student's competence in locating features on a world map. The purpose of the first analysis was to see whether some features were located more accurately than others were by the participants. The purpose of the second analysis was to identify the range of general locational competence among the sample group. The scoring system is given in Figure 2.

Task 2: Open recall

In the second task students were required to select features whose location they felt they knew, without the pressure of locating features chosen by another person. The purpose of this test was to find out whether they exhibited greater accuracy in their location of their self-selected features. It was open to the students to recall and locate the features they chose. Again, they were given a blank equal area world map. They had ten minutes in which to locate and name their selected features on the world map. The same instruction was given about identifying the features they chose, by shading, a line, ringing or marking in some other way and naming those features. They were asked to be as accurate as possible in locating the features. The students were told that they could include any ten features whose location they knew; they could chose which features and there was no requirement to spread them around the world; the only constraint was that they should be features another person could check up on (to avoid the inclusion of idiosyncratically named features, personal to that individual).

The intention for this task was to enable a comparison to be made with the outcome of the first task, focused on the general accuracy in locating features. Each map was scored for accuracy in locating features and given a general score of accuracy. The scoring system used was the same as that applied to the analysis of the first task (see Figure 2). A limitation was that the two maps by each student could not be compared, but the intention in this study was to make a general comparison between the number of students who could locate features selected by another person and those they self-selected. It was predicted that the location of features and places based on self-selection would be more accurate.

The scoring of individual features on the world map

Quality of feature accuracy

5	Accurate
4	Acceptably close
3	Approximate area of location
2	Same continent/region of world
1	Wildly inaccurate
0	No attempt to locate on map

The scoring of general competence in feature location on the world map

Levels of personal accuracy

A	all locations within accurate/acceptably close
B	all locations within accurate/acceptable close/approximate area of location
C	90% locations within accurate/acceptably close/approximate area of location
D	70% locations within accurate/acceptably close/approximate area of location
E	50% locations within accurate/acceptably close/approximate area of location
F	30% locations within accurate/acceptably close/approximate area of location
G	10% locations within accurate/acceptably close/approximate area of location
H	0% locations within accurate/acceptably close/approximate area of location

---

Figure 2: The scoring scales used for Tasks 1 and 2

In considering the results it is important to bear in mind that scoring at level 5 meant pinpoint accuracy and that at level 4 it was a good approximation of the location. Level 3 shows that the student has a clear idea of the general location of the feature or place they have identified. At level 2 the inaccuracy of location is at least off-set by locating the feature or place in roughly the correct region of the globe, while at level 1 there is complete inaccuracy. It is considered that accuracy at levels 4 and 5 is to be prized, while accuracy at level 3 should be thought of as generally acceptable. Scoring of the maps was undertaken by the author, using a template for Task 1 and a number of advanced atlases for Task 2. While there is a limitation to such qualitative judgements of accuracy by one assessor, it provided for consistency in the use and interpretation of the scoring scales and guides.

The initial analysis of the maps indicated that there were other aspects of these maps that should be examined. It was decided that the types of features and places students included should be noted; that is, whether the feature and places named were continents, oceans, cities or physical features, and so forth. This provided the opportunity to examine the balance of types of features and to see whether there was greater accuracy for some features than for others. The balance of global location was also thought worth examination to see whether the students exhibited any regional bias in the selection of features and places. This was undertaken using reference to the generalised notion of the 'North/South' divide (Johnston, Gregory, Pratt & Watts, 2000).

Results

No distinction is made between male and female students or between 'mature' (ie over 23) and 'young' undergraduates. All were over 18 years old, with the large majority between 18 and 23 but included several students aged in the 30s and 40s. Almost all the participants were female (there were only 5 men), reflecting the recruitment to primary initial teacher education. It was, in this, sense a broadly representative sample of undergraduate student teachers.

Task 1: Specified recall

Two analyses of the accuracy of location of the features and places in the Recall task were undertaken. First, the findings in relation to the accuracy of location of the individual features and places are noted. Second, the competence of the students in locating features and places on the world map are outlined.

Only three features and places were not so well known by the students. These are three places that are in the news or conversation with some regularity. There must be concern that less than one-fifth know the location of the River Amazon, though two-thirds are aware of which continent it is in. Two-fifths have a sound idea of the whereabouts of New York, but almost all the rest place it inaccurately in the USA (and some in Canada), though a fair number of these have it at least in the correct half of the continent. All the students knew that Moscow is in the area of the Russian Federation, but it most often was located much further east in Siberia.

World map features	5	4	3	2	1	0
Australasia	-	41%	54.5%	1.5%	1.5%	1.5%
Arctic Ocean	68.5%	10.5%	3%	3%	13.5%	1.5%
Madagascar	51.5%	-	6%	4.5%	24.5%	13.5%
River Amazon	-	9%	9%	45.5%	29%	13.5%
Himalaya mountains	7.5%	20%	25.5%	20%	12%	15%
Sahara Desert	21%	18%	11%	15%	23%	12%
China	-	29%	41%	18%	6%	6%
UK	15%	85%	-	-	-	-
New York	3%	12%	25.5%	58%	1.5%	-
Moscow	-	3%	30%	67%	-	-

Figure 3: Student primary teachers' accuracy of location of specified features in Task 1

There are several striking findings in the results shown in Figure 3. The student primary teachers achieved a competent level of accuracy in locating the majority of features and places they were given. In particular, all students in the sample knew the correct location of the United Kingdom. The reason for the difference between those who were absolutely correct and those who were not was that the former marked the UK to exclude the Republic of Ireland, while the latter circled the British Isles to show where the UK is. In effect, nineteen out of every twenty students know where Australasia is, though just over half of them limit the continent to Australia and New Zealand, whereas conventional wisdom includes a wider area into nearby Pacific islands. Similarly four-fifths of students know the location of the Arctic Ocean. Half the sample could locate Madagascar, the Himalayas and the Sahara desert very or reasonably accurately. Though there was no student who could draw China's border accurately, four-fifths of students know where in the world it is. Thus, four of the features and places are well known to almost all students and three more are accurately located by half the sample.

Three features were very inaccurately located by around a quarter of the sample, and three were not marked at all by over one-tenth of the students. It should not be entirely surprising that Madagascar's location is not really known to almost two-fifths of students, but it may be of more concern that the location of the Himalayas, the River Amazon and the Sahara Desert are not known to a third of students.

Broadly these findings indicate a reasonable level of knowledge of the individual features and places used for this task. The four places well known to the students might suggest that they have a basic mental map of the world, in which the British Isles forms an integral part.

Level of individual accuracy	% of students achieving each level	
	Task 1: Specified Recall	Task 2: Open Recall
A (very high)	-	14.5%
B	6%	37.1%
C	9%	32.3%
D	24.5%	12.9%
E	31.5%	3.2%
F	24.5%	-
G	4.5%	-
H (very weak)	-	-

Figure 4: Student primary teachers' levels of personal accuracy in Tasks 1 and 2

Each student's map was analysed for overall accuracy of locations. While no student could be classified (could any of us?) as being able to locate with virtually pinpoint accuracy 'unseen' specific features and places from memory, one in seven got close on nine or all ten of the features and places asked of them. In fact, two-fifths could locate seven or more of the features and places very or reasonably accurately. Seventy percent of the students could locate half or more of the features and places. In effect, this group of UK student teachers, largely female, would appear to be better informed about locational knowledge than Chiodo (1993) found in his USA sample. The overall level of accuracy is similar in outcome to that found in the recent National Geographic survey for essentially the same age group (National Geographic/RoperASW, 2002).

Nonetheless, Figure 4 also shows for Task 1 that almost three in ten students have a poor mental map of world locations. Indeed those at the lowest level would seem to indicate that they do not have a clear appreciation of even a basic world map framework to which to link other locational information.

Task 2: Open recall

The findings from Task 1 raised the speculation that if student teachers selected their own places and features to locate on a world map, there might be some improvement in the overall level of accuracy. The purpose of this task was to examine this speculation. Several other matters, which the examination of the maps raised, are also noted.

It is quite clear from Figure 4 that student primary teachers, when asked to locate features and places of their own choice, can do so accurately. Indeed, about one in seven students could locate all ten of their self-selected features and places with considerable accuracy. Taking the approximate area of location into account, about two-fifths of students showed themselves to able to place features on maps with a clear idea as to where they are. If a 90% or better success rate is used, almost seventeen out of twenty students can be classified as 'accurate' locators of features and places. Clearly, this result challenges, at least in relation to prospective primary teachers, the findings of both the national survey of UK adults (Gallup, 1988; National Geographic/RoperASW, 2002) and those of other researchers examining student primary teachers' locational knowledge (Drumheller, 1968; Cross, 1987; Chiodo, 1993; Gregg, Stainton & Leinhardt, 1997).

An important finding from these maps is that almost all the students included features and places which might figure in a list of someone else's 'specified' locations. In other words, it is clear that the large majority of students have an effective mental map of the world. Figure 4 shows clearly that all the students in the sample could locate with reasonable or better accuracy at least five features and places. It would seem that some doubt can be cast on the highly critical and negative use of findings of research in which locations are specified by the researcher, rather than left to the choice of the subject (Wilby, 1988; Radford, 2002). That the sample group of student teachers selected features, in the main, which provide them with a framework outline of the world, would support the view, tentatively, that the survey and other findings should be questioned.

The opportunity was taken to analyse the students' open recall maps further. Several other tentative findings emerged. Figure 5 shows both the areas of the world in which the features students selected were located and the accuracy of their location of these features and places. Locations in Europe were clearly dominant. Two-thirds of all the features and places named by the sample were in this continent. Around 10% of locations were in each of the continents of Africa, Asia, Australasia and North America. Interestingly, this would seem to support Wiegand's (1992) findings about primary children's balance of knowledge and Saarinen's (1976) conclusions about the focus of locational knowledge in relation to home country.

The general high level of accuracy in locating features and places is shown by the scoring at levels 5 to 3 (very accurate location to approximately the correct location). Interestingly, a fifth of the features and places in Asia were inaccurately located, though self-selected by students.

% of World cover	Regional location of features	Level of accuracy of location				
		5	4	3	2	1
11.8%	Africa	66.7%	16.7%	13.9%	2.7%	-
0.5%	Antarctica	100.0%	-	-	-	-
10.3%	Asia	22.2%	41.3%	15.9%	19.0%	1.6%
12.5%	Australasia	92.2%	2.6%	1.3%	1.3%	2.6%
40.7%	Europe	33.1%	44.0%	18.5%	4.4%	-
13.1%	North America	32.5%	33.8%	25.0%	6.2%	2.5%
7.4%	South America	57.8%	20.0%	15.5%	2.2%	4.5%
0.8%	Arctic Ocean	80.0%	-	-	20.0%	-
1.6%	Atlantic Ocean	80.0%	-	10.0%	10.0%	-
0.2%	Indian Ocean	100.0%	-	-	-	-
0.8%	Pacific Ocean	80.0%	-	-	-	20.0%
0.3%	Southern Ocean	-	100.0%	-	-	-

Figure 5: Accuracy of location of features by student primary teachers in Task 2

The features and places which students included were categorised in terms of the type of feature they are. Figure 6 lists the six main types of feature that could be clearly identified from the students' world maps, though one type of feature predominated. The 'other features' noted covered states in the USA, a canal, seas and a regional name.

It would seem that the major feature that underpins students' world mental maps is countries. Every student in the sample included at least one country (see: Figure 7), with 79% of students listing five or more countries in their chosen locations. Only 3% of the sample listed only countries. At least three different types of feature were included by 79% of the sample. Over 90% of the countries located by students were reasonably accurately marked, of which one-third were shown very accurately with their borders. There is a possible connection here with student primary teachers' ideas about geography, where many of them see geography as about countries and the world at large (Catling, 2002b, forthcoming).

% of types of features	Type of features	Level of accuracy of location				
		5	4	3	2	1
10.6%	Continent	93.7%	3.1%	1.6%	1.6%	-
3.3%	Ocean	80.0%	10.0%	-	5.0%	5.0%
62.8%	Country	32.9%	42.1%	18.2%	5.5%	1.3%
8.1%	City/town	18.4%	44.9%	20.4%	14.3%	2.0%
11.9%	Island	83.3%	5.6%	8.3%	2.8%	-
1.2%	Physical features	28.6%	42.8%	14.3%	-	14.3%
2.1%	Other features	53.8%	15.4%	15.4%	15.4%	-

Figure 6: Student primary teachers' levels of accuracy of location by types of feature in Task 2

Around one-tenth of the features marked were continents, islands or cities and towns. As with countries these were very largely accurately located on the world map. While Figure 3 indicates that students had some difficulty in locating the cities of New York and Moscow accurately, Figure 6 shows that self-chosen cities and towns are able to be much more accurately located. There seems to be little trouble in locating the continents or oceans; yet, as with the Arctic Ocean in the Task 1, knowledge is sometimes adrift for a very few students.

The information provided in Figure 7 indicates that many students included either continents or islands (or indeed both: 37%) on their world maps, alongside countries. It would seem that these three types of feature are also part of most student teachers' mental maps of the world. Some two-fifths also use cities/towns to help 'frame' their sense of the world.

It was clear that European locations dominated the students' world mental maps (see: Figure 5). Figures 7 and 8 provide strong evidence for not just the Eurocentric balance of their world maps, but of the dominance of The North (or Western World) in their 'view', and perhaps experience, of the world. Discounting oceans, which cannot be readily classified as in The North or The South (or Third World), from Figure 7 it can be seen that for continents it is The South which predominates, though this is the only southern feature which does. Of the 'southern' continents, Africa is mentioned more than South America. Three-fifths of the sample listed one or more 'southern' continents, while just less than one-seventh of students included 'northern' continents.

While all students included countries, three-fifths of the sample list countries from The North and The South and one-third list only countries from The North. Though, given the sample numbers, it is problematic to assert that there is no really significant difference in the accuracy of the location of the countries mentioned, it would seem that countries in The North are more accurately known than those in The South. About 60% of Third World countries were accurately mapped, while nearly 80% of Western countries were located accurately. 14.5% of countries in The South were very inaccurately located; about 6% were in The North.

% of types of features	Type of features	% listing features only in The North	% listing features in The North and The South	% listing features only in The South
63%	Continent	3%	23%	74%
21%	Ocean	-	100%	-
100%	Country	36%	61%	3%
40%	City/town	68%	16%	16%
61%	Island	45%	31%	24%
10%	Physical features	50%	-	50%
24%	Other features	75%	-	25%

Figure 7: % of student primary teachers including types of features on their world maps

While about half the sample located an island in The North (essentially, either Greenland or Iceland), just over one-third mapped an island in The South (usually Madagascar, indicating some influence perhaps from Test 1, undertaken a week before). In fact, only 20% of the students included islands from both the North and The South. The cities included by two-fifths of the sample are dominated by The North.

Balance of mentions	Location of countries	5	4	3	2	1
80%	Countries in The North	39.9%	39.1%	16.1%	3.9%	1.0%
20%	Countries in The South	5.3%	54.0%	26.3%	11.9%	2.6%

Figure 8: Accuracy and balance of countries mentioned by student primary teachers

Further evidence of the dominance of a Western world-view is shown by Figures 9 and 10. Figure 9 shows that almost nine-tenths of students included six or more features and places from The North, while less than one-tenth of students 'favoured' The South. Figure 10 indicates that almost half the sample had at least eight of their ten self-selected features and places from The North. This evidence does not just simply reinforce the sense of Western dominance in our world-view; it demonstrates that it is already very strongly embedded in many younger adults. Less than 7% of the sample have a world mental map which has 'Southern' dominance.

Emphasising The North	Equally North and South	Emphasising The South
87.1%	4.8%	8.1%

Figure 9: % of student primary teachers emphasising North or South

Balance of North/South features	% of student teachers
North 10/0 South	5.1%
9/1	16.9%
8/2	27.1%
7/3	16.9%
6/4	22.0%
North 5/5 South	5.2%
4/6	1.7%
3/7	1.7%
2/8	3.4%
1/9	-
North 0/10 South	-

Figure 10: Balance of North/South Features mentioned by student primary teachers

Conclusion

This study was deliberately limited in scope. It has, as a result, limitations, including the lack of comparability of the two Tasks at an individual level, no background information about individuals which might indicate influences on their world map and locational knowledge, and the limited size and scope of the sample of first year undergraduates. While the results provide some very tentative but stimulating outcomes, more importantly, perhaps, the study raises several questions.

The first question is this: is students' knowledge of the world as limited and inaccurate as earlier research might indicate that it is? There have been claims made that it is essential to include the learning of 'key' locations in national curriculum geography for key stages 1 and 2 (DES/WO, 1990), because concerns exist about the quality and depth of adults' world locational knowledge (Gallup, 1988; Chiodo, 1993; National Geographic/ RoperASW, 2002). The findings from Task 1 in the research reported here would appear initially to substantiate the national survey views of adults' world map/locational knowledge. However, Task 2 allowed student teachers to demonstrate that they not only know of places and features but also very largely can locate these accurately on a world map. It might be considered that students are advantaged in selecting their own locations, but the variety of places included by students indicates that they use a variety of features to frame their mental maps of the world. As such, the findings of the national surveys and other research become less clear-cut than the interpretations of their findings would seem to indicate. It would seem that some questions must be asked about the validity of the selection of places by researchers for others to specify on maps. In Task 1 five of the ten locations were in The South; in the national surveys, only a third of the sixteen places to locate were in The South (Gallup, 1988; National Geographic/RoperASW, 2002). Task 1 also contained a greater variety of features: five were listed as physical features, including the island of Madagascar. Of the national survey's sixteen, only two (1988) and one (2002) were not countries. There is some synergy here in that in Task 2 the student teachers demonstrated that their world maps are, for many, framed around countries, echoing the focus of the national surveys.

The second question concerns how students' world maps are framed: what are the types of places and features which adults use to build up their mental maps? If it is the case that student teachers have a basic framework for their world map knowledge, there is a need for more research to identify what this might be. Certainly, from Task 2, there is the implication that knowledge of countries plays an important role. If Weeden (1996) is correct in arguing that an understanding of 'country' is a challenge for primary children when building their understanding of 'nesting' relationships, and that these understandings are essential to developing an effective framework of locational knowledge, it may well be that the foundations of a world map are only laid rudimentarily at primary school level and are actually built up effectively during adolescence, in secondary school. A linked question must concern when it might be best to expect achievement by children in their world map knowledge. But is it secondary education, with its increased study of countries in geography, which helps to frame pupils' world mental maps? Does topical information in day-to-day life as a young and older adult have an impact? If so, how? Might the process be complex? How people develop their world mental maps is still not well understood (Gould & White, 1974; Kitchen & Freundschuh; Kitchen & Blades, 2002).

The third question concerns perspectives on the world reflected through world map knowledge: what is the impact of a Eurocentric background and context on developing an informed and balanced world mental map? There is evidence (see Gould & White, 1974; Saarinen, 1976; Wiegand, 1992) that our knowledge of the world is influenced by our perceptions of it, and that these perceptions in turn influence the knowledge which we 'accept' about the world at large, basic knowledge which is reflected in our mental maps. The evidence from Task 2 in this study indicates that a Northern/Western perspective dominates student teachers' mental maps of the world. As a result, the concern must be that those who are training to teach, as well as experienced teachers, carry a Eurocentric perspective into the classroom unconsciously, which will influence their teaching, even of world map knowledge. If a Northern bias is the way teachers 'see' the world, how will they really enable children to develop a more global sense of the world? Indeed, should world map knowledge in national curriculum geography be oriented more towards knowledge of places and features in The South to counterbalance the Western worldview?

Finally, there are the questions that this study did not set out to consider. Is there a gender issue for primary pre-service teachers in learning place knowledge? Is there any difference in the knowledge of 'mature' and 'young' student teachers? More valuably, if individual student maps were collected with this and other data to enable comparison of individual performance on both the map tasks, what further information and understandings might come to light? Given the teaching of national curriculum geography in primary and secondary schools, is it possible to discern any improvement in pupils' world map knowledge, and will this filter through into the teaching profession? However, could this simply reinforce the current world map knowledge limitations rather than challenge them?

This small, initial study has identified some tentative conclusions and several further avenues for research. It would seem that relatively straightforward tasks, such as those described above, with student primary teachers can provide insights which other more focused and rigorous studies may well have not considered! Were these task to be undertaken as part of a primary geography programme for prospective teachers and examined and discussed by the students, might they not provide for them some direct insight into what they know and what they might need to consider in heir tmental world map?

References

Anon (1988), Here be foreigners, *The Economist*, July 30, 42

Catling, S. (2002a), *Placing Places*, Sheffield: Geographical Association

Catling, S. (2002b), English Primary Trainee Teachers Ideas about Geography: A Sense of Environmental Concern? In Mngoma, W. & Hattingh, P. (eds.), *Education for Sustainable Living*: Proceedings of the International Geographic Union Commission on Geographical Education, Richards Bay, August, 27-32

Catling, S. (forthcoming), An Understanding of Geography: The Perspectives of English Primary Trainee Teachers, *GeoJournal*

Chiodo, J. J. (1993), Mental Maps: Preservice Teachers' Awareness of the World, *Journal of Geography*, May-June, 110-117

Cohen, L., Manion, L. & Morrison, K. (2000), *Research Methods in Education*, London: RoutledgeFalmer

Cross, J. A. (1987), Factors Associated with Students' Place Location Knowledge, *Journal of Geography*, March-April, 59-63

DES/WO (1990), *Geography for Ages 5 to 16*, London: DES/WO

DES (1991), *Geography in the National Curriculum (England)*, London: HMSO

DfE (1995), *Geography in the National Curriculum (England)*, London: HMSO

DfEE/QCA (1999), *The National Curriculum for England: Geography*, London: DfEE/QCA

Drumheller, S.J. (1968), Conjure up a map: A crucial but much neglected skill, *Journal of Geography*, February, 140-146

Elkin, S. (1997), Youngsters don't know their place in the world, *The Times*, January 31

Gallup (1988), *Geography: An International Survey*, Princeton: The Gallup Organization

Giannangelo, D.M. & Frazee, B.M. (1977), Map reading proficiency of elementary educators, *Journal of Geography*, February, 63-65

Gould, P. & White, R. (1974), *Mental Maps*, Harmondsworth: Penguin

Gregg, M., Stainton, C. & Leinhardt, G. (1997), Strategies for Geographic Memory: Oh, What a State We're In!, *International Research in Geographical and Environmental Education*, 6(1), 41-59

Helgren, D.M. (1983), Place Name Ignorance is National News, *Journal of Geography*, July-August, 176-178

Johnston, R., Gregory, D., Pratt, G.& Watts, M. (eds.) (2000), *The Dictionary of Human Geography*, Oxford: Blackwell

Kapp, B.M. (1991), 'A Magic Carpet Trip to Learning Geography', *Journal of Geography*, July-August, 174-178

Kitchen, R. & Blades, M. (2002), *The Cognition of Geographic Space*, London: I.B.Tauris

Kitchen, R. & Freundschuh, S (eds.) (2000), *Cognitive Mapping: Past, present and future*, London: Routledge

Lewis, M.W, & Wigen, K.E. (1997), *The Myth of Continents*, Berkeley: University of California Press

Lockledge, A. (1991), Elementary Place Geography: Beyond Memorization, *Journal of Geography*, January-February, 33-36

National Geographic/RoperASW (2002), *National Geographic-Roper 2002 Global Geographic Literacy Survey*, http://www.nationalgeographic.com   accessed November 24, 2002 and July 9 2004

Radford, T. (2002), Adrift on an ocean of geographic ignorance, *The Guardian*, November 21, 8

Saarinen, T.F. (1976), *Environmental Planning: Perception and Behaviour*, Boston: Houghton Mifflin

Schneider, D.O. (1976), The Performance of Elementary Teachers and Students on a Test of Map and Globe Skills, *Journal of Geography*, November, 326-332

Stimpson, P.G. (1991), Is It a Long Way to Tipperary? Suggestions for Improving Students Locational Knowledge, *Journal of Geography*, March-April, 78-82

Weeden, P. (1996), What is the capital of France and where is Burkina Faso?, *Primary Geographer*, July, 12-13

Wiegand, P. (1992), *Places in the Primary School*, Lewes: Falmer

Wiegand, P. & Stiell, B. (1997), Mapping the Place Knowledge of Teachers in Training, *Journal of Geography in Higher Education*, 21(2), 187-198

Wilby, P. (1988), British know little about the world and care even less, *The Independent*, London, December 29th

Chapter 16

Knowledge Bases for Effective Teaching: A case study of one beginning teacher's development as a teacher of primary geography

Fran Martin

Introduction

Research into the quality of teaching has focused on the relative importance of different types of professional knowledge (Smyth, 1987; Novak, 1998; Turner-Bisset, 2001), and some have suggested that enhanced subject content knowledge is most influential in teacher effectiveness (Alexander, Rose & Whitehead, 1992). At the same time other research has shown that good subject knowledge is not necessarily the most influential factor (Bennett & Carré, 1993). Bennett and Carré's research on student teacher learning showed that students enter Initial Teacher Education (ITE) courses with 'strong ideas' about subjects, teaching and the role of the teacher and that these can affect what students learn and accept as valid knowledge (Tillema & Knoll, 1997).

An important part of these 'strong ideas' is the set of values a student, or teacher, holds. It has been demonstrated that there is a relationship between teachers' values and their professional development (Lewis & Cowie, 1993), but one of the difficulties is that values are frequently implicit and therefore hard to articulate. In addition, professional values are highly contestable. However, research has shown that where practitioners are enabled to become aware of, and criticise, their tacit frames this has been a critical part of the process of professional development (Beyerbach, 1988; Ghaye, et. al., 1997).

Background to the project

Previous research (Martin, 2000) in the field of primary geography showed that, while the majority of primary students are 'novice' geographers, even those who held a geography degree seemed to have difficulties putting their image of geography into practice. The tentative conclusion, at the time, was that students' images of, and beliefs about, *teaching and learning* were also a key factor.

The conclusions drawn from this research led to a restructuring of the geography component of a primary PGCE course in a higher education institution. The revised programme sought to elicit students conceptions of geography *and* teaching and learning at the outset and to use these conceptions as the basis for comparison with each other, with experienced geography educators, and with images portrayed in the media and so on. The key aim of the geography component was now 'to develop students' deep, flexible knowledge of geography in order to enhance their capacity to plan, teach and assess pupils' geographical knowledge, understanding and skills' (UCW, 1999). The principles underpinning this are stated in the programme outline, received by all students:

Children, students, teachers and geographers are all learners of geography. The ideas we each construct about the world will differ according to previous experience and may be alternative to standard geographic accounts. Accordingly, the course promotes a challenging yet supportive learning culture in which personal meanings can be acknowledged and evaluated openly. (UCW Geography Component Outline, 1999)

In short, the course aimed to develop students' subject and pedagogical content knowledge by encouraging them to act as geographers themselves, to reflect on their learning and to apply this to:

- their understanding of children as learners,
- how they might transform their geographical knowledge into forms that are understandable to young children.

The aims of the research project stemmed from the need to address students' poor subject knowledge (and the negative attitude that was often associated with this lack of knowledge), from the wish to examine to role of pedagogical content knowledge in students' development, and finally to provide an empirical base upon which critically to evaluate the course. The aims were, thus, to:

- identify student teachers' conceptions and values about geographical education in ways that allow them to be appropriately represented, understood and acted upon;
- explore the impact of student teachers' conceptions and values on their development as teachers of primary geography;
- consider the impact of the findings for ITE course design and implementation.

Methodology

In essence, the methodology is *interpretative* in nature and falls broadly within the phenomenological tradition. As it is a piece of interpretative research it seeks to generate knowledge (Corney, 1998) and makes use of a multi-method approach, advocated by Reid et. al. (1997, 228) as a means of motivating 'participants to explore and make explicit thoughts and feelings of a personal nature ... that are not normally the subject of routine, conscious reflection'. In this respect the methods are drawn from various traditions and are designed to collect both qualitative and quantitative data. A summary of research tools is shown in Figure 1.

The concept mapping elicitation tasks were developed according to advice from Novak (1998) and Ghaye & Robinson (1989). They were chosen as a research tool for their ability to 'portray ideas, beliefs, values and attitudes and their relationship one to another in a form which is amenable to study and analysis' (Northcott, 1996, 457). All students were given the same eight *geographical terms* – physical features, environment, local, global, mapping, climate, people and places – which were the eight most commonly used terms in the pilot project conducted in 1998-9. The reason for providing some initial terms was that, in the pilot phase, feedback from students who had little background in geography indicated that they found it hard to even get started. Other drawbacks to note about using concept maps are:

- The act of creating a concept map can lead to students recognising 'new relationships and hence new meanings they did not consciously hold before making the map (Novak & Godwin, 1984, 17). *The concept mapping task had the joint purpose of being a teaching as well as an elicitation tool, so this was not perceived as an issue.*

- Some students may find it harder to represent their ideas in a graphical format than in other ways (Baugh & Mellott, 1998). *The interviews asked, 'do you feel the concept map enabled you to represent your conception successfully?'*
- Attention, therefore, needs to be given to the developing students' concept mapping skills if they are to be used as a formal assessment tool (Caelli, 1998). *This was built into the beginning of the course.*

Tools for gathering data	Purpose of tools	Tools for analysing data
1. Concept map made before geography component, concept map annotated after geography component.	To elicit conceptions of geography To identify changes in conception after input.	Use of scoring system to develop categories for whole cohort. Category 1 = most sophisticated; category 4 = least sophisticated conception of geography.
2. Written accounts of learning and teaching.	To elicit conceptions of teaching and learning	Analysed against classification system 'theories of teaching'.
3.Use of theoretical frameworks to stimulate students' thinking during interviews (Barrett Hacking, 1996; John, 1996; Fien, 1993).	To elicit values and beliefs underpinning conceptions To aid analysis of data	Used as part of coding systems for analysis of data gathered in 1, 2, 4 & 6.
4. Stimulated recall interviews – semi-structured, using tools 1-3 above as the basis for discussion.	To gain insight into students' perspectives and to validate researcher's interpretation of elicitation data	'Eye ball' analysis to give focus for school observations and interviews. Microsoft WORD – index and cross-referencing functions to analyse against coding system.
5.Observation of teaching, recorded in note form focusing on actions and talk.	To provide a stimulus for discussion which focuses on students' conceptions in action	Analysed qualitatively through discussion with participant during post observation interview.
6. Post observation interviews – semi-structured, using tools 1-3 & 5 above as the basis for discussion.	To explore with students their conceptions in action and the values that underpin these	Microsoft WORD – index and cross-referencing functions to analyse against coding system.
7. Research diary.	To record ongoing ideas, reflections, evaluations throughout the whole process, including initial formulation of research proposal.	

Figure 1: Research tools

The elicitation of conceptions of geography, teaching and learning was conducted with the whole cohort [n=79] in September 1999, the analysis of which enabled the identification of four groups of students whose conceptions of geography ranged from most to least sophisticated. From this a smaller sample [n=10] was selected who agreed to participate in the research in greater depth. These were chosen to be representative of the following:

- geographer or non-geographer,
- Early Years or Later Years specialist,
- traditional/non-traditional entrant,
- degree of sophistication of geographical conception,
- conception of teaching and learning.

Of these, four students participated in the project for a two-year period, one of whose case study is presented below.

Data for the case studies were gathered using steps 4-6 in Figure 1. Stimulated recall interview is a technique that has been employed in a number of different ways but 'generally involves the replay of videotape or audiotape of a teacher's lesson in order to stimulate a commentary upon the teacher's thought processes at the time' (Calderhead, 1981, 211). Clearly, elicitation data are not the same as video or audiotaped material. However, since the purpose of the interview was partly to try to explore the students' thought processes when they were making their concept maps, it seemed to distinguish the technique being used from the usual structured, semi-structured or unstructured type. The stimulus for recall was thus either the concept map or the classroom observation notes.

Case study of D

D has been selected as the case study to report here because his conception of geography was seen to be among the most sophisticated in the cohort, but he had had little experience of working in primary schools beyond the requisite two-week period prior to starting the PGCE course. The purpose of this particular case is, therefore, to show how his gradually developing understanding of pedagogical knowledge enabled him, over a two-year period, to utilise his sophisticated conception of geography more and more successfully in his teaching.

D is a mature student in his mid-thirties who had a career in ballet dancing before taking a BSc in Geography and Sociology during 1995-7. He studied geography at school between the ages of 7-16 and achieved an 'O' level Grade B. As a result of his experiences at school D developed a very positive attitude towards geography. He particularly remembers enjoying learning about different parts of the world and about environmental issues.

D's conception of geography and geographical education at the start of the course

D's initial concept map (Figure 2) has a clear structure, which is cyclical rather than hierarchical in nature. It shows a conception of geography that is centred on the inter-relationship between three key elements of people, place and environment. D's map shows these elements as being affected by a number of physical and social processes and the degree of impact of these processes being determined by the scale at which they occur. Of the eight terms provided D chose to use six, and added three of his own – *scale*, *processes* and *social*.

D's concept map appears to have elements of both the scientific and humanistic/welfare persuasions (Barratt Hacking, 1996). The map reflects a conception of geography that identifies and examines a variety of processes; it also has a clear focus on people, and their cultural and social organisations. Although D's concept map did not reflect the active enquiry element, it did represent complex geographical relationships within a clear structure. The fact that he had also not slavishly used the key terms provided is also an indication of a higher level of understanding

(Ghaye and Robinson, 1986), and his concept map was accordingly placed in Category 1 – the most sophisticated conception of geography.

D's written accounts of how and why he might teach elements of his concept map indicated an implicit theory of teaching that was a mixture of transfer (teacher imparts knowledge to passive child), shaping [moulding child to preconceived pattern] and travelling [acting as 'expert' guide, but letting child choose path] (John, 1996). An interesting element of the written account was that the question, 'what would be the benefits for children's learning?', elicited a conception of geography that was more values based and incorporated a more active, investigative approach than was evident in his concept map.

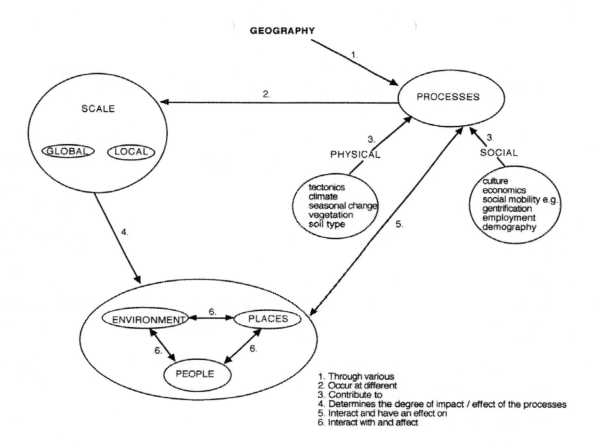

Figure 2: D's concept map elicited September 1999

What conceptions were evident in his interview?

D's interview revealed a conception of geography broadly similar to that inferred from his concept map. It was clear that he had drawn extensively on his geography degree

> *I remembered this model I'd seen [at university] and I thought – that'll be an easy way of doing it,*

but was then concerned about the limitations of models in general for representing highly complex ideas

The more I looked, the harder it got because I found it more difficult to make it clear exactly what I was thinking. ... I thought at one point that perhaps I knew too much.

D's expressed theory of teaching, on the other hand, was quite different to that inferred from the data. He was adamant that he did not adhere to a transfer theory of teaching, but indicated that he believed in aspects of all the others

Perhaps more ... the growing theory [resource provider, facilitator, social context], but I like some bits of shaping and travelling.

D indicated that the inclusion of values in geography was important to him, but that it was quite a novel idea that this could legitimately be part of primary school children's geographical education.

Teaching children to investigate their own values through the village task thing ... I thought was a really good way of developing geographical knowledge ... which I hadn't really thought about.

It was evident in the interview that D had some clear ideas about what to teach in geography and why, but he was hazy and muddled in his thinking about *how* to do so. This indicates a fairly narrow pedagogical base in contrast to his broad and complex geographical base.

D's conceptions in action

Examination of D's observed teaching episodes revealed other aspects of his understanding and application.

Teaching episode 1 June 2000
D was observed teaching a Y6 class in an inner city school. During his interview there is evidence that D is drawing on his humanistic/welfare persuasion in his focus on different people's perceptions of what makes a good environment,

I was trying to get out the distinction between different people's perceptions of what a good environment is;

the decision-making process,

what we were doing was looking at lots of different ways to deal with one problem ... then think of ways of improving, bearing in mind that one solution may not be enough;

and his desire to raise pupils' awareness of the social side,

one of the things that came up was about feeling safe. I thought it would be a good thing to do ... it's not just the physical environment, it's also your attitudes and all the rest of it towards it. If you don't feel safe then for you it's not a good environment no matter how pretty it is.

D was also drawing on his knowledge of educational theory in his ideas about how to help children learn these things.

I was also trying to develop the thinking that I was telling you about ... making that link with science where we looked at the results and then we considered the evidence, and so in geography we could just as well do the same. We've got evidence from the fieldtrip and now we need to consider it.

But the reality was very different because this evidence [pupils' notebooks, photographs, posters] was either not available or not explicitly drawn on during the lesson, so the pupils worked from memory.

Yes, ... but it was there for them to refer to, and in any case from their memory they were fine ...

The activity sequence also jumped from identification of a problem to asking the pupils to design a way of communicating a solution, thus missing out the skills of identifying a range of solutions, evaluating them and deciding which was the most suitable alternative.

It seems as though D's experience as a learner still predominates, and so his pedagogical content knowledge [PCK] is relatively small because his conception of teaching and learning does not help him to utilise his geography content knowledge base effectively. The key teaching strategy he said he was using during the introduction was

mainly teaching, I suppose, but not direct teaching, just sort of question and answer, discussion ... discussing issues that arise out of whatever it is we're looking at,

and during the activity phase, he said he was

just on hand if they wanted anything, different resources than the ones I'd planned. But mainly I wanted to ensure they were all not messing about, that they were co-operating.

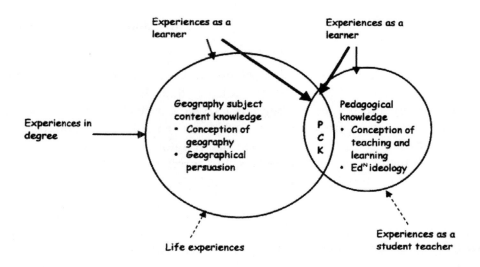

Key: PCK = Pedagogical Content Knowledge
........▶ = these experiences, are having less impact than solid lines;
━━▶ = these experiences are being most heavily drawn on in the act of teaching

Figure 3: Teaching episode 1 – D is working from the base of learner

It is possible to hypothesise that D is working from the base of learner in the conceptions of teaching and learning he is using (Figure 3), and that this not only prevents him from being able to transform his geographical knowledge into a form that is understandable to pupils, it also appears to be affecting how he makes sense of other experiences he has in school. For example, he interprets his observations of an experienced teacher scaffolding pupils' learning as 'clever questioning'.

> *With the class teacher I've seen that through her questioning techniques they [pupils] do ... the thinking is prompted so they do get there. She hasn't sort of given them the answers but through clever questioning they get there.*

Yet when applying this to his own practice, he transforms it into a teacher-led, question and answer session. His personal theory appears to be that learning should be child-centred, but his understanding of this is that 'you can't tell them things'. He wants the children to learn (gain knowledge) but thinks they should come up with the ideas themselves.

> *I wanted to see what they would come up with. I didn't want to influence them.*

Finally, his view of successful learning at this point is product orientated

> *It worked out alright because they all finished the task.*

As in his original interview, D continues to place value on developing pupils' thinking skills, but he does not seem to have a range of useful conceptual frameworks at his disposal to do this, and his knowledge of the range of teaching strategies he could employ is limited. The predominant experience he has to fall back on is that of learner of geography.

Teaching episode 2: March 2001
In September 2000, D took up his first teaching post in a small, catholic primary school. He had responsibility for a Year 1 class.

The lesson observed in March 2001 was on the local area and focused on land use and associated jobs available. Analysis of the data for this lesson indicates that D's knowledge of teaching and learning strategies is growing and that this is beginning to have a positive effect on his teaching, as well as on the children's engagement in the activities. It could be hypothesised that the growing pedagogical knowledge meant that more of his geographical knowledge was useful to him because he could see better how to transform it into forms that are helpful to children – in other words, his pedagogical content knowledge had increased.

Evidence of this can be seen in the way that the learning activities had shifted from requiring children to recall [as they were in June 2000] to enabling them to recognise (see Matthews, 1992, for research on recall and recognition tasks) and develop their own meanings about geographical phenomena. For example, the children were organised in groups for the introduction; each group had a set of photos [not the same for each group] and D's first comments to the class were:

> *Now give yourself about two minutes to remind yourself what we took on the photos.*

D was using maps and photos as a way of representing the local environment [visited for fieldwork the previous week] in a concrete way for young children. In this way, consciously or not, the activity automatically became more enquiry based and child-centred, as the children's cognitive processes were more focused on 'making sense of', [using the questions "What is it used for?" and "Who uses it?"] than 'remembering'. D was also recorded as saying:

We can work it out together.
We're all detectives now.

However, after an interesting mixture of group and class interaction for the first part of the lesson, the remainder [35 minutes] was still a teacher-led, question and answer discussion.

During the post observation interview, D's thoughts indicate that while he is beginning to be better able to draw on his geographical base, he is still unclear about what conceptual frameworks might help scaffold children's learning and this has led him to using tried and tested approaches, rather than taking more risks and trying out new approaches.

Yes, and I've done that a lot. I've just repeated something that's worked almost to death and now they're bored with it. But I have started to try new things ... I sort of feel like I should be doing a better job helping them, but I haven't got the skill or the experience or even the confidence maybe to try a certain way.

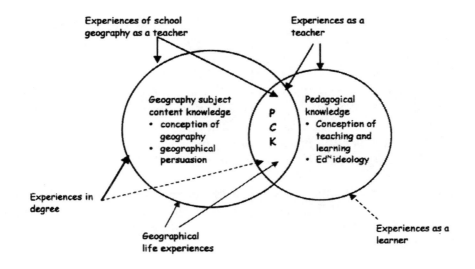

Key: PCK = Pedagogical Content Knowledge
............▶ = these experiences, are having less impact than solid lines;
──────▶ = these experiences are being most heavily drawn on in the act of teaching

Figure 4: Teaching episode 2 – D beginning to make the transition from base of learner to base of teacher

This could be evidence that he is shifting from the base of learner to teacher (Figure 4), but that this is causing him dissatisfaction [perhaps similar to the deconstruction stage in constructivist theory] and a loss of confidence at this stage. Nonetheless, he is organising the children's thoughts in some way, and this seems to be due to his pedagogical notion of 'readiness'. He is doing this in a way that indicates he is drawing much more successfully on that part of his pedagogical knowledge base that is informed by his educational ideology. For instance, he chose to organise the children in mixed ability, friendship groups because

They would have supported the people around them;

and

> *I did two sets of photos but I didn't give them all the same, so they've all got a different selection ... so they weren't all talking about the same thing.*

Later on, when discussing the fieldwork undertaken the previous week, D spoke about his teaching strategy.

> *I purposely never answered anyone's questions. I just posed questions ... and a little ripple would go back down and they'd stop and think and shout out answers, but I never actually said, I never agreed or disagreed.*

This was the first indication that he is encouraging the children to generate their own meanings and that knowledge is not certain, but open to interpretation. As the interview progressed, D was asked

> Do they know when you're doing these things that these are called geography lessons and that geographers think in different ways to ... scientists?

He did not think they did. But he then reflected on this and why it might be an appropriate strategy to use, and reached what might be called a 'road to Damascus' moment when he said,

> *but then half of that is also ... it's not just the intention, I mean it's not a conscious intention for me not to do it but I am aware that I don't do it. But the thing of saying ' this is what geographers do' is perhaps because I'm not even thinking like that myself! I'm not even thinking right, maps, that is what geographers do, so you see what I mean? So I need to. ... So I need to put my geography hat on and say right, I've got to think for this session I've got to think like a geographer haven't I?*

This could be interpreted as D being at a stage in his development where he has moved from the base of learner to teacher, but that this has not yet incorporated his geographical base. However, the comments above indicate that he is becoming aware of how he might incorporate the base of geographer within his teaching.

Teaching episode 3: June 2001
This lesson was observed at the end of June, almost 4 months after the previous one. The geography unit continued to focus on the local area, and the lesson itself had the aim of helping children explore who visits their school and what the implications of this are.

Analysis of the data for this lesson indicates that D's area of pedagogical content knowledge [PCK] has grown. This is characterised as 'working from the base of geography teacher'. The key elements he appears to be drawing on to inform his PCK are his degree geography, his and the children's geographical life experiences, his growing experiences as a teacher and an accompanying broader theoretical base [personal and established theory]. It could be hypothesised that this growing pedagogical knowledge has enabled him to utilise more of his geographical knowledge (Figure 5). Geographical and pedagogical knowledge, therefore, begin to blend together, creating a larger area of PCK; and his geographical knowledge begins to be embedded in his practice. In terms of his conceptions, this is evident in the match between his preferred ways of working and what is observed in action.

The lesson was introduced by D saying,

This afternoon we're carrying on the work we've started in our Geography. [Writes geography on the board, reminds children of last week's work on traffic survey]

As for the lesson observed in March, the children worked in groups and have photographs of various people [or in some cases artefacts that represent people – such as the milk crate] to work from – a recognition task. The whole approach was then, through a careful interchange of collaborative group and teacher-led/whole class activities, to enable the children to develop their own set of criteria that would help them to identify what a visitor is. D records on the board examples offered by children:

They knock on the door.
They don't work here all the time.
People who come from outside the school.
People who come from far away.

And this is achieved through an enquiry approach.

Today we're going to think about people who visit the school. What's that special word we use?
Identify
Yes! I was going to write investigate but identify is better.

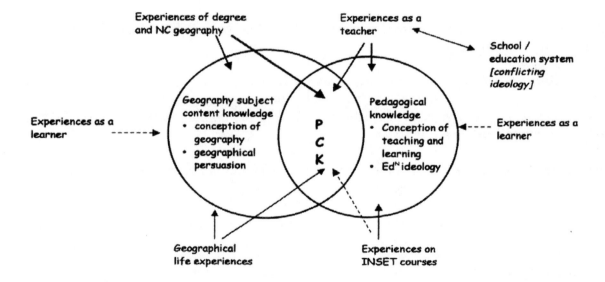

Key: PCK = Pedagogical Content Knowledge
┄┄┄► = these experiences, are having less impact than solid lines;
——► = these experiences are being most heavily drawn on in the act of teaching

Figure 5: Teaching episode 3 – D working from the base of geography teacher

The activity enabled them to do this by sorting the photos into sets of their own choosing and, reflecting his socially critical ideology, D was communicating the message that there is no right or wrong answer – but a range of alternatives that can be discussed and evaluated for their usefulness.

I said we were going to generate a definition of a visitor. I didn't want to come up with one. I just wanted to think about it ... I didn't want to tell them, I wanted them to work it out.

The focus for the lesson indicates that his humanistic/welfare persuasion was still very influential in this:

And the sort of humanistic/welfare bit is, I feel, the challenging stereotypes and the subjective nature of the whole thing, that just because one book or one person says such and such, your experience might be totally different ...

Evidence that his pedagogical knowledge base was growing can be seen in his comments:

They would have to have it sorted out I their minds if they had to tell me. If I'd just told them it would have been more passive wouldn't it?

Yeah, a thing I picked up from a conference about children and their concentration levels. I have major concentration problems here, so just change the strategy – have a chat to your partner about it

This growing pedagogical base is, perhaps, what has helped him create clearer conceptual framework for both his planning.

Following today's session, next week we're going to look at – well, if these people come every day as visitors what are the implications of that? Where do they stop? Do they all use a car, do they come on bikes? What are the implications for the school?, which is going to lead on to the issue.

and his teaching [his talk during the activity phases is predominantly about teaching/scaffolding rather than monitoring/managing, as it was in June 2000].

It gave me a nice opportunity to go round and get the specifics. I did go round all the groups and structure the conversation in that way.

The growing PCK also means that he is now better able to identify what are more appropriate ways of representing geographical knowledge. [He has a more developed understanding of the concept of 'match' or 'fitness for purpose'.]

I had that dilemma – should I chop them up, the little pictures ... obviously was more of a literacy skill so I chose not to do that ... cutting and sticking wouldn't have been appropriate.

To sum up, D's growing pedagogical content knowledge helps him to envisage better what his conceptions might look like if put into practice in his classroom.

Conclusion and implications

This chapter has set out a conceptual model for representing the development of one primary geography beginning teacher over the course of two years – the PGCE and NQT years. The model is an attempt to illustrate how D draws on different knowledge bases to inform his teaching, and that the ways in which he is able to utilise these bases changes as he appears to go through stages in his transformation from the base of learner to the base of geography teacher.

D, unlike many primary teachers, has a geography degree, so his conception of geography is sophisticated and complex from the beginning. However, his experience as a teacher at the beginning of the two years is limited, as a result of which he tends to draw on his experiences as a learner in the initial stages. This is unhelpful to him in terms of his ability to utilise his geographical knowledge.

As D's experiences as a teacher expand *and* because he is able to reflect on and evaluate these experiences, he begins to work from the base of teacher. This, then, enables him to begin to incorporate his geographical base into his teaching [PCK] until he begins to work from the base of geography teacher.

Two pieces of research seem to support this theory. Work undertaken by Berliner (1987) shows that the difference between experiences and expert teachers is that the latter are able to learn from their greater experience. D appears to be such a teacher. The 'effective teachers of literacy' research (Medwell et al., 1998) showed that effective teachers found it very difficult to articulate their subject content knowledge because it was embedded in their practice. Their subject content knowledge was their PCK.

This model is now being applied to the case study of a beginning teacher, B, who did not have a formal geographical background, but who was a nursery assistant for some time before starting her training. In B's case, her pedagogical base is large from the outset, but her geographical base is fairly limited. Initial analysis suggests that, because the PGCE course and subsequent experiences in school did not enable her to develop her geographical base, after a promising start B's geography teaching did not develop to the same extent as D's.

The implications for policy and practice have yet to be considered in depth. Yet, it seems clear that there are implications that go beyond the initial stages of teacher development in terms of the focus of, and pedagogical approaches used in, CPD training.

Within ITT there seems to be a clear need to address the conceptions of geography held by students when they begin their PGCE course. These are the teachers of tomorrow, and if we are to influence the subject's image in school, with parents, and with the public and the media, it is paramount that Initial Teacher Training challenges primary student teachers' images of geography and gives them sufficient opportunities to explore the nature of the subject, its benefits to children's development and its role in modern society. In conjunction with this it is as important to address students' conceptions of teaching and learning and to develop their pedagogical knowledge in such a way that enables them to better utilise their content knowledge. In both cases, tutor knowledge of students' degrees and prior experience in schools is also going to be a key factor.

Once qualified, there are implications for Continuing Professional Development and, particularly, for the NQT year. A student such as D will need further support to enable him to continue developing his pedagogical knowledge. On the other hand, a student such as B, mentioned above, will need professional development that focuses on raising her levels of subject knowledge.

References

Alexander, R., Rose, J. & Woodhead, C. (1992), *Curriculum Organisation and Classroom Practice in Primary Schools*, London: HMSO

Barratt Hacking, E. (1996), Novice Teachers and Their Geographical Persuasions, *International Research in Geographical and Environmental Education*, 5 (1), 77-86

Baugh, N. G, & Mellott, K. G. (1998), Clinical Concept mapping as Preparation for Student Nurses' Clinical Experiences, *Journal of Nursing Education*, 37 (6), 253-256

Bennett, N. & Carré, C. (eds.) (1993), *Learning to Teach*, London: Routledge

Berliner, D. C. (1987), Ways of thinking about students and classrooms by more and less experienced teachers, in Calderhead, D. (ed.), *Exploring Teachers' Thinking*, London: Cassell, 60-83

Beyerbach, B. (1988), Developing a technical vocabulary on teacher planning: preservice teachers' concepts maps, *Teaching and Teacher Education*, 4 (4), 339-347

Caelli, K. (1998), Shared understandings: negotiating meanings of health via concept mapping, *Nurse Education Today*, 18, 317-321

Calderhead, J. (1981), Stimulated Recall: a method for research on teaching, *British Journal of Educational Psychology*, 51, 211-217

Corney, G. (1998), Learning to Teach Environmental Issues, *International Research in Geographical and Environmental Education*, 7, (2), 90-105

Fien, J. (1993), Ideology critique and environmental education, in Fien, J. (ed.) *Education for the Environment: Critical curriculum theorising and environmental education*, Geelong: Deakin University Press 14-49

Ghaye, A. L. & Robinson, E. G. (1989), Concept Maps and Children's Thinking: A Constructivist Approach, in Slater, F. (ed.), *Language and Learning in the Teaching of Geography*, London: Routledge, 115-130

Ghaye, T., Cuthbert, S., Danai, K. & Dennis, D. (1996), *Learning Through Critical Reflective Practice. Book 1: Professional Values*, Newcastle-upon-Tyne: Pentaxion Ltd

John, P. D. (1996), 'Understanding the apprenticeship of observation in initial teacher education' in Claxton, G. Atkinson, T., Osborn, M., & Wallace, M. (eds.), *Liberating the Learner: Lessons for professional development in education*, London: Routledge, 90-107

Lewis, J & Cowie, H. (1993), Cooperative Group Work: Promises and Limitations - a Study of Teachers' Values, *Education Section Review*, 17 (2), 77-84

Martin, F. (2000), Postgraduate Primary Education Students' Images of Geography and how these affect the types of teachers they become, *International Research in Geographical and Environmental Education* 9 (3), 223-244

Matthews, M. H. (1992), *Making Sense of Place: Children's understanding of large scale environments,* Hemel Hempsted: Harvester Wheatsheaf

Medwell, J., Wray, D., Poulson, L. & Fox, R. (1998), *Effective Teachers of Literacy: A report of a research project commissioned by the Teacher Training Agency*, University of Exeter

Northcott, N. (1996), Cognitive mapping: An approach to qualitative data analysis, *Nursing Times Research*, 1 (6), 456-463

Novak, J. (1998), *Learning, Creating and Using Knowledge*, New York: Lawrence Erlbaum Associates

Novak, J. & Gowin, D. (1984), *Learning how to learn*, Cambridge: Cambridge University Press

Reid, A., Scott, W. & Oulton, C. (1997), The Contribution of Geography Teaching to Pupils' Environmental education: Methodological Considerations and Issues for Researching Teachers' Thinking About Practice, *International Research in Geographical and Environmental Education*, 6 (3), 222-233

Smyth, J. (ed.) (1987), *Educating Teachers: Changing the Nature of Pedagogical Knowledge*, London: Falmer Press

Tillema, H. H. & Knoll, W. E. (1997), Promoting Student Teacher learning through Conceptual Change or Direct Instruction, *Teaching and Teacher Education*, 13 (6), 579-595

Turner-Bisset, R. (2001), *Expert Teaching: Knowledge and Pedagogy to Lead the Profession*, London: David Fulton Publishers

Chapter 17

Student Teachers' Understanding of Locality

John Halocha

Introduction

Since 1991 the English National Curriculum Geography Order has required primary teachers to include a range of locality studies within the curriculum at key stages 1 and 2 (DES, 1991; DfEE/QCA, 1999). The majority of the primary school teachers are not geography specialists. Indeed, most stopped studying the subject at age 14. Current regulations for the initial training of teachers require that, by the end of their courses, trainee primary teachers have secure knowledge and understanding in the teaching of core and non-core subjects.

Many teacher training providers offer introductory courses in all subjects, including primary geography. However, these are often allocated a small proportion of the total course time (Norman, 2004). In addition, the *Qualifying to Teach* (TTA, 2003) standards state that courses may include either history or geography. This raises two issues: if geography is allocated time in an initial teacher training [ITT] course, the tutors must be sure that the time is being used to maximum benefit. Secondly, if geography is not chosen by an institution, can evidence be found to show that future members of the teaching profession do benefit from an introductory course in primary geography in those education departments where it has been included within the total course experience?

The research discussed here investigated the development of student teachers' understanding of localities within an introductory course in primary geography that had to be followed by all primary ITT students.

Literature Review

There has been limited research conducted into teachers' perceptions of geography as a subject (Barratt-Hacking, 1996; Walford, 1996; Martin, 1997, 2000). The focus has been on possible relationships between subject knowledge and teaching styles. Bowles (1997) examined issues of defining localities from pupils' perspectives. This work was developed into comparing pupils' knowledge and understanding of locality with that of student teachers. She concluded that

> The evidence is also there to suggest that the new, young primary school teacher with little specialist training is ill equipped to deliver either the geography curriculum or cross-curricular citizenship curriculum in that both demand an understanding of the environment within which their pupils are developing. (Bowles, 2003, 21)

This raises the question of what happens when trainee teachers, in fact, do have a structured introduction to the study of localities.

Martin's (1997, 2000) study of students' understanding of geography showed that the majority saw the subject as being knowledge-based, rather than focussing on enquiry and fieldwork. If trainee teachers do experience fieldwork and enquiry in the locality, can this change their perception of the subject? This needs to be seen in the broader context of the whole of the initial teacher training curriculum which is strongly knowledge-based. Edwards, Gilroy and Hartley state that

> in England there now exists a national curriculum for teacher education, supported by an audit culture to ensure that the curriculum is in fact delivered, which suggests that some at least feel that they can dictate what that knowledge-base is. (Edwards, Gilroy and Hartley, 2002, 51)

In the Geography Order that knowledge can be developed through the study of localities. A careful reading of the Order does not appear to limit what learning may take place within those locality studies. There may well be scope for teachers to develop children's geographies, thinking skills and understanding. But if they do not have the opportunity in their training to explore the opportunities provided by the study of locality, they may not make or have that opportunity once they begin their busy careers.

Catling argues that such experiences are important if future primary teachers are able to 'encompass a values perspective and an appreciation of geography's role in understanding place and environmental issues' (Catling, 2003, 16). But we also need to consider the effect of the learning experiences on children that these teachers will provide in the future. Holloway and Valentine (2000, 16) claim that children in contemporary Britain have limited spatial experiences that are based on the home, rather than exploring the wider world of their locality. In an attempt to help them think further afield, Martin (2001) encouraged pupils to think about how their own locality might be connected to other places by using their own personal geographies as starting points. In reporting her research on a Cambridgeshire village Massey suggests that 'localities are much better conceptualised as meeting places' (Massey, 1999, 6). If primary children are to develop a sense of how their locality is linked to other places and how these links have allowed it to change over time, it is perhaps important to understand how their teachers are prepared to help them understand their own worlds.

A further dimension in the study of localities is the way in which the cultures within them are examined. Bordieu (1977) suggests that the dominant group in, for example, a school, will control the knowledge and values contained in the curriculum. However, by starting with pupils' questions and experiences, Morgan (2001) argues that *critical multiculturalism* may be a way forward in helping pupils understand that cultures change over time and may be contested. He cites the research of Holloway and Valentine (2000) into how British and New Zealand children were encouraged to develop 'imaginative geographies of the other' by trying to understand the cultures present in other localities across the world. This implies that teachers' understand the potential in using studies of the locality to go much further than the facts that may be found there, by encouraging pupils to think, question and challenge; this is a very different interpretation of the subject that Lambert describes, where 'geography fundamentally fulfils the requirements of an 'answer culture' ' (Lambert, 2004, 78).

From this background of research and debate, the geography team at the research institution set out to study how trainee primary school teachers developed their understanding of locality studies while taking part in a generalist geography method course. In order to justify the amount of time taken up on such activities, it was necessary to analyse some of the underlying processes taking place in student learning.

Research method

The research context

The course team began the academic year with the specific intention of investigating processes at work in students' understanding of localities. This was felt necessary as the primary geography course on which they worked had evolved into having approximately one third of the time devoted to locality studies. To what extent did students really develop their professional understanding of the nature of locality studies, and how was their capacity to use them as an effective vehicle for developing children's geographical understanding actually extended?

The course took students through a number of stages. The first stage was to examine their own understanding of what was meant by *locality*. The second stage was to examine the range of literature in geographical education on children's developing understanding of place. They were then introduced to 'official' versions of the meaning and definition of locality studies. They also evaluated a range of resource materials available for use in schools.

Students next formed small groups and identified a locality that they would examine in depth. Their focus would be the identification of how it might be used with primary children, along with a detailed consideration of the pedagogical and practical issues involved. Following fieldwork, each group prepared and made a presentation in which they analysed their chosen locality and discussed the implications with other students. This was also an opportunity to develop practical skills. In addition, it was a chance to develop practical skills in designing resources to support locality studies with primary children.

The research process

Data was collected from 160 postgraduate students throughout their one-year PGCE course. Evidence was compiled in the form of field notes, observations and small-scale interviews with individuals and groups of students. At the start of the course, data was collected in the form of whole group and individual discussions, analysis of drawings, notes, maps and sketches provided by the students. The author attended student planning sessions and made field notes. In particular, student group presentations provided an extensive source of data on how their perceptions of locality studies had developed, along with the professional thinking, knowledge and understanding they possibly possessed. These presentations were an opportunity to demonstrate what they perceived to be appropriate geographical resources for use in locality studies. It also showed to some extent their ability to analyse the appropriateness of such resources.

It was also possible to track the application of these into school placements where students had the opportunity to plan and implement locality studies. In addition, the research team informally observed how students' understanding of localities was expressed in other parts of the geography programme.

Ethnographic methods were used to analyse the data. The relatively large sample of students and the number of group presentations enabled a number of patterns and trends to be identified as the students completed the various parts of the course. Once all the presentations had been completed and the data analysed, a number of clear patterns appeared in the changing understanding of students' perceptions of locality studies in the primary school.

Findings and discussion

Analysis of the data revealed eight main areas of interest. The account of these below is not presented in any particular order of priority. Each finding may have implications both for the design and content of a geography teacher training course and offer insights into students' developing thinking about locality studies. Taken together they present an interesting insight into the way students reflect on and develop their sense of *locality*.

What is a *locality*?

The course took students through a number of stages in thinking about what a *locality* is. Their first exposure was to ask them to identify, define and explain a locality they knew well from their own experience. They were then introduced to the 'official' national curriculum and QCA definitions of localities. Finally, in their presentation, they had to justify to fellow students the extent and content of the locality they had identified as their chosen place, as well as the geographical aims they could identify in using such a locality.

Group discussion revealed that while they understood the thinking behind official definitions, in practice it was often far harder to identify the precise extent and content of a school's locality, for both key stages 1 and 2. Each group offered a range of evidence, providing examples of parameters which might be used in defining a locality. Size, shape, communication systems and patterns, density and variety of features, school catchment area and the physical landscape were all identified. Having been able to focus on an area and analyse it from that perspective, the quality of debate, level of understanding and concepts used was judged to be higher than that used in the discussions which they undertook at the start of the course when using areas they said they were familiar with. They demonstrated an understanding that a chosen locality could be a fluid concept as events and resources within it change. At the start of the course a much more fixed concept was expressed, both in terms of size, shape and content of a locality. Having experienced the variety and potential for change taking place within their research locality, many expressed a greater understanding and confidence in being able to identify what might be selected for the effective teaching of geographical skills and concepts.

Linking a locality with the wider world

The key stage 1 programme of study requires pupils to 'recognise how places are linked to other places in the world' (DfEE/QCA, 1999), while at key stage 2 pupils should be able 'to recognise how places fit within a wider geographical context' (DfEE/QCA, 1999). When this was raised early on in the course, many students were very unclear about what this actually meant. They were searching for practical examples of what happened in the real world. For instance, non-specialist geographers found it hard to identify examples of how a local factory might be connected both with its suppliers and the places to which the finished products went. In the presentations, the majority of students were able to explain how they had identified real processes taking place in their locality, which they could use with children in order to extend their geographical understanding of how local people and activities were connected with the wider world. Some students went through a stage of attempting to increase vastly the size of the locality as they grappled with this idea. In the main, this was resolved through a discussion both of how much primary children might understand as well as the time constraints on the timetable.

The process of thinking through the various ways in which people and places might be linked proved to be a useful activity for many students whose previous experience had not exposed them to thinking about the world in this way. In two groups that did include specialist geographers, fascinating discussions developed in which they were able to analyse how non-specialists had begun to grasp these concepts. It helped them to realise the importance of not assuming that fellow teachers arrived at geography teaching with the same background knowledge or experience, or the same understandings about key elements of the subject.

How we 'know' a place

Relph (1976) suggests that we can experience places both as an *insider* and as an *outsider*. One of the strongest patterns to emerge from the data analysis was the way, following their fieldwork, in which students discussed with enthusiasm and confidence the ways in which they had 'got to know' more about their chosen locality. In analysing the data students provided, it became clear that it was not a straightforward process of 'coming to know' a locality but involved a complex set of developments. This category can be described through four sub-sets of the process.

1. Making contact with people in the locality
Fieldwork exposed the students to meeting many people who lived and worked in the locality. Before going out, many non-specialists had been very sceptical about both the level of support they might receive and the ease with which resources could be found to develop locality studies in school. Every group presentation included examples where students had made contact with a range of people who were both willing and interested in offering help. They were very encouraged by this. They also had first hand experience of seeing how a network of contacts might be established from one carefully chosen (or sometimes chance) meeting. Many students had expressed disbelief about the potential of this process when it was raised early on in the university-based parts of the course. By beginning to work with people in the locality, they were introduced to ways in which teachers might become *insiders* within the local community, gaining a deeper understanding of how it is seen by residents.

2. Perceiving and knowing a locality
Some students chose localities they thought they knew well, while others deliberately chose unknown areas, arguing that this is how it might be when they take up the teaching posts.

Many students who investigated an apparently familiar locality were able to discuss ways in which their knowledge had been extended. Using maps and plans, they walked the areas in detail. This raised the issue of what experiences and understanding their pupils would bring with them to school. Until that time, the majority explained that they had not considered the need to understand how pupils perceived their locality. They were also surprised to realise how little they might know as teachers if they did not live in the locality or had not worked there for some length of time. Some students were also able to discuss this in a broader professional context in terms of the benefits of being able to understand the catchment area of a school and the implications of this for their work as teachers. Their awareness of even small points such as the possible benefits of being able to discuss with their pupils where they played or where their grandparents lived, was identified in a small number of student presentations and discussions.

3 Accessing locality resources.
A further dimension in their awareness of how well they knew a place was related to the confidence and success they perceived in relation to gaining access to resources. During the presentations, students frequently remarked on how much their knowledge had developed about where to find geographical resources. Within this knowledge, they also gained first hand experience of successfully identifying unusual or unexpected resources.

4. Personal confidence in locality studies
The majority of students included examples of how a greater practical understanding of a school's locality gave them more confidence to initiate local geographical enquiries rather than simply using existing materials or base their work solely within the classroom. They felt that their confidence to undertake locality work with children had been increased by the experience because they accepted that as they got to know an area, their resources, contacts and understanding would accumulate.

Cross-curricular issues

During the student presentations there were many references to sources and opportunities they had identified related to local history work. The majority of these statements included a sense of insecurity about how curriculum design and planning might be tackled. The well-rehearsed questions of 'What is history?' and 'What is geography?' were asked by the students as they attempted to grapple with cross-curricular issues. Examples included studying old maps and plans of a village. As their debate extended, students began to justify ways in which relevant links might be made between the subjects and expressed their concerns for a rigid subject focus found in some schools.

A number of students were able to give examples from their school placements where they felt they had observed teaching in which relevant links had not been made because their teachers had said they were deliberately keeping history and geography separate to facilitate management or because they felt there was not enough time to spend on lessons where cross-curricular issues were introduced. These observations led to extensive discussions about the current subject divisions and ways in which they affected young children's growing understanding of the world.

The English *Geography Order*

Student teachers, especially those on PGCE courses, are exposed to the orders for all national curriculum subjects, often in an intensive way. Students talk of overload and anxiety about being able to absorb and understand all the primary subjects. Although the geography methods course attempted to assist them through this process, they were still critical of the methods and were concerned that their limited understanding would inhibit their performance in schools.

Their viewpoint changed considerably on return from their locality visits. Built into the presentation requirements was the need for them to show other students how they might use their locality to cover the geography curriculum and related cross-curricular issues. The great majority of students explained that by looking at practical examples from the real world, they were able to interpret the sometimes vague content of the Geography Order (DfEE/QCA, 1999). For instance, statements such as 'how settlements differ and change, including why they differ in size and character' (DfEE/QCA, 1999, 20) were seen as less than helpful when read out of context. But when they saw for themselves how a place was changing, almost as they observed it, they began to understand what such statements might mean.

The students also gave examples of how they were beginning to see patterns and processes in the world. In this context, some non-specialists felt that early on they had had a mental block about being able to transfer geographical concepts between ways in which they had already attempted to organise and understand the world. For example, many had created constructs for 'urban' and 'rural'. What they admitted they had initially found hard was the thought that some geographical ideas could be located within these apparently differing concepts. Communications is an example: As they began to understand how transport patterns developed, how people used them and links between physical and human processes, they felt that their confidence to introduce these concepts to children was increased. At a more global scale, some began to discuss how children might begin to compare their findings in the locality with evidence from studies of more distant places.

The enquiry process

At the start of the geography course students were questioned about their understanding of the enquiry process. This was approached from two perspectives. The first was to establish precisely what the enquiry process was. The second was to establish their understanding of possible links to scientific and historical enquiry processes being introduced in those method courses.

Analysis of the notes taken during student presentations reveals that by conducting their own investigations in a locality, the majority of groups had both identified opportunities for developing enquiries, as well as giving specific examples of how they might work. Some evidence of understanding the relationships with historical enquiry were found but very few examples could be identified in relation to the process of scientific enquiry. In particular, many presentations noted their wish to ensure that the enquiries were relevant to pupils and based on their own questions.

Physical processes

Very few presentations offered more than a passing reference to physical processes in a locality or how they impacted upon people. Local weather was totally ignored and some potentially useful links with science were not discussed. This may have implications for the way in which physical processes are covered in the geography course as a reading of the course materials does suggest that most time is spent on human and environmental issues. It may also be important to consider ways of developing students' understanding of the relationships between physical and human patterns and processes.

Values, attitudes and personal preferences

Students were introduced to ways in which these ideas could be found in geographical activities. A common student response was that this might be dangerous ground for teachers and that appropriate examples may be hard to find in a locality, especially ones which primary children could understand. However, in 30% of the presentations, students included values and attitudes that they said they would be prepared to develop as they arose from studying a locality. By the presentation stage of the course, these students thought that children would in fact see the relevance to their own lives. They showed an understanding that the locality could provide a range of points of views surrounding an issue and liked the approach, explaining that children would be working with sources at first hand. These students also explained that the process might begin to introduce children to the idea of having some input into decision-making and the potential for cross-curricular links with citizenship.

Conclusion

This research was developed from the need to assess the effectiveness and value of devoting one third of the generalist geography methods course to locality studies. The evidence suggests that it provides non-specialist students with an opportunity to take part in a number of valuable learning experiences:

- They can take into school an ability to assess critically a locality and begin to understand the place in which they work;
- They are able to apply national curriculum requirements in a practical context;
- They can extend their own understanding of key concepts such as enquiry in geographical education and able to perceive what a locality might be;
- Their personal confidence and subject knowledge can be developed within a practical and meaningful context.

Ofsted has recently expressed concerns over the quality of geography teaching in primary schools (Ofsted, 2003, 2004). If schools are predominantly staffed with teachers who have limited experience of the real potential localities have for learning, there may be a real danger of losing the battle for a secure place for geography. A supply of enthusiastic newly qualified teachers who have had such positive experiences may help the situation. This research has provided evidence to support the case for including geographical education in all courses of training, and it has enabled the course team to adapt geographical elements such as physical processes to ensure students have a broad and balanced understanding of the real potential for geography in the primary school curriculum.

References

Barrett-Hacking, E. (1996), Novice teachers and their geographical persuasions, Journal of *International Research in Geographical and Environmental Education*, 5,1, 77-86

Bordieu, P. (1977), *Outline of a Theory of Practice*, Cambridge: Cambridge University Press

Bowles, R. (1997) Defining Localities, in Scoffham, S. (ed.), *Primary Sources: Research Findings in Primary Geography*, Sheffield: Geographical Association, 24-25

Bowles, R. (2003), *The role of locality understanding in primary teaching: Contrasts in child and adult locality knowledge*, Paper presented at Charney Manor Conference, March 2003

Catling, S. (2003), *Geography as understanding the environment? - The perspectives of English trainee teachers*, Paper presented at Charney Manor Conference, March 2003

DES (1991), Geography in the National Curriculum (England), London: H.M.S.O.

DfEE/QCA (1999), *The National Curriculum for England: Geography*, London: DfEE/QCA

Edwards, A., Gilroy, P. and Hartley, D. (eds.) (2002), *Rethinking Teacher Education: Collaborative Responses to Uncertainty*, London: Routledge

Holloway, S. and Valentine, G. (2000), Children's geographies and the new social studies of childhood, in Holloway S. and Valentine,G. (eds.), *Children's Geographies: Playing, Living, Learning*, London: Routledge, 1-26

Holloway, S. and Valentine, G. (2000), Corked hats and Coronation Street: British and New Zealand children's imaginative geographies of the other, *Childhood*, 7, 335-358

Lambert, D. (2004), Geography, in White, J. (ed.) *Rethinking the School Curriculum: Values, Aims and Purposes*, London: Routledge, 75-86

Martin, F. (1999), Contrasting views on locality between child and adult, *International Research in Geographical and Environmental Education*, 8, 1, 78-81

Martin, F. (2000), Postgraduate primary education students' images of geography and the relationship between these and students' teaching, *International Research in Geographical and Environmental Education*, 9, 3, 223-244

Martin, H. (2001), Personal geographies, *Primary Geographer*, 45, October, 17

Massey, D. (1999), The social place, *Primary Geographer*, 37, April, 4-6

Morgan, J. (2001), Teaching multicultural geographies, *Primary Geographer*, 45, October, 4-5

Norman, M. (2004), The state of primary geography in ITE, *Primary Geographer*, 54, January, 43

Ofsted (2003), *Geography in primary schools*; Ofsted subject reports 2001/02, http://www.ofsted.gov.uk/publications/index.cfm?fuseaction=pubs.summary&id=3163 accessed 2 Nov 03

Ofsted (2004), *Geography in primary schools*, Ofsted subject reports 2002/03: http://www.ofsted.gov.uk/publications/index.cfm?fuseaction=pubs.summary&id=3523 accessed 24 Feb 04

Relph, E. (1976), *Place and Placelessness*, London: Pion

TTA, (2003), *Qualifying to Teach*, London: TTA

Walford, R. (1996) What is geography? An analysis of definitions provided by prospective teachers of the subject, *Journal of International Research in Geographical and Environmental Education*, 5 (1), 69-76

Chapter 18

Comparing Children's and Adults' Understanding of Locality

Rachel Bowles

Introduction

This paper takes as its starting point the view that geography, of all the national curriculum subjects, is, at the primary school level, most dependent upon both teachers' and children's own knowledge of the geography of their local area. It is argued that because younger children live, play and move through their local geography on a daily basis, it is the child who has the more detailed knowledge than the teacher even at an early age (Moore, 1986; Matthews, 1992). Moreover, Palmer (1998) has shown that

> four year olds are active thinkers in the realm of environmental issues and are constantly trying to relate the ideas they encounter to their own experience…in short they possess the knowledge, ideas and values which formal education can build upon in a sound and progressive way. (Palmer, 1998, 33)

It is, therefore, this knowledge which must be used to enable progress in children's understanding of geographical processes and patterns. It is also this knowledge that informs citizens of the future, both children and the teacher.

The discrepancy between child and teacher knowledge has been measured from evidence gathered by interview and questionnaire. This empirical evidence has been analysed simply through themes and quantified where appropriate. National Curriculum 2000 geography is content rich through its requirements for both knowledge and skills (DfEE/QCA, 1999). Yet, to be taught effectively, it demands that the individual teacher, though given some latitude, must understand their local geography. This is over and above whatever specialist subject knowledge they may have acquired at school or in their initial and continuing professional development as a teacher.

Teachers' understanding of locality

Matthews (1992) and others have drawn attention to the considerable variation between individuals understanding of the geography of their locality. The child's view has been placed in context in Chapter 2. The context for considering the adult view is less straightforward. Children need and must try to understand the world within which they find themselves. They have to learn how to keep safe, to notice change and consider aesthetics. Gradually they are put to using this knowledge and understanding by being given responsibilities; they are expected to complete tasks within a time scale and to standards agreed by consensus in the family and the community and by society. By the time they reach adulthood the child's view seems to have been considerably changed.

Initial teacher trainers have investigated the geographical understanding that trainees bring to their intended career. McPartland (1996) and Barratt-Hacking (1996) looked at secondary PGCE students' memories of being taught and, amongst other observations, have noted these experiences appear to have no bearing on the way they think and plan in the classroom. Similarly, Martin (1999, 2000; chapter 16) and Halocha (1998; chapter 17), in studies with Primary PGCE students, have shown, along with Shulman (1987), a lack of correlation between image and teaching style. Martin points out that 'people perceive phenomena differently in different contexts; geographer and geography teacher are two very different roles which may lead to very different views of the subject' (Martin, 1999, 80), and these adults already had some notion of geography. Halocha (1998) showed that though primary initial teacher training [ITT} students appeared to have a greater variety of geographical experience and understanding than many experienced teachers, it was still vital that fieldwork experience was provided in their programmes before the trainees understood how pupils perceive the locality. One of the conclusions drawn by Martin was that it is vital to know the nature of the images and perceptions that teachers have of their pupils' locality.

Martin (1999) points out that:

> Planning geographical enquiries in the local area requires teachers to have some knowledge of the locality. In general, teachers do not live in their locality and so their perception of the opportunities there are for geographical enquiries may be limited. However, these perceptions may also be limited by their image of geography as a subject and their image of teaching. As non-geographers (as the majority of primary teachers are), can they identify aspects of the locality that would make a suitable focus for enquiry? In turn, can they pose suitable geographical questions or hypotheses that would drive the enquiry and enable the children to develop as geographers? (Martin, 1999, 80)

Adult interest in locality geography was not always evident in the schools used in the children's' perception research. The use of the lunch hour by the researcher, on the day of the interviews, to verify the location of the places the children had mentioned, was regarded as eccentric by some staff in more than one school. This in turn raised the query – how much do these teachers know about the locality in which they teach? Do they know more or less detail than the children? These questions were further strengthened when three inner city school geographers mentioned that, because most of the staff lived in the suburbs, they were conspicuously ill-informed about the geography of the school locality and of the out-of-school life that was possible (or not) for the children. This led to a lack of understanding and co-operation required to develop the cross-curricular aspects of geography in the support of citizenship and sustainability (think globally, act locally).

Research approach

Obtaining children's views

The evidence for the children's views about their locality came from a national survey of 25 schools in widely varied localities (see chapter 2). Semi-structured interviews based upon four questions were taped with groups of five children. The questions, supported by scaffolding questions, elicited where they lived and how they got to school, where they played and shopped, which were special places for these activities, and, finally, where would they take visitors to show them the most important features of their locality. Aerial photographs and 1:25,000 OS

Explorer maps were used as support and for showing locations. The interview transcripts were then coded, categorised linked to themes and charted. The children interviewed ranged in age from Reception to Year 8. There was a predictable change in answers with age, with the children becoming less egocentric, more proud of leaving behind 'childish' matters, and more interested in providing precise detail. For this study, key stage 2 children's interviews only were used.

Obtaining adults' views

ITT students were the adult sample for this study. There were 50 first year student teachers in the sample.

The locality elements elicited from the children were used to devise a questionnaire to which were added further questions to review the knowledge that ITT students should have obtained about the locality of their school experience school. The students were expected to include a locality resume in the school experience file as a programme requirement. In effect this profile of their school experience school and its area, together with map availability on the web, provided a skeletal *locality* study. While they were at an early stage in their ITT programme, because of the focus of this requirement, it was felt that the students could be 'seen' as surrogate teachers in terms of their locality experience and knowledge.

After their first block school experience three teaching groups of first year undergraduates completed the questionnaire, in February. It was hoped to see how far, having regularly visited one school environment since mid-autumn, before a full block experience in March, the responses might reflect some detail of the school environment. During the block school experience it was not unusual for a number of students to have been placed at the same school. It is recognised that this might have an affect on the results but it is not thought to be sufficient to negate the development of theoretical ideas about adult knowledge.

Once returned, the questionnaires were coded and analysed by theme and age group. The themes for analysis (see below) were informed by similar work by Barratt and Hacking Barratt (2000) with Year 7 children. The themes were indicated in detail on the student questionnaire, particularly with reference to landmarks, features, places visited locally and change in the locality, in order to elicit how many features were actually noticed. The students were also interviewed in groups and their responses similarly categorised and analysed.
Article I.

Findings

An overall picture of the results can be provided initially. For each theme the children of all ages showed the greatest knowledge, over 40% alluded to each element of the locality. By contrast, the adult feedback rarely achieved more than 30 % and usually only 20% of the interviewees made comments. Of these, the young adults, the Under 21's indicated no interest in open space, took transport for granted, were more concerned with people, had little interest in employment, and had not developed a feeling for place through natural features, though they knew much about built environment leisure features. It appeared that this group were also oblivious to change, history and comparisons between places.

Adults' knowledge

The findings from the student teachers' questionnaire provided evidence of six groups of adult locality information, which complemented those identified by the children. Where appropriate reference is made to the children's understanding and preferences alongside those of the adults, for comparison. In that many of the student teachers were young adults, reference is also made to them in the context of 'under 21s'. 'Mature' adults – over 31 – are also referred to.

School Context
This group included housing character and the journey to school. The former was not fully understood by adults under 21. The journey to school figures showed the presence of 'green' schools as well as the 'career/suburban adults' enhanced need to use the car for practical reasons, primarily linked to parenting responsibilities.

Neighbourhood features
This group included playing areas, places which could be visited, places which the children said they had visited and places which the student would take visitors to. The under 21s were generally unimaginative, and uncaring, about visitor possibilities despite the children talking about more features than the students knew. In part this can be explained by probable differences in understanding: 'Country Park' to the young adult is not regarded as countryside – countryside is further away! For some under 21s local museums were not significant – the nearest are Central London (60mins transport time away). Distance is an unknown quantity for many children and adults, both in time and miles. The suburban children on the whole had visited a greater variety of places.

Neighbourhood features
These were concerned with shopping and were, on the whole, consistent in all age groups with common sense answers given. This is unsurprising, considering this is the most consistent locality feature of living requirements. There was confusion over the meaning of the word 'regional'. Answers revealed that inaccurate knowledge and assumptions were made, which indicated the influence of motorway/premier route access to out-of-town retail parks, of which some of the largest are in the south-east. Children's' evidence from other regions also showed this kind of influence.

Immediate school features
Knowledge of features such as buildings and their associated spaces is required for curriculum work in both core and foundation subjects; this includes building age and materials, building style, garden and parking space. When detail seems accurate for the locality, usually in the 21-31 age group, there was little recognition of subject significance. Outside this age group there is generally a considerable lack of knowledge in all areas, indicating poor observation skills generally. For example, parking and gardens received scant attention.

Understanding of generic locality features
This group focused on features that might be used for comparison with contrasting areas, such as places of worship, meeting places, health and beauty centres, garages and physical features. Knowledge seemed minimal. In completing the questionnaire, both interest and knowledge seems to wane at this stage. The reason for this section was lost on most of respondents.

Social characteristics

These included the state of repair of buildings, employment, and ethnic mix and character of the locality. It provided for geography in context, but these elements barely received a comment despite the fact that this was specifically asked for in the education programme requirements.

Figure 1 indicates a number of features of the adult group surveyed in this study. Of the 50 students, only a handful provided reference and distance to every locality feature though there was space to show this in terms of time and distance to travel. Each attraction, which covered leisure, educational, built and natural features, was based upon the types of attraction described by the children in their group interviews. Each could be visited within the whole school experience school area. This area, for the first year undergraduates, covers South Essex, West Kent and the Outer London boroughs of Bexley, Bromley, Greenwich and Lewisham. The school localities ranged in type from urban Inner London through inter-war, post-war and late 20th century suburbs to Thames estuary industrial towns and villages. All were within 90 minutes of the coast and open countryside – a fact noted mostly by the mature students with families.

The under 21's knew least about the out of town attractions and most about the venues catering for the under 25's.

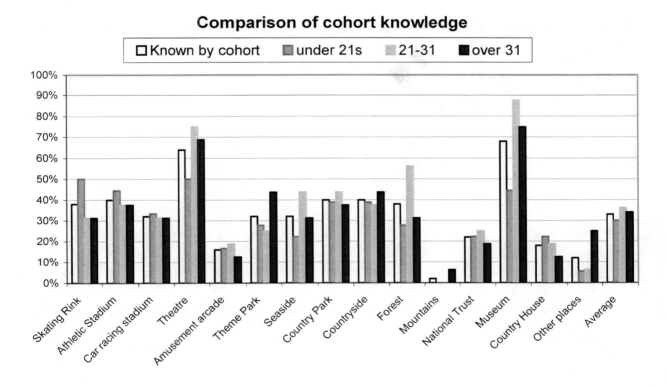

Figure 1: Comparison of cohort knowledge of places to visit

The majority cohort lacked knowledge on countryside activities compared with urban attractions, such as theatres and museums. Only a third of the sample provided such knowledge, the greater part of this coming from the 21- 31 and over 31 age groups. The least observant adults were those who had come directly from school to university (c.6%), the under 21s. The most observant were the mature adults whose life style is much more likely to be dependent upon suitable housing and parking, for instance mature students with families. Just under half of that age group made detailed observations.

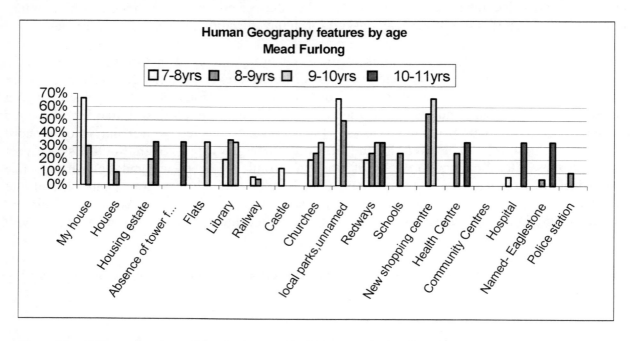

Note the differences in percentage knowledge between urban (70%) and rural (100%)

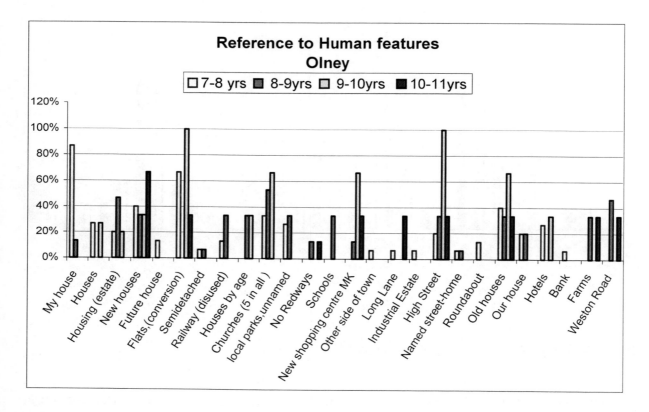

Figure 2: Human Geography features mentioned by the children

The children's knowledge

Responses by all the children (Figure 2) showed a steady move away from personal space to community features with increasing age. The city children showed more awareness of community health and policing features than the market town children, but the latter showed more awareness of the varied land use of a small town

Overall, the number of locality features mentioned increases with increasing maturity and, presumably, increased sense of responsibility. By implication, by the time children reach Year 7 in secondary school, there may well be a sound understanding of the main facets of the locality, which should be developed further through geographical enquiries rather than by instruction.

Comparison of children's knowledge with undergraduate knowledge of leisure features

The children's themes were matched with those used with the adult undergraduates and considered in detail for leisure features reached by car, for local leisure features and activities and for reference to physical features (Figure 3). When undergraduates' knowledge is compared with children's knowledge, while allowing for the difference between the leisure activities described by the children and noted by the undergraduates, there is still a remarkable mismatch between the generations' perception of leisure features and activities. Group activities centred upon stadia, theme parks and other well advertised venues (40% or over for the adults) received scant attention from the children, who preferred more open out-of-town activities. It is salutary to notice that adult ideas about children's activities only coincide with the children's with theatre and museum visits. The children value the countryside and country parks much more than the adults.

This preference is reinforced by the collation of references to observing leisure activities and local leisure features when cycling and walking. Even when allowance is made for the fact that children's perceptions of activities and what adults think are possible or generally viable, there remains the disquieting thought that the life of the children outside school is largely unconsidered, or at the worst discounted, as of being of no value for teaching purposes.

Comparison of Undergraduate and children's reference to physical features

Consideration of the knowledge of physical features compounds the difference in knowledge between adults and children. This evidence concerns references to physical features. Here the children, who need to understand the potential of slope and water for so many play activities, completely outclass the adults in wealth of knowledge and understanding. Barely 10% of the adults considered physical features, yet over 40 % of the children in both rural town and city communities were aware of the value of views from hill tops and of the effects of flooding.

Matthews and Limb (1999, 64) point out that children, when they

> see the world around them, recognise that part of what they 'see' are structures which constrain them. These may include the adult values imprinted upon the physical and built landscapes in which they live, or the social constraints imposed by the adult gaze.

They go on to point out that there is a considerable difference between children's conceptions of space and place, their environmental competencies, and their levels of spatial cognition, grouped by Hart (1979) into *children's geographies* and *the geography of children*. Hart continued to develop the ideas generated by his two-year study of children's day-by-day movement about their local community. Hart (1997), along with Spencer & Blades (1993) and Matthews (1992), shows that local places matter to individuals, that in belonging to a place one develops an identity by participation and involvement with local resources. This has been repeatedly emphasised by the children in all the interviews. The city children emphasised the significance of the major leisure foci. The market town children meticulously described the relationship of a major national poet and the historic buildings in the High Street, as well as the annual community gatherings often based upon the river. Similar references can be made for all the school localities visited. Yet for all of the children in these primary schools, when this was mentioned to their teachers, they – with the exception of the teachers who were geographers – showed surprise at the local knowledge the children knew and thought worth telling a stranger.

What images or perceptions do children have of their own locality?

Overall, age for age, children have a very clear view of the nature of their locality. As Barratt and Barratt Hacking (2000, 18), in their study of Year 7 children, point out:

[children's] understandings of the local environment are individual…and [they] interpreted 'my locality' in different ways and at different scales.

In this study group interviewing smoothed out the variety in interpretation and scale. The macro development from isolated, individual recognition of features to a reasoned consideration of features in relation to each other is observable from Year 1 through to Year 7 and 8. Where there had been good geographical input by teachers, by Year 4, the evidence was *ordered* in the children's minds rather than anecdotal, but even the anecdotal evidence was far more detailed than that of adults.

Section 1.01   Both Matthews (1999) and Hart (1997) make a case for the need to research the environment as children 'see it'. In pursuit of this Matthews has drawn up a research agenda, two of the seven topics of which are used here to unravel the information given in the interviews and questionnaires. These concern how children see and use their locality.

Children's 'ways of seeing' differ from those of adults
Play Areas by Age: City. There are differences between the city and country town child's use of public play space even in unplanned urban environments. As would be expected, local parks figure large in urban localities, not just for the playground or ball game element. In the city detailed descriptions of the wild life to be seen in the large parks were given. It is clear that the older children range far and wide, aided in the city by its system of designated paths for pedestrians and cyclists which lead from the housing estates, through the parks to different parts of the city and which include the centre, shopping areas and major parks.

Play Areas by Age: Country town. Country town children, on the other hand, hardly consider the planned play areas. The recreation ground figures in the older children's references, but because it is the flattest place for ball games being at the edge of the local river's flood plain. The other open space for kicking a ball about is up on the valley side in the 'Bonfire field' – the children's name, not the adult name for this place. Just going 'out' of town into the fields was a favourite occupation whether with cycle, skate board or just messing about. With the older children, this was a freedom they could see being lost with the growth of more housing estates and the changes in infrastructure that new development involves.

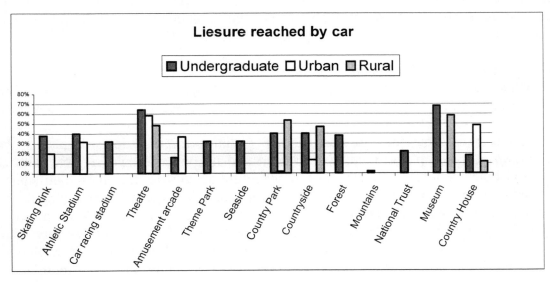

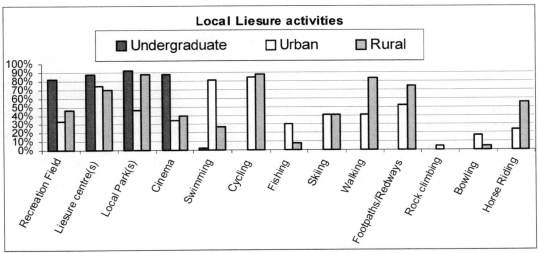

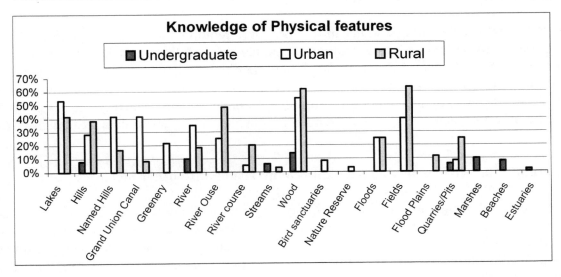

Figure 3: A comparison of children's locality knowledge with that of ITT adults

Tuan (1977) suggests that this early reluctance to give detail about public places is because few public places are 'made to the scale of young children'. Yet this is the area where the undergraduate teacher has greatest perception of local features – this is where you can play; it is so designated; as a mother that is where you take a young child and to where you are expected to go when unaccompanied, not the street or 'any old place'.

Children's place use differs from that of adults
> Children play anywhere and everywhere often venturing to places where their environmental needs have seldom been recognised. (Matthews & Limb, 1999, 68)

The literature points out that the conventional planning response towards play spaces is to provide hard surfaced playgrounds within sight and hearing of adults, replete with climbing frames and other commercially constructed adventure activity forms. It is significant that the city centre children's favourite play area was a large open field waiting for building development but allowed in the meantime to be open space. There was no regular mention of the playgrounds thoughtfully provided in each urban neighbourhood area and marked on the city map with a seesaw. The parks and spaces about the lakes were appreciated, especially for cycling and skate boarding, but there was always mention of having to avoid adults following more conservative activities.

In the country town, similarly, the greatest enthusiasm by the youngest children was reserved for the 'Bonfire field' again, an open space which presumably was occasionally grazed but, because of its slope was usually left unfarmed. The older children, however, roamed further and gave excellent descriptions of the bridleways, footpaths and the route of the dismantled railway. In addition, great discussion was occasioned about the safety or otherwise of a certain bathing place along the local river and the availability of 'loop' walks about the town. One sensed that here was freedom from adult interference and a chance to 'stand and stare' judging by the whispered confidentialities of what could be seen of wild life and vegetation. This sense of freedom was not so freely expressed by the city children though the older ones appreciated the bird sanctuaries and nature reserves available on the city's edges – again provided for adults, not children on their own.

Trainee teachers' knowledge of the built environment

The challenge of developing enquiry in the local area requires more attention to local detail than would appear to be known by the undergraduate teachers. In this study they were asked to give information about features which would define the characteristics of the locality in both social and built environment terms (Figure 4). Overall, only 50% were able to give any detail – after over ten weeks of regularly passing through the immediate school locality. It is significant that the least observant age group are the under 21's whilst the greatest detail came from the over 31's.

Community knowledge needed to enable comparisons with other localities

In the geography programmes of study for key stages 1 and 2 the study of contrasting localities is required (DfEE/QCA, 1999). Locality photo packs and videos used in these studies include reference to the pattern of school day, the means of getting to school, the distances travelled to school, health care, social attractions and the physical landscape, as well as the built environment. Only 14 percent of the study cohort returned information upon these features. The country town children took community features for granted, as one would expect in a rural town.

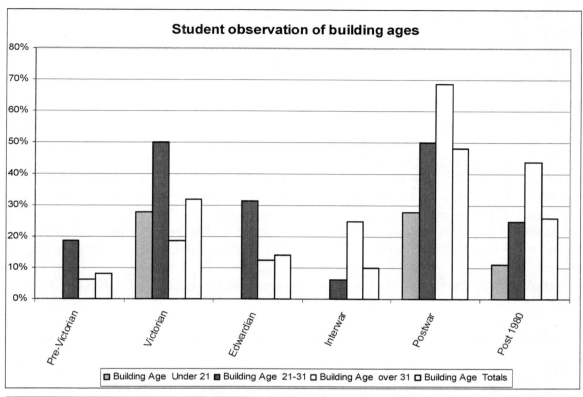

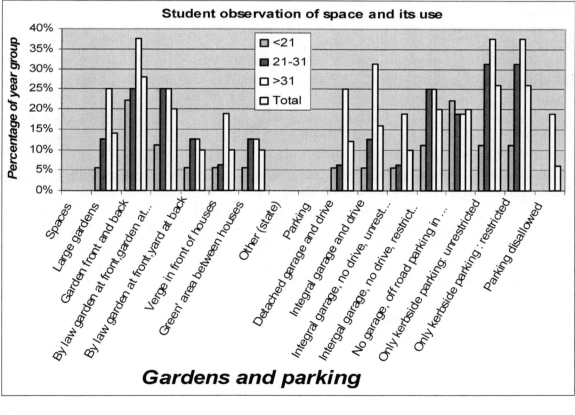

Figure 4: Student observation of locality features for curriculum use

They were more concerned that they had to travel some distance for swimming facilities. City children were conversant with the location of both health and policing points – as were other classes of inner urban children elsewhere. The country town children, on the other hand, were very clear about meeting places and clubs, which for the urban children did not seem to happen outside Cubs and Brownies unless one went to the organised leisure centres.

Discussion

The evidence presented by the children shows they have and develop locality awareness in their primary years. The teacher must recognise this spatial and environmental awareness. Martin (2000) has shown that this is problematic even for the geographically knowledgeable primary PGCE student. How much more difficult must it be then for the primary undergraduate whose specialist training is confined only to one of the core subjects. Children's cognitive spatial awareness 'concerns putting together personal knowledge and understanding of spatial layout, patterns and processes, and use' (Catling 2001, para 9). Catling continues, pointing out that

> ...spatial awareness cannot be divorced from place experience and environmental perceptions, which link to our sense of place and concern for the quality of the environment. Experience and interaction about the physical and social environment enables development of mental awareness of the spatial nature of the environment.

Unfortunately, this study provides evidence that with advancing maturity adult cognition of spatial layout, patterns and processes would appear to become less acute. This may be because, on entering adulthood, social environments, which influence an individuals' understanding of the physical and social environment, change. Personal concerns appear to be more focused on how and when people react within the social environment.

It would seem that to remedy this break in environmental perception it is vital to redevelop spatial awareness on three fronts:
- increased experience in and of the environment, i.e. increased time in the field during the ITT programme for all students, whether this is for scientific, historical, geographical, artistic or physical education reasons.
- increased movement about the environment – in the case of the student teacher and certainly the NQT, an observant walk about the locality encountered by the children they teach. This is not just the streets immediately about the school but the whole school catchment area as designated by the streets in the children's addresses.
- discovering how others see, understand and use the environment. This, in the local area of the school, requires specific abilities, many of which need to be used for cross-curricular purposes and all of which are dependent upon geographical understanding of the environment and its depiction by and with map and graphic. Moreover, these are abilities expected as outcomes from the activities associated with the geography programme of study, such as way finding, map reading, locating oneself, and understanding settlement hierarchies and place connections.

Conclusion

In the current educational environment, within the curriculum, developments being called for in primary education are that:

- geographical work should involve children in effective enquiries (and thus strongly support the development of thinking skills),
- primary schools should develop cross-curricular competences in citizenship and sustainability understanding, and
- primary children should become more involved in their community through citizenship and sustainability activities.

From the evidence it would seem that this is possible, taking account of the cognitive development of children's understanding of the environment in which they play and move about. However, the evidence also points out that:

- the new, young primary school teacher with little specialist training appears to be ill-equipped to deliver either the geography curriculum or a cross-curricular citizenship and sustainability curriculum, in that both demand an understanding of the environment within which their pupils live and are growing up;
- the lack of knowledge and understanding of locality features, necessary to appreciate similarities and differences with distant localities, also highlights the deep lack of background among potential primary teachers for delivering citizenship and sustainability as well as for developing geographical understanding.

If it is the case that adult knowledge and understanding of the localities in which they work is limited, and if, in particular, this situation is particularly the case amongst primary teachers and trainee primary teachers, it must be a matter of major concern in the geography and geography education communities that this situation is remedied. This study has raised a particular issue, in that it seems that while primary age children may be reasonably knowledgeable about their locality, many of their teachers may not be but, perhaps more worryingly, may lack the stimulus to remedy this. This is not a situation that need remain as it appears. The opportunity to develop in-service courses to help teachers build their local area knowledge and their skills in teaching geography can be used to tackle this. While challenges remain for time and quality in the primary geography curriculum, it is, nonetheless, the case that there are many schools which have shown what can be achieved (Ofsted, 2002, 2003).

Some schools have effective enquiry and locality study work in place. There are also effective networks being established to ensure the young primary teacher can improve both their specialist and professional competencies. These approaches need to be monitored as does the contrast in attitudes, particularly of adults, shown in the children's survey and undergraduate study. Most certainly, more detailed studies of primary teachers and children's locality knowledge, understanding and attitudes are needed. These concerns raise also some interesting areas for further investigation in their own right, in that they have a bearing upon willingness or otherwise of primary teachers to consider the wider world, global citizenship and issues of sustainability.

References

Barratt, R. and Barrett Hacking, E, (2000), Changing my locality: conceptions of the future, *Teaching Geography*, 25 (1), 18

Barratt Hacking E. (1996), Novice Teachers and their Geographical Persuasions, *International Research in Geographical and Environmental Education*, 5 (1), 77-86

Caputo, V. (1995), Anthropologies silent 'others, in Amit-Talai, V. and Wulff, H. (eds.), *Youth cultures: a cross cultural perspective*, London: Routledge

Catling, S. (2000), What is the purpose of teaching geography in school? in Moon, B., Brown, S. & Ben-Peretz, M. (eds.), *Routledge International Companion to Education*, London: Routledge

Catling S. (2001), *Children's Developing Spatial Awareness*: *Notes for presentation to GeoVisions Project Working Group Geographical Association*, www.geography.org.uk/project/geovisions/places.html   accessed 0n 18 Oct 03

DfEE/QCA (1999), *The National Curriculum for England: Geography*, London: DfEE/QCA

Halocha, J. (1998), Primary school teachers understanding of localities, unpublished paper presented at the 1998 UDE Geography Tutors Conference, Bath.

Hart, R. (1979), *Children's Experience of Place: A Development Study*, New York: Irvington Press

Hart, R. (1997), *Children's Participation*, London: Earthscan Publications

Martin, F. (1999), Contrasting Views on Locality between Child and Adult, *International Research in Geographical and Environmental Education*, 8 (1), 78-81

Martin, F. (2000), Postgraduate Primary Education Students' Images of Geography and the Relationship between these and Students' teaching, *International Research in Geographical and Environmental Education*, 9 (3), 223-244

Matthews, M. H. (1992), *Making Sense of Place: Children's understanding of large scale environments*, Hemel Hempstead: Harvester Wheatsheaf

Matthews, H. and Limb, M. (1999), Defining an agenda for the geography of children, *Progress in Human geography*, 23 (1), 61-90

McPartland, M. (1996), Walking in our own Footsteps: Autobiographical memories and the teaching of Geography, *International Research in Geographical and Environmental Education*, 5 (1), 57-62

Moore, R.C. (1986), *Childhood's Domain*, London: Croom Helm

Palmer, J. (1994, *Geography in the Early Years*, London: Routledge

Shulman, L.(1987), Knowledge and teaching: Foundations of the New Reform, *Harvard Education Review*, 57 (1), 1-22

Spencer, C. & Blades, M. (1993), Children's understanding of places: the world at hand, *Geography*, 78 (4), 367-373

Tuan, Y. (1977/2001), *Space and Place – the Perspective of Experience*, Minneapolis: University of Minnesota Press

Chapter 19

Student Teachers' Attitudes towards Education for Sustainable Development

Alison Ryan

Introduction

In 1992, the need for sustainable development was endorsed at international level when 180 world leaders signed up to Agenda 21 (UNCED, 1992). Education was recognised as crucial to its achievement and, in September 2000, education for sustainable development [EfSD] became an explicit feature of the statutory primary curriculum. In practice, however, the implementation of measures outlined in Agenda 21 has been slow. Rhetoric about the need for sustainable development abounds but this is not universally understood, acknowledged, nor converted into practice. Ofsted has only recently indicated its support for whole school commitment to EfSD and there is little in the national curriculum (with its emphasis on transmitting factual knowledge and raising standards in basic skills) to support pupils' active participation. The government's latest primary strategy (DfES, 2003) mentions neither EfSD nor Geography, which has a major role in promoting it.

Nevertheless, issues such as the development of genetically modified crops have prompted 'genuine misgivings about food, nature, progress, science and technology . . . even democracy itself' (Vidal, 1999, 6). In 2002/3, 4000 primary schools registered to take part in the Eco Schools programme, and primary age children have consistently voiced their concerns about sustainability issues. If teachers are to capitalise on this concern and introduce effective EfSD, they need to possess appropriate knowledge and understanding, along with certain values and attitudes. This research aimed to elicit initial teacher education [ITE] students' understanding of sustainable development and their attitudes towards EfSD and how these related to their perception of the primary teacher's role. These findings would be used to inform the planning of new ITE modules in geography and in the wider curriculum.

Literature review

Attitudes to sustainability issues

Commentators fail to agree on the meaning of sustainable development and how it might be achieved (Redclift, 2002). Definitions of sustainable development reflect different ideological positions and interests. Many would agree with the Qualification and Curriculum Authority's [QCA] statement that it involves ensuring a better quality of life for everyone now and for generations to come whilst protecting the environment (http://www.nc.uk.net/esd). However, that this should also include high levels of economic growth is not so generally accepted.

Steiner (1996) claims that through events such as Band Aid more is known about inequality and positive development than ever before. Environmental groups also flourish. Social theory suggests that as societies are modernised and as environmental risks increase, people become more reflexive and critical (Huckle, 1996). However, other commentators perceive a 'sense of despair and apathy' about the state of the environment (Plant, 1995, 253) and sustainable development is viewed as an impossible goal, given today's consumer society. Moreover, many people lack understanding of the complexity or relevance of global issues and the close ties between human activities and the environment (Norris Nicholson, 1996). Maiteny (2002) suggests that pro-environmental behaviour will only endure if it is rooted in a significant personal experience rather than a response to regulations, incentives or anxiety.

A high level of awareness or knowledge, or even the 'right' values do not necessarily lead to 'informed behaviour'. Posch (1993) discovered many inconsistencies between ITE students' 'values in action' and their espoused values and for a variety of reasons such as the cost of 'green' products, as well as laziness and apathy. The type and level of concerns expressed by ITE students appear to be no different from those of the public at large. They seem to have little awareness or understanding of issues such as power relations, which cause or contribute to the world's resource problems, and are confident that science and technology will solve environmental problems (Hicks & Holden, 1995). 'Green citizenship' is seen in terms of individual action, maintaining the status quo and involving activities such as recycling rather than political action (Campbell & Davies, 1995). Wilkins' study (1999) of student teachers revealed a high level of political disenchantment and cynicism. They felt powerless to effect change and found citizenship a negative concept.

Education for sustainable development

Different assumptions are made about EfSD theory and practice. For some, it involves simply acquiring knowledge of issues and developing concern. The DfEE/QCA (1999) state that pupils should be taught the skills, knowledge, understanding and values to participate in decision-making as part of education for active citizenship. Others see it as a process involving personal and societal change. It should be holistic, action-orientated, issues based, socially critical, participatory, empowering and reflective, and incorporate a futures dimension (Tilbury, 1995). Some commentators maintain that education should advance particular ends or ideologies such as sustainable development (Fien, 1993; Huckle, 1991). Jickling & Spork (1998) on the other hand assert that education should teach about sustainable development and develop skills to participate in debate about its nature. Several problems associated with innovation in formal education have been raised and there is no agreement as to whether formal education can actually achieve sustainable development. Standish (2003), for example, is critical of 'new agenda' geography with its emphasis on values and attitudes. He favours a 'traditional' approach: pupils should be taught about systems and different countries and develop skills to formulate their own opinions rather than be told how to think and act in relation to the world around them. Several commentators observe that ITE students (and teachers) are rarely involved in critical reflection concerning wider ethical, social and political issues and abstract concepts (Dunne, 1993) and indeed find it difficult when asked to do so.

Concepts of education

Several different ideological orientations (which are influenced by strongly held values) as to the nature and purpose of education have been identified. Theories of teaching and learning are likewise expressed in different ways. Biggs (1994), for example, describes a quantitative theory which involves transmission of facts, skills and competencies and a 'surface' approach to learning. A qualitative theory on the other hand, involves 'deep learning' within a constructivist model, with pupils learning actively and the teacher scaffolding their learning. In practice, however, neither ideological orientations nor theories of teaching and learning are exclusive. A strong form of EfSD would favour a constructivist model but in practice this may also involve the transmission of facts.

ITE students' perceptions of teaching

People enter teaching for a variety of reasons, from influencing children's thinking to the prospect of long holidays. Some see it as an 'ethical endeavour' (Steiner, 1996). Most students enter ITE courses with fixed ideas about teaching which are resistant to change when challenged by either their tutors or school experience (Bramald et al., 1995). Students also reveal a limited and unproblematic view of teaching and learning: learning, for example, is equated with the acquisition of factual knowledge and the use of traditional methodologies is favoured. QCA schemes of work should be followed to the letter to avoid criticism from Ofsted (Townsend, 2001). Other researchers have identified discrepancies between students' beliefs and practice. Their beliefs are unobservable until translated into practice, yet practice does not necessarily indicate their beliefs (Dunne, 1993).

Research method

Methodology

The research was undertaken using a qualitative or interpretative approach. This was seen as appropriate mainly because the aims were to identify, describe and understand individual perceptions and seek insight rather than focus on statistical analysis. A qualitative approach can also incorporate a flexible research design: theory need not be superimposed on the data collected but can emerge from it (Burgess, 1985). It is also an appropriate approach to use within research concerned with EfSD, which has a strong values base and emphasises personal as well as societal change.

The sample

The research involved ten volunteer students in their final year of a three-year ITE course. It was felt that third year students would have more 'life experience' and would have begun to formulate ideas about the role of a primary teacher. They represented a range of ages and backgrounds.

The method

The key research method used was semi-structured interviews. This was used for a number of reasons. It is seen as a particularly appropriate strategy within a research methodology with essentially interactive and interpretative characteristics. It is also often used in a small-scale enquiry with limited time and resources in a situation where the researcher is an actor (Robson, 1993). Used rigorously, qualitative interviewing 'combines the complexities of factual and emotional responses in a richness of communicated understandings which can't be found in other technical rational means of data collection' (Day, 1993, 126). In the event, it proved to be a flexible method, enabling interesting or unexpected responses and underlying motives to be explored and producing a large volume of 'rich' data from a small number of individuals. Each student was interviewed for approximately half an hour. They all agreed to the interview being tape-recorded. This was felt to be the most unobtrusive and straightforward method of data collection and worked well, enabling the interviewer to concentrate on what the interviewee was saying and respond appropriately.

Qualitative interviewing has potential problems of bias and the legitimacy of qualitative data has often been questioned. However, Gilbert (1993) considers that the effects of interviewers on the validity and reliability of data can be overstated: limited guidance and direction from an interviewer do not constitute misdirected probing. Moreover, a desire for objectivity can sometimes be unproductive, producing a conventional and unreflecting answer rather than evoking a deeper and more thoughtful response. Cohen, Manion & Morrison (2000) point out that interviewees rarely have insight into the causes of their behaviour. They may be unaccustomed to putting their feelings into words; they may not admit to socially undesirable traits; or they may be over-polite, answering what they anticipate the interviewer wants to hear. The former did arise during the interviews and students struggled to answer some questions. However, their responses did include comments with which they knew I would not agree or which could be considered as not 'politically correct'.

The interview

Piloting enabled research questions to be refined, probes to be tested and techniques to be evaluated and modified. Subsequently, a framework of mainly open ended and exploratory questions was prepared in which the students could elaborate their ideas but which would also to provide the data required. The questions focused on their perceptions of education and teaching and their knowledge and understanding of sustainable development.

- What do you see as the primary teacher's role? Which values and attitudes do you want to teach or develop?
- What do you think about the future? Do you think that sustainable development is achievable? How much do you think you know about global issues? Do you do anything to be a 'green citizen'?
- Do you think that EfSD should be a feature of primary education?

Analysis of the data

The analysis of the data was consistent with the general underlying philosophy of the research, that it is descriptive and interpretative. The interview tapes were transcribed in full. The data were divided into sections and each section was coded in order to identify categories. Descriptive codes were used which were mutually exclusive and covered all options. Patterns or themes were then identified in the data. Some codes, categories and themes had been suggested by theory, intuition and piloting but others were generated by the data: for example, it had not been anticipated that students would raise introducing a whole school initiative as a significant problem. The findings are presented in terms of impressions which were gained. Little reference is made to numbers as the main concern was to identify and describe a range of behaviour and opinions rather than how many hold the view or how strongly.

Findings

A number of findings emerged from the study. Those discussed here relate to the role of primary education, sustainability issues and attitudes to education for sustainable development. Student comments are used to inform the findings.

The role of primary education

Most students were adamant about the importance of teaching children 'basic skills' (literacy and numeracy) either because that was what was expected of them or because they saw them as crucial to children's future.

> *'you can't get anywhere in this world (without them)'*

Some also saw social skills as a basic skill. However, the provision of a 'broad and balanced curriculum' was also seen as essential, as was the development of 'the whole child'. Teaching children to be reflective and critical was seen as fairly important, helping them to become independent thinkers.

> *'so they can reflect on a variety of issues and ideas and be critical about them, how it relates to their own lives'*

Most students appeared to see themselves as transmitters of society's values, with parents receiving little recognition of the part they might play in this.

> *'children don't always come to school with the right values'*
> *'you do have to teach children things (values and attitudes) - you can't just let them develop it themselves all the time'*

The students were unanimous in identifying attitudes towards other people ('respect') as the most important area to be developed. They all saw addressing values and attitudes as something they would be proactive about, by including it in their planning where appropriate as well as a more unstructured, informal approach.

> *'presenting alternatives to what they've experienced and letting them make their own minds up about different issues'*

Most of the students hoped that their teaching 'would make a difference' but they disagreed over the influence that a teacher has over children.

> *'a lot of children think that what the teacher says is gospel'*

Sustainability issues: knowledge, understanding and attitudes

All except one of the students were unreservedly positive and optimistic about their personal futures. In terms of the future of the planet and the human race, there was a mixed response and most felt it was out of their control.

> *'nah - don't believe a word of it (media reports on predicted ecological disasters) - it will happen one day but not while I'm alive - hundreds, maybe thousands of years down the line'*

Most students tended to see any problems as 'out there' and not really relevant to them. There was, however, some indication that they felt they should 'do something'.

> *' this is a really bad attitude - by the time anything awful happens we won't be around but I do think we should make more of an effort for future generations'*

229

Issues like war, ethnic cleansing and the unequal distribution of wealth were identified as the most significant, rather than environmental problems.

> *'so many people with so much, so many with nothing'*
> *'(global warming) doesn't worry me . . .I'm sure technology will grow and solve problems'*

Sustainable development was seen as idealistic and everyone saw it as difficult to achieve.

> *'it's a nice idea but unrealistic'*
> *'if it's not happened up to now with all the attempts that have been made I can't see it happening in the future'*

Numerous obstacles were identified, including lack of interest (unless the effect could be seen locally) and expense as well difficulty in understanding the issues involved and knowing what to do.

> *'if I could afford it I would have solar power on my roof'*
> *'is buying an artificial Christmas tree best?'*
> *'I'd like to do something but I don't know what'*

'Human nature' was seen as the main obstacle: people were selfish or too set in their ways and would not be prepared to change. Some students also believed firmly in the status quo.

> *'people wouldn't be prepared to make a conscious effort - drop in standard of living - only little things like energy saving light bulbs - people aren't willing to give up their creature comforts'*
> *'you've always got to have rich and poor people for society to work'*

The students acknowledged that many people had little control over their lives, but thought that this did not apply to them. Some saw voting as important; others expressed political disenchantment, lack of interest, cynicism and powerlessness to effect change.

> *'I don't get too involved - it's a bit of an ostrich thing - I suppose it's wrong and this is why things don't get altered, it's out of your immediate control - other people will sort it out'*

Although most of the students claimed to watch or listen to news programmes or glance at newspapers, no one could recall, for example, demonstrations at the latest world summit. They all considered their level of knowledge about global issues to be limited although this was not necessarily a concern. Acquiring knowledge was mainly seen as information for teaching rather than as knowledge which an individual should have.

> *'I feel I should know more - children are expected to discuss and debate current issues'.*

All except one of the students undertook one or more 'green' activities such as consciously seeking out recycled and CFC products; recycling newspapers, bottles and plastic bags; saving energy (switching off lights). One student demonstrated an awareness of 'fair trade' products. However, environmental considerations were not necessarily the driving force but rather lack of choice or financial reasons. A range of obstacles was identified, from inertia to lack of money.

'it's difficult when values are one thing and money's another'

Attitudes to EfSD

There was unanimous agreement that, in terms of process, EfSD was highly desirable. Each student highlighted one or more features such as active or collaborative learning.

> *'active learning - (children) learn and remember by doing something'*
> *'collaborative learning . . . I like the idea of that . . . if you believe in change, then people have to work together'*

For most students, their responses reflected at least some of the ways in which they already approached teaching and learning. They thought that EfSD could be satisfactorily included not only within geography but across the curriculum in spite of the subject focus of the national curriculum.

> *'children seem to get more out of (cross curricular work)'*

The idea the EfSD was not just cross-curricular but should permeate a school's ethos was also received positively: it would make the experience 'real' for children and thus be more motivating.

> *'otherwise it would be hypocritical - you can't just talk about it in the classroom and not do anything'*

There were, however, some reservations about whole school initiatives.

> *'it wouldn't be easy to implement in schools - it would need . . . the support of all the staff which is not always easy'*

None of the students dismissed the socially critical dimension of EfSD as inappropriate.

> *'it's good to encourage children to think that they could make a difference'*
> *'I really like the idea of kids getting involved in life, in society, in the issues involved'*

However, they expressed a number of reservations. They thought the teacher's agenda should not be paramount and there were mixed feelings about investigating local issues.

> *'they're not just kicking up a fuss because the teacher's learning objective is to write a letter of complaint'*

All students identified the potential for clashes between school and parents or other members of the local community. Doubt was also expressed about children questioning the way they live, which could be interpreted as critical of parents.

> *'you wouldn't want a child to be ostracised because he comes to school in a car'*

The importance of a carefully thought out and 'balanced' approach was emphasised: teachers should have sufficient background knowledge, and children adequate information to listen to each other then make up their own minds. A need for training, for example on dealing with controversial issues in the classroom, was identified.

Discussion

The students' responses suggested that they saw a primary teacher as a 'reflective practitioner' with a moral purpose, engaged in the development of the whole child and not merely as a technician, which much of their training might have led them to believe. They drew from different theories as to the role of education and approaches to teaching and learning. For example, they considered that some transmission was necessary but that a constructivist approach was also appropriate, with children being involved in active, reflective and co-operative learning. Developing values and attitudes was viewed as important as teaching what they saw as 'the basics' although this was seen in terms of people and their relationships with each other, rather than attitudes towards the environment. They demonstrated some inconsistencies in their belief in children's autonomy. Initially it would appear that they would support a liberal approach as proposed by Jickling & Spork (1998). However, in then stating that certain values and attitudes should be taught they seemed to be leaning towards the deterministic approach of commentators such as Fien (1993) or 'well intended indoctrination'. There seemed to be an assumption that their values were the 'right' ones, acceptable to all.

The students' responses to questions about sustainable development supported much of the literature. Their views ranged from denial of any crisis to concern; any problems were in the future, elsewhere or not relevant to them, and would probably be solved by science and technology. This perhaps could be explained by Cross' notion (1998) that teaching is an 'optimistic' activity. Human nature and society were viewed as incapable of change and people's basic greed was seen to conspire against sustainable development ever being achieved. They appeared to have little awareness of current events or issues. As their information came largely from 'low-level' media information they were not aware of global systems and the structural forces which circumscribe people's choices and actions. They equated quality of life with consumption and although they undertook a variety of 'green' activities, these were seen in terms of individual action, rather than involvement in political action and questioning the status quo, very much supporting Campbell & Davies' findings (1995). These were also activities which involved little effort or changes to their basic lifestyles and seemed to be quite arbitrary, unrelated to any knowledge they might have had of particular issues. Their reasons for not doing more are similar to those [such as helplessness, inertia and cost] identified by other researchers. Although some were more interested in voting than others, their feelings of cynicism, disenchantment, disempowerment and inability to effect change also reflect other findings.

In terms of EfSD, the students did not appear to regard education as an opportunity to 'change the world'. They were in favour of several features of EfSD, such as collaborative learning and learning actively through enquiry in geography or investigation in science, and in most cases were already using these approaches. Cross-curricular work was seen as something which should be developed rather than as problematic. This is, perhaps, somewhat surprising, given the focus on subjects both in school and in the students' training and the difficulties other students have identified in implementing cross-curricular themes (Lyle, 1996). However, the students interviewed had all recently been assessed as very competent teachers and perhaps they were now able to make links between subjects as an effective approach to teaching and learning. They were realistic about the difficulties of introducing innovation into primary schools, especially if this involved whole school commitment. They expressed some reservations about encouraging children to be socially critical but had no hesitation in stating that this was an appropriate approach to take and that children should become involved in real issues. This was seen as an empowering experience for children which would demonstrate that 'active citizenship' could make a difference as well as making learning more relevant and meaningful. However, they did emphasise a balanced approach rather than Fien's (1993) commitment to promoting actively values and attitudes which are seen as essential to sustainable living.

Conclusion

Much research suggests that a verbal response is a problematic indicator of action (Gilbert, 1993). The students may have claimed that they would engage their pupils in, say, practical, issues-based learning, but there is no way of knowing whether this will be the case. Whether or not they will engage with any form of EfSD can only be inferred from their responses as it concerns a hypothetical situation in the future.

The students' responses indicated that they would be predisposed towards a committed form of EfSD, at least in terms of process. However, they demonstrated little of the requisite knowledge, understanding and attitudes. Little concern or awareness of the need for sustainable development was evident and although they might have been happy for their pupils to take a socially critical approach, the students did not appear to see the need to engage in the process of change themselves.

The research only considered the views of a small group of students who may not be representative of all those engaged in ITE. However, the findings suggest that considerable input would be required to enable these students to engage effectively with EfSD. To make EfSD solely schools' responsibility would seem to be problematic, given the patchy nature of good practice. For ITE to enable students to prepare their pupils for life as global citizens requires developing both their subject knowledge and pedagogic skills. Suggestions have already been made as to how EfSD could be addressed within ITE (Shallcross & Wilkinson, 1998). It is perhaps now time to move on and evaluate the impact and effectiveness of input on EfSD within ITE. This research could be seen to imply that if ITE students emerge with the knowledge, understanding, skills, values and attitudes to address EfSD once in the classroom, then all will be right with the world. However, it should be noted that if EfSD is to be pursued with some hope of progress, then it needs to be seen as part of a process involving the whole school community.

References

Biggs, J. (1994), The research context: student learning research and theory where do we currently stand?, in Gibbs G. (ed.) (1994) *Improving student learning*, Oxford: Oxford Brookes University

Bramald, R., Hardman, F. & Leat, D. (1995), Initial teacher trainees and their views of teaching and learning, *Teaching and Teacher Education,* 11 (1), 23-31

Burgess, R. G. (ed.) (1985), *Strategies of Educational research: Qualitative Methods*, Lewes: Falmer

Campbell, B. & Davies, I. (1995), Education and green citizenship: an exploratory study with student teachers, *Journal of Further and Higher Education,* 19 (3), 20-31

Cohen, L., Manion, L. & Morrison, K. (2000), *Research Methods in Education*, London: RoutledgeFalmer

Cross, R. (1998), Teachers' Views about What to do about Sustainable Development, *Environmental Education Research*, 4 (1), 41-51

Day, C. (1993), The development of teachers' thinking and practice: does choice lead to empowerment?, in Elliott, J. (ed.) (1993), *Reconstructing Teacher Education: Teacher Development*, London: Falmer Press

DfEE/QCA (1999), *The National Curriculum: Handbook for primary teachers in England*, London: DfEE/QCA

DfES (2003), *Excellence and Enjoyment: A strategy for primary schools*, London: DfES

Dunne, E. (1993), General beliefs about teaching and learning, in Bennett, N. & Carré, C. (eds.), *Learning to teach*, London: Routledge

Fien, J. (1993), *Education for the Environment: critical curriculum theorising and environmental education*, Victoria: Deakin University Press

Gilbert, N. (ed.) (1993), *Researching Social Life*, London, Sage

Hicks, D. & Holden, C. (1995), *Visions of the Future*, Stoke-on-Trent: Trentham Books

Huckle, J. (1991), Education for sustainability: assessing pathways to the future, *Australian Journal of Environmental Education*, 7, 43-62

Jickling, B. & Spork, H. (1998), Education for the Environment: a critique, *Environmental Education Research*, 4 (3), 309-327

Lyle, S. (1996), Environmental education for sustainable futures: Developing an action-research model for primary initial teacher education, in Steiner, M. (ed.), *Developing the Global Teacher*, Stoke-on-Trent: Trentham Books

Maiteny, P. (2002), Mind in the Gap: summary of research exploring 'inner' influences on pro-sustainability learning and behaviour, *Environmental Education Research*, 8 (3), 299-306

Norris Nicholson, H. (1996), Crossing points and meeting places: geography and global perspectives in initial teacher education, in Steiner, M. (ed.), *Developing the Global Teacher*, Stoke-on-Trent: Trentham Books

Plant, M. (1995), The Riddle of Sustainable Development and the Role of Environmental Education, *Environmental Education Research*, 1 (3), 253-266

Posch, P. (1993), Approaches to Values in Environmental Education, *OECD/ENSI Values in Environmental Education Conference Report*, SCCC

Redclift, M. (2002), Pathways to Sustainability?, *Geography*, 87 (3), 189-195

Robson, C. (1993), *Real World Research: A resource for social scientists and practioner researchers*, Oxford: Blackwell

Shallcross, T. & Wilkinson, G. (1998), The primacy of action: the basis of initial teacher education for sustainability, *Environmental Education and Information*, 17 (3), 243-256

Standish, A. (2003), Constructing a value map, *Geography*, 88 (2), 149-5

Steiner, M. (ed.) (1996), *Developing the Global Teacher*, Stoke-on-Trent: Trentham Books

Tilbury D, (1995), Environmental Education for Sustainability: defining the new focus of environmental education in the 1990s, *Environmental Education Research*, 1 (2), 195-212

Townsend, C. (2001), Initial teacher training at the CREATE Course, *Environmental Education*, 68, 9-10

United Nations Conference on Environment and Development (UNCED) (1992), *Agenda 21*, London, Regency Press

Vidal, J. (2000), Century of the environment, in WWF/The Guardian, *A new century a new revolution*, London: WWF/The Guardian, 5-6

Wilkins, C, (1999), Making 'Good Citizens': the social and political attitudes of PGCE students, *Oxford Review of Education*, 25 (1-2), 217-230

Chapter 20

Student Teachers' Perceptions of Geographical Enquiry

John Halocha

Introduction

The thinking behind the enquiry process and practical ways of developing it with pupils are a central part of many primary geography courses in initial teacher education. At several higher education institutions a '3+1' degree is offered in which students study a main subject and education studies with equal weighting for the first three years of the programme, completed by a fourth year PGCE qualifying them to teach. Students studying Geography as their main subject are prepared to become effective subject leaders. The research described here was set up to investigate the students' level of understanding of geographical enquiry in order to make some assessment of the effectiveness of the geography modules taught in the 3-year programme. These students may have an impact on their future colleagues, who may well have limited experience and little expertise in geography, and it was considered important to investigate how the students understood, defined and explained the nature of geographical enquiry.

Year three undergraduates were selected as they had completed both a level 2 module called 'Children and Places' and a level 3 module focussing on geography subject leadership in primary schools. In these modules, they consider the rationale for geographical enquiry and have opportunities to develop their practical skills in planning, conducting and evaluating enquiries appropriate to the primary curriculum.

The research was carried out in order to assess their levels of understanding of enquiry, as well as some of the issues that arise when such approaches to learning are adopted. The findings were intended to inform the geography tutors on the programme of the effectiveness of inputs on enquiry in order to improve the quality of training for future geography subject leaders.

Literature review

The concept of geographical enquiry may be traced back to secondary school curriculum development activities in the 1970s and 1980s (Roberts, 2003). The Geography 16-19 Project used the phrase 'enquiry-based teaching and learning', while The Geography for the Young School Leaver Project included the words 'areas of enquiry'. Although the contributors to *Geographical Work in Primary and Middle Schools* (Mills, 1988) make no direct reference to it, an embryonic form of enquiry is provided in Williams & Catling (1985) in which they identify basic communication skills, intellectual skills and social skills as experiences children should be systematically exposed to in order to carry out geographical studies. Storm (1989) perhaps set the framework for geographical enquiry with his five key questions to be used to focus the study of places (Figure 1), building on an outline of geographical questions first put forward in Storm & Catling a year earlier (1988, 306-307; see also, Catling, 1988, 253). These *enquiry questions* have been included in the key texts that focus on the methodology of primary geography teaching since the late 1980s (eg Blyth & Krause, 1995; Foley & Janikoun, 1996; Owen & Ryan,

2001). By 1991 the Geography orders stated that 'Enquiry should form an important part of pupils' work in Key Stage 2' (DES, 1991, 35). Foley and Janikoun (1992) argued for the addition of two further questions in the light of the wording of the 1991 geography orders. The 1995 revised Geography order actually included some of the enquiry questions developed by Storm. *The Handbook of Primary Geography* (Carter, 1998) includes a whole chapter on geographical questions and enquiry. QCA (1998) commences their discussion paper No. 3 on geographical enquiry with the statement that

> Geographical enquiry is an integral part of the geography national curriculum requiring pupils at key stages 1, 2 and 3 to be given opportunities to ask geographical questions and investigate places and themes. (QCA,1998, iii)

The current order, published in 1999, states clearly that 'teachers should ensure that geographical enquiry and skills are used' at both Key Stage 1 and 2 (DfEE/QCA, 1999, 16, 18). Foley (1999) suggests that English primary teachers should see geographical enquiry in much the same way as they do mathematical and scientific investigations.

Key questions to pose in the study of any place

What is this place like?
Why is this place as it is?
How is this place connected with other places?
How is this place changing?
What would it feel like to be in this place?

Figure 1: Storm's five geographical enquiry questions for the study of places (Storm, 1989, 4)

Although the *enquiry process* was being adopted in geography teaching in primary and secondary schools, the only published research into how teachers actually put it into practice was conducted in some secondary schools by Roberts (1998, 164-167; 2003). The findings were used to inform the 1998 QCA discussion paper. Her data revealed that secondary school teachers of geography interpreted the term *enquiry* in a variety of ways. She suggested that these teachers had been affected by their own past geographical experiences as both students and teachers.

Most recently, Lambert argues that with the many changes which have taken place in the national curriculum since 1991, and alongside other issues affecting schools,

> Despite lip service paid to techniques to promote 'enquiry learning', geography fundamentally fulfils the requirements of an 'answer culture'. (Lambert, 2004, 78)

If Lambert is correct, then attention should be paid to how trainee teachers are introduced to the concept of *enquiry* and develop their understanding of the term. The research reported here examines this within the context of a course for primary geography specialist students.

Research method

In year 2 of the Bishop Grosseteste College '3+1' honours degree programme, geography students follow a module entitled 'Children and Places', in which they examine the practicalities of teaching the National Curriculum orders in primary schools. The year 3 module 'The Geography Subject Leader' examines in depth the role of a subject leader. Towards the end of their 3-year degree programme, seventeen geography subject specialists were asked to complete a questionnaire designed to collect data on their understanding of the term *geographical enquiry*.

Students were told that the questionnaire was designed in order to help the course team improve further the quality of experience offered to geography specialists. It was handed out towards the end of a timetabled teaching session in the module 'The Geography Subject Leader'. Students were asked to sit alone to complete the form. No tutor was present while the forms were completed. The forms were designed to be anonymous. Students were asked to leave the completed forms in a box when they left the session.

The questionnaire consisted of five questions. Each question is stated below, together with the reasons for the use of that question.

Q 1. As a geography specialist, what does *geographical enquiry* mean to you for your work so far with official sources?

This question was designed to assess the extent to which students' reading of a wide range of statutory and non-statutory documents may have influenced their understanding of the concept of enquiry.

Q 2. How would you know when enquiry was actually being used in primary school geography lessons?

Here, students were encouraged to consider the evidence they thought they would need to show that children were engaged in an enquiry process. It was also included to help them think about the evidence they might collect as geography subject leaders.

Q 3. What evidence have you seen of geographical enquiry during school placements?

If Roberts (1998) is correct, it was considered to be relevant to consider the possible impact of what students observe taking place in schools.

Q 4. Many sources suggest that the most effective enquiries are those generated by the pupils themselves. How can this actually be achieved, while at the same time ensuring the national curriculum orders are covered in full?

This question encouraged students to comment on the extent to which pupils' own questions about the world may or may not be connected with the statutory content of the national curriculum. It was also included to see if students challenged the validity of a centrally imposed curriculum.

Q 5. Just imagine that in a future review of the foundation subjects, it was decided that teachers could re-define the concept of *geographical enquiry*. What would you do and why would you do it?

The final question was included to encourage students to break away from what they had read and seen in schools. It was intended to be an opportunity to express their own views on what geographical enquiry might be.

The replies to each question were analysed separately and collated to build up a picture of the range of responses. This also provided an opportunity to identify patterns of response. Words, phrases and ideas were grouped together where similarities were identified. Students' comments were read carefully for any evidence of how tutor opinion may or may not have been transmitted during the taught modules.

Links across the questions were also examined; for example, if a response to one question might also be linked to a similar response to another question. An example of this was whether students who had seen very little enquiry taking place in schools had a particular picture in their minds of what they might actually identify as enquiry.

The data was examined for any evidence of language from various sources being drawn on or used in the students' own writing. For instance, were Storm's original set of enquiry questions (Figure 1) a major part of their vocabulary?

Written responses can only provide part of the picture of student understanding. However, it was decide not to interview students since it was felt that anonymous replies might result in more honest and realistic answers. At the time the research was conducted, the cohort still had to have an interview as part of their assessment for the year 3 module and the subject team decided that it would be inappropriate and unethical for students to feel that interviews for the research might influence how they were formally assessed.

Findings

Overall, there was considerable conformity across the responses. This created a number of patterns that are discussed below. However, some interesting individual statements offer insights and raise issues about the teaching and learning in the 3-year programme.

Question 1: Personal understanding of the meaning of 'geographical enquiry'

Almost all students placed emphasis on the need for children to pose geographical questions based on their own interests. They justified this by the need for children to 'make it their own learning', 'to try out their ideas', and how such enquiry 'promotes curiosity'. They did not go into detail about the questions and there were no examples of Storm's enquiry questions used for illustration. The emphasis was very much on children posing their own questions. They did, however, suggest that the pupils' questions would be of a 'geographical nature'. They did not discuss how pupils might actually know what type of questions to be asking.

Although this *liberal* approach dominated their replies, more than half the students also stated that the teacher would have some form of control over the process of selecting the questions that children would follow. The process would be 'structured by the teacher', 'discussion - directed by the teacher although children would not realise this', and 'can be structured as much or as little as a teacher thinks necessary' are examples of their thinking on this process. There appears to be some tension between wanting children to learn how to pose questions independently while at the same time allowing the teacher to control the process in some way. This is developed further in replies to question 4.

Question 2: Knowing geographical enquiry is being used in a geography lesson

This question asked students to identify evidence they might see in school to show whether or not enquiry was being used. It was also included to encourage students to think for themselves how they might do this as a geography subject leader.

Although they stated that they would be looking for pupils asking geographical questions, they included more precision by suggesting that the types of questions should be studied: were they open or closed? Replies to this question also showed more detail about the role the teacher might play in developing enquiry questions. The majority of answers suggested that pupils would ask the initial questions and teachers would help them to clarify what they wanted to find out and how they might do it. The teachers' role appears to be one of ensuring that geographical learning is developed and that it is clearly focussed. Further evidence, they suggested, would come from seeing much practical activity and the use of a wide range of resources. A further trend was that there would be evidence of pupils demonstrating a change in their thinking about the area of geography being investigated. For example, after studying a river they would have clear ideas about how water flows and changes the landscape.

Question 3: Evidence seen in school of geographical enquiry in practice

Just over half the replies stated that no geographical enquiry had been observed during school placements, nor had they been asked to teach any themselves. These responses were followed up in some cases with examples of practice they had observed: 'most geography prescribed - little or no scope for geographical enquiry', and 'children answering questions set by teacher'.

However, those who said they had seen effective enquiry work gave examples taken from practical fieldwork activities in schools, for instance 'asking questions about why Cleethorpes had developed as a tourist place' and 'traffic survey - parking controls - testing ideas against reality'. This cohort of students appears to have had strongly contrasting experiences on school placements.

Question 4: Involving pupils in geographical enquiry generation

This question allowed students to respond in more depth to the tension between the need to provide a learning environment in which children can develop geographical enquiry, while at the same time ensuring the geography national curriculum was covered in full.

The majority of replies suggested that the teacher creates the overall framework within which pupils develop their geographical enquiries. They justified this by recognising that time was limited. Most replies provided evidence of how teachers might do this: 'teacher guides children's thinking', 'teacher gives children ideas of the issues', 'teacher is the most important person', and 'teacher checks children's enquiries before they go off to ensure within guidelines'. The overriding message to this question was that the teacher creates and controls the overall framework for enquiry learning to ensure statutory requirements are met. Alongside this, students also expressed the clear desire for children to develop their own questions and interests within this framework.

Reading the detailed responses to this question gave a sense of how students were trying to ensure that the nature of geographical enquiry would not be lost within the demands of legal requirements and other school pressures. Some were able to suggest ways of achieving this. Using literacy time to develop enquiries that also fulfilled NLS objectives and to think creatively and be flexible. Some replies also suggested that teachers could be secretly directive in making children think they had chosen an enquiry when they had not: "this will actually be decided by the teacher who will lead the children in a certain way during their discussions". Other replies were not as direct as this but perhaps suggested this method may be behind some of their thinking.

Question 5: Redefining geographical enquiry

Half the students wrote that they were 'unsure' about how to respond to this question.

Those who did offer some ideas covered a range of ideas. The predominant word was 'freedom' for teachers to allow children to develop their own lines of enquiry based on their interests. This would then require more time for meaningful enquiries to develop. It is interesting to compare this with recent views expressed by the chief HMI on how the primary curriculum might develop, particularly in relation to increased cross-subject interaction (DfES, 2003).

Discussion

A recurring theme throughout the responses was how the teacher reconciles the need for genuine geographical enquiry within the practical constraints imposed by the school and legislation. Many geographical sources (eg. *Primary Geographer*, No.38, July 1999) provide extensive and challenging ideas on how enquiry can be developed in school, while perhaps not taking into account the context in which this teaching might take place. Perhaps specialist courses need to take this reality into account and provide opportunities for students to reflect on how they might respond. Rawling (2001) points out that the time available for proper and in depth consideration of both theory in education and the basis for academic subjects is limited in initial teacher education courses. As geography discipline specialists, may this be an appropriate time to ask critical questions about the nature of geographical enquiry? Might there be new ways of looking at how primary children develop an understanding of the world? Indeed, Catling (2003) argues that the time may be right for teachers and researchers to look more critically at such concepts as enquiry by considering how children view their worlds. If we are to develop a curriculum that takes into account what children wish to find out, we may be able to offer experiences they can see the point of pursuing.

The responses to Question 2 suggest that students are developing some critical skills in assessing how enquiry may be identified in school. The programme appears to be successful in preparing them to judge practice against some currently held views on the nature of enquiry. However, responses to Question 3 raise some concerns. Half of these specialists did not observe or teach enquiry methods on placements experienced by all students. The placement of students may need to address this, for both geography specialist students but equally with regard to non-geography specialist students. Should, as a minimum, geography-based school experience be built into the specialist course in years 1 and 2?

Responses to Question 4 included phrases such as 'guided by the teacher' and 'teacher guides thinking right direction'. They reveal opportunities to draw out the underlying meanings of such statements to enable students to justify their points of view and understand more deeply why they hold them. This in turn may enable them to work alongside colleagues in school with greater confidence, having worked through their own positions on these issues. This in turn may help them raise questions about the essential nature of enquiry and why we actually believe it aids the development of geographical thinking.

Half of replies to Question 5 suggested students had difficulty in making a response. Initial teacher educators have become experts in training students to meet the Standards for QTS. But, surely a reflective practice model also needs to ensure that students have the ability to think and reflect on current received wisdom and educational theory? Are current programmes really preparing students for a world in which they may be able to influence the nature of primary education? Catling's (2003) notion of starting from the child's perspective may help students avoid taking for granted official notions of concepts such as enquiry. However, is this an approach that students will find in other modules in their programmes and, indeed, when they are on school placements?

Conclusion

Taking all the responses together, it appears that students are increasingly aware of what enquiry might look like if the model of primary geography suggested by Catling (2003) were to be adopted in schools. However, they may be reluctant, or indeed feel powerless, to challenge 'the current adult-orientated sense of geography' (Catling, 2003, 204) as their awareness grows of the influence of teaching for SATS, inspections and the current perceptions of some headteachers and teachers. However, many programmes do work with some partnership schools where increasingly the headteachers and governors are encouraging and supporting their staff to adopt new approaches to learning and teaching, now encouraged by the recently published strategy for primary education, which seeks to support children's learning and experience more explicitly and to see teachers engage in thinking about learning and teaching across the curriculum, not simply in subject boundaries (DfES, 2003). As a result of this research, the geography team is looking at ways to ensure that geography students have the opportunity to meet people from primary schools who are working to develop critically and imaginatively the nature of primary education. Hopefully, the lack of confidence that came through in many of the responses may be addressed by meeting people who have the confidence and initiative to innovate and show that it can work in the real world. In this way it may then be possible to look afresh at the notion of enquiry.

> Asking questions about the world, investigating and exploring it directly and discussing one's discoveries with one's peers, are surely survival skills programmed into the young of our species. (Spencer, 2003, 233)

Spencer argues for education to work *with* children rather than to be about imposing concepts, knowledge and systems from outside upon them that in many ways are alien to the worlds in which children, in reality, live. However, one of the main structures imposed from beyond the child is the current Geography Order. We have a rapidly growing body of literature (Catling, 2003, 205-210) in the world of geographical education that argues for us to develop geographical experiences based more on children's own worlds and questions. Perhaps it is now time for the geography education community (teachers, researchers, headteachers etc.) to research and develop a very clear model of what an alternative to the current order might look like in practice and how geographical experiences really are a vital part of children's education in the primary school.

References

Blyth, A. & Krause, J. (1995), *Primary Geography: A developmental approach*, Sevenoaks: Hodder & Stoughton

Carter, R. (ed.) (1998), *Handbook of Primary Geography*, Sheffield: Geographical Association

Catling, S. (1988), Geography within environmental studies, in Mills, D. (ed.), *Geographical Work in Primary and Middle Schools* , Sheffield: Geographical Association, 252-264

Catling, S. (2003), Curriculum contested: Primary geography and social justice, *Geography*, 88 (3), 164-210

DES/WO (1991), *Geography in the National Curriculum (England)*, London: HMSO

DfEE/QCA (1999), *The National Curriculum for England: Geography*, London: HMSO

DfES (2003), *Excellence and Enjoyment: A strategy for primary schools*, London: DfES

Foley, M. and Janikoun, J. (1996), *The Really Practical Guide to Primary Geography*, Cheltenham: Stanley Thornes

Foley, M. (1999), Using the enquiry approach in primary geographical education, *International Research in Geographical and Environmental Education*, 8 (1), 82-85

Lambert, D. (2004) Geography, in White, J. (ed.), *Rethinking the School Curriculum. Values, aims and purposes*, London: Routledge, 75-86

Mills, D. (ed.) (1988), *Geographical Work in Primary and Middle Schools*, Sheffield: Geographical Association

Owen, D. & Ryan, A. (2001), *Teaching Geography 3-11: The Essential Guide*, London: Continuum

Primary Geographer (1999), Focus on Enquiry, *Primary Geographer*, 38, July

QCA (1998), *Geographical Enquiry at Key Stages 1-3*, London: QCA

Rawling, E. (2001), *Changing the Subject: The impact of national policy on school geography 1980-2000*, Sheffield: Geographical Association

Roberts, M. (1998), The nature of geographical enquiry at key stage 2, *Teaching Geography*, 23 (4), 164-167

Roberts, M. (2003), *Learning through Enquiry*, Sheffield: Geographical Association

Spencer, C. (2003), Why has the geography curriculum been so little attuned to the child's geographical enquiry? *Geography*, 88,3, July, 232-233

Storm, M. (1989), The five basic questions for primary geography, *Primary Geographer*, 2, Autumn, 4

Storm, M. & Catling, S. (1988), Evaluating your geography curriculum: a checklist, in Mills, D, (ed.), *Geographical Work in Primary and Middle Schools* , Sheffield: Geographical Association, 304-307

Williams, M. and Catling, S. (1985), Geography in primary education, *Geography*, 70, 243-245

SECTION 3

DEVELOPMENT OF THE SUBJECT

The state of geography

Chapter 21

Geography Subject Leaders' Perceptions of the State of Primary Geography

Simon Catling

Introduction

Since the introduction of the national curriculum in England towards the end of the 1980s, primary schools have been required to teach geography to pupils from 5 to 11 years old. For geography to develop effectively since its full introduction in 1991 (DES, 1991), primary teachers needed access to expertise in their schools. To support teachers each school would require a geography subject leader or co-ordinator (Alexander, Rose & Woodhead, 1992). By the late 1980s less than half of primary schools had subject co-ordinators for geography or social or environmental studies (DES, 1989); this was only a limited improvement on a decade earlier (DES, 1978).

The need to support the development of primary geography in the early 1990s, together with the pressure on primary schools to engage in teaching a subject-based curriculum, led to schools appointing or allocating teaching staff with responsibilities for each of the curriculum subjects. Depending on the size of the school, the experience of the teachers and their expertise and interests (or not), there might be a teacher solely responsible for geography, or with geography allocated as part of a humanities set, or with geography as one subject in a disparate portfolio of responsibilities. Because of the very varied nature of school contexts in England, there was no discernible pattern that could be identified across the country. By the mid-1990s every primary school at least had a named member of the teaching staff who was responsible for overseeing geography throughout the school: the geography co-ordinator (Ofsted, 1999). Such geography subject leaders have now become a potential source of information about development and practice in geography in primary schools, as well as a matter of study in their own right.

Alongside Ofsted's inspections of primary schools, which provide an evaluative picture of the state of primary schools, the Qualifications and Curriculum Authority (QCA), responsible for the national curriculum, began to undertake its own monitoring studies of the school subject curriculum in the early 2000s. The role of these studies was to obtain a differently focused perspective on the state of the primary subjects, through small-scale sample study interviews with subject leaders. In view of the development of QCA's work in geography, for example the publication of schemes of work for primary geography (DfEE/QCA, 1998/2000), and of their role in redrafting the geography programmes of study (DfEE/QCA, 1999a), the QCA Geography Officers' interest in monitoring lay in gathering information to give both a broader and a more detailed picture than the Ofsted reports provided. QCA's subject monitoring programme is the origin of this study.

This study sought to monitor the situation in primary geography through the eyes of the geography subject leaders in a sample of schools. In initiating it, the QCA Geography Officers wanted to gauge three things:

- the impact of recent changes and developments to the primary curriculum – such as the literacy and numeracy strategies – on geography;
- the geography subject leaders' sense of their own situation and the standing of geography in their schools;
- the support for geography teaching provided through services and resources for geography subject leaders and their colleagues.

The Approach to the Research

The study was commissioned in 2001, to be undertaken during the year 2001/02 (see Catling et al, 2002). The guidance provided was that a small number of schools should be used, and that a similar approach might be followed to that of a previous study (Halocha & Richardson, 2001). Given that the study was to be focused through the perspectives of geography subject leaders, several alternatives were possible, including, for instance, the shadowing of subject leaders for a period, the use of questionnaires, the use of interviews and the study of documents and records (McKinley, 1996; Cohen, Manion & Morrison, 2000). However, the limited funding available for the study and the request to use a variety of schools in more than one area of the country created a clear constraint on these possibilities.

To meet the requirement for at least a limited national spread and to obtain as broad and balanced a picture as possible, the following criteria for selection of the sample of schools were decided upon:
- that there should be schools covering inner city, urban , suburban and rural catchment areas;
- that the schools should be spread across England, but in selected regions;
- that the study should include large, medium and small schools;
- that there should be a range of quality of schools;
- that almost but not all should be primary schools.

Working with colleagues based in five higher education institute Schools of Education across England, twenty-five schools were identified to meet these criteria, drawn from the North-East, across Central England, and in the South-East. This number reflected the funding available. The sample included two first schools and one middle school, alongside the twenty-two primary schools, of which ten had nursery classes. Nine schools were located in rural areas, seven were in suburbs, seven were urban schools and two were inner city schools. On the basis of advice from local education authority inspectors and advisers, the experience and knowledge of the colleagues involved, and from Ofsted inspection reports, schools demonstrating a range of overall educational quality and achievement were identified, from highly rated providers to one school in special measures.

In order to ascertain the perspective of the geography subject leader in each school, it was decided that the study would be conducted through *structured interviews*, rather than through questionnaires. The latter was rejected on the grounds of probable limited responses and because of perceived limitations in ensuring clarity of the responses. However, the use of interviews has its limitations, in that the responses to questions are dependent, still, upon the interpretation of the respondent, can be constrained by personal interests and biases, and may be limited by the respondent looking to provide a 'correct' or most positive response, as well as being subject to the ways in which the questions are interpreted and put by the interviewer (Cohen, Manion &

Morrison, 2000; Hoggart, Lees & Davies, 2002). Nonetheless, the strengths of this research method lie in being able to personalise the questions, prompting and probing the responses to gain clarification, and to ensure data gathering. In that the study was to involve five interviewers, each interviewing five geography subject leaders, there was the added complication of ensuring consistency across the group, so that the information gathered and its interpretation would have validity. To overcome this difficulty, a *structured* interview schedule was devised and the interviews were set up in the context of *respondent* interviews (McKernan, 1996; Wiegand, 1996). A respondent interview is one in which the interviewer retains clear control of the interview, seeking responses to direct questions from the interviewee. In addition, guidance on the purpose of each question and on ways each might be followed through was provided. While the interviewers were each known to each other and had common interests, a structured interview was used to attempt to ensure that as greater consistency as possible across the team and the interviewees could be achieved.

The use of a *respondent* interview enabled the interviewers to control and structure the interview to a predetermined agenda. This was essential to be able to meet the requirements of the study contract. The preparation of a *structured interview schedule* followed naturally, as a mechanism to provide for consistency of questions across the interviewing team. The schedule was produced through consultation with the QCA Geography Officers and across the five interviewers. The result was a detailed and extensive schedule of some twenty-five pages and nine sections, a version of a very thorough questionnaire (McKernan, 1996). The questions sought straightforward factual information as well as personal responses and evaluations concerning the geography practice in the subject leaders school. Both closed and open questions were used. For the latter, the interview allowed the possibility of following up the responses with probing questions to clarify them and seek reasons and explanations. *Information-oriented* questions focused on such matters as contextual information about the school and the subject leader, her/his knowledge of particular services and resources, involvement in in-service activities, the purchase of resources for school, and so forth. Questions which sought *perspectives*, *opinions* and *judgements* covered such topics as the clarity and value of aspects of national curriculum geography, the impact of national strategies on geography, the benefits and limitations inherent in changing the curriculum, the standing of geography in the school and the subject leader's perception of the strengths, weaknesses, threats to and opportunities for geography in the school.

All twenty-five interviews were carried out successfully. They averaged between two and three hours in length. In order to encourage the geography subject leaders in the selected school to participate, each was paid for their time from the funds for the study. All interviews were carried out thoroughly and geography subject leaders reported that they valued the process, finding it informative and enabling them to reflect on their own situation. To support the geography subject leaders, a copy of the completed interview was left with them. The completed interview schedules were returned to the team leader, who undertook the analysis of the data provided. A great deal of material emerged from this study and only some of the findings are reported below.

While the findings of this study are informative and have some consistency with the findings in Ofsted primary geography reports before and during the period of study (Ofsted, 2000, 2001, 2002a, 2003; Catling, 2003), no claim is made that what emerges is representative of the national picture. In that the schools were selected, albeit against criteria, in relation to colleagues engaged in the study rather than randomly, it may be that they do not reflect fully the breadth of quality and the state of affairs in geographical education in primary schools nationally. This is a possible limitation of the study.

Key Findings

About the subject leaders

The geography subject leaders in the sample schools varied in their experience and background. Just over half had been in post for one or two years, of whom two were newly qualified teachers. Only one had held her post since pre-national curriculum days. Of the twenty-five subject leaders, only four were responsible solely for geography, while eleven covered one other subject, and ten held between two and four responsibilities other than for geography; of these five were head or deputy head teachers. While four also held history subject leaders roles, four were responsible for mathematics, three for physical education and three for religious education. There was no consistency in subject links, such as geography in the context of a humanities leadership role. More than half the geography subject leaders held geography qualifications, one at Master's degree level. However, five had not taken geography beyond fourteen years of age. Of this sample, just over two-thirds had received some in-service training in geography in the 1999-2002 period. Of these, half had been on courses linked to subject leadership or on planning for National Curriculum 2000 geography changes. The other half had completed a mix of courses, in which there was no particular pattern. Only one subject leader had attended a national conference in which primary geography pathways could be followed.

Geography's standing

Generally geography's standing in the primary schools was no greater or lesser than that of other primary non-core subjects. However, in three schools geography was held in high regard and linked to the environmental and Eco-school ethos of the schools' mission. In a third of the schools, geography's status was seen to be improving, but in two the opposite was felt to be the case. In these two schools, the time to teach geography remained an issue, with only one main topic taught in one term during the year. In over a third of schools the time allocation for geography fell below the recommended time for teaching the subject (QCA/DfES, 2002). However, almost a third of the schools devoted more than the key stage 2 time norm, teaching over forty hours of geography a year.

The standing of geography was also reflected in its timing. Geography has become an 'afternoon' subject in 96% of the schools; the mornings were set aside for the core subjects, taught, it was explained, when the children were fresher and more alert and able to concentrate better. In almost all schools geography was taught in blocked periods in alternate terms or half-terms, or quarter-term blocks for the youngest children, often alternating with history. Two-thirds of the schools justified this approach as allowing a more cohesive approach to children's learning and in that it enabled greater depth of study. However, schools were not able to show *how* this supported consistency and progression in children's learning, although two-thirds also stated that they provided for curriculum continuity through the use of continuous units and 'genuine' links with other subjects, indicating that they felt this provided for progression of the subject.

The geography curriculum

Curriculum development in geography was mixed across the schools. While the geography subject leaders judged that there were some positive benefits in the redrafted Geography Order in National Curriculum 2000 (DfEE/QCA, 1999a), it was the geography scheme of work for key stages 1 and 2 that had the greater impact (DfEE/QCA, 1998/2000). However, there were concerns that the national primary strategies had had a negative impact generally, though they were not without benefits to geography planning and teaching.

Following the introduction of the modified geography programmes of study in 2000, two-thirds of schools had revised their geography policies. Of these, seven schools had instituted a rolling programme of revision every two to four years. The programmes of study had helped about half of the schools to respond to new developments, such as the emphasis on *sustainable development*, the greater clarity of the *patterns and processes* aspect of geography and the reference to *decision making* skills in geography. Some four-fifths of the subject leaders felt that the programmes of study were clearer to understand and use. However, the marginal notes in the programmes of study were not seen as informative by two-thirds of the subject leaders. While the programmes of study were felt to be helpful by most subject leaders, they were little used beyond the revision of school policies and in checking that the scheme of work covered the requirements.

The scheme of work for geography for key stages 1 and 2 (DfEE/QCA, 1998/2000) had much greater credibility in supporting curriculum improvement. Indeed, it has had a significant impact on modifying the planning of the geography curriculum in schools. Four-fifths of schools had updated their geography scheme of work since 2000, and all but two schools in the sample drew on the scheme. Five schools had moved from their own geography curriculum, with which they were dissatisfied, to full adoption of selected units from the QCA guidance scheme for their whole geography curriculum. Two-thirds of schools either had adopted some and adapted others to create their scheme or had taken some, adapted others and linked these with their own units in revising their geography schemes. In all, somewhat over half the school had drawn fully on the QCA scheme to revise their own. Of the two schools that had retained their own geography schemes, one was now planning to use the QCA guidance scheme, following the arrival of a new headteacher.

Schools judged the value of the QCA geography scheme to be that there was a good range of choice on which to draw, that units could be contextualised locally, that there were close links to current school schemes that could be adapted, and that adaptation would be helpful in improving their own scheme. In selecting particular sets of units, subject leaders commented that this enabled a balanced geography curriculum to be developed, teachers' familiarity, confidence and interests could be followed, current resources could be used, links with other subjects could be exploited best, and they could build on good practice in the school. Units linked to the study of the local area and other localities, to environmental awareness and to the study of rivers proved to be the most popular, all taken up by two-thirds or more of schools. Least popular were the units published in 2000, perhaps because many schools did not have copies of them.

The impact of government initiatives

One of the impacts of the introduction of the *literacy* and *numeracy* strategies in 1998 (QCA, 1998) was to lift the requirement to teach the full programme of study for each of the foundation subjects. Most geography subject leaders identified the loss of time for teaching geography as a strong negative impact, particularly since just under half of the schools had yet to regain all of that lost teaching time. Inevitably, this was seen by these schools to be the core reason why they could not cover the geography curriculum and teach it as well as they wished to do. Nonetheless, the majority of schools felt that the development of the strategies had helped them to improve their approach to planning lessons, which had rubbed off on geography, and that the development in particular of literacy skills had supported both enquiry learning and the use of non-fictional texts in geography. Numeracy was seen to have supported improvements in work linked to mapwork as well as with data handling. The later introduction of the *ICT* strategy was also seen to have been helpful in this context by a few subject leaders. But they valued much more the widening access to resources through CD-roms and the internet, and considered that both they and colleagues as well as pupils were building greater competence and confidence in the use, understanding and appreciation of technologies.

Other opportunities to make further cross-curricular connections were also emerging, something that has more recently been encouraged (QCA/DfES, 2002; Ofsted, 2002b; DfES, 2003). In almost all schools, formal subject connections have been created between geography and one or more subjects. These connections relate to particular units and themes. By far the most connections were made with history and science. Four-fifths of schools noted ways in which geography and history supported each other, for example in the use of enquiry methods, in local area topics and through fieldwork and mapping skills. In about three-fifths of schools geography and science connections linked to such topics as water, rivers and landscape processes, the weather, and environmental change and issues, as well as with enquiry and investigative approaches. But three-fifths of subject leaders identified links with other non-core subjects. For instance, in religious education, the contemplation of landscape and the challenging of stereotypes; in art there were links made between geography and landscape sketching and in locating places where artists worked; in design and technology the making of weather equipment and landscape models was linked to geographical studies; in music, the landscapes that have inspired composers were examined; and in physical education movement activities linked into directions and distance understanding.

While more than half of schools were beginning to make connections in geography with *thinking skills*, only a minority of schools had begun to consider links between geography and *citizenship*. For those schools that were pursuing thinking skill development actively, the subject leaders saw the key value in extending geographical enquiry. In the context of citizenship, few subject leaders had developed clear curriculum connections, though these had been in the context of decision making and the quality of the school environment. Items in the national curriculum subject handbook for geography and in the primary teachers' handbook (DfEE/QCA, 1999a, 1999b), such as the *inclusion* statement and the reference to *key skills*, had had negligible impact on subject leaders. Inclusion was considered in terms of a whole school policy and approach, not specifically in the context of geography by the large majority of subject leaders.

Using support services and resources

It has already been indicated that either the national curriculum geography handbook or the national curriculum handbook for primary teachers (DfEE/QCA, 1999a, 1999b), as well as the QCA geography scheme of work for key stages 1 and 2 (DfEE/QCA, 1998/2000) have been used by almost all geography subject leaders. However, the large majority has only used the printed versions, and has not referred to the web sites containing these documents. Indeed, web sites supporting the national curriculum were not used, except by just one or two subject leaders. As to the other published support materials from QCA, there was little if any knowledge of them, let alone use made. While the subject leaders were more aware of Geographical Association publications, only about half used *Primary Geographer* and a third had copies of the Association's primary geography handbook (Carter, 1998). Locality packs and Barnaby Bear publications were the other publications noted by more than the occasional individual. There was equally limited use of LEA geography and/or humanities support services, with less than half the geography subject leaders having had any contact with their LEA inspector or advisor.

Less than a sixth of primary schools were involved in geography subject liaison either within primary school partnership groups or with their local secondary school and its feeder primary schools. Very limited use appears to have been made of other LEA services, though just under half of schools used LEA-run field centres. The indication is that while specific key national geography documents are known to and largely used by geography subject leaders, there is less knowledge and use of materials from the Geographical Association and even less information about geography support at a local level.

The role of the geography subject leader

Geography subject leaders recognise the limitations to their own situation and activities. While many of them have put time into updating either the schools' geography policy or the geography scheme of work, which they see as the core priority, they tend to feel that geography comes lower down their list of essential activities, especially for the large majority for whom geography is just one responsibility. In about a third of schools this is reinforced by the low priority given to geography, and for almost half it is made difficult by their perceived lack of time to undertake their role effectively. In about a third of schools, geography subject leaders identified specific time during the year for monitoring geography; for a third of this group, there was about half-an-hour each week. Another fifth considered that they might be able to negotiate time during the year; the rest saw no opportunity at all. This information linked closely with the perception of subject leaders about their impact on the quality of geography teaching and learning throughout the school. Only three subject leaders judged that they had a strong impact, while over a third commented that they had negligible if any impact at all; of these two felt particularly unsupported in the school. However, most subject leaders felt they had some impact, and that they achieved this through monitoring colleagues' geography unit plans and through advising about and purchasing resources for geography teaching. Again, there were connections here with those who held a budget for geography resources and support, which just over half did; another quarter of the subject leaders had to bid for funds to their head teacher, while one sixth had no responsibility for purchases whatsoever.

The limitations in geography's development in school are indicated further by the lack of in-service training opportunities. In almost two-thirds of the schools, there was no geography INSET for the school's staff provided by the subject leader or anyone else. Where there was opportunity, the focus was on the revised geography scheme of work. Several more geography subject leaders undertook *informal* support through discussions and feedback with colleagues, but this occurred in less than a quarter of schools. While this is a depressing scenario, subject leaders indicated that it was no worse than for other non-core subjects.

However, most geography subject leaders were keen to develop their role and to work to priorities they had identified. The key priorities were: to update the school geography policy and scheme of work and to maintain this; to monitor the teaching of geography throughout the school; to audit, identify need and purchase further appropriate teaching resources; and to support and advise colleagues about planning and teaching. The majority of subject leaders judged that their colleagues viewed geography positively, and in many cases felt that the pupils enjoyed and benefited from colleagues' geography teaching. But in over a quarter of schools, there was concern that a number of staff lacked both confidence and the appropriate level of knowledge and understanding to teach geography effectively.

The geography subject leaders were open and informative about the possibilities and limitations in their schools. Considering weaknesses, one-third felt that their geography curriculum and teaching needed further development, while a quarter were concerned about the nature and quality of assessment in geography. Time to teach geography effectively remained a concern for a third of schools. Other issues identified by a small number of subject leaders included limited time for fieldwork, the quality of resources, the lack of INSET and the need to be more challenging in geography teaching. On a more positive note, all subject leaders felt they could identify strengths in their provision. Almost half felt that their colleagues enjoyed and were clearly committed to teaching geography. A similar number commented on the enjoyment pupils gained from their geographical learning. Likewise, half referred to the quality of their resources; a third noted that they had a good level of fieldwork; and about half valued the geography scheme of work they had in place. Half the subject leaders expressed clearly that they enjoyed their role.

Subject leaders were beginning to detect some positive signs for the future as well. For example, in a sixth of schools head teachers were expressing an interest in developing the wider curriculum much more fully. Almost half considered that the time was right for further developments in the geography curriculum to be made, and a quarter felt that they could build further on their colleagues' experience and achievements. A few others saw the allocation of some time for monitoring during the school day as a realistic possibility, and some were hopeful that INSET possibilities might be emerging for themselves and the whole school staff. This sense of optimism was not without threats, however. Over half of the subject leaders were concerned about the potential continuing impact of the primary strategies and other government initiatives on time for geography teaching, and a very few saw this as inhibiting any improvement in their limited current situation. For three schools the turnover of geography subject leaders was of concern, since they were uncertain as to the continued support for geography in the school. Overall, the outlook was more positive than critical.

Conclusion

This study did not examine the teaching and learning of geography in primary schools. It concentrated on the perspectives of geography subject leaders about their own context and tried to identify an overview of the range of situations in primary schools. There is much that emerges from this study. In particular, the following outcomes are noted and considered:

- In the majority of the primary schools, geography is a valued curriculum subject, though it seems that it has still, like other foundation subjects, a relatively low priority when it comes to development and resources. The status of geography remains fragile, but there is evidence that heads are developing an interest in improving the role and contribution of the foundation subjects. This is leading, it would appear, to a slow but steady increase in the status of geography, though, as yet, it is only having a marginal impact on the quality of geographical learning and teaching in primary schools (Ofsted, 2002a).
- The introduction in 1998 of the option for two years for primary schools to suspend the foundation subjects' programmes of study had a clear impact on the schools in this study, in that the time for geography was reduced and still has not been fully regained in many of the schools.
- The reintroduction of teaching to the full geography programmes of study for key stages 1 and 2 in 2000 led to some rethinking by very many schools of their geography schemes of work. This appears to have been influenced much more strongly by the QCA *A Scheme of Work for Key Stages 1 and 2: Geography* (DfEE/QCA 1998/2000) than by the revised Geography Order (DfEE, 1999a).

- Primary schools appear in their post-2000 revisions of their geography schemes of work to have made much greater use of the QCA guidance on a geography scheme of work. Thus, this guidance has been a major influence. Schools' development of their geography schemes have largely been in terms of modifications to their existing curriculum and the adaptation of the QCA scheme Units to their own circumstances. Almost all schools use a variety of the Units, but it is clear that they see themselves adapting rather than adopting them unchanged.

- Where geography subject leaders are making reference to the geography programmes of study, the majority view the structure of the programmes of study as clear and informative. In particular, they value the emphasis now placed on sustainable development, decision making and geographical patterns and processes. However, limited use is made of the programmes of study other than in checking curriculum coverage and in drafting school geography policies. The most popular Units used and adapted by schools are those associated with localities, the environment and rivers.

- Effectively, the QCA geography scheme of work is *the* resource used by geography subject leaders to support geography planning in most schools. Other QCA materials are little known, as are many other publications to support teachers in relation to geography. But the Geographical Association's *Primary Geographer* and *Handbook for Primary Geography* are known to up to half of subject leaders. It would seem that these two key publications are serving a clear purpose. This indicates that there is a need for these and other organisations to make the value of their materials and services much more widely accessible and known.

- There is evidence of a revival taking place in the linking of curriculum subjects, supporting developments being encouraged by QCA and the government (QCA/DfES, 2002; DfES, 2003). It appears that these are more thoughtful and relevant than they may have been in the past (DES, 1989). While more than half the schools are making progress in linking thinking skills into geography, less than half of the schools have yet undertaken any developments relating to citizenship.

- There is a clear variation between schools in the time given to teaching geography. About one-third of schools allocate considerably less time than is recommended as an appropriate starting point, but two-fifths give more time. However, geography has become an 'afternoon' subject in almost all primary schools.

- The national literacy and numeracy strategies have also begun to affect the style of geography lessons, which increasingly have introductory, group/individual work and plenary sections, a pattern for all lessons that appears to be developing across schools. Broadly, the literacy and numeracy strategies are seen to be supportive for geographical work that uses information texts and in linking mathematical understanding and skills to such areas as mapwork.. ICT is also seen to support access to geographical resources through skills, as well as providing useful resources in itself. CD-Roms are the most fully used resource, but the use of web sites is increasing.

- While the geography scheme of work in a primary school provides a clear outline of the content and structure through its units of what to teach, the organisation of that teaching in geography lessons is left in the hands of individual teachers in the large majority of schools. Very few schools use pre-planned lesson materials consistently. Nonetheless, geography teaching is based on explicit lesson objectives.

- There are geography subject leaders in all the schools in this study, but almost all of them hold other subject or school responsibilities. Over half of them have their main teaching qualification in geography. However, many of the geography subject leaders are concerned about the limited impact they have on geography teaching in their school. One third of them have some designated time for their role and just over half of them have a budget responsibility, but there is clearly an inconsistency of approach to the role across schools. Though there have been INSET opportunities for geography subject leaders in most schools, this is not seen as a strong element of support by the subject leaders. The issue of effectiveness is also demonstrated in the lack of INSET opportunities that the geography subject leaders provide for colleagues in their schools.

- Very many geography subject leaders are confident about the future of geography in their schools, and all schools see strengths in what they do in geography. In about half the schools the enthusiasm of staff generally is evident, as it is among the children. But there is concern about the effectiveness of some teachers in about one-third of the schools. Geography subject leaders see opportunities for development, particularly through their monitoring of the geography curriculum and the provision of INSET for colleagues if these develop. While the majority of subject leaders see a need still for curriculum development, two-fifths of subject leaders are confident in the geography scheme of work that they have in place.

Ofsted have identified a steady, if uninspiring and only incremental, improvement in the teaching and learning of primary geography in recent years, but have raised concerns about the effectiveness of subject leadership in many schools (Ofsted, 2001, 2002a; Catling 2003). This study supports the general perception that geography has a reasonably sound foundation on which to build in primary schools, according to subject leaders. What it is not able to do is comment on the competence of the subject leaders who participated. There are clear indications that more remains to be done to develop primary geography. Geography subject leaders do not appear to be complacent about the state of geography in their schools, even where they feel reasonably optimistic in its future. What is less clear is where the real encouragement to improve is to come from, even though the government's recent primary strategy is focused on curriculum improvement and on enjoyment and rigour in learning and teaching (DfES, 2003). This study indicates that challenges still lie ahead and that positive decisions to support geography teaching and learning more effectively and *explicitly* are needed in all primary schools and from the government and local authorities, as well as by other organisations, such as QCA and the Geographical Association.

References

Alexander, R. Rose, J. & Woodhead, C. (1992), *Curriculum Organisation and Classroom Practice in Primary Schools: A Discussion Paper*, London: DES

Carter, R. (ed.) (1998), *Handbook of Primary Geography*, Sheffield: Geographical Association

Catling, S. (2003), *The State of Primary Geography*, paper presented to the Geographical Association Annual Conference, 'Valuing Geography', University of Derby, 24 April, unpublished

Catling, S., Bowles, R. Halocha, J., Martin, F. & Rawlinson, S. (2002), *Monitoring Geography in Primary Schools: 2001/02 – A Report for the QCA Geography Officers*, London: QCA, unpublished

Cohen, L, Manion, L & Morrison, K (2000), *Research Methods in Education*, London: RoutledgeFalmer

DES (1978), *Primary Education in England*, London: HMSO

DES (1989), *Aspects of Primary Education: The teaching and Learning of History and Geography*, London: HMSO

DES (1991), *Geography in the National Curriculum (England)*, London: HMSO

DfEE/QCA (1998/2000), *A Scheme of Work for Key stages 1 and 2: Geography*, London: DfEE/QCA

DfEE/QCA (1999a), *The National Curriculum for England: Geography*, London: DfEE/QCA

DfEE/QCA (1999b), *The National Curriculum Handbook for Teachers in England*, London: DfEE/QCA

DfES (2003), *Excellence and Enjoyment: A strategy for primary schools*, London: DfES

Halocha, J & Richardson, P (2001), *Geography in Key Stage 2*, London: QCA, unpublished

Hoggart, K, Lees, L & Davies, A. (2002), *Researching Human Geography*, London: Arnold

McKernan, J. (1996), *Curriculum Action Research*, London: Kogan Page

Ofsted (1999), *Primary Education 1994-98: A Review of Primary Schools in England*, London: Ofsted

Ofsted (2000), *Standards in Geography, 1998/99*, London: Ofsted

Ofsted (2001), *Ofsted Subject Reports, 1999/2000: Geography*, London: Ofsted

Ofsted (2002a), *Primary Subject Reports 2000/01: Geography*, London: Ofsted

Ofsted (2002b), *The Curriculum in Successful Primary Schools*, London: Ofsted

Ofsted (2003), *Geography in Primary Schools: Ofsted subjects reports series 2001/02*, London: Ofsted

QCA/DfES (2002), *Designing and Timetabling the Primary Curriculum: A Practical Guide for Key Stages 1 and 2*, London: QCA/DfES

Wiegand, P. (1996), Interviews, in Williams, M. (ed.), *Understanding geographical and Environmental Education: The Role of Research*, London: Cassell

Acknowledgement
I would like to thank Rachel Bowles (University of Greenwich), John Halocha (Bishop Grosseteste College), Fran Martin (Worcester University College) and Steve Rawlinson (Northumbria University) for their support and work as interviewers in this project, which was part funded by the Qualifications and Curriculum Authority of England.

Chapter 22

Pupils' Perceptions of Geography: KS2/3 transfer issues

Lorraine Harrison & Melanie Norman

Introduction: Why is geography in a poor state of health?

In *Changing the Subject: The impact of national policy on school geography 1980-2000*, Rawling (2001) uses Ofsted data on 'progress and achievement of pupils' and 'quality of teaching', to exemplify the status of geography in comparison with other subjects. During the period 1993-1997 it is noted that for geography,

> in KS1and 2, teaching is now good in one third of schools and satisfactory in most of the rest; a steady improvement in recent years. (cited in Rawling, 2001, 93)

However, these positive trends take a turn for the worse during the 1998-2000 period of inspections,

> much work in geography is satisfactory but not enough is good or very good. (Ibid.)

The requirement to teach the geography programmes of study was suspended, alongside all the other foundation subjects, in the primary sector from 1998 to 2000 to create space for the government's initiatives to improve the standards of literacy and numeracy in primary schools. Although the programmes of study returned as statutory requirements in the primary sector in *Curriculum 2000* (DfES/QCA, 1999a) geography and the other foundation subjects have found themselves marginalised by the emphasis on literacy and numeracy ever since.

The debate about provision for geography in schools continues to influence teaching and learning at all levels. The impact of National Curriculum Geography across the primary phase has resulted in curriculum delivery that has been described as descriptive and outdated. The recent debate led by Brown (2002), Huckle (2002) and Stannard (2002) echoed a similar situation at Key Stage 3 and 4. Indeed, Huckle reports that

> too many pupils are left alienated, bored and disenchanted by geography lessons that do not answer their need to understand their present and likely future place in the world. (Huckle, 2002, 71).

Stannard was concerned that geography is losing its 'centrality' in education and describes the subject as being in a state of 'crisis'. The nature of this crisis, however, is seen to focus 'chiefly on secondary schools' (Stannard, 2002, p.73). A recent Chief HMI's Annual Report (Ofsted, 2003), however, suggests that a similar 'crisis' is evident in primary schools as well. The report indicates that a gulf exists in the quality of teaching in the core subjects and the foundation subjects and states that

> in two thirds of schools....the teaching of English and mathematics is good or better whereas in under half of schools, the teaching of geography was good or better. (Ofsted, 2003)

The report goes on to argue that in primary schools:

- teaching often fails to enthuse or challenge pupils;
- weaknesses exist in teachers' long term planning with insignificant recognition of what pupils have already learned;
- particular time pressure exists for geography and history (Ofsted, 2003)

There is a suggestion from Ofsted, however, that the situation is improving and there is evidence that pupils can experience a broader, more balanced timetable. Some schools are able to combine high standards in both the core and foundation subjects and are characterised by:

- a curriculum planned and taught as discrete subjects, yet with effective links across subjects that facilitate coherence;
- good use of first hand experience;
- curriculum design and timetabling that embraces high quality teaching and pupil motivation (Ofsted, 2003)

Recent emphasis on the development of creativity (Scoffham, 2002) and thinking skills through geography (Parry, 2002) support the need for teachers to develop innovative practice. This might involve teachers discarding the 'notion of the curriculum as a course to be run and think of it as a network of ideas to be expanded' (Prawatt, 1992, cited in Parry, 2002, 128).

Previous research into pupils' perceptions of geography

This small research project explores pupils' perceptions of geography and is intended to provide an insight into their views about the subject from key stage 2 to key stage 3. It contributes to the debate about the development of geography and emphasises the need for good geographical provision within and across key stages.

It was surprising to find that very little research has been carried out with regard to pupils' perceptions on the way that they learn in geography. Dowgill (1998) notes studies by Scarfe in 1949, Long in 1964, Naish in 1972, and Corney in 1987, all of which included some reference to pupils' attitudes towards geography. But Lidstone, also quoted in Dowgill (1998), said, in terms of all of these research projects, that the research

> has not made major contributions to the improvement of either geography as taught in schools or of education systems in general. (Lidstone 1988, in Dowgill 1998, 56)

Dowgill's work focused on the pupils' perspective of learning geography through what was then the new Geography National Curriculum. He examined pupils' perceptions as they studied geography in key stage 3 during the period from 1991 to 1993. He noted:

> Interestingly, although perhaps not a surprise, the one major group rarely considered during the discussions surrounding the National Curriculum and geography in particular was the pupils. Little reference was made to their experiences and the Geography Working Group consciously made a decision 'against undertaking a substantial programme of visits; (DES, 1990, 1)'. Thus the research undertaken on pupils' experiences of geography, it seems, had little impact on the development of the Geography National Curriculum. (Dowgill 1998, 5)

The fact geography finds itself in a crisis has generated debate and discussion about the future of the subject. The discussion was initiated after an article entitled *The Erosion of Geography* was published in the *Education Guardian* on November 20th 2001.

> According to the government, the point of education is to develop our critical faculties. – But the government seems to have lost sight of its own objectives. With the emphasis on core subjects, the one that is most help in getting to grips with the important issues of the day – geography – is being squeezed. So much so that geographers everywhere are alarmed that this vital discipline is under attack, not as a deliberate policy, but by default, because the government's priorities are elsewhere. (Brown, 2001)

Contributions to the debate have been published in *Geography,* the academic journal of the Geographical Association. However, in the column inches generated there is only one direct reference to the pupils themselves. Grimwade writes (2002):

> We will never know what is 'relevant geography' to the lives of young people unless we ask them.

The research project

The research reported here is part of a larger project on secondary school pupils' perceptions of geography. As a key part of the study, evidence of their views was sought from Year 7 pupils about their primary geography experience.

The framework

The research was undertaken through a survey of a large number of pupils to gain an overall idea of pupils' perception of school geography. Noting trends from the survey, interviews were planned with a sample of pupils to refine further their ideas on the positives and negatives of school geography. The aim was to find out from the pupils themselves what they liked and disliked about geography.

Research methodology

The research was conducted in secondary schools within Brighton and Hove. Of the research strategies suggested by Denscombe (1998), a survey seemed the most appropriate. Obtaining a viable number of responses from key stage 3 pupils in a number of schools could only be achieved manageably through a survey.

Denscombe (1998) notes that social science researchers frequently face the problem that they cannot collect data from everyone, so sampling techniques have to be adopted. The sample needs to be carefully selected, as it cannot be assumed that the sample will reflect the opinions of the whole population. This sample fell into the category of probability sampling, since the pupils surveyed were likely to be a representative cross-section of the key stage 3 population within the Brighton and Hove area and generally representative of key stage 3 pupils in similarly sized urban areas in the south-east of England.

The approach to probability sampling used here involved multi-stage sampling (Denscombe, 1998). Following the initial survey, a further sample from within the original sample was targeted for more in-depth research. The sampling frame was pre-determined since the research set out to focus on a group of key stage 3 pupils. The response rate was not a matter of concern as the pupils were required to respond by their teachers during lesson time, and a 100% response was achieved. The size of the sample was not an issue in this research project since the pupils were required by their teachers to undertake a response. The sample size was dependent upon the number of pupils required to participate, in this case 1172 across years 7, 8 and 9. This is over the suggested size for a small-scale research project but not sufficiently large to be called any thing other than small-scale.

Although Denscombe (1998, 25-27) suggests that qualitative research *tends* to use non-probability sampling techniques, this was not the case with this research. The methods adopted allowed the collection of quantitative and qualitative data which although cumbersome to analyse, gave a balance to the results. However, the second stage of the research, which focused on qualitative data from a small sample of key stage 3 pupils, is more in line with expectations for qualitative research.

The questionnaires

Denscombe (1998) suggests that certain research strategies tend to be associated with particular research methods; for example, surveys tending to be linked with questionnaires. However, all research methods have advantages and disadvantages, none necessarily being better or worse than another. The researcher needs to be aware of the strengths and weaknesses of the selected approach before finally deciding upon the method to be used. It is also recommended that more than one method might be adopted to corroborate or question the data produced by using different methods. In order to achieve this, having analysed the questionnaires, interviews were conducted with a selection of pupils.

The questionnaire was designed to be as simple as possible to be answered by mixed-ability pupils across key stage 3. The selection of words to convey intended meaning was difficult to achieve and not entirely successful despite best efforts. Some questions sought straightforward answers that could easily be quantified. Other questions asked pupils to give their thoughts and opinions about the subject of geography. Hence, both quantitative and qualitative data were collected.

The length of the questionnaire was kept to a double side of A4, so that pupils did not feel daunted by the prospect of completing it. Several designs were constructed before deciding upon the final version. The questionnaire was piloted in a local school outside the research area. This was a valuable exercise and the design and the wording were altered as a result of this pilot. The questionnaires were distributed to the schools and collected after half a term had elapsed.

The heads of department had made the necessary arrangements within their schools with regard to obtaining permission for the questionnaires to be completed. Although pupils were asked to write their names on the sheets and the name of the school, this was purely for purposes of identification for follow-up interviews. A covering letter addressed to the pupils was read out by class teachers so that the pupils were aware of the purpose of what they were being asked to do.

The interviews

Later in the same year a group of pupils who had said they would be willing to talk in further depth about their responses to the questionnaire, were interviewed. An interview was a logical progression from the questionnaire in that 'it lends itself to being used to follow-up a questionnaire' (Denscombe 1998, 112). However, the interviews targeted year 9 pupils so are not reported on in this chapter in which the focus is on some of the year 7 responses to the questionnaire (but see Norman & Harrison, 2004).

Results

No analysis was planned based on the sex of the pupils. Pupil perceptions of school geography were sought from a general pupil perspective, and there were no single sex schools in the survey. However, it is worth noting that the 450 responses from year 7 pupils were split, with 215 from males and 227 from females. Eight respondents did not write their name or sex on their questionnaires.

The pupils were invited to give their views about school geography. They were asked to respond to a range of questions. Within the overall questionnaire, the questions listed in Figure 1 were used as the basis for this investigation.

---

1. Please **underline** a) b) c) or d) to show your interest in school geography:
   a) very interested   **b) interested**
   c) not very interested   **d) not at all interested**

   Now write a few words to describe why you have underlined the words(s) you have.

3. What types of things do you **like** that you do in geography lessons?

4. What types of things that you do in geography do you **dislike**?

7 If you can remember, please write down anything you learned about geography when you were at primary school.

Figure 1: The questions used in the questionnaire for the perception of geography study

The responses to these questions were analysed to establish:
- levels of interest in the subject;
- justification for levels of interest;
- geographical likes and dislikes;
- geographical experiences gained at Key Stage 2.

The following discussion explores the relationship between the pupils' levels of interest, experiences at Key Stage 2, and their overall views about the subject. In order for some comparisons of responses to be made, the questionnaires were analysed according to pupil responses to question seven. The pupils' responses were grouped into the following categories:

Response Category One
Pupils who did not respond to question seven.

Response Category Two
Pupils who either could not remember doing any geography or who stated that the subject had not been studied at primary school.

Response Category Three
Pupils who could recall studying a range of isolated geographical experiences, normally related to a specific concept or aspect of the subject. For example, 'natural disasters', 'maps', and 'drawing charts, graphs and diagrams'.

Response Category Four
Pupils able to contextualise their experiences or link geographical concepts. For example, 'we learnt about the differences between hot and cold climates and the way people live in them', and 'we learnt about regions of Wales and London, we had to compare it to each other'.

Perceptions of Geography at Key Stage Two

Figure 2 provides an overview of pupil perceptions of geography according to response category and school. It is interesting to note that an average of 43% of all pupils either did not respond or perceived that they had not experienced geography at Key Stage 2. An average of 57% of pupils were able to recall some geographical experiences. Of these only a small proportion of pupils could place these experiences within a wider geographical context.

Pupil responses across schools are similar, apart from those in school D which has a high proportion of pupils who did not respond to question seven. These pupils were, therefore, not able to draw from their primary school experiences.

School	Pupil Perceptions [Categorized]			
	1 No Response	2 No Recollection or Experiences	3 Isolated Experiences and/or Concepts	4 Linked Experiences and/or Concepts
A	15%	17%	63%	5%
B	13%	17%	58%	12%
C	15%	26%	57%	2%
D	43%	24%	31%	2%
Average %	22%	21%	52%	5%

Figure 2: Overall Percentage of Pupils Perceptions of Geography at Key Stage Two

Levels of interest in geography at key stage 3 compared with pupil perceptions at key stage 2

Figures 3, 4, 5 and 6 compare response categories, schools and levels of interest in geography. An interesting relationship exists between these response categories and levels of pupil interest.

Those pupils who were unable to recall any geographical experiences from Key Stage 2 have the highest proportion of responses indicating disinterest in the subject. Many of these pupils reported that the subject was 'boring' or could not cite a geographical reason to justify their views. Very few pupils in this category identified geography as interesting.

Those pupils from response category two have the highest proportion of responses in the interested category. This group was able to justify their views, and some of their ideas linked the subject matter with a level of understanding about places within the wider world and the environment. Typical responses here were: 'I am interested in geography because you can learn about the world around us and different places', and 'You learn about your surroundings. It's different from any other subject. There are lots of different types of geography.'

Less sophisticated responses indicated the individual's ability to connect with specific tasks, learning experiences or their desire to learn. Typical responses included, 'I'm not amazing at geography but I'm interested so I can get better. I like it when we draw pictures', 'I like geography but I don't like drawing all the maps and things like that', and 'Because it's interesting in some ways but some of the work is either quite hard or a bit dull.'

School	Levels of Interest [No Response]			
	Very Interested	**Interested**	**Not Very Interested**	**Not At All Interested**
A	9%	55%	27%	9%
B	12%	47%	29%	12%
C	0%	42%	42%	16%
D	4%	38%	41%	17%

Figure 3: Levels of current (key stage 3) interest in geography (expressed in percentages) from those pupils in *response category one*

School	Levels of Interest [No Recollection and/or Experiences]			
	Very Interested	**Interested**	**Not Very Interested**	**Not At All Interested**
A	8%	23%	54%	15%
B	4%	35%	48%	13%
C	18%	39%	36%	7%
D	0%	13%	56%	31%

Figure 4: Levels of current (key stage 3) interest in geography (expressed in percentages) from those pupils in *response category two*

School	Levels of Interest [Isolated Experiences/Concepts]			
	Very Interested	**Interested**	**Not Very Interested**	**Not At All Interested**
A	2%	54%	44%	0%
B	9%	54%	30%	7%
C	10%	60%	23%	7%
D	14%	48%	33%	5%

Figure 5: Levels of current (key stage 3) interest in geography (expressed in percentages) from those pupils in *response category three*

School	Levels of Interest [Linked Experiences/Concepts]			
	Very Interested	**Interested**	**Not Very Interested**	**Not At All Interested**
A	0	1	3	0
B	1	9	5	2
C	0	2	1	0
D	0	1	0	0

Figure 6: Levels of current (key stage 3) interest in geography (expressed as raw data) from those pupils in *response category four*

Pupil likes and dislikes of geography at key stage 3 compared with pupil perceptions at key stage 2

Figures 7 and 8 reveal a broad picture of likes and dislikes. Significant findings here are:
- the overwhelming number of references to map-work, associated with both likes and dislikes;
- a significant dislike of writing in response categories one and two;
- references related to learning about the world/other countries and cultures appear only in response categories three and four.

School	Likes			
	1 No Response	**2 No Recollection or Experiences**	**3 Isolated Experiences and/or Concepts**	**4 Linked Experiences and/or Concepts**
A	Mapwork	Mapwork	Mapwork	Making maps
B	Map/Atlas work	Map/Atlas work	Learning about other countries & world events	Learning about other countries & world events; Mapwork
C	Mapwork	Mapwork	Mapwork	Mapwork
D	Mapwork	Mapwork	Learning about other cultures & countries	Learning about other cultures & countries

Figure 7: Top geography *likes*

School	Dislikes			
	1 No Response	**2 No Recollection or Experiences**	**3 Isolated Experiences and/or Concepts**	**4 Linked Experiences and/or Concepts**
A	Written work	Everything	Mapwork	Mapwork
B	Writing	Writing	Mapwork	Mapwork
C	Mapwork	Mapwork	Mapwork	Looking things up about other countries; Mapwork
D	Writing	Writing	Mapwork	Weather

Figure 8: Top geography *dislikes*

Significant differences in responses were noted between schools. For example, those pupils in response categories one and two from school C made comparative judgements about the same concept related to both likes and dislikes. Some pupils liked drawing maps, yet disliked six figure grid references, whilst others liked six figure grid references yet disliked scale. It is possible that their preferences could be linked to levels of challenge and that these views represented an inability to place their experiences within a wider geographical context. Indeed, the majority of responses from this school referred exclusively to map-work!

Pupils in response categories one and two from school B frequently expressed their pleasure in 'drawing maps' as opposed to their dislike of 'doing' map work. This may indicate a more interactive level of engagement here. Some references were also made to undertaking local fieldwork and learning about geographical patterns and processes. The overwhelming dislike among pupils in this school was writing. The pupils did not offer specific examples here but their views might relate to preferred learning styles or a particular kind of teaching and learning strategy.

Pupils in response categories three and four from schools B and D could identify a range of likes and dislikes with generally more references made to likes than dislikes. Typical responses here are: 'Compass points, physical geography (likes).... drawing, because I'm not talented at drawing (dislike),' 'Going outside and seeing what things are human or physical (like) ....writing (dislike)', and 'I like looking at places and things about them, also I like looking through atlases. I like finding out why things happen e.g. volcanoes, earthquakes (likes).... none (dislike).' A more sophisticated view of the nature of the subject is beginning to emerge here. Pupils seem to be drawing on previous experiences to build an increasingly complex and accurate geographical understanding.

In a few cases, pupils were beginning to make links between experiences/activities and could identify the geographical purpose for their work. For example, one pupil stated, 'I like to know about the environment, how people react to things and why they do things. I like looking up information in books and atlases.' This pupil had already begun to make links at primary school and identified the following experiences: 'where countries are and names of continents, the link between people, pollution and environment.'

Conclusions

This investigation has provided some understanding of pupils' views about geography and identifies a clear link between perceptions at Key Stage 2 and the ability to make sense of and enjoy geography at Key Stage 3. It also reveals a discernible difference between the range and nature of perceptions between schools. Those pupils in response categories three and four in schools B and D were able to identify and justify their likes and make links with prior experiences. This may reflect the breadth and variety of the curriculum provision experienced by these pupils.

There is no doubt that the quality of geographical opportunities afforded to pupils are vital at both key stage 2 and key stage 3 if they are to be given opportunities to develop a secure understanding of geography's subject matter. This will enable them to make sense of those characteristics that define and distinguish the subject as a 'vital component of the present curriculum' (Stannard, 2002, 81).

References

Brown, P. (2001), The Erosion of Geography, *Guardian Education* 20 Nov 01, London: Guardian Newspapers

Brown, P. (2002), The Erosion of Geography, *Geography,* 87 (1), 84-85

Cohen, L., Manion, L. & Morrison, K. (2000), *Research Methods in Education,* London: RoutledgeFalmer

Denscombe, M. (1998), *The Good Research Guide*, Buckingham: The Open University Press

DfEE/QCA (1999a), *The National Curriculum Handbook for Primary Teachers in England*, London: DfEE/QCA http://www.standards.dfes.gov.uk/schemes, Accessed: 18.Feb.03

DfEE/QCA (1999b), *The National Curriculum for England: Geography*, London: HMSO/QCA, http://www.standards.dfes.gov.uk/schemes, Accessed: 18.Feb.03

Dowgill, P (1998), *Pupils' Conceptions of Learning Goegraphy under the National Curriculum,* Unpublished Ph.D. thesis: University of London Institute of Education

Geographical Association (2003), Making a Case for Geography, *Teaching Geography*, 28

Grimwade, K. (2002), *The Future of Geography*, Geography, 87 (2)

Huckle, J. (2002), Reconstructing Nature: Towards a Geographical Education for Sustainable Development, *Geography*, 87 (1), 64-71

Norman, M. & Harrison, L. (2004), Year 9 students' perceptions of school geography, *Teaching Geography*, January, 11-15

Ofsted (2003), *Annual Report of Her Majesty's Chief Inspector of Schools: Standards and Quality in Education 2001/02* London: Ofsted available from: http://www.ofsted.gov.uk/publications/index.cfm?fuseaction=pubs.summary&id=3144– accessed 18 Feb 03.

Parry, J. (2002), Developing Children's Thinking Through Multimedia in the Context of Local Wildlife Areas, *Geography*, 87 (2), 125-131

Rawling, E. (2001), *Changing the Subject: the impact of national policy on school geography 1980-2000*, Sheffield: Geographical Association

Scoffham, S. (2003), Thinking Creatively, *Primary Geographer*, 50, 4-6

Stannard, K. (2002), Waiving, not Drowning Geography – Challenges and Opportunities, *Geography*, 87 (1), 73-83

Walford, R. (2001), Geography's Odyssey: The Journey so Far, *Geography*, 86 (4), 305-317

Chapter 23

Don't Forget the Trainees: Issues relating to the recruitment of geographers into primary teaching

Steve Rawlinson

Introduction

The decline in the numbers of geography graduates entering primary and secondary school teaching (Rawlinson et al., 2003) raises issues that should concern all geographers. Taken from the perspective of one teacher training provider this chapter offers explanations for this decline, indicates its significance, especially to the primary sector, and considers a particular programme, which aims to encourage more geographers to consider teaching as a career.

In the last 10 years anecdotal evidence from Initial Teacher Training [ITT] providers has suggested a decline in the numbers of geographers entering both primary and secondary teacher training. In 1999 the shortage of geography trainees in the secondary sector was officially recognised with the Teacher Training Agency [TTA] designating geography as a shortage subject. In response a TTA/RGS (with IBG) funded project was developed both to examine the nature of the problem and to develop strategies to halt the continuing decline in geographers applying for PGCE programme places (TTA, 1999; Thorne 2001 & 2002), in order to produce effective and exciting geography teachers who can inspire the positive feedback model for developing geography teachers illustrated in Figure 1.

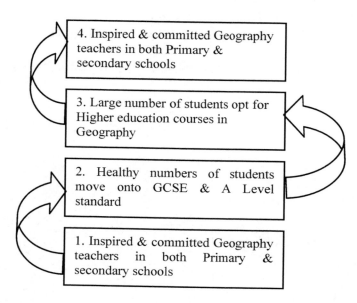

4. Inspired & committed Geography teachers in both Primary & secondary schools

3. Large number of students opt for Higher education courses in Geography

2. Healthy numbers of students move onto GCSE & A Level standard

1. Inspired & committed Geography teachers in both Primary & secondary schools

Figure 1: Positive Feedback Model (Rawlinson et al., 2003, 40)

However, the decline in numbers entering ITT with geography qualifications does have worrying implications for the continued health of the subject at all levels, since it can all too easily lead into the alternative spiral of decline – the negative feedback model – illustrated in Figure 2 (Rawlinson et al., 2003).

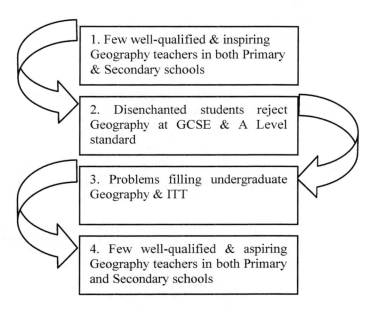

1. Few well-qualified & inspiring Geography teachers in both Primary & Secondary schools

2. Disenchanted students reject Geography at GCSE & A Level standard

3. Problems filling undergraduate Geography & ITT

4. Few well-qualified & aspiring Geography teachers in both Primary and Secondary schools

Figure 2: Negative Feedback Model (Rawlinson et al., 2003, 41)

With fewer geography specialists entering the classroom greater numbers of children are finding their geography taught by non-specialists. The problems this can lead to have already been identified by Ofsted (2002). Although this should not imply that all geography teaching raises concern, from the primary perspective there is an issue that receiving a poor experience of the subject in the early formative stages may have a negative effect on a child's perception of the subject and consequently in the choices made for further study – early impressions can have life long repercussions.

The reasons behind the diminution of geography's representation in teacher training and the need to consider it as a 'shortage subject' is an amalgam of many factors (Catling, 2003; Rawling, 1996; Rawlinson et al, 2003), but key issues appear to be:
- the impact of the national curriculum in schools, particularly the emphasis placed on the *core* subjects to the detriment of the *foundation* subjects such as geography, which in turn leads to
- decreasing entries for Geography at GCSE and A level – perhaps reflecting a decline in the quality of the teaching and also the rise of 'sexier' subjects such as psychology, likewise leading to
- declining numbers taking geography degrees – again as a result perhaps of 'poor experiences' in geography and the greater attraction of alternatives.

An additional subject specific factor impacting upon the numbers of geographers entering ITT must also be considered. This relates to the skill base that geographers develop during their studies, either at secondary or tertiary level. The modern geographer is able to offer a wealth of transferable skills, such as problem solving/decision making, ICT and inter-personal skills. These are highly desirable commodities in many professions where pay and conditions of service are often better than in teaching. In these circumstances entering the classroom appears less attractive and exciting to the new geographer (Rawlinson et al., 2003).

Further exacerbating the situation is the host of other generic issues that have seen teaching lose its attractiveness as a profession. High amongst these perceived barriers are:
- concerns over behaviour management;
- dissatisfaction with pay and, increasingly, conditions of service;
- discontent with the status of teachers within society.

(Rawlinson et al., 2003)

Yet despite these concerns, in the primary sector the number of trainees wishing to enter primary ITT continues to be healthy. At Northumbria University the ratio of applicants to places continues to be 12:1, for the 3-year BA Early Primary Education and 4:1 for the PGCE Primary programmes. For the undergraduate programme, the number of students with 16+ and 18+ geography qualifications is indicated in Figure 3. It should be stressed here that there has been no diminution in the quality of either the applicants or the trainees in the last few years.

Subjects	2002 entry	2001 entry
Article II. Geography A	23	19
Geography GCSE	47	29
History A	16	6
History GCSE	57	31

Figure 3: Geography & History entry qualifications of BA Early Primary Education ITT trainees at Northumbria University: 2001 & 2002 entries (percentage of intake)

Subjects	2003 entry	2002 entry	2001 entry
Geography	4	3	2
Geography related	8	3	5
History	5	4	5
English	9	11	13
Maths	-	1	1
Science	4	5	3
Art	3	4	3
Music	-	-	1
D & T	-	-	1
PE	3	2	3
RE	1	1	-
ICT	1	-	-
Psychology	12	5	17
Other	50	61	46

Figure 4: Entry qualifications of PGCE Primary ITT trainees at Northumbria University: 2001-2003 (percentage of intake)

Whilst the representation of geographers on the Northumbria University BA primary programmes appears relatively strong, the 'poor' showing of the number of geography graduates on the PGCE course must raise some concern (see Figure 4).

Whilst there have been some studies on the causes and effects of shortages in specific subject recruitment in the secondary sphere (eg Constable et al., 1999), there has been less emphasis on subject shortages in the primary sphere. Yet, children's early experience of subjects such as geography can determine attitudes and perceptions of that subject for life. It is, therefore, for the geographical community to recognise there is a need to encourage geographers to enter teaching in both spheres of education. So far attention in recruitment has focused specifically on the secondary sector but, given the importance of early educational experiences, it could be argued that more geographers should be encouraged to enter the primary sector.

This chapter considers how more geographers could be encouraged to enter teaching by examining how the issue is being addressed at Northumbria University. The approach outlined offers a model that other institutions, and indeed other subjects, could readily adapt.

The geography education module

Given the decline in numbers entering secondary geography ITT training and the continued small representation of geographers entering primary training, an innovative programme *module* was developed at the university to appeal to geography undergraduates (and students in related subjects) to enable and encourage them to consider teaching as a career

Most universities have schemes encouraging students to visit and help in local schools. This experience benefits both the students and the schools. The students gain valuable life skills while being able to 'try out' the school experience perhaps with an eye on a future career in teaching. For the schools the arrival of students into the classroom brings help in the form in the enthusiastic, knowledgeable and interesting young people. However, the vast majority of these university schemes is voluntary in nature and does not always enable the student to maximise the opportunities offered.

The *Students into Schools* [SiS] scheme at Newcastle and Northumbria universities is almost unique in that it offers credit for undertaking this work (Students into Schools website). Students are able to gain 10 programme credits for making nine weekly visits to schools, helping in classes and submitting a reflective learning log of these visits for assessment. The scheme also enables participants to work towards the SiS Graduate Employability Standards, which, from previous experience, have considerably enhanced their CV's and increased employability. Each year over 150 students successfully undertake the programme, a figure that is growing annually. Some students go on to take more advanced modules that increase their skill base further.

It was by utilising the experience and organisation of the SiS Project, and by focusing the student experience in schools on the teaching of geography, that Northumbria's *Geography in Education* module was developed. By giving the students experience in schools with a specific subject focus, it was intended that those students undecided about teaching would see the profession in a new light where they might both use their expertise and have their subject's intrinsic value recognised. To ensure they understand the nature of geography in today's schools a co-requisite 10-credit module on *Geographical Education* offered practical guidance on the nature of the school subject and about effective learning strategies in both the primary and secondary age phases.

The fundamental aim of the 20-credit package is to offer a positive experience in schools, with a real focus on the subject the student is studying. This will either encourage a teaching career to be pursued further or will end such ambitions at that point – either result is seen as a successful outcome. If a participant can make an *informed* decision about teaching prior to applying for a

PGCE place, it should ensure that those on such courses are not just taking it as a 'stopgap' or 'fall back position'. In turn, this should lead to greater retention on those courses and, therefore, a higher output of secondary geography teachers as well as primary teachers who have gained a sound knowledge of geographical education.

In the light of research undertaken as part of a wider project into the shortage of geography trainees (Rawlinson, et al., 2003) the module was offered to second year students. However, during the first year of delivery of the programme, it emerged that third year students would also have taken the module had it been available to them. Accordingly the module was modified and is now available to both second and third year students, with full credit.

Module organisation

The module has been designed with an equal balance of university-based *academic* study (the subject specific component – worth 10 credits) and school-based *professional* experience (the professional component – worth 10 credits). The programme for the module is outlined in Figure 5.

The subject specific component
The subject specific component consists of consideration of:
- the evolving nature of geography education;
- the implementation of the Early Learning Goals, the National Curriculum and relevant examination syllabi as they apply to geography;
- the methods and techniques for teaching geography in both primary and secondary schools.

This component is taught through a mixture of lectures, seminars and fieldwork, highlighting the practicalities of geography teaching and emphasising good practice.

The professional component
Using the SiS organisation enables both efficient and effective placement of the students. The students are able to choose whether to have a mixture of experiences – primary *and* secondary – or concentrate on just one schooling phase – primary *or* secondary. All students are encouraged to consider the former approach as it is felt that this offers:
- experience in an age phase they would not have previously considered;
- the opportunity to confirm their perceived choice of age phase;
- insurance that whichever phase of ITT training the student undertakes in future they will have had experience in the alternate phase. Given the current concern over the KS3 transition problems this is seen as a particular strength of the module.

Each year a third of the group elect to take the former option either because they wish to confirm their choice of age phase or simply to 'test the water' in both age phases.

The placements also provide the opportunity to:
- experience teaching in different localities;
- work with good role models;
- develop teaching skills alongside an experienced teacher;
- address and correct preconceptions.

These are all factors that enable the students to make an informed choice about entering the teaching profession.

The Geography in Education/Geographical Education module (20 credits)

The taught module consists of 12 sessions of 2 hours each, plus 2 field visits of 4 hours each.

The first three sessions set the context of the module.

Session
1. Introduction – the nature of geography and geography in education
2. The National Curriculum and Geography Examination Syllabi – implications for teaching geography
3. What is 'good geography'? What makes a good geography lesson? How to plan for teaching good geography. Survey of the techniques used and how they might be applied in different circumstances and levels, e.g. including enquiry approach, fieldwork, data recording, use of the Internet, and role play

The following nine sessions address the teaching of specific topics, to various ages, and involve both staff inputs and student presentations.

4. Undertaking locality studies
5. Settlement studies, followed by:

   Fieldtrip 1 to Felton - an environmental geography simulation exercise

6. Simulation presentations
7. Resourcing geography
8. *Assessment 1* – student presentations
9. Practical Physical geography, followed by:

   Fieldtrip 2 to Marsden - coastal fieldwork for all ages

10. Safety on fieldwork
11. ICT in the geography classroom – session led by geography PGCE tutor at Newcastle university
12. *Assessment 2* – student presentations. Unit review.

Figure 5: The Subject Specific Programme

Module assessment

The assessment of the module is divided equally between the module's two components, and this enables students to claim 20 credits – 10 for each component. For the *academic* component students undertake two presentations of lessons they have planned and taught. They are also asked to submit a written justification of their approach. For the *professional* component students produce a written reflective learning log and oral presentation of their school experience.

Evaluating the student experience of the geography education module

In order to understand the impact of the module and to recognise the perspectives of the students who took it, an evaluative approach was used to elicit student views. This involved seeking through a questionnaire, interviews and assessment data information about:

- students' understanding of the nature of geography in school education;
- their response to working with children in school, teaching geography and more broadly;
- their interest in continuing towards a primary or secondary PGCE programme;
- their sense of the nature and demands of primary and/or secondary teaching generally.

An evaluative approach to such a study is often seen to be more judgmental and qualitative in style (Cohen, Manion & Morrison, 2000; McKernan, 1996). It is also seen to be more *political* in interest – in a professional context – in that it may well be used to make decisions in relation to key activities which there is interest in maintaining and developing for extrinsic as well, perhaps, as intrinsic reasons.

In that this module was developed to provide experience and possible encouragement for undergraduates to consider entering the teaching profession, this approach was considered to be a valid means to research the benefits and limitations of the module. In this case the focus for evaluation was on *student evaluation*, complemented by evidence through the assessment of student presentations, written justifications and reflective logs. While the former provided information about student perceptions and value judgements in relation to the experience and the module as a whole, the latter enabled judgements to be made about the quality of their understanding of the required learning and of their attempts to make sense of their experience.

Discussion of the findings and the value of the research

This module had a very specific rationale, arising from a real need and based upon research findings (Rawlinson et al., 2003). Evaluation suggests that it appears to have lived up to expectations. The module aimed to provide the students with a solid grounding in the nature and purpose of geography education together with practical experience to enable them to confidently enter initial teacher training. It ensured they achieved a good profile of experience in both primary and secondary schools to enhance their application for a PGCE ITT programme if they desired to take that career option. So far it appears to have achieved a 100% success rate in placing those students who wish to do so onto primary or secondary ITT programmes.

It is interesting to note that the numbers expressing a preference for the primary age phase are consistently higher than those opting for the secondary phase (Figure 6). Though the numbers entering PGCE courses directly from the module are modest, many students now opt to take gap year(s) after graduation. However, from student feedback about career choices, it would appear that the numbers likely to enter PGCE training from this route might well rise. However, identifying whether these students do enter ITT will raise some difficult career tracking problems for the university.

The feedback from the students during the first 3 years of the module has been positive and the particular strengths of the module that students have identified have been:
- familiarity with the subject content ensures understanding of what is being taught and why – this removes much of the initial fear of entering the classroom;
- feeling valued, by being able to offer not only subject knowledge but geographical pedagogy as well ;
- feeling confident about applying for a PGCE place;
- understanding the demands of teaching in both the primary and secondary phases.

Student Characteristics	Year of entry			
	2003	**2002**	**2001**	**2000**
Males	5	4	9	2
Females	5	8	4	9
Yr. 2	4	9	10	11
Yr. 3	6	3	4	N/A
BA Geography degree	6	8	8	7
BSc Geography degree	4	4	4	4
Initial preferred age phase - Primary	6	5	6	5
Initial preferred age phase - Secondary	4	4	4	6
Unsure of preferred age phase	-	3	3	-
Applied/Entered/ completed Primary PGCE course	N/A	1	1	1
Applied/ Entered/ completed Secondary PGCE course	N/A	1	2	2
Qualified teacher in employment	N/A	N/A	1	2

Figure 6: Profile of the *Geography in Education* Students 2000 – 2003

A concern that was expressed (by university geography staff) during the development of the module related to the effect that taking this module would have on degree classification, a perennial problem for students taking a module outside their specialist area of study. Though the students were geographers, or from related disciplines, an educationally focused module was not seen as clearly able to connect with their geographical studies. The results from the three cohorts that have completed the module show that it mirrors the marks they have achieved in other aspects of their studies and that it has not in the least disadvantaged them. Indeed, some participants have suggested that it has helped them achieve better marks in other modules, since its approach has considerably enhanced their presentational skills.

There have been several positive benefits to the students from taking the module. These include:
- Several students have gone on to take further SiS modules, such as student mentoring, and thereby enhanced their management skills and consequent PGCE applications.
- A number of *Geography in Education* students have now successfully completed undergraduate dissertations based on geographical education themes.
- The module enables schools and children to benefit from the input of 'cutting edge' geography from current undergraduates.
- It has strengthened the link between the university's education department and the subject department, a point that was positively commented on by Oftsed in a recent inspection of initial teacher education. There are obvious staff development and research advantages in continuing and developing this link.
- Other subjects in the university have expressed interest in the way this module has been set up and developed.
- The programme contributes to the university's Widening Participation agenda by enabling children to work and talk with undergraduates. Informal discussions lead to the children exploring the nature of university education and, therefore, perhaps considering such a step themselves. The fact that these 'model' students are geographers may raise ambitions in these subjects.

Enabling students to make an informed choice of career is a key aspect of the module. By offering them the chance to try out teaching with no loss to them in terms of time or degree credits, students feel 'safer' in opting to undertake the module. At the first meeting for those planning to take the module, it is made clear to participants that if at the end they decide not to go into teaching then this is a successful outcome. If they subsequently decide not to apply for a PGCE place then this means that such a place is not wasted on someone who may leave that course before completion.

The participants value being able to undertake experience in both age phases. Three students began the module convinced that secondary teaching was for them, but changed their minds and moved on to train as primary teachers.

Students taking the module report that they feel very well prepared for their school experience – the academic component takes them through school organisation, lesson planning and innovative techniques in geography teaching. They, therefore, seem able to contribute significantly to the schools in which they work. In addition, the attention given in the academic component to broader educational issues they say enables them to perform well at both primary and secondary PGCE interviews.

This evaluative research has shown that one method of overcoming the shortage of graduates entering a teaching career in specific subjects may be to offer them a good experience in school, backed up with sound knowledge of their subject's educational theory/methodology/pedagogy as a fully accredited component in their undergraduate degree programme.

Experience at Northumbria University of such specifically targeted courses show that these modules work. Courses targeted at men into primary ITT and ethnic minorities into teaching generally have shown that by addressing the specific fears, concerns and perceptions of the target groups, many of these can be overcome (Rawlinson & Soni, 2002). Such 'taster' courses specifically encourage participants to consider what they could bring to the classroom. For geographers, especially those who take a year out between graduation and PGCE training, this consideration is especially significant.

The work of the *Geographers into Education* project (Thorne, 2001, 2002) raised awareness of the shortage of geographers issue amongst HEIs, who are now more conscious of the need to recruit to their courses and to sell the value of the subject. Modules such as that offered by Northumbria University, or the similar module at Manchester Metropolitan (Gibson, 2003), take this initiative to its next logical step in attempting to ensure there is a steady supply of good quality enthusiastic geographers able to enter the teaching profession.

Conclusion: where next?

Geography in primary schools should be exciting and dynamic and central to the curriculum, but the lack of specialist support in schools, either from an in-house teacher or via LEA support, often raises a fear in teachers of tackling it. This may result in children having a poorer experience in the subject and setting in train a spiral of decline, which may have serious consequences for the subject's survival (see Figures 1 and 2).

Addressing the declining spiral of geography's representation in teaching and raising the quality of geography teaching is not easy, especially in relation to the primary field. However, there are three strategies which could be more widely adopted to address this concern:

- *The development of more undergraduate geography in education modules*, such as the Northumbria *Geography in Education* module or that offered by Manchester Metropolitan (Gibson, 2003). The geography in education module course provides a model that other institutions (and other shortage subjects) might follow. By allowing students to have both a primary and secondary experience it gives students the opportunity to ensure that they *really* want to go into teaching and that they choose the age phase most appropriate to them.

- *The provision of geography taster courses*, which target particular groups such as men (with geography qualifications). These should be designed to ensure that the school experience attached to them is undertaken in a school where the candidate will experience high quality teaching of the subject, be that primary or secondary. These would seem to be a cost effective way of offering a 'good experience' for those who are thinking of entering the profession. There are a number of markets for potential recruits that ITT providers could now consider – mature geographers now thinking of a career change, those about to leave the armed services, and those who have been made redundant. Appropriate courses and support will perhaps encourage them to join the profession. The 'hidden' geography that such people bring to the classroom as result of their life experience is invaluable.

- *Raising the profile of geography in the local area*, by utilising contacts with Geographical Association branches. The work of each university geography department's Teaching Liaison Officer in ensuring the relevance to the school curriculum of the branch's programme of activities is essential in this respect. An exciting and relevant programme may encourage more students to go on to take a geography degree and thereby stimulate the positive feedback model (Figure 2) of recruitment into (geography) teaching.

The key to success in all these strategies is the first school experience that these potential teachers have. It is essential they are able to work alongside experienced practitioners who are able to allay fears and who encourage them seriously to consider the profession. This necessitates careful organisation on the part of the provider and close liaison with schools and staff. For the participant, taking part in lessons where the subject matter is familiar, ensures that the fear of lack of subject knowledge does not overpower the experience to the detriment of all other aspects.

A recent survey of the state of primary geography in schools offers some scope for optimism (Catling et al., 2003; see also chapter 21). While there are concerns, it indicates that the majority of primary school geography subject leaders feel that the subject is in fair health and that geography offers much to the children, although further help and support in the form of more in-service training would be very much appreciated.

The long-term future of the subject in the primary sector depends on the continuation of this positive feeling about geography's worth. It also needs all members of the geography community to consider the issues of teacher recruitment and retention and to develop appropriate supportive strategies in their own situations. Above all, it is essential to offer a positive picture of teaching as a profession. Do we always realise that the 'off the cuff' remark, such as 'why on earth do you want to become a teacher?', can stifle the ambition at birth? The best advocate for teaching should be the teacher, but evidence from interviews with students suggests otherwise (Rawlinson et al., 2003).

If the geography community itself does not take seriously the shortage of geographers entering the classroom, then it is certain that no one else will.

References

Carter, R (ed.) (1998), *Handbook of Primary Geography* Sheffield: Geographical Association

Catling, S., Bowles, R., Halocha, J., Martin, F. & Rawlinson, S. (2002), *Monitoring Geography in Primary Schools: A report for the QCA Geography Officers*, London: QCA, unpublished

Cohen, L., Manion, L. & Morrison, K. (2000), *Research Methods in Education*, London: RoutledgeFalmer

Constable, H.; Bolden, D.; Howson, J. & Spindler, J. (1999), Physics Teachers: Supply, Training and Retention, unpublished Report for the TTA

Craig, L. & Lenon, B. (eds.) (1997), *Directory of University Geography Courses 1997*, London, Royal Geographical Society with The Institute of British Geographers

DES (1991), *Geography in the National Curriculum (England)*, London; HMSO

DES (1995), *Geography in the National Curriculum (England)*, London: HMSO

DFEE/QCA (1999), *Geography: The National Curriculum for England*, London: HMSO

Gardner, R. & Craig, L. (2001), Is Geography History? *Journal of Geography in Higher Education*, 25 (1), 5-10

Gibson, C., (2003), Geographers into Teaching at Manchester Metropolitan University, *Planet* 10, 16 - 18

McKernan, J. (1996), *Curriculum Action Research*, London: Kogan Page

Moran, A. (2001), Training to teach: motivating factors and implications for Recruitment, *Evaluation and Research in Education*, 15(1), 17-32

Ofsted (2002), *Secondary Subject Reports: Geography*, London: HMSO

QCA (1998), *Maintaining Breadth and Balance at KS1 & KS2*, London: QCA

Rawling, E. (1996) School geography: some key issues for higher education, *Journal of Geography in Higher Education*, 20(3), 305-322.

Rawlinson, S., Essex-Cater, L., Bolden, D. & Constable, H. (2003), Have geographers lost their way? Issues relating to the recruitment of geographers into school teaching. *Journal of Geography in Higher Education*, 27 (1), 39-56

Rawlinson, S. & Soni V. (2002), Improving the Recruitment of Ethnic Minorities into Primary Teaching; Developments in the North-East of England in *Emerging Issues in Teacher Supply and Retention: Proceedings of the second conference of the Teacher Supply and Retention Project*, University of North London, IPSE

Spear, M., Gould, K. & Lee, B. (2000), Who would be a teacher? A review of factors motivating and demotivating prospective and practising teachers, *National Foundation for Educational Research*

Students into Schools (2003), http://www.ncl.ac.uk/sis/home.phtml accessed 17 Dec 03

TTA (1999), *Understanding Teacher Supply in Geography*, The report of a conference organised jointly by the Teacher Training Agency and the Royal Geographical Society (with IBG), April 1999

TTA (2002), http://www.canteach.gov.uk/ accessed 17 Dec 03

Thorne, F. (2001) News on Geographers into Teaching, *Planet Special edition One*, 16

Thorne, F. (2002), Geographers into Teaching Report *Royal Geographical Society with the Institute of British Geographers*

Thornton, M. & Reid, I. (2001), Primary teacher recruitment: careers guidance and Advice, *Education 3-13*, 29 (2), 49-54

Walford, R. (1996), *Is geography still on the map?: An analysis of the summer 1996 examination results*, Paper presented to Council of British Geographers, October 1996, unpublished

Walford, R. (1997), *Geography, still hanging on!: An analysis of the summer 1997 examination results*, Council of British Geography, unpublished

Walford, R. (2000), Geography Examined 1850-2000, *Geography*, 85 (4), 303-310

Whitehead, J. & Postlethwaite, K. (2000), Recruitment, access and retention: some issues for secondary initial teacher education in the current social context, *Research in Education*, 64, 44-55.

DEVELOPMENT OF THE SUBJECT

Resource and curriculum development

Chapter 24

Researching the Development of a Primary Geography Resource: Why, how, issues and implications.

Jane Graham and Greg Walker

Introduction: Why did we develop the resource?

As education lecturers with a primary geography specialism, a major focus of our work is showing trainee teachers appropriate ways to teach geography, enabling them to work with confidence in school. We have noticed the increasing use of the Qualifications and Curriculum Authority [QCA] Geography Scheme of Work (DfEE/QCA, 1998/2000) in whole school planning. A popular unit is number 3, *An island home*, which seeks to link geography and literacy. The unit purports to show 'how a storybook can be used to develop children's understanding of geographical features and ideas' [Unit 3, 'About The Unit' (QCA, 1998/2000)]. The unit is focused on the imaginary island of Struay and what it is like to live there. The unit prompts children to investigate similarities and differences between their home and Struay and consider whether they would like to live there.

Some Roehampton trainees had been asked by schools, where they were completing school experience, to teach this unit with the single resource, the storybook *'Katie Morag and the Two Grandmothers'* (Hedderwick, 1995). They were not given 'pictures and photographs of Coll in the Inner Hebrides, on which the island of Struay is based' [Unit 3, Resources (QCA, 1998/2000)]. Whilst the story offers a range of opportunities to explore a sense of what it might be like to live on a remote island, photographs of the real place, the Isle of Coll, would greatly extend the range and potential for children's geographical learning.

We decided to give tangible support to both trainees and teachers by developing resources for use with unit 3. We wanted to retain the use of the popular Katie Morag story but to complement it with resources about Coll. Photographs and associated activities, including those that would probe values and attitudes, had the potential to enhance teaching and learning opportunities within this unit. Our aim was to meet the aims of the National Curriculum Geography Working Group (DES, 1989) enabling children to view the place from the perspective of people who live there.

What principles guided the process of compiling the pack?

We wanted to produce a resource that would:
- Motivate and challenge children to learn about this locality;
- Encourage discussion and exploration of ideas and thoughts and feelings;
- Develop conceptual understandings;
- Support the development of enquiry skills;
- Be seen to be relevant by classroom teachers offering links to programmes of study, relevant practical ideas and a range of approaches with accurate up to date information.

Catling (2003) argued persuasively for the importance of children being involved in decisions about what should be studied in geography and he suggested criteria that might be used to provide a geographical framework for them:

- A focus on real places, from local to national scale, and/or on elements of real environments, such as types of environment, human settlements or activities, physical and human processes creating and changing environments;
- The use of resources such as maps, the real environment beyond the classroom (and school), photographs of various sorts, information books and technological sources such as CDs, the internet and email;
- Reflection on key geographical ideas, including location, patterns and environmental processes;
- The recognition of environmental concerns and issues;
- The development of a sense of the world, its cultural and environmental variety and of the interdependence of people, places and environments;
- The examination of personal positions and values and of those held by others and of the views and reasons for them. (2003, 193-4).

Although the resource pack would clearly be presenting children with a locality to explore, we found it useful to take account of these criteria in developing the pack.

Our aim was to produce a resource that would offer opportunities to explore the geography of the real Scottish island of Coll, whilst retaining the valuable literacy links with QCA Unit 3 and the imaginary island of Struay. Norris Nicholson has stated that 'stories can supplement other geographical resources to help children visualise different places and lifestyles' and that 'they offer children windows and doors upon other worlds beyond their own' (Norris Nicholson 1994:5). The detailed illustrations and content of the Katie Morag stories, produced by the author and artist Mairi Hedderwick and based on her own experiences of living and working for many years on Coll, would provide a springboard for children to share ideas and to 'generate valuable discussion with strong geographical elements' (Palmer 1994, 130).

As well as using *Katie Morag and the Two Grandmothers* to introduce the unit of work in an enjoyable way, other links to this story and other Katie Morag stories were made in the resources to offer children mapping opportunities, placing geographical vocabulary and ideas in a meaningful context, following routes, actions and events and sharing their ideas and feelings about other people in other places. Wiegand highlighted the importance of opportunities in place studies to be 'able to think and feel yourself into them' (1993, 65). We wanted to offer activities that would focus on, and allow children to explore ideas in relation to themes presented in the Katie Morag story, that is, of a remote island, its environment, weather, wildlife, transport and the daily lives of the people who live on or visit the island.

Whilst literary links were to be important in motivating and challenging children, the use of photographs would be central to the resource. Young and Commins (2002) have stressed the importance of presenting positive images of people in distant places. We sought to do this by giving an all-round view of the place, by finding out as much information as possible about it and the people who live there and presenting images that treat both sensitively. We felt that this necessitated developing resources that offered a range of honest representations for children to explore, resources that would not only engage them but also offer access to the thoughts and feelings of people who lived there. This in turn would encourage children to express ideas and be able to make reasoned judgements from accurate and comprehensive evidence. Our set of photographs, background information and activities would focus on the real, named people who live, work and visit Coll. In this way the resource would provide opportunities for children, most importantly, to answer the questions about what life on Coll might be like.

The evidence of Shevelan et al (2002, 3) highlighted more recent thinking in the use of simple maps and aerial photographs by young children. Children can start with an aerial view and a map of an unfamiliar place as 'establishing shots' and, as Spencer (1998, 17) noted, teachers can then confidently promote and encourage geographical discussion and ideas. Catling agreed that the use of a vertical aerial photograph and matching pictorial map would allow children to build a sense of place of a locality they could not visit. (Catling1995, 12). The publishers provided us with the A3 aerial photograph of the island and we designed a simple pictorial map to be used alongside.

The work of Mackintosh on children learning from photographs highlighted the need to select photos that not only interested children but also challenged them by 'exploiting their curiosity and flexible attitudes about other people and cultures'(Mackintosh, 1998,18). We needed to offer teachers' ideas that would include photograph and map content to promote graphicacy, to encourage identification, decoding, interpreting, predicting, observing, supposition and narrative. Our photographs should offer opportunities for line drawings, sketching, annotation as well as allowing children to appreciate that what is not in the photograph is just as important and that a photograph may offer only a partial representation of a place or of the people who live there.

Central to planning active, practical and meaningful geography that would motivate children to find out more about the world around them is the enquiry process. This process involves encouraging children to ask questions and to look for answers to them. Whilst this is not the place to discuss the nature of geographical enquiry, or issues of teachers' understanding of enquiry (Martin, 1999; Carter, 1998; Owen and Ryan, 2001; Catling, 2003,) we felt our resource needed to exemplify an enquiry approach, stressing the importance of children raising their own questions and using evidence to seek to answer them. Catling highlighted a structure for geographical enquiry: 'to cultivate children's learning by working from their own interests to explore, understand and learn further from the world, as well as to contribute to it through active engagement and participation.' (2003, 192).

The work of Davidson & Catling (2000, 280) in examining further the process of enquiry and a question led curriculum, was also to prove useful in the planning of the resource as was Catling's work (2002:7) on thinking geographically. The work, providing geographical examples to promote thinking skills, was particularly helpful when we considered the activities for using the photographs. Scoffham (2002, 6) also reminded us, in his review of recent work on brain function that 'these skills, which are crucial to meaningful learning, can all be developed and promoted through primary geography. We need to keep them high on our agenda.'

The importance of a value - based approach to learning (Scoffham, 2000; Owen and Ryan, 2001; Catling, 2003) guided us to offer activity ideas that would allow individual responses and discussion from children based on images and information about the real people of Coll. These would include children, individuals and families expressing their thoughts and feelings about work, home and leisure on Coll as well as from visitors to the island. A consideration of the way people interacted with their surroundings was also important, for example, what children had written about living on Coll and what tourists valued about the island. There was also the notion of safeguarding special places on the island such as the Royal Society for the Protection of Birds (RSPB) Reserve at Feall beach whilst also allowing locals and visitors to use it.

When we developed our ideas based on the photographs we sought to make explicit links with the Key Stage 1 programmes of study (DfEE/QCA, 1999). For teachers using the resource who might have limited confidence in teaching geography we sought to highlight clearly key geographical skills, knowledge and concepts whilst trying not to be prescriptive in terms of what children should do. We did not offer ideas for differentiation as, with any resource pack, teachers need to be selective and amend ideas to cater for the needs and learning styles of their own children.

Owen and Ryan (2001, 60) argued that in order to motivate all pupils it is important to provide a variety of approaches to teaching and learning and we incorporated a number of their ideas into the pack:

- Following a map/drawing a map/using a CD-Rom atlas;
- Interpreting photographs;
- Making a model;
- Reading a reference book;
- Designing a poster;
- Undertaking traffic and land use surveys;
- Assessing environmental quality;
- Searching the World Wide Web
- Sketching;
- Discussing an issue;
- Taking photographs.

We aimed to promote cross-curricular links including the use of ICT throughout the pack. The resource would be QCA unit specific and consequently seen as relevant and appropriate by schools who chose to purchase the photo pack. We hoped it would offer resources that would enhance the teaching and learning for any teacher using unit 3 *An Island Home*. Integrating the many ideas from our literature review provided a structure when we began the process of creating the resource.

When and how did we produce the resource?

The following outline sets out the sequence of the events in the development of the pack from origination to publication.

October 2001: Origination
- Initial discussions about the project and contact with the publishers to gain their approval in principle.

November 2001: Proposal outline
- Written outline proposal presented to the publishers.

January 2002: Proposal acceptance
- Approval gained from the publishers, including funding for a visit to the Isle of Coll.

February 2002/June 2002: Preparatory work
- Selecting suitable dates for the fieldwork – this was guided largely by a desire to take photographs during the summer with the likelihood of better weather conditions;
- Contacting the primary school and an island family on Coll;
- Carrying out research on Coll – this was largely through internet sites and OS Landranger map 46;

- Research into the most appropriate structure for the resource pack.

June/July 2002: Fieldwork.

- 28 June: Travel to Oban – gathered information and photographs about Oban that would represent the reality of Mairi Hedderwick's 'mainland';
- 29 June: Ferry to Coll – drove / walked around the island locating areas of particular interest for photograph locations – meetings with key people e.g. the tourist family and shop, hotel and holiday home owners;
- 30 June: Whole day taking photographs (in excess of 60 in number with 2 copies at each site) – each site marked on the OS map and relevant notes taken - visited the holiday home;
- 1 July: Further photographs taken and held a meeting with Mairi Hedderwick – return to mainland.
- We discussed the nature of the project with those individuals who featured in our photographs and sought permission to use their image in the pack.

July to August 2002: Photographs

- July: Publishers developed and return photographs.
- August 2002: Selected the 24 most suitable images, the limit set by the publishers. *We wanted photographs that would capture children's imagination and prompt them to want to know more about this place and the people who live there.*

September to December 2002: Devising the pack

- The substantive work on devising the activity ideas, the resources and other details for each photograph, finalised the exact choice of photographs. Extensive email contact with both the island and tourist families, including acquiring further resources from them, produced a revised version of QCA unit 3 that would best utilise the photo pack resources.

January 2003: Piloting the pack

- Resources piloted in a Year 2 class and feedback received from the class teacher and one other experienced infant teacher who reviewed the resources;

February 2003: Completion

- Final version of the resource pack completed;

April 2003: Publication

- Publication of *'Discover Coll: the real Struay'* (Graham & Walker, 2003)

Article III.

What were the constraints on the project and how did they affect the outcomes?

In spite of the considerable time spent in discussion, research and preparation whilst aiming for the best possible final product, we inevitably faced constraints that limited our ideas and the final outcome.

Time constraints

There were time constraints in our work.

- The publishers were willing to fund one short visit to Coll but this meant that taking photographs, direct contact with people and further research and data collection had to be completed in a restricted timeframe;

- Work commitments and a desire to visit in summer made it impossible to visit the island's primary school whilst children were present and a key opportunity for comparison / contrast was therefore limited.

Privacy/sensitivity constraints

There were sensitive issues to ensure we took careful account of.

- Discussions with the headteacher of the island's primary school prior to the visit revealed that the introduction into the curriculum of QCA unit 3 had led to a deluge of letters, from schools all over England, for information about the school and requests for twinning links. This was particularly problematic for such a small school since they had neither time nor resources to respond to requests. It was clearly a very sensitive issue and one that we did not wish to further complicate. It became essential to dissuade schools purchasing the pack from seeking contact with the school by highlighting this issue strongly in the resource introduction. The headteacher did, however, feel that once the resource had been published that this might reduce unsolicited contacts;
- Whilst the contributions of real people on Coll would be invaluable to a case study approach we were concerned not to exploit their goodwill nor to compromise their privacy.

Organisational/resource constraints

There were organisational and resource constraints in the development of the pack.

- Researching Coll prior to the visit gleaned limited information and, with no existing first hand experience of the island or similar islands, we approached the trip with restricted background knowledge;
- Internet information was largely aimed at tourists and was not representative of daily life on Coll;
- The weather for most of the visit was grey and wet and meant that not all the photographs taken were of sufficiently good quality to reproduce at A3 size. Additionally, content showing a dull, damp place had the potential to tell a biased story. However, this type of weather is representative of periods of time in the Western Isles in summer, including the years 2000 to 2002. The gift shop owner in the village of Arinagour mentioned this in terms of its adverse affect on her livelihood. Fortunately our 'tourist family' contributed a number of photographs of family members engaged in outdoor leisure activities on the island taken in bright sunshine in May 2002 and these helped to give a more balanced view of the island's weather;
- There was much we hoped to include in the final product but the limit of 24 photographs with key written information and photocopiable resources, confined to the reverse side of each A3 photograph, proved a challenge. Whilst we wanted to give teachers a structured pathway through the resource to enable them to enhance geographical learning rather than merely give out information we did not want to convey the idea that this was the only way to use the materials;
- Significant island events like the Coll Show were omitted because we had no access to appropriate resources;
- Insights we gained were often intangibles such as the friendliness of the people, a lifestyle quite at odds with the urban experiences of most of us and we had difficulty in conveying a sense of these intangibles through pictures and words;
- Presenting sensory dimensions like sounds and smells were problematic.

Meeting all our objectives in just 24 photographs was a challenge and the end product is inevitably partial – it is after all the photograph selection and activity ideas of just two adults, neither of them island inhabitants, and our own values inevitably come through. As with any writer or photographer we are all interpreters.

Conclusion

In conclusion we feel that the visit to Coll gave us invaluable insights into a previously unknown place and consequently we would advocate first hand experiences as part of distant place studies whenever possible. We are concerned that time constraints will find teachers using the resources in a limited way and just 'scratching the surface' of a fascinating place, missing opportunities for an in-depth exploration of Coll. Additionally, by relying on the ideas in the pack and not giving the work a personal dimension the ideas of both teachers and children' may not be effectively explored.

We believe that with time and inclination, and at no great expense, teachers could use some of our ideas for their own distant place photograph resource. If the place were not too distant it would enable children to have invaluable first hand experiences. Such a resource would have a personal dimension, would make it possible to add resources over time including photographs taken by children and to explore their ideas and enquiries. A locality in the UK that contrasts with the children's locality does not have to be *very* distant or *very* different. The majority of UK primary schools are probably no more than a short distance from a place that has characteristics that would allow children to find both differences and similarities with their own place. Moreover the processes involved in producing a photo pack are largely similar for all localities.

References

Carter, R. (ed.) (1998), *Handbook of Primary Geography*, Sheffield: Geographical Association
Catling, S. (1995), Mapping the environment with children, in de Villiers, M. (ed.), *Developments in primary geography, theory and practice*, Sheffield: Geographical Association, 12-16
Catling, S. (2002), Thinking Geographically, *Primary Geographer* 47, 7-9
Catling, S. (2003), *Curriculum Contested: Primary Geography and Social Justice*, Geography, 88 (3), 164-210
Davidson, G. & Catling, S. (2000), Towards the question-led curriculum 5-14, in Fisher, C. & Binns, T. *Issues in geography teaching*, London: Routledge
DES (1989), *National Curriculum Geography Working Group, Interim Report*, London: HMSO
DfEE/QCA (1998), *Raising Standards: Geography*, London: DfEE/QCA
DfEE/QCA (1998/2000), *A Scheme of Work for Key Stages 1 & 2: Geography*, London: DfEE/QCA
DfEE/QCA (1999), *The National Curriculum: Handbook for primary teachers in England*, London: DfEE/QCA
Graham, J. & Walker, G. (2003), *Discover Coll, The Real Struay,* Coalville: Wildgoose
Hedderwick, M. (1995), *Katie Morag and the Two Grandmothers*, London: Bodley Head
Mackintosh, M. (1998), Learning from photographs, in Scoffham, S. (ed.), *Primary Sources: Research findings in primary geography*, Sheffield: Geographical Association, 18-20
Martin, F. (1999), The enquiry approach: What, Why and How, *Primary Geographer* 38, 4-8

Norris Nicholson, H. (1994), *Place in Story-time*, Sheffield: Geographical Association.

Owen, D. & Ryan, A. (2001), *Teaching Geography 3-11: The Essential Guide,* London: Continuum

Palmer, J. (1994), *Geography in the Early Years*, London: Routledge.

Scoffham, S. (ed.) (1998), *Primary Sources: Research findings in primary geography,* Sheffield: Geographical Association

Scoffham, S. (2000), Environmental Education: a question of values, in Fisher, C. & Binns, T. *Issues in geography teaching*. London: Routledge

Scoffham, S. (2002), Neuro-geography, *Primary Geographer*, 47, 4-6

Shevelan, C. et al (2002), Learn to look down, *Primary Geographer* 47, 30-31

Spencer, C. (1998), Aerial photographs and understanding places, in Scoffham, S. (ed.) *Primary Sources: Research findings in primary geography*, Sheffield: Geographical Association, 16-17

Wiegand, P. (1993), *Children and Primary Geography*, London: Cassell

Young, M. & Commins E. (2002), *Global Citizenship: The Handbook for Primary Teaching*, Cambridge: Chris Kington Publishing

Chapter 25

Developing a Locality Resource Using ICT to Support Staff Development and Primary Children's Geographical Thinking

John Moore

Introduction

The context for this research project began initially as the result of an approach by the headteacher of a local primary school to a humanities tutor in the Department of Primary Education at Nottingham Trent University. The school had been invited to join a project to develop twinning links with a school in Harare, Zimbabwe in the summer of 1998. Earlier in that year a member of the management committee of the local Development Education Centre (DEC) had visited Nottingham's twinned city in Africa, with a view to identifying two primary schools in the suburbs of Harare that might be interested in making links with schools in Nottingham. On returning to Nottingham the DEC committee wrote to several schools asking if any would be interested in being involved in developing a school link. Two Nottingham primary schools agreed to become involved and coincidentally were based together on the same campus on the Clifton Estate, which is adjacent to The Nottingham Trent University Clifton Campus.

Three events occurred almost simultaneously that created the context for this study. The first, briefly mentioned above, when the head of one of the two schools contacted the humanities education tutors to seek help with the development of a locality resource park based on the catchment area of his school. This approach coincided with the announcement that the Department of Primary Education at Nottingham Trent would be relocating some half a mile to the main campus which would ultimately necessitate the adaptation of the humanities programme and the focus of the local studies module. The third event was the intention by the University to initiate a partnership programme focusing on developing joint research activities with local schools and to therefore invite bids for collaborative project ideas.

In liaison with humanities tutors a bid proposal was submitted to the Project Committee of the Faculty of Education by the two schools, for consideration under the title of:

Resourcing the local area: a collaborative approach to using the locality as a foundation for the development of global citizenship.

The aims off the project were to:
- Develop high quality resources with a geographical perspective for the study of a local area;
- Provide opportunities for school-based staff to develop their knowledge and understanding of how local area resources can be used to support children's learning in geography;

- Provide the context for university staff to further their knowledge and understanding of how primary aged children make sense of their local area and in particular to deepen their understanding of progression from Key Stage 1 to Key Stage 2;
- Provide a relevant context for university and school staff to develop specific Information and Communications Technology (ICT) skills;
- Provide an opportunity for the students to develop subject expertise in a context which is relevant to their professional development;
- Further develop the links between partner schools and the department of Primary Education;
- Support the development of links between two Nottingham Primary schools and two primary schools in a suburb of Harare.

The bid was accepted and £2,500 was allocated to the project, the majority of the money being mainly for teaching cover in order to enable one teacher from each school and two university tutors to have time to plan, investigate and produce the resource pack.

Review of the literature

The teachers from the two schools wanted to create a locality pack based on the catchment area of their two campus schools so that the children in Harare would have some idea of the environment in which the majority of English children lived. The project initially appeared to be a straightforward task of collecting a series of photographs and maps on the local area and putting some background contextualisation together. At the planning stage it was decided to model the resource pack on ones that had already been professionally produced.

In the last decade there has been a plethora of published material on locations both near and far and the better locality packs have provided a range of high resolution A4 photographs of various aspects of everyday life, in small locations on most of the continents. The initial aim was therefore to identify those that had been produced by the Geographical Association [GA]. The GA had published distant locality packs on Kaptalamwa (Weldon, 1994) and Malawi (Bowden & Trill, 1995) which offered models to consider. However, Jackson & Morgan (1994) produced a contrasting UK locality pack that offered the most useful way forward.

It was important to ensure the theoretical basis on which the pack would be developed was based on sound educational and geographical criteria. Geographers ask questions about places and an enquiry approach was fundamental to the study of the Clifton location. Storm (1989) indicated there were five key questions when studying a location, which provided a structure for a geographical investigation. Good practice in geographical education recognises the learning needs of primary children and stresses that children's learning about a distant locality should be based on a sound knowledge and understanding of their local area. Both the Clifton schools involved their children in studying aspects of their local environment and had collected a range of local photographs. However, these were neither comprehensive nor of the quality required to be included in the pack. A review of the general literature on this aspect indicated that photographs should represent the typical range of houses, shops, amenities, parks and play areas in the immediate vicinity the schools.

One of the main aims of the project, particularly for the tutors, was to develop ICT both in the production of the pack and in personal terms, for the tutors. Digital cameras were becoming more accessible and affordable thus offering an alternative to the usual photographic approach.

New computer software enabled easy and quick downloading of images into a computer, creating an inexpensive way to store and edit the photographs. Developing this aspect of the project was essential from both the tutors' and the teachers' point of view, especially as Pickford (1999) contends that ICT can support children's learning by enabling them to carry out mundane and time -consuming tasks quickly and easily which ultimately allows more time for in depth analysis and drawing conclusions. Also several writers in May (2000) justify the increased use of ICT to develop geographical skills, knowledge and understanding. In the article 'Our Street', Ryan (May 2000, 13) summarises the range of cross-curricular learning opportunities that also arise from linking ICT and geography.

The tutors needed to develop ideas and strategies to integrate ICT into their humanities modules, and developing the knowledge and the basic ICT skills was an important consideration for the future planning of the teaching programme for students. Many of the schools in which the students undertake their School Based Training [SBT] placements were developing ICT suites and it was important to ensure students were both knowledgeable and confident in using this new technology to develop geographical thinking. However before this could be introduced into the course, tutors had to become confident and conversant with these new developments and getting familiar with digital cameras was an appealing starting point.

Research methodology

The first meeting of the teachers and tutors began by considering the proposed aims for the project. These had been developed as a 'best guess' in order to meet the deadline for completing the bid. The detail had now to be discussed and agreed upon in order to move forward. The initial discussions were related to how the local area might be represented and how the data could be gathered. It was felt that the first National Curriculum Geography Order (DES/WO, 1991) provided the most effective breakdown of geography and it was decided to use the five distinct geographical categories within the Attainment Targets to study the locality. Skills (1), Knowledge and Understanding of Places (2), Physical (3), Human (4) and Environmental (5). The latter three categories were seen as useful ways of initially dividing the task of gathering information and best fitted the strengths of the team. Human geography would be the largest section given the range of services on the estate and the two teachers decided to focus their data gathering on this aspect. The two university tutors each took one of the remaining two categories- physical and environmental geography. The estimated time for undertaking this initial photographic survey, which involved familiarisation and walking the area around part of the estate, was half a day each.

The next item for discussion was ICT support. It was evident that no one was knowledgeable or proficient enough to develop the ICT resource aspect of the project, so it was decided to approach a university technician in order to give guidance and advice.

Setting some deadlines and a notional time scale was discussed but no definite decisions were made. We had nine months to complete the project but until we had more information and data, those decisions had to be left to the next meeting.

Four weeks later we reconvened having completed our individual data gathering. During this period several technicians had been approached but none were available. It was therefore decided to approach an IT consultant. There were several possible contacts in schools around Nottingham but it was realised that obtaining their services would have an impact on the budget.

The most likely candidate was a recently retired head teacher who was at the forefront of ICT developments within the LEA. He was available and was invited to the meeting. His involvement proved to be very significant in terms of determining the future direction the project would take.

Figure 1: The area of the Clifton Estate, Nottingham

The map in Figure 1 indicates the area that the team was initially investigating. The Clifton Estate was built in the 1950's and when completed was the largest council estate in Europe. It was a green field site where planners visualised an estate that catered for 30,000 people with schools, shops, and services conveniently located and interlinked.

The IT consultant felt that to only focus on one part of the estate would not give a true picture of the locality, especially as it was built as an entity and should therefore be studied in its entirety. This suggestion, whilst appropriate, meant a significant 'ratcheting up' of the project in terms of the demands on time as well as the knowledge required to address the original criteria. An increase in the ICT element was also essential if all this new information was to be recorded in a manageable and organised way. It was argued that the children on the estate as well as the children in Harare should be able to access the information using the latest available technology.

The team felt these suggestions were valid but were concerned that the proposed budget would not meet these new initiatives. There was uncertainty that if this new proposal was accepted by the group there would not be the money or the time to complete the project. Assurances were given that the available technology was more than capable of managing the increased amount of information. All the photographs, maps, documents would be stored on a CD-Rom which would eventually be able to produce the paper version in a visually stimulating way.

Debate centred around the most effective way of representing the mass of information that would be generated by more than doubling of the area to be studied. The IT consultant had a very clear idea from the outset as to how the data would be represented. His ideas initially were conceptually difficult to grasp especially as the team was still struggling with the complexities of 'computer speak'. A comic strip approach was used in order to explain how a series of visual filing cabinets would be formatted in order to help to organise and store the information.

It was finally agreed to increase the study area to the whole estate and whilst the extra data was being gathered, the IT consultant would create a CD-Rom and install the information already gathered in order to demonstrate, at the next meeting, the structure and layout of the data.

The thinking behind the project was moving from just providing a 'paper pack' for the children of Harare towards a more general ICT resource database for use by children in all the primary schools on the estate as well as students. This shift in emphasis is not untypical of most projects as the potential inherent within them is realised. The initial idea to create a small-scale locality pack was now becoming one part of a much bigger project.

Developing the ideas

It was apparent that the methodology for developing this resource was changing to a more action research approach of plan, do and review. We were not sure exactly what the final outcomes would be and most certainly unsure as to how we would get there.

The initial set of information, maps and photographs collected by the team were stored in Word files and a disc was 'burnt' showing the basic structure and format of the package. From this point it became an iterative process of subtle adaptation and enlargement as more and more possibilities emerged as the research revealed more information and the bounds of technological possibilities increased.

The original monies were quickly swallowed up in these new developments and a further bid was developed in the next round of projects. This bid was submitted with some adaptation from the original, the main aims still intact but with increased emphasis on staff development in ICT, more student involvement, trialling the CD-Rom with a class of children and increasing the range of visual resources. Also a subtle change to the title of the project was seen as necessary. It was modified to:

> *A collaborative approach between two primary schools and The Nottingham Trent University to develop a CD-Rom for a local locality study.*

A presentation was prepared for the committee using the mark 1 version of the CD-Rom. The potential was acknowledged, the bid was accepted and £3,000 was allocated.

Once the initial CD-Rom had been developed an additional aspect of the methodology was agreed upon. It was decided to approach a year 3 student to trial the disc whilst on Teaching Practice. The student selected had good ICT skills, was placed in a school with a new ICT suit and felt confident in working with a whole class. Tutors gave support in the planning process and it was decided initially to let the children explore the content of the disc with only a brief explanation about the practicalities of accessing the information.

In the first lesson the children were excited and quickly began to move around the different areas of the disc. Much of what happened was serendipitous with them coming across photographs of places they recognised and sharing this with their neighbours. They explained to each other how to find a particular photo or showed the route they had followed on the screen. In the 30-minute session they had individually explored large parts of the disc, had shared information they found with their neighbours, explained how to find particular things and were generally very motivated by this experience. This basic unstructured familiarisation was seen as essential in order to ensure the children could find information quickly when more organised work was undertaken in the future.

The next lesson was more structured in that they all received a base map of the estate and were given the task of locating certain features from the disc and marking particular locations on the map. This proved more challenging but with support and encouragement most located the position of the school, a local garage, and the shopping arcade. It was clear that the class needed more practice on basic map skills but the disc was the stimulus and developed the motivation for this to be followed up.

The first part of the process of working with children had shown that with minimal input from the teacher, the disc was presented in a way in which children could find information by trial and error initially, and then quite quickly become to understand which particular information could be found in the 'virtual filing cabinets'.

The next step was to add more information to the disc. Some of the money paid for a series of aerial photographs to be taken, transport information on how the estate was serviced to be gathered, and additional photos of all the shops, public houses, schools and general amenities to be taken. The final version of the disc became a comprehensive resource pack of information on the whole estate.

It had gradually become evident to the team that the crux of the project was leading towards being able to draw on the CD-Rom's bank of information to develop children's thinking skills.

Discussion centred around how best to finalise and draw to a conclusion the project. All the files on the CD-Rom had been created in order that they could be easily downloaded in other software packages. The IT consultant had always had in mind the idea of making all the data available to use with *Textease*. This is a software package that allows files to be imported and then manipulated. Whilst the downloading process is relatively simple once it is understood, training and practice is required.

Promoting the capabilities of the disc was seen as an essential extra development to the project. In order to do this and ensure the full potential of the disc was appreciated, the decision was made to invite a teacher from each of the eight primary schools on the Clifton estate for a half-day workshop. The teacher selected by the school needed to be ICT conversant, which in some cases was not always the Geography coordinator. The team felt it was important that the teacher was ICT literate so the session could concentrate on the conceptual possibilities of the disc rather than the mechanics of teaching the basic processes. It was hoped that the teachers would then go back into school to run workshop sessions for interested staff.

The tutors wanted the teachers to see the learning potential inherent within the package so that their children could develop stories, plan routes, identify patterns, think about the location of shops, consider whether there was a reasonable distribution of facilities and generally be able to use the technology to solve geographical problems within their catchment area.

Discussion

There were several outcomes to this project that were not foreseen at the outset. As with any project keeping it to manageable proportions *was* a real challenge. A modest set of aims became an ambitious project that pushed the finances, time and skills of the teachers and tutors to the limit.

The major decision to increase the area of study to the whole settlement made geographical sense. The estate was built as an entity, if asked people say they live in Clifton regardless of their postal address. All the eight primary schools serve different areas of the estate but many of the facilities would be used by all the children, e.g. the leisure centre, and the main shopping centre with the large supermarket. In order to be able to make judgements about services, for example, the location and type of every shop, park, playing field, etc. had to be recorded accurately This all round increase in workload delayed the timescale for the completion of the project which was initially nine months but eventually became eighteen months.

However, the delay was offset by the greater opportunities the range and scale of information about the whole estate gave to the schools, and the increased opportunities to add to the ICT developments. For those directly involved, the ICT component had the most significant incremental impact in that we, the teachers and tutors, all started with simple word processing skills and an ability to point a conventional camera and press. This quickly moved onto to using digital cameras, downloading, editing, scanning and cropping, moving files and being able to use *Textease,* to name but a few examples. This confidence led to simulating the types of activities students and children could do when exploring the geographical potential of the files where maps, photos and text could be merged.

The final version of the disc was piloted by one of the teachers with their class of year 5 children. She reported that their interest was captured the minute they realised that the photographs displayed were places they recognised and knew. This led to linking that knowledge to exact locations on a map. This familiarity with subject content demonstrated the importance of using the immediate environment and the importance of allowing children to explore within a structured framework.

The challenge for teachers using the disc will be to set structured activities which encourage the children to think, speculate and develop opinions. The disc should be able to be used easily by any primary aged child because in the end it is only a resource, the skill comes from a teacher who will be able to devise activities that draw on this database and who will help children download information into *Textease* in relation to a specific geographical task.

An example might be to solve the following problem:

- Your Uncle's car has run out of petrol outside your house, he needs to walk to the nearest petrol station to fill his can. What is the shortest route for him to take?

The children download the estate map into *Textease*, select a photograph from the files of the nearest petrol station and superimpose this at the side of the map, mark a route between the two locations on the map and write a piece of text to explain the route to take. A useful additional development for the teacher to consider would be to have a digital photo of the front view of every child's house. This would also help to personalise their work and be a useful starting point for geographical work on their locality.

The project overall offered the opportunity for the team involved to become more conversant with ICT, develop more in depth knowledge of the estate and create new teaching ideas for both the children and the students. The outcome was a 'win, win' situation in which all the schools on the estate benefited from a comprehensive research project that had a tangible piece of software; the Primary Department developed closer links with the partnership schools and the humanities tutors developed a teaching package that would benefit future students and, not forgetting the raison d'être for all this work, the schools in Harare got their resource pack. However, the key aspect to emerge from all of this work was the realisation of the way ICT is capable of promoting geographical thinking

Conclusion

The project was finished in 2000, which coincided with the Estate's golden jubilee celebrations. The content of the CD-Rom was a snapshot of the whole estate at the beginning of the New Millennium and, although changes will continue to take place, it will be a useful archive which will offer the potential for developing further geographical understanding, such as the concepts of change and continuity, similarity and difference.

The salutary aspect highlighted from the whole project was how time consuming it would be for teachers to develop an in depth knowledge of the local area. In the past it was very glib to identify the local area as a useful learning resource and the tutors have realised that to ask students to consider using the catchment area of their placement school, in order to develop their geography planning, is not a small undertaking. Likewise for the NQT or the non specialist teacher, the time and effort required to undertake this locality research would not be practical unless it could be built on existing information and resources, otherwise if attempted, it would at best, be only superficial. However, if done properly by the whole school and linked to ICT, real value could be accrued for developing geographical thinking.

A school needs to invest time and money in supporting the whole staff to be involved in order to provide the knowledge and range of resources necessary for teachers to feel confident in being able to challenge children's thinking about why places are as they are. Using the new technology to store data and software packages to manipulate and represent different scenarios should be an exciting prospect. It was clear from children's responses that geography and ICT sat very comfortably together and, when combined particularly with the children's own local knowledge, provided the opportunity for more demanding activities to be undertaken.

References

Bowden, D. & Trill, J. (1995), *Localities in Malawi*, Sheffield: Geographical Association

DES/WO (1991), *Geography in the National Curriculum (England)*, London: HMSO

DFE (1995), *The National Curriculum for Geography: Key Stages One and Two*, London: HMSO

Jackson, E. & Morgan, W. (1994), *Flatford: A contrasting UK locality,* Sheffield: Geographical Association

May, S. (2000), *High-tech Geography: ICT in Primary Schools*, Sheffield: Geographical Association

Pickford, T. (1999), *ICT: An enquiry approach*, Sheffield: Geographical Association

Storm, M. (1989), Five basic questions for primary geography, *Primary Geographer*, 2,4

Weldon, M. (1994), *Kaptalamwa A village in Kenya*, Sheffield: Geographical Association

CONCLUSION

Chapter 26

Future Developments and Directions for Primary Geography Research

Fran Martin & Simon Catling

Introduction

The opening chapter gave an overview of the methodological and substantive areas that have been the focus of primary geography research over the last 20 – 30 years. It also outlined some areas where there are gaps. With the exception of research conducted within the field of developmental psychology, none of that which is reported here has secured large-scale research funding. As one might expect, therefore, the contributions to this book confirm that research in primary geography is largely small-scale and reflects the interests, enthusiasm and commitment of a relatively small band of individuals. However, these interests are not divorced from a context in which there is concern about the image of the subject, its status in England, and a period (1990 – present) of almost constant curriculum change.

Geographical education appears to be in crisis. Geographical education, and primary geography in particular, has a status at all levels in society that makes it hard to reach the top of major research funders' lists of priorities, yet a key question raised in Chapter 1 concerned the lack of access to sufficient resources to conduct the research that needs doing. Without funding even research which is being conducted will have difficulty reaching a wide audience, so whilst this book is a testament to the very real benefits that children can gain from geographical study, this message remains within the geographical community which is not where it is most needed. This is particularly so in primary education because the majority of primary school teachers are not geographers.

This concluding chapter therefore sets out to establish what might be appropriate future developments and directions for the subject, as this will, in part, determine possible developments and directions for research within it. The previous chapters suggest a number of implications for curriculum, pedagogy and research methodology; these will be synthesised in order to identify possible priorities for the future. However, there is a debate ranging within the geographical education community itself about the nature, purpose and relevance of the subject which is in danger of subverting any attempts to raise its profile (Rawlings, 2001; Catling, 2003; Standish, 2003, 2004). Unless the geographical education community can agree on, and convey, the central importance and relevance that geography has in children's learning and development, there is little point setting out a future research agenda because the funding will not exist to support it. For this reason, a brief overview of this debate will be given.

Geography: *Curriculum contested* in the 21st century.

During the late 1990s Kent (1999:103) called for geographers 'around the world ... to research the perceptions [of the discipline] held by non-geographers in our respective societies and based on these, propose, share and carry out strategies for promoting an up-to-date and accurate knowledge, understanding and thus perception of the study of geography'. This plea echoed a concern among many geography educators that the image of geography among non-geographers is often perceived as being 'a burden on the memory rather than a challenge to the mind' (Kent, 1999, 103). This populist view of geography as a body of factual knowledge, rather than a means of understanding how the world works, has had a powerful effect on the development of the National Curriculum for Geography not least because non-geographers had a role in the decision-making process. Rawling (2001) gives a comprehensive account of the influences affecting the development of National Curriculum geography, showing how, despite a promising initial draft (DES/WO, 1990) the final orders (DES/WO, 1991) were content-laden, over-prescriptive and, as perceived by some, less relevant to children and education than certain other subjects. Each major review (DFE, 1995; DfEE/QCA, 1999) then created opportunities for those both within and beyond the geography community to have another chance at influencing the curriculum.

Kent's plea was aimed at non-geographers. However, there is by no means agreement *within* the geography community about the nature of the subject and its role in the curriculum. This has been evident in a recent debate played out, in the first instance, in the geography forum pages of a web-based geography network (Staffordshire Learning Network, 2003) where twenty-five entries were made over a period of six weeks (26-11-02 to 06-01-03), and subsequently in the pages of *Geography* (2003-4), the Geographical Association's international journal. The debate was on the subject of 'Teaching values rather than skills' and led the Chief Executive of the Geographical Association to question whether 'the source of geography's uncertain position in the curriculum is the lack of clarity not only among the public but also teachers of geography, as to the identity of the subject' (Lambert, 2003, 47). There is not space to go into detail here, but at it's core the debate concerned the revised curriculum's (DfEE/QCA, 1999) focus on environmental change and sustainable development. The thrust of the argument (Standish, 2003) is that the revised curriculum promotes 'green politics' where the 'knowledge content of the geography curriculum is being replaced by a 'New Agenda' of values and attitudes (for example, environmentalism, sustainability and cultural tolerance) and personal life skills' in which teachers 'are more concerned with telling pupils how to think and act in relation to the world around them' (Standish, 2003, 149). In response, Morgan (2003a) points out that Standish is making a false distinction between factual geographical knowledge, and a geography that focuses on values and attitudes. In Morgan's view, 'the apparently 'factual' always involves particular ways of selecting, valuing and understanding experience' (2003a, 151) so Standish's argument is therefore about the replacement of previously agreed sets of 'facts' with new sets of 'facts'. What Standish fails to acknowledge is that no selection of content or knowledge is value free, and that his preferred facts are based on old values about what is desirable in education, while the New Agenda 'facts' are based on new values about the purpose of education that have currency in the twenty-first century. Ellis (2003), on the other hand, criticises Standish's narrow portrayal of values education and specifically the pedagogical approaches that might be employed by teachers. He identifies five distinct objectives for teaching about values – values inculcation, values analysis, moral reasoning, values clarification and action learning – and suggests that Standish focuses on values inculcation and ignores the other, more complex, approaches (Ellis, 2003, 234).

The debate continues in a later issue of Geography (Standish, 2004) with misunderstanding between the different viewpoints appearing to remain. Whilst debate within a subject community is no doubt healthy and a reflection of the dynamic nature of the subject, it does seem as though there is a difference of opinion which is not helpful in the context of a climate in which geography has very low status and a poor image in terms of its relevance in a school curriculum for the 21ˢᵗ century, concerns highlighted by many authors in this publication (Catling & Martin, Chapter 1; Catling, Chapter 21; Halocha, Chapter 20; Rawlinson, Chapter 23). Perhaps the lack of clarity and degree of misunderstanding is because the debate is really about something more fundamental than geography's identity. It is about the purpose of education itself.

Geography and the purpose of education.

Within the fields of geographical and environmental education educators have identified different ideologies, or orientations, in education (Fien, 1993, 1998; Huckle, 1993; Naish, 1996; Sterling, 2001). The one chosen here (Figure 1) is selected because it also explicitly demonstrates the impact of each orientation on how knowledge is perceived which will, in turn, affect the content considered appropriate within a curriculum and the pedagogical approaches that might be utilised in practice. If this classification is applied to the debate about knowledge or values in geography, the criticism of 'New Agenda' geography (Standish, 2003, 2004) appears to come from a vocational/neo-classical position:

> *...the only value that matters is knowledge. Other values, such as concern for the environment, social justice and a respect for diversity are about moralising and have no place in a curriculum with the goal of intellectual and personal development of the individual'.* (Standish, 2004:89)

It is made clear that this knowledge is held by teachers and other authoritative sources. Implicit in this is criticism of both the liberal/progressive ideology (the geography curriculum should be an adult, not child-centred) and the socially critical ideology (which is tantamount to indoctrination). These criticisms focus on (a) the *perceived* content focus of the New Agenda geography, and (b) the teaching approaches he assumes this will imply. Because of a lack of understanding of (a) assumptions about (b) are mistaken. If the *only* focus of the New Agenda was values and beliefs then this *would* lead to values inculcation because the knowledge that originally led to those values and beliefs would be hidden; pupils would be asked to behave in certain ways without having access to the 'facts'. This would be action predicated on stereotypical beliefs, not knowledge. Standish would be right to be critical of such approaches, and he has some evidence to suggest that these *are* approaches used by some geography teachers. However, this is *not* what liberal/progressive or socially critical approaches imply.

Both liberal/progressive and socially critical geographers have as their goal that pupils should adopt certain values and attitudes, but the means by which they seek to achieve this is on the basis of knowledge. The question is: whose knowledge? Both groups seek to 'problematise' knowledge by providing a number of different perspectives, including those that are non-Western and that draw on children's geographies (Catling, 2003; Morgan, 2003b); the purpose is to raise awareness that not everyone 'knows' the world in the same way and, as a result, to encourage pupils to revise their frames of reference or '... to travel with a different view' (Slater, 1992). Up until this point the goals of liberal-progressive and socially critical geographers are similar.

However, a liberal-progressive believes in the right of free choice for the individual, whereas for socially critical geographers this is not an option because they believe that there are some actions that are fundamentally wrong (for example, in the context of human rights) because they lead to injustice in the world. For this reason they go further to encourage pupils to be openly critical of social, economic, political and environmental structures that have led to these inequalities and injustices. In this sense they have as their goal not only individual change, but social change.

	Vocational/Neo-classical	**Liberal/Progressive**	**Socially Critical**
Educational orientation	Sees education as a preparation for work; it views socialisation, education and training as similar processes and seeks to help students to find their place in society by providing them with the skills required to fulfil their work roles. It is an education that accepts technocratic and managerial values and, insofar as it uncritically accepts existing social structures and hierarchies, may perpetuate injustice, inequality and the status quo.	Sees education as preparation for life rather than work. It seeks to help students fulfil a wide range of life roles through a broad general education based as much upon the humanities and liberal arts as upon science and technology. This orientation seeks development and improvement of society through the education of autonomous individuals. It values individual excellence and achievement and adopts a reformist approach to social change.	Sees education as a challenge to social injustice and the status quo. It is founded upon a belief in the need for education to play a role, along with other social institutions and agencies, in creating just and democratic societies. Personal development is valued, but seen to be insufficient in a world that is structurally unequal.
Nature of knowledge	Knowledge is objective - a public matter; exists in books; mostly described as skills and information, (facts, concepts) which have their meaning and significance in occupational or disciplinary contexts; special concern is for the technical/rational/scientific/managerial interest of knowledge (knowledge for control).	Knowledge is subjective, a 'private' or individual matter; exists in accomplishments or 'in the head' of the individual; mostly described as learning, attitudes and living skills which have meaning and significance in individuals' life context and culture; special concern is for the practical / expressive / cultural interests of knowledge for communication, deliberation and refinement.	Knowledge is dialectical, an interplay of subjective views of the world and the historical and cultural frameworks in which they are located. Sees knowledge as socially constructed. Thus, knowledge is not easily specified: its meaning is context specific. It places a central value on the role of knowledge in social action: the emancipatory interests of knowledge.
Learning theory	Behaviourism: deficit models of the learner, transmission theories of learning	Constructivist-interactionist: sees the learner as building cognitive structures through interaction	Social constructivist-interactionist: sees the learner as reconstructing a social reality that is socially constructed and subject to reconstruction through historical and political processes
Teacher's role	An authority, transmitting knowledge, structuring and sequencing what is known to allow the learners to achieve mastery	A 'mentor' or facilitator, organising learning opportunities to allow the learner to take advantage of opportunities and achieve autonomy	A project organiser and resource person, organising critical and collaborative projects in negotiation with learners and community
Learner's role	A receiver of transmitted knowledge, more or less prepared or motivated to achieve within the framework of what is taught	An active constructor of knowledge through experience and opportunities to discover and enquire, more or less able to take advantage of opportunities in terms of preparation and own previous experience	A co-learner, using available knowledge through interaction with others in socially significant tasks of critique or collaborative social action

Figure 1: A classification of orientations (or ideologies) in education (Fien, 1993, 17-22)

This is *informed* action for social change that involves the agent of change in a critical analysis of the sources of this information, and is very different to indoctrination. It is akin to values analysis, clarification and action learning and, as such, focuses on learners 'having a *reasoned* base for whatever actions they might take in relation to specific social and environmental issues' (Ellis, 2003:234).

To summarise, the geography curriculum continues to be hotly contested, each argument being underpinned by sets of assumptions and principles that relate to particular ideologies and paradigms. These assumptions and principles are not always acknowledged, often being part of that tacit knowledge referred to in chapter 1 and, in the case of classroom teachers it could be argued that the level of awareness of the relationship between ideology and practice outlined by Fien (Figure 1) is not necessary. However, in the case of educators who are responsible for the development of geography teachers, whether at the stage of initial or in-service training, such a level of awareness and understanding could be considered crucial. What are the implications of this for the future direction and development of primary geography?

The future of primary geography research: setting an agenda

A number of possible directions and developments can be identified from the contributions in this publication. Top of this agenda is the need to be clear about the nature of geography and its role in the curriculum, and then to convey this to others – primary practitioners, government, and society in general. As mentioned earlier, some disagreement within a subject community is inevitable and a reflection of a healthy dynamism where a subject is constantly changing and developing as knowledge and understanding about it and its contribution to society grows. However, the polarised nature of the views expressed in the current debate is indicative of a fundamental difference about the subject's identity which should not be ignored as it is potentially divisive and may contribute further to the state and status of geography as outlined in Chapter 21.

Once a degree of clarity is established and communicated, it is then possible to propose an agenda for research that relates to the gaps identified in Chapter 1:
- Geography curriculum and planning
- Teaching geography
- Aspects of geographical learning

The sections of this book in themselves [children and pedagogy, teacher development and the development of the subject] indicate that current research in primary geography is directly related to these areas. Chapters within each section report a range of research projects that suggest a number of directions for the substantive, pedagogical and methodological aspects of primary geography research. For example, an overview of the chapter titles shows that all four key elements of learning – knowledge, understanding, skills and attitudes & values (DES, 1985) – are the focus of attention and this applies equally to teachers and learners, whether in Foundation Stage settings or in Higher Education beginning and In-service training courses. What follows is a brief synthesis of the research findings and implications under each heading.

Geography curriculum and planning

It seems clear from a number of the research projects reported here is that teachers' knowledge, perceptions and beliefs about geography and substantive areas within it have a profound impact on the ways in which they interpret the National Curriculum, their planning, teaching and assessment. Martin highlights a concern about beginning teachers' subject knowledge when, on PGCE primary courses, geography has between 4 and 14 hours allocated to it depending on the institution, a concern which is echoed by Bowles, Halocha and Scoffham. If this is the case, there is little time to do anything about the concerns raised by Bowles and Moore who identify teacher subject knowledge as an issue in locality studies. Bowles points out that if teachers' local geographical knowledge is poor this will have a negative impact on children's learning and form a poor basis for contrasting locality studies, while Moore shows how developing teachers' in-depth knowledge of the local area is far more complex and time consuming that had been thought. Macintosh, on the other hand, sets out a possible series of activities and experiences that might enhance children's understanding of rivers, river systems and river processes all of which demands not only a certain level of subject knowledge on the part of the teacher, but also a level of pedagogical knowledge that enables the teacher to use appropriate analogies, metaphors and representations that help to transform the complex subject matter into forms that are understandable to children. It is the integration of these two types of teacher knowledge that form pedagogical content knowledge, the knowledge base Martin suggests is the most appropriate for successful teaching and learning. This level of training takes time and, set against the backdrop described by Catling in chapter 21, has implications not only for initial teacher training but also for continuing professional development of primary school teachers throughout their careers.

Research into teachers' knowledge and attitudes within the field of geographical and environmental education is not unknown (Barratt Hacking, 1996; Leat, 1996; Walford, 1996), although very little has been done in the field of primary education. However, there is a case for synthesising and disseminating the findings that do exist and using these as the basis for future research. An example of this is the work currently being done by the Irish Association of Scientific, Social and Environmental Education (IASSEE). Members of IASSEE have begun synthesising the research into teachers' knowledge, attitudes and beliefs about geography (Greenwood, 2003). This, along with reviews in the others subjects, is underpinning a major research project that will ask every primary teacher trainee in Eire and Northern Ireland to complete a questionnaire about their knowledge, and sources of knowledge, in geography, history and science as well as their attitudes towards these subjects.

Curriculum development, the resources that are available to support teaching and learning in geography, and how these are interpreted and used by primary teachers are vital further areas for enquiry. Geography is taught with and through a variety of resources within and beyond the classroom. It is essential to understand much more clearly what is the use of these resources, and how teachers consider and value them in relation to their planned teaching – as well as what they see are the limitations of the resources and their accessibility to be – in and outside the classroom.

Chapters in this book attest to the direction primary geography seems to be taking in the early 21st century. Primary geography educators and researchers have not appeared to question the relevance of the New Agenda to the geography curriculum or children's learning and development. For example, Catling (2003) has recently called for a primary curriculum that not only embraces the New Agenda, but also recognises, values and builds on children's geographies. In short, he argues for a *child-centred* geography curriculum, an argument predicated on a deep understanding of *children as active agents* in constructing their own geographies and geographical learning, linked to the literature on children's geographical experience, the geographies that affect children and how children learn. This has found broad support by others (Mackintosh, 2003; Morgan, 2003b; Spencer, 2003), and there is a remarkable degree of consensus among authors in this publication about both the focus on child-centred geography (Bowles, Halocha, Owens, Scoffham, Spencer, and Storey) and the New Agenda of sustainable development (Bloomfield, Bowles, Owens and Ryan) and citizenship (Bowles, Disney, Owens and Catling). However, this understanding of the relevance and importance of geography is held within the geographical community; the research that has been conducted is not *sufficient*, and it exists in forms that are not accessible to the majority of primary school teachers. There are implications here for both the development of the curriculum and the ways in which research findings are disseminated. Perhaps one of the more successful ways is by developing geographical resources that take account of previous research as described by Walker and Graham. Not only have they shown how research findings can be applied to the development of a resource, but also they, and Moore, have made the process of developing such a resource open and transparent providing a model that others could follow.

Teaching and learning in geography

Teaching and children's learning are taken together because, as identified in chapter 1, what appears to be missing from primary geography research at the moment is a focus on the *process* of learning and an integral part of that process is the teaching of the subject, in whatever context, as a single subject or through inter-subject topics. Many of the research findings reported in this book suggest that there is a need to use learners' current knowledge, understanding, skills and attitudes as a *starting point* for teaching, and this applies at all levels of learning from teacher education to children in the Foundation Stage. Several studies, such as those outlined in Chapter 1, have identified such starting points (although more work is required, particularly in the field of teacher education) but there is currently a gap in our knowledge of how to develop learning *from* this point – research is needed into what is an appropriate and helpful progression in geographical learning at all levels. Mackintosh, in her discussion of progression in children's understanding of rivers, shows how we can learn much from research in other subject areas – in this case science.

This same research (Mackintosh) draws on a Piagetian model of how children learn through constructivist approaches [reflecting the liberal/progressive ideology in Figure 1]. Constructivist approaches to learning are evident in other chapters, but these also highlight the power of collaborative learning (Disney, Moore, Owen, Storey and Wilmot), and collaborative learning in situations that have a real sense of purpose whether creating an ICT learning resource (Moore) or deciding on a route for newcomers to an area (Owen). In the case of Wilmot's research, she goes further to suggest that research into social constructivist approaches 'support the growing body of international opinion which challenges the orthodoxy of traditional theoretical perspectives on learning and development' – i.e. that children progress through certain stages, and the notion of 'readiness' which has led to teachers being mis-informed about children's spatial ability in general (also confirmed in Plester's research) and contributed to the low expectations that are often identified in Ofsted reports.

Social constructivist approaches identify scaffolding and the use of language as two key processes in enhancing learning. As Scoffham notes, geography is the only subject that distinctively explores the notion of location and spatial awareness and the tools geographers make extensive use of are graphical (including maps) and visual representations. Storey draws on linguistic acquisition research to show that young children already have the symbolic tools (language) when they begin primary schooling. They therefore have the foundation for tackling more sophisticated and challenging ideas than is usually recognised which, if applied to graphical symbolic representations, suggests that the use of symbolic texts could enable a far greater degree of abstract thought about space and spatial representation; another example of research (supported by Plester and Francisca de Azevado) challenging teachers' assumptions (derived from Piagetian stage models) that young children's experiences need to be predominantly concrete.

The interesting thing about all these examples and the learning processes suggested or explored is that, while they are clearly learner-centred and use socially constructivist approaches, they all emphasise the importance of subject knowledge. In any teaching and learning situation, the teacher's knowledge of the syntactic and substantive frameworks that help us to make sense of the world as a geographer are crucial. They underpin the following aspects of teaching geography that were identified in Chapter 1, Figure 2:

- Teachers' perceptions and expectations of children in geography
- The use and impact of enquiry-led teaching in geography
- The role of effective questioning in geography teaching
- The use of ICT to enhance geographical learning
- The use of differentiation in geography teaching
- How teachers identify children's misconceptions and use strategies to overcome these
- Teachers' use of explanation in geography teaching
- Teachers' application of higher order thinking skills in geography teaching
- Approaches to assessment in geography teaching and learning

However, as outlined by Scoffham, advances in brain research have helped us to recognise the importance of the affective as well as the cognitive ways of knowing the world. There is a growing realisation that unless feelings and attitudes about places, people and environments are taken into account, as demonstrated by Francisca de Azevado, these can provide real blocks to learning in the cognitive domain. For example, Spencer demonstrates the importance of place attachment and the role of geography teaching in the enhancement of personal wellbeing. When this is taken together with the New Agenda for geography, it highlights the need for research such as that being conducted by Disney which questions the 'wisdom' that school linking between the UK and economically developing countries is automatically going to promote international understanding and positive attitudes. A further issue identified in Disney's research is that primary teachers tend to avoid confronting real issues such as poverty, perhaps because of their lack of knowledge of the underlying causes as well as a lack of confidence in how to teach about controversial issues, both of which take us back to the debate about geography and what might be considered a suitable curriculum.

It seems appropriate here to provide another example of research that meets the criterion of being *sufficient* and which is highly *relevant,* but which has been conducted outside the geographical community. The Global Education Research Group (GERG) has done a pilot study with 586 primary and secondary trainee teachers in four HEIs in the south west of England. The focus of the research was trainees' knowledge and understanding of global issues and their motivation to teach about them (Holden et. al, 2003). The group is now seeking funding to broaden both the scale and scope of the study.

Primary geography research methods.

Issues concerning methodology have already been addressed in Chapter 1. However, there are a number of specific issues that have been identified within each section of the book that it is worth summarising here:

- Ryan reminds us that, when researching attitudes and expressions of intent, a verbal response is a problematic indicator of action. This suggests the use of methods other than interviews, such as those used in personal construct psychology, and the need to gather data that provides evidence of action.

- On a related point, if research is to investigate not only the relationship between intent and action but also the impact of that action on learners in the classroom, Owens identifies a difficulty in defining and measuring, for example, pro-environmental behaviour because the outcomes of experiences are often only truly gauged in the long term. This was evident in Martin's research which, if it had been confined to a year, would have resulted in very different findings to those that were revealed from data gathered over two years, suggesting the need for longitudinal studies.

- Spencer demonstrates how important it is to define terms clearly within any research. There is a real need to be clear about, and have agreement over, what is understood by a term [eg enquiry, locality, sustainability] as well as the methods best suited to research it.

- Precisely because primary geography research is small-scale, reflects the needs of individuals, and is generally not funded, little agreement about methodological approaches exists at an explicit level. There are sources that have attempted to do this (see Chapter 1) but perhaps there is also a need for primary geography researchers to be more explicit about the process they go through at ALL stages, such as that provided by Owen.

- Also because of the nature of much primary geography research, it tends to be practitioner led which creates problems in (a) defining or setting boundaries to the researcher's role, since the researcher is usually a participant (Bloomfield, Disney, Martin) and (b) in encouraging those at the heart of practice, who have enormous amounts of wisdom based on experience, to become researchers themselves (Bloomfield).

- Finally, there is a wealth of information here about the range of methods which could be used for both teaching and research, not least those that reflect a liberal-progressive, child-centred agenda such as using vision maps, child-taken photos, child-led walks, and role-play (Bowles).

Conclusion

To summarise, while there are several directions that primary geography research could take. One of the most important might be to do some *joined up thinking and co-operative action*. This seems to be indicated on a several fronts:

- An understanding of the teaching and learning process cannot be separated from teachers' and children's knowledge and attitudes and the ways in which these affect how they interpret the curriculum.

- While past research in primary geography may mostly lack sufficiency, there is a wealth of information there that could usefully be synthesised and disseminated (using, for example, the model of Rickinson, 2001) in order to provide a sounder basis for decisions about future research.

- Developments in education in general – the global dimension, sustainability – have an impact on primary geography and these are areas where research and curriculum development is already taking place which should not be ignored.
- Equally, research that *does* meet the criterion of being sufficient (in terms of scale) has been conducted in areas (developmental psychology, science, environmental education) which has much to offer primary geography research both in terms of possible methodologies as well as implications for practice.
- Primary geography research that has drawn on knowledge in other areas (brain research, linguistics) has been strengthened both in terms of its substantive and methodological advancements.

There is no doubt that the energy, enthusiasm, commitment and experience exists to conduct research that will help our understanding of geography and pedagogy move from experience, personal wisdom and tacit knowledge to transparency, rigour and explicit knowledge. The energy, enthusiasm, commitment and experience also exists to agree on, and promote the nature of geography and its contribution to children's learning and development beyond the confines of the geographical community. The latter is going to be essential if we are to achieve the former and this book offers a further contribution to this process.

References

Barratt Hacking, E. (1996), Novice Teachers and Their Geographical Persuasions, *Journal Of International Research in Geographical and Environmental Education*, 5,(1), 77-86

Catling, S. (2003), Curriculum contested: Primary geography and social justice, *Geography*, 88 (3), 164-210

DES/WO (1990), *Geography for ages 5-16. Final report of the Geography National Curriculum Working Group*, London: DES/WO

DES/WO (1991), *Geography in the National Curriculum*, London: HMSO

DFE (1995), *Geography in the National Curriculum: Revised Orders*, London: HMSO

DfEE/QCA (2000,) *The National Curriculum for England: Geography*, London: HMSO

Ellis, B. (2003), Constructing a Value Map, *Geography*, 88 (3), 234-235

Fien, J. (1993), Ideology critique and environmental education, in Fien, J (ed.), *Education for the Environment: Critical curriculum theorising and environmental education*, Geelong: Deakin University Press, 14-49

Fien, J. (1999), Towards a Map of Commitment: A Socially Critical Approach to Geographical Education, *International Research in Geographical and Environmental Education*, 8 (2),140-158

Greenwood, R. (2003), Student attitudes to geography and environmental education – a review, Paper presented at the annual conference of the *Irish Association of Social Science and Environmental Education*, Dublin, June, unpublished

Holden, C., Clough, N., Hicks, D., & Martin, F. (2003) Education for Global Citizenship: the knowledge, understanding and motivation of trainee teachers, *Report to the World Studies Trust*, October, unpublished

Huckle J. (1993), Environmental education and sustainability: A view from critical theory, Fien, J. (ed.), *Environmental Education: A Pathway to Sustainability*, Geelong: Deakin University

Kent, A. (1999), Image and Reality – How do others see us?, *International Research in Geographical and Environmental Education*, 8 (2), 103-107

Lambert, D. (2003), Geography: A Burden on the Memory or a Light in the Mind?, *Geography*, 88 (1), 47

Leat, D. (1996), Geography Student Teachers and Their Images of Teaching, *Journal Of International Research in Geographical and Environmental Education,* 5 (1), 63-68

Mackintosh, M. (2003), Wither Primary Geography?, *Geography,* 88 (3), 228-229

Morgan, J. (2003a,) Comment on Standish 'Constructing a value map', *Geography,* 88 (3),151

Morgan, J. (2003b), Theory into Practice?, *Geography,* 88 (3), 230-231

Naish, M. (1996), The Geography Curriculum: A Martyr to Epistemology?, Gerber, R. & Lidstone, J. (eds.) *Developments and Directions in Geographical Education,* Clifton: Channel View Publications

Rawling, E. (2001), *Changing the Subject: The impact of national policy on school geography 1980-2000,* Sheffield: Geographical Association.

Rickinson, M. (2001), Learners and Learning in Environmental Education: a critical review of the evidence, *Environmental Education Research,* 7, 207-320

Slater, F. (1992), 'To Travel with a different view', Naish, M. (ed.) *Geography and Education,* London: Institute of Education, University of London

Spencer, C. (2003), Why has the Geography Curriculum been so little attuned to the child's geographical enquiry?, *Geography,* 88 (3), 232-233

Staffordshire Learning Network (2003), SLN Geography Forum: Teaching values rather than skills, http://www.sln.org.uk/ubb/forum/HTML/000416.html, accessed 20 April, 2004

Standish, A. (2003), Constructing a value map, *Geography,* 88 (2), 149-151

Standish, A. (2004), Valuing (Adult) Geographic Knowledge, *Geography,* 89 (1), 89-91

Sterling, S. (2001), *Sustainable Education: Re-visioning Learning and Change,* Totnes: Green Books, on behalf of The Schumacher Society

Walford, R. (1996), What is Geography? An analysis of definitions provided by prospective teachers of the subject, *Journal of International Research in Geographical and Environmental Education,* 5 (1), 69-76